Safeguarding the Stranger

Safeguarding the Stranger

An Abrahamic Theology and Ethic of Protective Hospitality

JAYME R. REAVES

PICKWICK *Publications* • Eugene, Oregon

SAFEGUARDING THE STRANGER
An Abrahamic Theology and Ethic of Protective Hospitality

Pickwick Publications
An Imprint of Wipf and Stock Publishers
199 W. 8th Ave., Suite 3
Eugene, OR 97401

www.wipfandstock.com

PAPERBACK ISBN 13: 978-1-4982-2461-1
HARDCOVER ISBN 13: 978-1-4982-2463-5
EBOOK ISBN: 978-1-4982-2462-8

Cataloguing-in-Publication data:

Names: Reaves, Jayme R.

Title: Safeguarding the stranger : an Abrahamic theology and ethic of protective hospitality / Jayme R. Reaves.

Description: Eugene, OR: Pickwick Publications, 2016 | Includes bibliographical references and indexes.

Identifiers: ISBN 978-1-4982-2461-1 (paperback) | ISBN 978-1-4982-2463-5 (hardcover) | ISBN 978-1-4982-2462-8 (ebook)

Subjects: LCSH: Hospitality—Religious aspects—Christianity.

Classification: BV4647.H67 R42 2016 (paperback) | BV4647.H67 R42 (ebook)

Manufactured in the U.S.A. 07/13/16

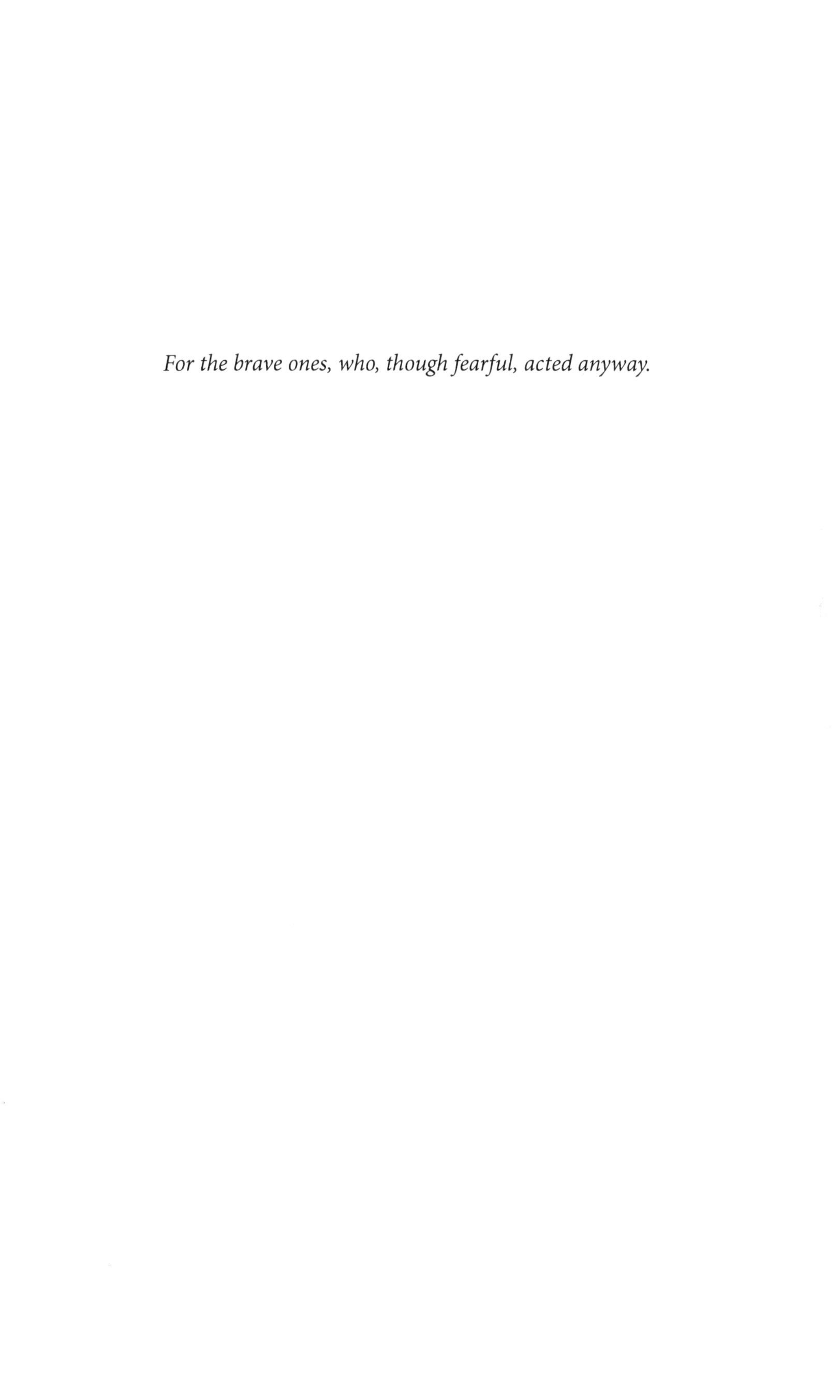

For the brave ones, who, though fearful, acted anyway.

Ar scáth a chéile a mhaireas na daoine.
It is in the shelter of each other that the people live.
—Irish Proverb

Contents

Acknowledgments

The Hebrew concept of *chesed*, חסד, is often translated as "steadfast love," but it gives a name for the quality of going above and beyond the call of duty or obligation, to bend over backwards, to do whatever it takes, to endure despite hardship, and to embody mercy and compassion in all that one does. I have been extremely lucky to be surrounded by people who have been full of *chesed*, and they deserve to be acknowledged.

I would first like to thank my colleague and friend David Tombs for his unfailing encouragement over the life of this project, as well as the staff and faculty at the Irish School of Ecumenics at Trinity College, University of Dublin.

While my years as an undergraduate in university are long gone, I must also acknowledge the influence of two particular professors who have shaped me in the most profound ways and set me on this path. Ann Livingstone taught this kid from small-town American South that an amazing, heartbreaking, complex world waited just beyond my doorstep, and that I need not be afraid of it. Likewise, David Gushee shepherded me through the horrors of genocide and taught me the power of a lived and dynamic faith, the love and healing of family, and the silly delight of Mr. Bean. Both Ann and David have given me myself, a self I doubt I would have known without their help.

I would also like to recognize the important contributions of individuals in Northern Ireland and the Former Yugoslavia who are on the frontlines of justice, peacemaking, and reconciliation work and, in that work, you have shown me the power of hospitality, giving me the inspiration to pursue this topic. In particular, I would like to thank Goran Bubalo, Randy Puljek-Shank, Entoni Šeperić, Eli Tauber, Moris Albahari, Zilka Spahić-Šiljak, and Bernadette Devlin McAliskey for their contributions of time, conversations, suggestions, and challenges which have given life to this research.

There have been friends and colleagues, too many to name here, who have given tremendous support over the course of this research. In particular, I would like to gratefully recognize the substantial contributions of friends from the Baptist Theological Seminary at Richmond and those who served as early readers for this project: Phyllis Rodgerson Pleasants Tessieri, Mark Biddle, Tracy Hartman, and Ana Karim.

Finally, I would like to thank my partner, James Pattison, who throughout this process has been ever-loving, ever-patient, and ever-supportive.

Introduction

...hospitality is not merely one ethics among others, but the ethics par excellence.

—Jacques Derrida[1]

Over the past fifteen years, there has been an upsurge of theological and religious writing on the topic of hospitality. On the whole, this body of literature reflects two primary approaches: either it discusses the theory of welcome and the other, or it attempts to recover what it perceives to be a forgotten spiritual practice. Yet, the discussions related to either of these facets are limited. In the theory-based literature, there is a lack of contextual evidence and lived experience that roots the practice of hospitality in everyday life. This body of literature also tends to focus on *why* the other should be welcomed rather than the variety of ways that welcome can be expressed and the realities faced when the other says "yes." In the practical literature, the reality is considered, yet its attempt to recover hospitality is primarily limited to interpersonal relationships or considering communal identity, extolling the virtues of inviting others into one's home, recovering the power the ritual of welcome as a personal spiritual practice, or challenging groups and communities who tend to be insular and homogeneous. This practical body of literature often speaks of hospitality in the context of issues related to immigration or homelessness, but it rarely goes beyond general "welcoming the stranger" scenarios as practiced by mainstream religious communities.

Perhaps because of the recent revival of the topic within scholarship or because of a lack of understanding as to the full potential hospitality entails, there appears to be a reluctance to consider hospitality's practicality beyond the already pre-determined scope. The potential for hospitality to impact

1. Derrida, "Hospitality and Hostility," quoted in McNulty, *The Hostess*, xvii.

and influence ethical behavior and theological understanding is limitless, yet the baggage the term "hospitality" carries with it and how it is interpreted limits how it is viewed and understood.

Therefore, this work is distinctive in that it extends the discussion related to hospitality beyond the usual topics of table fellowship and inclusion by considering the provision of refuge or sanctuary to an endangered other as a hospitable act. Throughout this research, the focus is on an exploration and analysis of protective hospitality and its faith-based motivations and resources. For clarity's sake, protective hospitality is defined as *the provision of welcome and sanctuary to the threatened other, often at great risk to oneself.*

When practitioners are questioned about why they provided a safe place for someone in danger, they often declare, "It is just what we do" or "It's what anyone would do." For religious practitioners of protective hospitality, their actions often appear innate, as a matter of course. Yet, to the keen observer, there is something more. This book seeks to explore what that is and how it can be applied in a variety of contexts.

Furthermore, the call to provide protective hospitality is found in all three "Abrahamic traditions" of Judaism, Christianity, and Islam. Yet, despite this common ethical imperative, there has been no sustained effort in the literature thus far to consider hospitality through an inter-religious lens. Therefore, an additional unique contribution of this work is that it considers the Christian practice of protective hospitality by also examining its practice in the Jewish and Islamic traditions, noting commonalities as well as differences which provide new perspectives or opportunities for renewal and growth. Such an analysis highlights the positive potential for a "cooperative theology" between the Abrahamic traditions through the practice of protective hospitality that could be used to address issues of peacebuilding, conflict, marginalization, oppression and threat to the vulnerable in meaningful and effective ways.

I approach this work from a specific context. My interest in hospitality and protection arises from a personal place. My family background was anything but hospitable or protective. I am the third generation (at least) of women who were sexually and/or emotionally abused by male authority figures (husbands, fathers, religious leadership, etc.); yet, despite the knowledge of the abuse, nothing was done within the family structure to protect the vulnerable. Relationships and abuse continued and so the threatened had to seek refuge elsewhere.

I am also a child of the racially divided American South and have been profoundly formed by witnessing the inequalities and cruelty inflicted by racism, albeit from the somewhat safer white female perspective. I grew up with both invisible and real boundaries I was forbidden to cross because people who had darker skin than I did lived on the other side. But also, in recent years, I have lived in two areas of the world—the Former Yugoslavia and Northern Ireland—where religion and its corresponding national identity has divided neighbor against neighbor, community against community as well, in very similar and yet very different ways.

My interest in hospitality began while living in the Former Yugoslavia. After residing in Sarajevo, Bosnia from 1998–2000 and in eastern Croatia in 2003–2004, the impact of hospitality made an indelible mark upon me. How could a society and all its constituent entities—be they Muslim Bošnjak, Orthodox Serb or Roman Catholic Croat—express such welcome to me and yet show such inhospitality to one another? How can such amazing warmth and generosity coexist beside hatred and xenophobia, even against those one had lived beside one's whole life? And what motivated those who risked their lives to save someone from the other side? I was perplexed and sought to understand more fully.

During and after my experiences of living in Bosnia and Croatia, a question began to form that this book seeks to address. Ethnic cleansing and genocide of the religious other in the Former Yugoslavia, Darfur, Rwanda, Iraq, Syria, and numerous other places is a well-documented reality. Yet, there are defiant examples of people reaching out beyond their own identity to welcome and provide safe haven or assistance to someone from the other side in practically every modern conflict narrative. I began to wonder why some choose to take others in for protection and some do not, and what is required for practitioners of protective hospitality to put themselves and their families at risk to give sanctuary to strangers. On a theological level, I sought to know what role faith plays in making these decisions, what resources were there to enable these actions to be fostered and utilized to make a difference in the future, and what the Abrahamic traditions might bring to this.

Therefore, the question addressed in these pages is as follows:

> *What are the resources and teachings in the Abrahamic traditions that take hospitality and, more specifically, its call to provide protective hospitality seriously enough to inform shared action and belief on behalf of the threatened other, often at great risk to oneself?*

To answer this question, this work aims to be both ecumenical and interreligious in its theological approach. While offering a Christian point of view, it seeks to broaden that same Christian theology by being in intentional conversation with the perspectives of other Christian denominations beyond my own Baptist background, as well as the other Abrahamic traditions of Judaism and Islam.

There are obvious limitations to this approach: I am neither Jew nor Muslim, and I have no Arabic and limited Biblical Hebrew experience, which requires me to rely upon English translations and interpretations. Therefore, when it comes to textual and interpretive work, I am aware that I am profoundly shaped by my own Christian, congregationalist, low-church background and training in hermeneutics and exegesis as well as my experience in inter-religious and international experiences.[2]

Thus, this research will primarily be an endeavor from an inclusive Christian point of view that utilizes resources from both Judaism and Islam to interrogate and challenge the Christian tradition's theology and practice of protective hospitality. I recognize that no religion is homogenous or monolithic, and that Judaism, Christianity, and Islam do not exist as single entities. Instead, there are a multiplicity of Judaisms, Christianities, and Islams, defined by the diversity of people who adhere to them. Muslim scholar Omid Safi writes that religions, as in Judaism, Christianity, and Islam, teach nothing. Instead, the "[i]nterpretative communities do . . . [as d]ivine teachings [are] achieved through human agency" and that religion "is always mediated" since "Islam says nothing. Muslims do."[3]

So, while I focus upon the Abrahamic traditions, I recognize my limits in speaking with authority beyond the Christian tradition. Accordingly, this research does not speak for all Christians or every Christianity. Instead, it recognizes the complexity within each identified tradition, but it also recognizes the clumsiness and unwieldiness that can come from over-precision in naming just which Judaism, Christianity, or Islam is being talked about at every point. Within the context of Christian theology and Christianity mentioned here, it will in most cases be limited to Western Christianity, recognizing that there are even a multitude of Western Christianities. However, as it would be impractical to similarly differentiate Judaism and Islam in this work of Christian theology (unless particular traditions such as Sufism

2. Another example of this approach in the area of textual scholarship can be found in Byrne's, *The Names of God in Judaism, Christianity and Islam.*

3. Safi, "The Times They Are A-Changin'," introduction to *Progressive Muslims*, 22. Similarly Kwame Anthony Appiah emphasizes the individual and personal, noting: "It's not Muslims; it's particular people now and it . . . gives it a kind of concreteness . . . What binds me to Islam is my Sunni friends and my Shiite friends, my Israeli friends, my cousins who happen to be Muslim, and strangers whom I've come to know and like who are Muslim. What I have in common with these very diverse groups of Muslims that I know is different in each case. So that breaks up the sense of them as a kind of monolithic 'them.'" Appiah, "Sidling up to Difference," http://www.onbeing.org/program/sidling-up-to-difference/transcript/5876.

may apply in a specific area), I feel it is appropriate to take a similarly broad approach to "Christianity." Therefore, the analysis of how protective hospitality is discussed in Judaism and Islam is intended as indicative rather than definitive. Whether adherents will wish to own it confessionally or not goes beyond the immediate task of excavating and identifying the resources to which this research appeals.

My argument will be as follows:

> *Protective hospitality and its faith-based foundations, specifically in the Abrahamic traditions of Judaism, Christianity, and Islam, merit greater theological attention. More specifically, the practice of protective hospitality in Christianity can be enhanced by better understandings of Judaism and Islam's practice of hospitality, namely their codes and etiquettes related to honor. Additionally, the positive potential for protective hospitality's contribution to peacebuilding, conflict transformation, and reconciliation and the possibility for development of a "cooperative theology" among the Abrahamic traditions are particularly valuable.*

Outline of Chapters

The book is divided into two parts. The first part is comprised of the first three chapters, focusing upon a greater analysis of hospitality, theology, and ethics. The second part, comprised of the final two chapters, look specifically at protective hospitality.

In Chapter One, I identify the theological movements and influences that shape the investigation to follow. I begin with contemporary examples of protective hospitality and then discusses two currents in contemporary Christian theologies—a contextual and political theological approach and a cooperative and complementary theological approach—that will shape a dialogical method to understanding faith-based hospitality. I then identify the capacity for complementarity in the theology of the Abrahamic traditions which lends itself to a shared heritage of ethical practice, emphasizing the voices within the traditions that seek to challenge rather than collude with the powers and national might. Lastly, I argue that a "hermeneutic of hospitality" is appropriate in order for the research to embody its contextual method and structure.

In Chapter Two, I extend hospitality through examination of its scope and complexity and highlight aspects that contribute its amorphous nature. Inherent tensions in hospitality's definition and practice are explored, as seen in the relationships between hospitality and hostility, particularity and universality, inclusivity and exclusivity, safety and threat, invited and uninvited, expected and unexpected, and culture and counterculture. I also argue in this chapter that three main themes can be identified in the practice of hospitality—table fellowship, intellectual welcome, and the provision of protection—and that hospitality is inextricably linked to the essence of ethics and ethical practice.

In Chapter Three, I analyze the practice of hospitality as exhibited in the Abrahamic traditions of Judaism, Christianity, and Islam, considering their shared cultural and geographic origins and patterns related to models of behavior and impact of early experiences of persecution. I also identify the traditions' own unique understandings that contribute to the practice of hospitality, highlighting the emphases missing or forgotten in Christianity's theology and practice in light of the contributions of Judaism and Islam, namely in the more clearly articulated obligations and etiquette related to hospitality which I suggest are associated with a more explicit honor code. It is understood, however, that Christianity is not alone in its neglect of certain aspects of hospitality, and that each religion is never pure in theological systems or ethical practices. Therefore, critiques expressed toward Christianity could be applicable to Judaism or Islam as well.

In Chapter Four, I examine the stages of hospitality and the role of protection in hospitable practice, while also noting the motivations for action on behalf of a threatened other that have been identified by other scholars. I also specifically argue that issues of protection, force, and violence give meaning to and limit the practice of protective hospitality, particularly in light of hospitality's emphasis upon life, freedom from cruel relationship, and openness to the other. Additionally, I consider the role of boundaries, risk, and concerns for purity that enable and hinder communities and individuals from practicing protective hospitality. Moreover, I examine the challenge of negotiating boundaries, risk and concerns for purity, which necessitates the need for an ethic of risk to be adopted to inform responsible action.

In Chapter Five, I identify and explore various texts from the Abrahamic traditions that illustrate the practice and limitations of protective hospitality pointing to an often conflicted and imperfect practice, but a practice authoritatively modeled in the traditions nonetheless. Texts from the Jewish and Christian traditions will be limited to the Tanakh / Hebrew Bible for two reasons. First, the limitation seeks to highlight the shared textual tradition between Judaism and Christianity that shapes the practice of protective hospitality. Second, the limitation is a practical one related to the need for brevity. While there are significant passages in the New Testament that could be included, this work is not an exhaustive survey of all texts but an analysis of sample texts that problematize, shape, and speak specifically to the provision of protection. From the Tanakh / Hebrew Bible, the texts to be analyzed are the Rahab narrative from Joshua 2; the Lot in Sodom narrative from Genesis 19; the Levite, concubine and Ephraimite in Gibeah narrative in Judges 19; and the cities of refuge texts in the deuteronomic witness. Analysis based in the Qur'an and elsewhere in the Islamic tradition center upon Lot/Lut's hospitality in the Cities of the Plain, God as protector, the Constitution of Medina and its implications for the *ummah* ("community") and the *dhimmi* ("protected people"), and a selection of other texts that address the issue of protection.

In the conclusion, I draw all of these elements together to present some distilled points that hopefully will be useful in moving forward with what has been presented. It is my hope that the future potential of this work is that it can contribute to the further development of a body of literature that encourages inter-religious cooperative action and the work of creating safe spaces on behalf of marginalized groups and individuals. Moreover, it ultimately aims to spark the imagination and provide a space to consider the development of a culture and cycle of courageous reciprocity and resistance through the memory of acts of protective hospitality provided in the past to counteract cycles of abusive power and violence.

PART ONE

Hospitality, Ethics, and Theology

1

Locating the Theological Approach

Theology begins with my life, but my life is inter-related with the lives of others.

Thus, "I am" is always also "we are."

—Jung Young Lee[1]

INTRODUCTION

This book is primarily a Christian exploration of protective hospitality informed by the Jewish and Islamic traditions. As such, it draws upon the hermeneutical principles and methodology of political theology as seen through the more specific lenses of liberation and feminist theologies in an inter-religious ethical context, and explores how the insights of political theology can be extended beyond the Christian tradition to explore the social issue of protective hospitality from an inter-religious perspective in an increasingly pluralist world.

What I seek to do here is to provide an analysis of Abrahamic protective hospitality in a way that is critical, creative, and constructive. I aim to accomplish this through the use of two currents in contemporary Christian theologies: a contextual and political theological approach and a cooperative and complementary theological approach. The first approach emphasizes the situating of this work upon context and lived experience

1. Lee, *Marginality*, 8.

and the methodologies of Christian political, liberation, and feminist theologies. The second approach emphasizes cooperative and complementary theological aspects that are informed by inter-religious, Abrahamic, and hospitable hermeneutics.

A CONTEXTUAL AND POLITICAL THEOLOGICAL APPROACH

A contextual and political theological approach is useful as it enables one to analyze and reflect on hospitality on three different levels—social, cultural and theological—taking into account both orthodoxy (doctrinal belief where it exists) and orthopraxy (practice and context). Starting with practical, contextual examples to set the stage, there will then follow an exploration of the political, liberationist and feminist theological foundations of these examples.

Arising from a Context: Contemporary Examples of Protective Hospitality

> *The highest virtue is always against the law.*
>
> —RALPH WALDO EMERSON[2]

This section presents two brief case studies as initial anchors to contextualize the practice of protective hospitality. There are many examples which could be used, but for the sake of brevity and for the role of theological development, the case studies of Le Chambon-sur-Lignon and the Sanctuary Movement have been chosen.

The Village of Le Chambon-sur-Lignon

One of the best-known examples of protective hospitality of the twentieth century are the relatively widespread actions of Christian, Muslim and other non-Jew rescuers[3] who provided sanctuary and assistance to Jews and other

2. Emerson, "Worship."

3. "Rescuers" is the common term used to refer to those who hid Jews or helped Jews escape during the Holocaust. They are also referred to as "Righteous Among the Nations" or "Righteous Gentiles." They are memorialized and remembered at Yad

threatened individuals and communities in Nazi-occupied Europe, North Africa and Palestine in the late 1930s and early-mid 1940s. The motivations for rescue and refuge given were varied, but the common narrative is that during this time, over twenty thousand people from forty-five countries[4] took in strangers, those who were different either religiously, politically, or ethnically, risking their lives for the sake of the other's well-being.[5]

Throughout the literature, however, the actions of the village Le Chambon-sur-Lignon (shortened to Le Chambon) in France are cited as a prime example of hospitality in the context of rescuers during the Holocaust. Under the primary leadership of Protestant pastors André Trocmé and Edouard Theis, the village rescued between three and five thousand Jews by providing sanctuary within the community, either by helping them get to safer locations (such as Switzerland) or by harboring them more long-term in private homes, local farms or public buildings in the village. Putting themselves in harm's way and giving up much of their own freedom while under the Vichy regime of World War II France, the villagers of Le Chambon, also referred to as Chambonnais, practiced hospitality in some of the most costly ways.

The understanding of protection for the Chambonnais was rooted in their own tradition as descendents of the Calvinist French Huguenots who had been severely persecuted during the European Reformation as a result of their criticism of the use of power by the kings of France and the Roman Catholic Church.[6] This use of historical memory informs what theologian Letty Russell refers to as their "heritage of resistance."[7]

Russell's term "heritage of resistance" encourages a discussion of the term coined by Christian political theologian Johann Baptist Metz—"dangerous memory"—which, for Metz, stems from Christian Eucharistic theology and the concept of *anamesis*, wherein adherents *remember* God's saving deeds as an act of worship.[8] From meaningful, healthy remembrance

---

Vashem in Israel, but certain criteria must be met for them to be officially recognized. See Yad Vashem's website for more details: http://www1.yadvashem.org/yv/en/righteous/about.asp.

4. The precise number recognized as "Righteous Among the Nations" according to Yad Vashem is 25,685 as of January 1, 2015.

5. For examples, see Hallie, *Lest Innocent Blood Be Shed*; Tec, *When Light Pierced the Darkness*; Fogelman, *Conscience and Courage*; Gushee, *Righteous Gentiles*; Hellman, *When Courage Was Stronger Than Fear*; and Satloff, *Among the Righteous*.

6. See Scoville, *Persecution of Huguenots*; Conner, *Huguenot Heartland*; and Sunshine, *Reforming French Protestantism*.

7. Russell, "Hot-House Ecclesiology," 50.

8. While this understanding is particularly relevant to Christianity, there is room for different foundations within non-Christian traditions as well. In fact, the term

of past events and the communal narrative comes action, and it is action that can be described as "dangerous" as it often challenges the status quo, highlights injustice and will, on many occasions, inform and motivate acts of resistance. It must be said, however, that this reliance upon memory as fuel for tradition of resistance as seen in the actions of Le Chambon is not unique to the Christian tradition in its practice of hospitality. There there are accounts of Muslims in South Europe, North Africa and Palestine conducting similar activities with similar motivations. Moreover, all three of the Abrahamic traditions have this "heritage of resistance" at its core and all subsequently advocate welcome and hospitality as a result, which will be explored later.

In the case of Le Chambon and their own dangerous memory, ethicist Philip Hallie notes that even the routes the Chambonnais used to take Jewish children and families through the mountains of southeastern France into the safety of Switzerland were the same routes their Huguenot ancestors took when fleeing persecution.[9] As such, that heritage formed memories and self-identification that enabled the community to wed hospitality, which often came at a great personal price, to the provision of protection as a "faithful response to new social, political and economic developments and to particular historical crises," resulting in the protection of thousands from death camps.[10]

This heritage of resistance also enabled the Chambonnais to understand "the importance of welcome and hospitality [as] . . . they stretched this welcome as far as they could."[11] Those rescued by the Chambonnais remarked upon the hospitality they encountered there, enabling them, even in the midst of their suffering, to "find realistic hope in a world of persisting

---

"dangerous memory" does not necessarily need a religious foundation at all to still be effective in its meaning, albeit different from Metz's original intent. The Christian understanding argued by Metz is based in Jesus' proclamation that when followers share bread or drink from the cup, they are to do it "in remembrance" of him (Luke 22:19; 1 Cor 11:24–25). God's saving acts include not just spiritual salvation, but also physical, as seen in deliverance of the Israelites from slavery and redemption from injustice. See also Metz, *Faith in History and Society;* and Metz, *A Passion for God*. However, it is worth noting here that the term "dangerous" can be problematic. Metz's understanding of "dangerous" meant "defiant" or "remembering that endangers the abusive status quo." Yet, "dangerous memory" in the minds of many can also refer to unhealthy memory, such as in relation to nationalistic, violent, martyr-related memories that divide and exclude.

9. Hallie, "From Cruelty to Goodness," 27.

10. Bretherton, *Hospitality as Holiness*, 141.

11. Russell, "Hot-House Ecclesiology," 50.

cruelty."[12] For example, when a new refugee family found protection in the village, it was customary on the following morning after their arrival to "find on their front door a wreath with '*Bienvenue!*' 'Welcome!' painted on a piece of cardboard attached to the wreath . . . [but] nobody knew who had brought the wreath; in effect, the whole town had brought it."[13]

Yet, in the midst of this hospitality, the Chambonnais were keenly aware of the risks they were taking on behalf of the threatened other in their midst. Russell refers to Magda Trocmé, wife of André Trocmé, as noting that "the righteous must often pay a price for their righteousness; their own ethical purity" when it came to affirming life by providing sanctuary.[14] Additionally, both André Trocmé and Edouard Theis along with others were arrested for their actions and sent to an internment camp. Upon their release, they were asked to sign a promise of obedience to the law, which they refused, and, as a result, were forced to go underground to continue their protection efforts after their release.[15]

Sanctuary Movement in the United States

The Sanctuary Movement in the United States in the 1980s "began as a movement of hospitality that aimed to provide for the humanitarian needs of vulnerable refugees" from Central America.[16] From that practice of hospitality, however, a political movement was born that sought to protest U.S. President Ronald Reagan's destructive policies supporting wars in Central America.[17] Refugees from the violence in Guatemala, El Salvador and Nicaragua who had entered the United States illegally lived "with the immediate expectations of death if they were deported back to their countries," yet the US immigration and Naturalization Service (INS) demanded their return. Hence, the Sanctuary Movement was born.[18] Churches, synagogues, and

12. Hallie, "From Cruelty to Goodness," 27.

13. Ibid.

14. Russell, "Hot-House Ecclesiology," 50.

15. See Hallie's *Lest Innocent Blood Be Shed* for the history of the village and the risks they took for their actions.

16. Smith, *Resisting Reagan*, 69.

17. Ibid. See also LaFeber, *Inevitable Revolutions*; Carothers, *In the Name of Democracy*; and LeoGrande, *Our Own Backyard*. For a theological perspective of the events in El Salvador at that time, see Romero, *Voice of the Voiceless*.

18. Golden and McConnell, *Sanctuary*, viii. For the sake of brevity, I will rely primarily on the Smith and Golden and McConnell texts for this section. However, see also Bau, *This Ground is Holy*; Crittenden, *Sanctuary*; Cunningham, *God and Caesar at the Rio Grande*; and Nepstad, *Convictions of the Soul*. For an exploration of feminist

community groups, and organizations responded to the needs of those fleeing the violence, torture, and trauma of their homelands by actively taking in and harboring the refugees.[19]

Members of the movement "declare[d] their buildings sanctuaries for refugees,"[20] and in so doing, their actions put them in direct defiance of the American government and its interpretation of the Refugee Act of 1980. The US government classed what the members of the Sanctuary Movement were doing in the 1980s as "criminal, punishable by a $2,000 fine and up to five years in prison," but "[b]y declaring sanctuary, white, middle-class congregations experienced something of the risk that the . . . church of Central America . . . [had] endured for years."[21]

The members of the Sanctuary Movement did not take risks and violate the law casually. The decision to enter into the work of providing sanctuary was a thorough and much-discussed process, with some communities taking a couple months and others taking almost a year to decide if they were going to become involved.[22] For those who decided to join the movement, their decisions were most often marked by a turning point upon which they refused to submit to secular authority, but only to God and the call for justice.[23] Golden and McConnell describe the decision to participate and conduct an illegal network of sanctuary as follows:

---

issues and the role of women in the movement, see Lorentzen, *Women in the Sanctuary Movement*. While it is not scholarly material per se, an interesting account of the Sanctuary Movement from the perspective of a thirteen year old Guatemalan refugee is found in Pellegrino's *Journey of Dreams*. For a more contemporary look at the movement and implications for more recent immigration policies in North American post-9/11 context, see García, *Seeking Refuge*.

19. Golden and McConnell note that Native Americans in the United States also participated in this movement, using their reservations as sanctuaries. They were "very much concerned about the plight of Guatemalan Indians," as "[o]ne branch of the Mohawk nation in upper New York state . . . declared its sacred land a sanctuary" and "near Indiantown, Florida, Seminoles . . . harbored hundreds of Guatemalan Indians," which "paralleled [their involvement] in the original [Underground] railroad when Seminoles harbored escaped slaves making their way to Oklahoma and Mexico" (*Sanctuary*, 60).

20. Golden and McConnell, *Sanctuary*, viii. The sanctuary, however, was not based primarily as a physical place but as a "collective will of a faith community taking a stand for life" and served as a safe place where truth could be spoken (ibid., 11).

21. Ibid., 1–2.

22. Ibid., 132. Golden and McConnell reference an article in the *Wall Street Journal* (June 24, 1984) where members of the sanctuary movement are accused of committing a "willful and casual violation of American law." It is noted that while the "willful" claim was true, casual it was not.

23. Golden and McConnel, *Sanctuary*, 134.

> The calls came, coded conversations—midnight emergency calls from a Colorado highway driver, from the Rio Grande valley, from a pastor in Ohio, from a Methodist housekeeper in Nebraska, from refugees alone in a room in a dark church, from the clandestine Mexican church, from a Trappist monastery, from an Amerindian tribe in upstate New York, from a Concordia, Kansas, retreat center, from a farm collective in Iowa, from a synagogue in Madison, Wisconsin . . . The decision was made to keep everything in the open, to allow the public to see as clearly as possible what sanctuary was and who was involved in it. But this did not preclude caution and security efforts to protect refugees from arrest, especially when they were en route to a sanctuary. To date [1986], no refugee has been taken from a sanctuary or the railroad and deported . . . from 30 sanctuaries in 1982 to 3,000 in 1984.[24]

A unique aspect of the Sanctuary Movement compared to other instances was its public aspect. While often the provision of protective hospitality is conducted in secret because it was often risky and/or illegal, leaders of the Sanctuary Movement recognized that if the provision of sanctuary were made public, it would "give the refugees a platform to tell their stories about atrocities experienced in Central America"[25] and bear witness to the brutality supported by the Reagan administration. Furthermore, the decision to remain public was an attempt by the providers of sanctuary to circumvent the INS and "claim the high moral ground [by] openly explain[ing] themselves to the media and their denominations."[26] As providers of sanctuary began to be arrested, the arrests "only served to increase the movement's visibility and produce an outpouring of support from around the country."[27] That support grew to include condemnation of the arrests and support of the provision of sanctuary from the National Council of Churches and groups of Roman Catholic bishops and religious orders. This support was followed by the announcement that "the city of Los Angeles and the state of New Mexico declared themselves Sanctuaries."[28] As a result, in 1987, the number of Sanctuary groups, according to Smith, totaled over four hundred:

24. Ibid., 52–53.
25. Smith, *Resisting Reagan*, 67.
26. Ibid., 66.
27. Ibid., 70.
28. Ibid.

Table 1.1—Types of Sanctuary Groups, 1987[29]

Types	Number	Percent
Protestant Churches	93	22
Anabaptist Churches	80	19
Unitarian Universalist Churches	67	16
Roman Catholic Churches	65	15
Jewish Synagogues	41	10
Ecumenical Religious Groups	25	6
Cities	24	6
Universities	15	4
Other Secular Groups	13	3
Total Religious Groups	371	88
Total Secular Groups	52	12

In 1984, the INS shifted its strategy toward the Sanctuary Movement and began arresting offenders who provided sanctuary to illegal refugees. When interviewed, Christians claimed in court that their motivation was that they were "fulfilling a Christian moral duty" by providing sanctuary.[30] One person in particular, Nena MacDonald from Lubbock, Texas, had been arrested with fifteen others for providing sanctuary and rationalized her actions by stating:

29. Table sourced from Chicago Religious Task Force Sanctuary Directory 1987 (table 7.7 in Smith, *Resisting Reagan*, 185). The numbers reflected here do not correspond with the numbers given in Golden and McConnell (*Sanctuary*, 53), which are much higher, but Smith's book looks at the group called Sanctuary through which primary provision was given, whereas Golden and McConnell register any church, synagogue or group that were primary or secondary providers of sanctuary, sometimes in connection with and other times independent of the organization Sanctuary. One should also point out that, as noted in the above table, the role of the secular groups in the provision of protective hospitality in the Sanctuary Movement was a small but important one. Nicaraguan theologian Juan Hernández Pico is referenced in Chicago Religious Task Force for Central America's 1986 organizing manual, stating that "those who are faithful to the God of history may be those whose motivating convictions stand outside religious categories" and "[In the revolutionary process] seeing people die for others, and not hearing any talk from them about faith in God being the motivating factor, liberates Christians from the prejudice of trying to encounter true love solely and exclusively within the boundaries of faith. It also helps to free them from the temptation of not considering a revolutionary process authentic unless it bears the label 'Christian.'" In *Organizing for Resistance*, 1.

30. Golden and McConnell, *Sanctuary*, 68.

> If I walked down a street in Lubbock and saw a person lying in the street hurt, people would think there is something wrong with me if I didn't help. What I have done with refugees is no different. If people come here to drink from the well of kindness and we turn them away, we will have poisoned the well. Someday when we ourselves may need to drink from that same well, we will find it poisoned with floating bodies.[31]

Similarly, one of the founders of the Sanctuary Movement, Jim Corbett, found that the laws that were broken as a result of his actions were of less importance compared to the moral imperative he felt to protect the endangered lives of Central Americans seeking safety in the U.S. For Corbett, the Nuremberg trials, which he had grown up hearing about because of his father's legal profession, had proven moral responsibility was greater than inhumane laws of a nation-state.[32]

While the churches and religious communities overall in the U.S. tend not to be particularly liberationist, Golden, McConnell, and Smith all noted they have a history which points to revolutionary tendencies at certain times when the need arose, seeking liberation for those who were victims of injustice and oppression.[33] The Sanctuary Movement also found inspiration in the "dangerous memory" of protective hospitality enacted by the faithful in times past, again highlighting a "heritage of resistance" that practicing communities claimed as their own. Smith, Golden and McConnell summarize these as:

- In the declaration of "entire cities as sanctuaries of refuge for accused criminals" in the Hebrew Bible[34]
- In Christian churches "during the Roman Empire and in medieval England [which] had offered themselves as sanctuaries for fugitives of blood revenge[35]
- In the early American colonial era when churches "protected escaped political prisoners from British agents" and Quakers were known for "harboring . . . religious dissenters"[36]

31. Ibid., 77.

32. Smith, *Resisting Reagan*, 65. For more information on Jim Corbett and his role in the Sanctuary Movement, see Davidson, *Convictions of the Heart.*

33. Golden and McConnell, *Sanctuary*, 4; Smith, *Resisting Reagan*, 65–67.

34. Smith, *Resisting Reagan*, 67.

35. Ibid.

36. Golden and McConnell, *Sanctuary*, 4.

- During the era of American slavery and the work toward its abolition, churches "provided refuge and protection to fugitive slaves in direct defiance of the Fugitive Slave Law of 1850" via the Underground Railroad[37]
- During World War II, religious communities harbored Jews and other threatened groups or individuals.[38]
- And during the Vietnam War, when "many churches sheltered conscientious objectors"[39]

In addition to the memories of these models of protective hospitality, the Sanctuary Movement also looked to the history of the religious traditions involved—primarily Judaism and Christianity—which were both "born in the travail of escape."[40] For those involved in the work of the Sanctuary Movement, liberation theology became more real as they came to see God as "the force acting in history on the side of those first refugees, leading them from slavery to freedom" and whose "identity was rooted in action and proclaimed in verbs of struggle—leading, delivering, freeing."[41]

Golden and McConnell also noted a paradigm shift among communities that participated in the provision of protective hospitality in the Sanctuary Movement. They noted that with the "learning process and the wrestling with faith that occur[s] before a declaration of sanctuary" came a process of conscientization, a "shift of consciousness," which signals a "change of understanding and a change of heart that leads to deeper commitment."[42] Concurrently, Smith argues the conscientization occurred because as more communities "considered declaring sanctuary, they were forced to learn the reasons why so many traumatized and anguished Central Americans were flooding northward."[43]

37. Ibid.

38. Ibid.

39. Smith, *Resisting Reagan*, 67.

40. Golden and McConnell, *Sanctuary*, 14–15. Islam also has this history, but there is no mention in the referenced materials of Muslim involvement in the particular actions of Sanctuary Movement.

41. Ibid.

42. Ibid., 135. Golden and McConnell refer to Paulo Friere's term *conscientization* as "a process of critical reflection at deeper and deeper levels about how human beings live and die in this world" as it "invariably destroys old assumptions and breaks down mythologies that no longer explain reality because of new information." Smith's use of the term is much more practical and concrete, utilizing it as a means of education that informs resistance and social action.

43. Smith, *Resisting Reagan*, 69.

Political, Liberationist, and Feminist Theologies

Now that the context has been set, let us now consider the theological foundations upon which such activities can be analysed. Political theology arises out of the reality of history, suffering, and memory usually connected with some form of political upheaval. As such, political theology has been defined as "the analysis and criticism of political arrangements (including cultural-psychological, social and economic aspects) from the perspective of differing interpretations of God's ways in the world."[44]

While the term "political theology" is most commonly used in the context of Christian theology, there is no good reason to argue Christianity is the sole proprietor of such theological thought. Nevertheless, in spite of this, the majority of the literature related to "political theology" is Christian. Therefore, as far as methodology is concerned, we will consider what is available, and expand and enhance it where applicable in relation to other religious traditions.

Political theology as seen in its early days, sometimes referred to as European or German political theology, began as an ecumenical endeavor developed as collaboration between Protestant and Catholic theologians. It arose from a context of post-World War II Europe as both churches faced the common problem of secularism and lack of capacity to respond to the horrors that the previous years of conflict had inflicted upon the continent and the rest of the world.[45] Two of its primary thinkers, Johann Baptist Metz and Jürgen Moltmann, who are Catholic and Protestant respectively, reflected the inter-church nature of this theological development. While context was not as specifically identified as it would be later in liberation and feminist theologies, political theology began to lay the groundwork for considering religion's role in a world of conflict, modern explorations of ethical behavior toward one's neighbor, and the social implications of theological belief albeit from a more theoretical approach. Utilizing Marxist criticisms and a hermeneutic of suspicion that refuses to take any underlying principles at face value,[46] political theology began to emphasize praxis, considering the effect theological teaching had upon the social and political as well as the spiritual

44. Cavanaugh and Scott, *The Blackwell Companion to Political Theology*, 1.

45. Moltmann, *On Human Dignity*, 98.

46. The origins of the hermeneutics of suspicion are discussed in more detail in the context of the thoughts and writings of Sigmund Freud, Friedrich Nietzsche, and Karl Marx in Ricoeur, *Freud and Philosophy*, 32–35; and Ricoeur, *Hermeneutics and The Human Sciences*, 34. See also Segundo, *Liberation of Theology*; O'Donnell, "Influence of Freud's Hermeneutic of Suspicion," 28–34; and Williams, "Suspicion of Suspicion," 36–53.

and psychological realms.[47] Through careful scrutiny, political theologians considered various theological doctrines and deemed them to be "oppressive or liberating, alienating or humanizing."[48] In this way, political theology as a method was seen as "a corrective to situationless theologies" as it counteracted naïve idealism and sought out the more difficult of human experiences for theological reflection.[49] Working particularly on the themes of memory, suffering and hope, Moltmann and Metz saw there was no such thing as an "*a*political theology"[50] and they began to formulate critiques of long-held concepts such as the nature of God, the nature of humanity, freedom, and interpretation of history necessitated by the manipulation of these ideas in war-time Europe in the early twentieth century.[51]

This early political theology had its weaknesses, namely in that it was predominantly androcentric *and* Eurocentric. It has been justly criticized as primarily reflecting "the voice of the bourgeoisie, questioning their own basic assumptions and seeking grace and hope in conversion."[52] These limitations meant political theology did not offer the full potential it encouraged when taken seriously. There were other voices to be heard other than European middle and upper class males. Over the years, the work of theologians such as Dorothee Sölle began to draw together the work of the German predecessors and the new theological voices arising from other parts of the world, and political theology's boundaries expanded into what would become known as liberation theology.[53]

Liberation theology was influenced by political theology as it took root as its own movement, but it evolved into something distinctive.[54] It carried with it substantial political and social critique, but increasingly focused upon the realities of poverty and oppression, namely in the development of the hermeneutic that emphasized God's preferential option for the poor and oppressed. It sought to go one step further than earlier European versions of political theology had done; it sought to put theory into practice

47. Moltmann, *On Human Dignity*, 98.

48. Ibid.

49. Metz, *A Passion for God*, 23–24.

50. Moltmann, *On Human Dignity*, 99.

51. Chopp, *The Praxis of Suffering*, 4.

52. Ibid.

53. See the works of Sölle: *Political Theology*; *Suffering*; *Celebrating Resistance*; and *The Silent Cry*.

54. All of these theologies (political, liberation, and feminist) could be discussed in the plural, rather than the singular, such as political theologies, liberation theologies, and feminist theologies. Usage of the plural reflects the understanding that even these different methodologies are not monolithic.

through creating base communities, fostering dialogue, and coordinating resistance around certain political issues such as social class and economic deprivation, oppressive government regimes, and the rights of indigenous and marginalized peoples. Yet, liberation theology would go through its own evolution; it was susceptible to the similar charge of androcentrism and was critiqued as being primarily Roman Catholic, particularly in its development in Central and South America.

Out of these critiques of male-centered theology both in the political and liberationist realms, feminist theology gained ground.[55] Believing women's experiences and issues related to women were not being adequately represented, feminist theologians asked serious questions about concepts of gender, power, violence, and trauma. Utilizing some of the same hermeneutical tools as liberation theologians, feminist theologians went further in that they sought to give voice and support not only to the case of the poor and the oppressed, but also to the experiences of women and the effects of women's issues upon on the faith community and society.[56]

All three of these theological approaches inspire, challenge, and borrow from one another, and the lines between them are continually blurred with the emergence of related theologies such as queer, womanist, mujerista, or Asian women's theologies.[57] Furthermore, it is possible that all three also fit within schema of contextual theology as one can interpret their theological hermeneutic as "explicitly [placing] the recognition of the contextual nature

55. Feminist theology in a variety of forms had existed previous to this time, as seen in Sojourner Truth's "Ain't I a Woman?" speech given in 1851, where she states: "[The preacher] says women can't have as much rights as men, 'cause Christ wasn't a woman! Where did your Christ come from? Where did your Christ come from? From God and a woman! Man had nothing to do with Him. If the first woman God ever made was strong enough to turn the world upside down all alone, these women together ought to be able to turn it back, and get it right side up again! And now they is asking to do it, the men better let them." See hooks, *Ain't I a Woman?*, for further information. Similarly, Elizabeth Cady Stanton's work with the Seneca Falls collective on *The Woman's Bible* was influential, as it was the first time the Christian Bible had been published with commentary and critique that spoke to the needs of women. Nevertheless, the modern period of feminist theology quickly developed with the works of Daly, such as *The Church and the Second Sex* and *Beyond God the Father*, and with Ruether's *Mary, the Feminine Face of the Church*.

56. See also Brown and Bohn, *Christianity, Patriarchy, and Abuse*; Phyllis Trible, *Texts of Terror*; Kyung, *Struggle to Be the Sun Again*; and Schüssler Fiorenza, *But She Said*.

57. For queer, womanist, mujerista, and Asian women's theology examples, see the following respectively: Althaus-Reid, *The Queer God*; Williams, *Sisters in the Wilderness*; Aquino et al., *Reader in Latina Feminist Theology*; Kyung, *Struggle to Be the Sun Again*.

of theology at the forefront of the theological process,"[58] whether it be in the form of a geographical, cultural, sexual, economic, or political context.[59]

While liberation and feminist theologies arguably lie under the more general umbrella of political theology, each have their unique place, and yet in cooperation with one another they each bring different aspects to the investigation of a theology and ethic of protective hospitality.

First, there is the issue of audience. My primary concern is to consider the needs of the powerless, marginalized, and threatened other by addressing those who are in the position to provide protective hospitality, those who have the power to host.[60] Those who are within the powerful mainstream are usually the ones who are in the easiest position to provide protection of the persecuted. Therefore, I wish to keep in mind the needs of the threatened other, which requires the tools of liberation and feminist theologies. Yet, it utilizes the tools of political theology by identifying theological and ethical imperatives that contribute to meaningful action for those who have the power to provide protective hospitality.[61]

Second is the issue of hermeneutics. Most useful are two particular hermeneutics within political theology: the hermeneutic of suspicion, found in all expressions of political theology, and the hermeneutic of liberation for all, found mostly in liberation and feminist theologies. The hermeneutic of suspicion can shed light on long-held, but often forgotten, ideas and traditions related to welcoming the other in the Abrahamic tradition of hospitality. Additionally, as the practice of protective hospitality calls into question ideas related to power and authority, both hermeneutics of suspicion and liberation are likely to be of particular value for theological analysis.

Third, the engagement with political, liberation, and feminist theologies highlights that the approaches here are centered upon social practice

58. Pears, *Doing Contextual Theology*, 1.

59. It is understood, however, that while all theology is contextual, not everyone recognizes it as such, *explicitly* emphasizing the context within theological construction. See ibid., 1–4.

60. Jacques Derrida argues that hospitality relies upon one having the "power to host," as noted in "Hospitality," 110–12. This acknowledgement to hospitality's need for "the power to host" is also referred to by Reynolds, *Merleau-Ponty and Derrida*, 177–79; Newlands, *Hospitable God*, 77–78; and Carroll, "Reimagining Home," 179–81.

61. Nevertheless, there are protectors as well as those in need of refuge who are part of the marginalized of this world. I think specifically of networks of women who have been victims of domestic abuse who join forces to protect one another. In their case, utilizing only general political theology as an approach can be lacking and would benefit from more specific feminist perspectives. Therefore, since this research seeks to address their plight as well, the more specific disciplines of liberation and feminist theologies are required.

and lived experience. The theological formulations presented here were not incubated in a vacuum, but were shaped and matured in response to concrete experience. Feminist theologians assert "[t]heology follows life; it does not precede it."[62] Moreover, this emphasis upon applied praxis understands that theological formulations are of no value to anyone if they are not disseminated and lived out in a constructive way. If left in the realm of doctrine only, theology becomes mere conjecture rather than practical, concrete expression of dynamic faith. Similarly, liberation theology exhorts contextual praxis, seeing everyday concerns as integral to theological formation and considering the recitation of creed and tradition without corresponding action as lifeless and empty. In this way, liberation theology sees itself not as "a new theme for reflection but as a *new way* to do theology."[63] Liberation theology does not, however, stop at reflection, but seeks "to be a part of the process through which the world is transformed."[64] Transformation is essential to the narrative of protective hospitality, and, therefore, should not be ignored.

Fourth, the emphasis upon violence, trauma, exclusion, and the needs for security as emphasized in feminist theology has a great deal to contribute to the discussion of protective hospitality. Whereas European political theology and liberation theology tend to give more patriarchal understandings of suffering, feminist theology takes a different approach by giving voice and bearing witness to those who have been abused and neglected, tortured, and persecuted. Feminist theology challenges justifications for suffering as a means of redemption.[65] The refusal to "grant [violence] power"[66] and, subsequently, the emphasis upon acts of resistance to power is a foundational concept of feminist theology that can offer crucial sensitivity. Likewise, issues of social inequality, systems of patriarchy, and exploitation of the weak and vulnerable are ever present in discussing the concept of protective hospitality, and so the feminist perspective is useful to this discussion.

Fifth, the use of other types of literature beyond simply the sacred texts as evidenced in feminist theological constructions is valuable. Particularly in the practice of hospitality, looking to other sources and authorities that challenge and shape cultural practice of welcome and safety is helpful. Furthermore, in light of the fact that those in need of protection are often those

62. Brown and Bohn, *Christianity, Patriarchy, and Abuse*, xii.

63. Gutierrez, *A Theology of Liberation*, 15.

64. Ibid.

65. See Brock and Parker, *Proverbs of Ashes*, for an example of how feminist theologians are questioning the role of violence, suffering, and trauma as being redemptive.

66. Brown and Bohn, *Christianity, Patriarchy, and Abuse*, xii.

who have been marginalized even by the formal structures of the religious traditions, feminist theology's inspiration from extra-textual sources and primary narratives is necessary to give voice to those experiences.[67] Such sources provide "helpful insights to the human condition" and can also articulate the "experiences of those who have been marginalized by the dominant tradition."[68] In turn, they have the potential "to challenge theology, deconstructing its authoritative status and 'unmasking' theological narratives."[69] Therefore, the stories of practitioners and other instances of protective hospitality to the threatened other during conflict, even in recent history and current events, are vitally important to theological analysis presented here.

Lastly, this work emphasizes the poor as found in liberation theology, but seeks to explore the definition of who exactly "the poor" are. It does not rely upon economic poverty, per se, as liberation theology practitioners have traditionally sought to do. Economic realities certainly play a role, but are not the sole contributing factor to the need for protective hospitality. One of the most valuable contributions to this discussion comes from the liberation theologian Jon Sobrino, who asserts "the poor are those who die before their time." For most of the poor, death comes slowly through grinding poverty. For a few, however, their death is a "swift, violent death, caused by repression and wars, when the poor threaten these unjust structures . . . [and] are deprived even of their cultures in order to weaken their identities and make them more defenseless."[70] According to Sobrino, those targeted for persecution in such a way that they need protective hospitality are, indeed, "the poor." Similarly, other liberation theologians such as James Cone and N. L. Eiesland define the poor as those who have been subjected to discrimination, marginalization, and dehumanization because of their race, ethnicity, class, or disability.[71] Therefore "the poor" are not simply the economically deprived, but are all who are oppressed or marginalized within a society, anyone who is suffering because of injustice or in need of protection.

Accordingly, what is presented in the following chapters builds upon the understanding that the respective Abrahamic traditions have a strong foundation in social justice traditions. While the three traditions carry out their commitments to social justice in a variety of ways, there is a shared end

67. Graham, *Theological Reflection*, 71–72.

68. Ibid., 72, referring to Walton, "Speaking in Signs," 2–6.

69. Graham, *Theological Reflections*, 72.

70. Sobrino, *The Principle of Mercy*, 50. Cf. Tombs, *Latin American Liberation Theology*, 213.

71. Eiesland, *The Disabled God*; Cone, *God of the Oppressed*.

result to these commitments: to live lives that honor God and the dignity of one's fellow human beings.[72]

A COOPERATIVE AND COMPLEMENTARY THEOLOGICAL APPROACH

In addition to a contextual and political approach, the second theological current drawn upon is a cooperative and complementary theological approach informed by three particular distinctive emphases identified as the inter-religious, Abrahamic, and hospitable. To succeed in this endeavor, both disciplines of Christian theology and religious studies are drawn upon, taking a step beyond a solely Christian outlook by seeking to engage more directly with lived experience in a pluralist world.

Towards an Inter-Religious Approach

The reality of a pluralist world and its role in developing self-understanding was acknowledged in the nineteenth century by thinkers such as Max Müller and Goethe, who both argued that "to know one is to know none."[73] Comparative religion scholar Ruth ApRoberts utilizes Müller's assertion, and declares "to know Judaism and Christianity we must study non-Jewish, non-Christian cultures, especially of the surrounding peoples."[74] Therefore, to truly understand Christianity's theology and ethic of protective hospitality, it is beneficial to consider other non-Christian traditions that shed light on particular aspects that may be invisible otherwise. Therefore, I seek to examine Christian theology and protective hospitality through the interpretative lenses of Judaism and Islam's own practice in such a way that is respectful of difference and highlights complementarity and enables cooperation for mutual benefit. More specifically, the theology analyzed and developed here seeks to emphasize complementarity in thought and identify potential cooperative action through extending protective welcome to the endangered other.

Furthermore, these two main theological approaches—the contextual and political, and the cooperative and complementary—are interlinked.

72. See Esack, *Qur'an, Liberation and Pluralism*; Ellis, *Toward a Jewish Theology of Liberation*; and Yong, *Hospitality and the Other*.

73. Müller made this observation in the area of religions; Goethe, in the area of language. This statement is credited to both in several sources, including ApRoberts, *The Ancient Dialect*, 28; and Courville, *Edward Said's Rhetoric of the Secular*, 66.

74. ApRoberts, *The Ancient Dialect*, 28.

The dual usage of these approaches of Christian political theology and inter-religious hermeneutics is considered a necessity by both Asian liberation theologian Aloysius Pieris and inter-religious scholar Paul Knitter, whose work argues that if inter-religious dialogue "does not come out of an experience of human suffering, and does not explore the this-worldly, liberative message of all religions, [then it] is a violation of the very nature of religion and interreligious dialogue."[75] Yet, Pieris also questions his fellow liberation theologians by questioning if their "vision of the kingdom of God [is] perhaps too narrow because it is too Christian."[76] Pieris, therefore, understands that if one is to consider political theology, one must also consider the inter-religious; and if one is to consider the inter-religious, one must consider political theology in light of "the many poor and the many religious"[77] of this globalized world. Those of different religious traditions still live in the same world, have the same human needs, have many of the same values, and suffer the same abuses. John Donne's classic assertion that "no man is an island"[78] rings true for the inclusion of religious traditions as well in the current pluralist and globalized context. Conversely, to try to control that which is different and enforce homogeneity is to dominate and control, which is unhelpful to dialogue.

Yet, in light of the practicalities of an inter-religious hermeneutic, it should be noted that those who profess a particular faith are "never innocent of other philosophical influences."[79] Whenever theological constructs are proposed, they are contextual in that they are based in a "specific place and time"[80] and are reflective of an individual's or community's experiences and world view informed by culture, national and political identities, and other self-defining factors. The key to constructing a socially relevant and contextually oriented approach is to be aware of those factors. If one seeks for that approach also to be inter-religious and cooperative in nature, then demonstrating inter-religious literacy, making "measured judgments within the bounds of [one's] learning," and knowing when "to stop speaking about things beyond [one's] expertise" are also required.[81] Therefore, what follows

75. Knitter, foreword to *An Asian Theology of Liberation*, xi–xii. See also Pieris, *Love Meets Wisdom*.

76. Ibid., xii.

77. Knitter, "Pluralism and Oppression," 198–208.

78. John Donne, "Meditation XVII," in *Emergent Occasions*.

79. Graham, *Theological Reflection*, 138.

80. Ibid., 138–39.

81. Clooney, *Comparative Theology*, 6.

seeks to highlight cooperation in ethical practice with a view to the context out of which it arises.

As Christian political theology in its various forms seeks to address suffering and violence, and no religious tradition's adherents are immune to suffering, it is no surprise that feminist and liberationist perspectives found in Judaism and Islam also take suffering, violence, and marginalization seriously. Such perspectives are relatively recent, but their existence is important.[82] While a variety of disciplines will be utilized to draw a variety of strands together, feminist and liberationist hermeneutics of the textual sources and tradition will most often prevail throughout this analysis.

A word regarding the feminist role in this discussion of suffering, solidarity, and inter-religious cooperation is required. Feminism is, according to feminist theologian Ursula King, "the missing dimension in the dialogue of religions," and "interfaith dialogue is mostly, at least on the official level, carried out by men, and gender issues have rarely been on the agenda."[83] Additionally, feminist theology fills a role in ethical formation that has been heretofore lacking: it is relational in its ethical constructions. Women tend to "develop . . . relation-centered ethics . . . [which] contrasts to the stress on rules and autonomy in male ethics."[84] As a result, the relational aspect of hospitality is attractive to many feminist-leaning scholars. Moreover, many feminist theologians emphasize "life" as the "key word," as the norm for evaluating "religious traditions in interfaith dialogue" wherein words such as "life-affirming," "life-enhancing," "survival-centered" often appear.[85] Concurrently, protective hospitality has, at its center, a dedication to the value and preservation of life, particularly on behalf of those who are threatened.

In some contexts, religious diversity is closely linked to liberation theology in that denying the need for diversity and insisting upon uniformity is to restrict life and "the right to full human and religious flourishing."[86] Likewise, feminist theology emphasizes both the global and the local as it

82. Their legitimacy in the overall presence and structure in the respective religious traditions cannot be debated at length here, but are understood. For liberationist perspectives in Islam and Judaism, see Esack, *Qur'an, Liberation and Pluralism*; Dabashi, *Islamic Liberation Theology*; Ellis, *Toward a Jewish Theology of Liberation;* and Ellis, *Reading the Torah Out Loud*. For feminist perspectives, see Wadud, *Qur'an and Woman* and *Inside the Gender Jihad*; Hassan, "Challenging the Stereotypes of Fundamentalism"; Plaskow, *Standing Against Sinai*; and Haddad and Esposito, *Daughters of Abraham*.

83. King, "Feminism," quoted in Engell, "Dialogue for Life," 249. Another version of King's article can be found in May, *Pluralism and the Religions*, 40–57.

84. Engell, "Dialogue for Life," 255.

85. Ibid., 256.

86. Phan, "Living for the Reign of God," 18. See also Phan, *Being Religious Interreligiously*.

is "trans-national, trans-regional, trans-cultural and trans-religious,"[87] it "recognize[s] the complex web of multiple oppression" and it "shift[s] from the politics of identity to the politics of solidarity."[88]

Additionally, solidarity with the suffering and oppressed in inter-religious spheres enables those "from diverse cultures and religions to come to shared conclusions about truth and value and action"[89] and it requires a "hermeneutical privilege" to be given to those who suffer.[90] The emphasis upon this commonality in approach is appropriate if the suffering are to be allowed to be a part of their own solution and the religious traditions represented truly seek to make effective changes against injustice.[91] In this way, then, "the questioning face of the suffering . . . enables religions to face and question each other and come to joint assessments of truth."[92]

Furthermore, as inter-religious scholar John D'Arcy May points out, "suffering poses an ethical question, to which the only appropriate response is action."[93] While what action is taken can differ depending upon the religious tradition, "the universal experience of suffering correlates with particular practical responses . . . because it is mediated to us in markedly different ways—called 'religions'—in which the common human lot is symbolised."[94]

Concurrently, Knitter states that "religions call on what is more than human (at least the human as we now experience it) in order to transform or liberate the human" and that "to transform the human context will mean, generally, to oppose or resist the forces that stand in the way of change or newness."[95] Knitter also refers to the work of David Tracy who notes "religions are exercises in resistance . . . which reveal various possibilities for human freedom . . . [w]hen not domesticated by sacred canopies for the status quo or wasted by their own self-contradictory grasps at power."[96] In the same vein, Mohandas Gandhi declared: "those who say that religion has nothing to do with politics do not know what religion means."[97] Yet, it is this

87. Kang, "Re-constructing *Asian* Feminist Theology," 49.

88. Phan, "Living For The Reign Of God," 49, referring to further arguments made in Kang, "Re-constructing *Asian* Feminist Theology," 222–24.

89. Knitter, "Responsibilities for the Future," 85, referring to Francis Schüssler Fiorenza's "Theological and Religious Studies," 133–34.

90. Ibid., 86.

91. Ibid.

92. Ibid., 85.

93. May, *After Pluralism*, 94–95.

94. Ibid.

95. Knitter, "Responsibilities for the Future," 76.

96. Tracy, *Plurality and Ambiguity*, 84.

97. Gandhi, *My Autobiography*, 504.

value of resistance that has been lost in mainstream Abrahamic traditions while still being so vital to its ethical framework, particularly on behalf of the poor, marginalized, and oppressed. It is this value of resistance on behalf of the threatened other that I seek to rediscover and illuminate in the context of protective hospitality.

Within the emphasis upon the social relevance of an inter-religious hermeneutic, there is also the need to acknowledge the existence and authority of the subversive and prophetic in the foundations of the Abrahamic traditions, found particularly in the intra-communal discussions regarding meaning, ethics, and use of power.[98] All three of the traditions have had national might on their side at one point or another. Yet, adherents of all three traditions have also tasted the humiliation and disempowerment of being a threatened other, an oppressed and persecuted minority.

To welcome and admit the threatened other and provide protection is to subvert the powers that call for their exclusion or demise. To cry out for inclusion in society, many times against popular opinion, is to be prophetic as it provides a vision for what the community can or should be. In light of this, I aim to emphasize the voices in the Abrahamic traditions that challenge rather than collude with the powers and national might. I also wish to highlight instances where the marginalized are subjected to rejection and oppression both in the halls of government and community as well as in the temples of religion.

This combination between the spiritual and political through the voice of the prophetic is reminiscent of Knitter's concept of the "*mystical-prophetic dipolarity*" that "vibrates and flows back and forth within all religious traditions."[99] This dipolarity

> animates a two fold project, each aspect essential, each calling to and dependent on the other, to transform both the within and the without, to alter inner consciousness and social consciousness, to bring about peace of the heart and peace in the world, stirring the individual to an earnest spiritual praxis and also to a bold political praxis . . . The dynamic and call of this mystical-prophetic dipolarity is what tells Christians that they can love God only when they are loving their neighbour, or Buddhists that wisdom is not possible without compassion . . . Neither the

98. See works such as Appleby, *Ambivalence of the Sacred*; Gopin, *Between Eden and Armageddon*; Kimball, *When Religion Becomes Evil*; Horsley, *Religion and Empire*; and Almond, Appleby, and Sivan, *Strong Religion*, for discussions on the social relevance of religion, particularly in relation to power, violence, and conflict, both for positive and negative impact.

99. Knitter, "Responsibilities for the Future," 77.

> mystical nor the prophetic is more fundamental, more important; each calls to, and has existence in, the other.[100]

While Knitter's dipolarity speaks to intra-religious dialogue more than inter-religious dialogue, it is not without applicability. The mystical and prophetic in each tradition oftentimes finds itself mirrored in other traditions in very similar ways. The emphasis upon doctrine and right belief is countered by a comparable emphasis upon personal and communal responsibility. When the balance is not maintained, Knitter asserts, there are "mystics whose spirituality becomes self-indulgent, insensitive, or irresponsible . . . [and] prophets whose actions become self-serving, intolerant, or violent."[101]

Testing this balance through exposure and cooperation with other traditions is beneficial as it tests the health of the religious tradition and its place in the world. Knitter explains this by arguing that if adherents from a variety of religious traditions "can agree in the beginning that [their faith] must always promote greater eco-human wellbeing and remove the sufferings from our world, then they have a shared reference point from which to affirm or criticize each other's claims."[102] In this way, "immediate solutions to interreligious disagreements" are not provided but a "path toward solutions" is made possible.[103]

Similarly, inter-religious scholar Hendrik Vroom asks a pertinent question: Is right conduct the criterion for true religion?[104] In working out answers to this question, Vroom refers to Knitter who names this particular criterion as being a "message [which promotes] the psychological health of individuals, their sense of value, purpose, [and] freedom . . . [promoting] the welfare, the liberation, of all peoples, integrating individual persons and nations into a larger community."[105] Furthermore, Vroom highlights Knitter's argument emphasizing liberation as "the possibility for religious traditions to understand one another [which] lies in a 'communion of liberative praxis,'" making dialogue, then, a "'shared praxis' from which a 'communication in doctrine' is possible."[106]

Vroom's assertions concerning right conduct are valuable. In this approach, the test of healthy theology is based in how it is practiced and the

100. Ibid.

101. Ibid.

102. Ibid., 85.

103. Ibid.

104. Vroom, "Right Conduct," 107.

105. Knitter, *No Other Name?*, 231. Cf. Vroom, "Right Conduct," 107.

106. Knitter, "Toward a Liberation Theology of Religions," 183. Cf. Vroom, "Right Conduct," 107.

effects it has not only on the believers themselves, but also on those around them. Therefore, if one were to form an inter-religious theology around the concept of protective hospitality, it can best be tested as it is formed into an inter-religious ethic.[107] If a theology has no valuable, corresponding ethic, that theology is practically meaningless. Conversely, if an ethic has no underlying system of belief,[108] it is often empty and simply duty for duty's sake.[109] In this way, religious ethics are deeply rooted in spiritual belief and practice and to separate the two is to misrepresent both.[110] Theory and practice, or theology and ethics, "mutually drive each other forward" and "do not belong in two different kingdoms," but at the same time, they also "never wholly correspond with each other . . . [and] do not come to a unity in history."[111] Instead, as Jürgen Moltmann asserts, theology and ethics "constantly overlap so that theory must incorporate practice and practice must incorporate theory."[112]

Furthermore, a cooperative ethical hermeneutic rooted in Abrahamic theologies takes into account and shows sensitivity to the diversity of traditions and approaches found in Judaism, Christianity, and Islam. All three traditions uphold the imperative of "prophetic responsibility" when it comes to developing the links between theology and ethics,[113] and yet each is particular in how that prophetic responsibility is carried out. As such, the effort toward pluralism in order to illustrate the positive potential for an Abrahamic theology and ethic of protective hospitality needs to consider those particularities and the "apparent mutual incompatibility of cultures and religions, presenting its ethical credentials precisely in its sensitivity to differences and its solidarity with the marginalised."[114]

While they are often unable to be uniformly changed, particularities can be "imaginatively transcend[ed]" when it is realized that "there are aspects

107. With "ethic" being defined as the code of behavior one has toward others—both on an individual and societal/communal level.

108. Whether it be based in "theology" per se—meaning a belief in God and a view of God's place in the world—or in humanism or some other similar value system.

109. However, duty for duty's sake should not be summarily discounted, as it is a recognized value system stemming most familiarly from the work of Immanuel Kant and the development of deontological ethics. Despite its noble intent, it does not, nevertheless, point to the ideal of religiously-motivated ethics and lacks in authority to maintain practice, particularly in more dangerous or conflicted contexts.

110. May, *After Pluralism*, 84–85.

111. Moltmann, *On Human Dignity*, 107–8.

112. Ibid.

113. Esack, *Qur'an, Liberation and Pluralism*, 17.

114. May, *After Pluralism*, 60–61.

of them which are philosophically limited or ethically unsatisfactory."[115] It is here where the cooperative and inter-religious nature of this ethical formation is useful, in that where there are weaknesses in one tradition, another tradition may be utilized in order to teach, challenge, and strengthen. May considers this in the context of inter-religious communication, noting interaction between traditions "can transform both persons and situations . . . [because] by acting together on behalf of the suffering . . . religious people, no matter how different their backgrounds, truly come to know what they believe."[116]

May's consideration of inter-religious communication necessitates a discussion related to the method of inter-religious hermeneutics in general. There are a variety of ways in which inter-religious communication takes place. Comparative theologian Catherine Cornille identifies them as the following:

1. the hermeneutical retrieval of resources for dialogue within one's own tradition;
2. the pursuit of proper understanding of the other;
3. the appropriation and reinterpretation of the other within one's own religious framework; and
4. the borrowing of hermeneutical principles of another religion.[117]

The first approach identified by Cornille emphasizes the internal dialogue—or intrareligious dialogue—that occurs as a result of exposure to or desire to interact with the other. As a result, a number of hermeneutical tools can be utilized to examine the resources within one's own tradition that may inform and foster "greater openness toward other religions."[118] This work relies upon the conversations previously conducted within the boundaries of this approach in each of the traditions and upon the centuries of theological debate that has addressed issues of exclusivism and pluralism, and discussions of supercessionism, soteriology, revelation, and religious authority.

The second approach is, perhaps, the most common hermeneutic in inter-religious dialogue as it focuses upon learning about the other as a means of gaining understanding. The Qur'anic admonition that each

115. Ibid., 99–100.

116. Ibid.

117. Cornille, "On Hermeneutics in Dialogue," introduction to *Interreligious Hermeneutics*, edited by Catherine Cornille and Christopher Conway, x.

118. Ibid., xi.

tradition was created "so that you may know one another" encapsulates such an approach."[119] Yet, over the years, optimism has battled with pessimism as to whether or not such understanding can ever really be achieved. Cornille points out that the experimental and affective dimensions of inter-religious study where ideas and teachings that resonate with one's experience are secondary to "rational comprehension or historical knowledge"[120] have been neglected.

Yet, comparative theologian Samuel Youngs argues such a process is becoming more popular as the global nature of "contemporary religious and secular pluralism . . . is having a marked influence on the ways in which academia studies religion and theology," causing a move "beyond a typically Christian way of studying religion and theology in order to advocate a more sympathetic outlook and approach with regard to other religions."[121] Youngs identifies this process as one whereby "a religious scholar or theologian reaches out from their own faith tradition—without denying that tradition—in order to intentionally and sympathetically interact and exchange with other systems of theological belief in a comparative way."[122]

The third approach looks to gain "not only proper understanding of the other religion but also mutual enrichment and growth in truth" through appropriation and reinterpretation.[123] It looks for the original meanings in the religious contexts from which certain truths and teachings arise, while utilizing those same teachings to enhance, challenge or integrate into one's own religious tradition. In this approach, there is the acknowledgement that traditions borrow from, are in conversation with, and transform because of other traditions, both from within and without. Some find this approach disturbing, labeling such practices as syncretism, spiritual colonization, or simple theft. The comparative theologian Francis Clooney writes of the "persistent colonialist tendency to co-opt . . . others, consuming them simply for our own purposes."[124] His concern is valid and should serve as a corrective, ensuring appropriation is not consumption, but careful consideration, dia-

119. Qur'an 49:13. Muslim scholar Reza Shah-Kazemi notes the Arabic meaning for *ta'arafu* (know one another) does not refer only to "knowledge in the ordinary sense, but to spiritual knowledge." See Shah-Kazemi, "Light upon Light?," 121.

120. Cornille, "On Hermeneutics in Dialogue," xv–xvi. Cornille has written about this further in her 2008 book, *The Im-Possibility of Interreligious Dialogue*, 137–76.

121. Byrne, *The Names of God*, 3, referring to the work of Youngs, "The Frontier of Comparative Theology," 1–10.

122. Youngs, "The Frontier of Comparative Theology," 4. Cf. Byrne, *The Names of God*, 3.

123. Cornille, "On Hermeneutics in Dialogue," xvii.

124. Clooney, *Comparative Theology*, 52.

logue, and integration for shared benefit. However, from a more positive perspective, this particular inter-religious hermeneutic, Cornille asserts, also has a greater capacity to "lead to the rediscovery of certain forgotten, neglected, or implicit dimensions"[125] in the traditions being explored and providing "opportunity for continuous growth."[126] Ricoeur's version of linguistic hospitality most likely resembles appropriation[127] according to Ricoeur scholar Marianne Moyaert who notes appropriation is "never an act of 'absorption,' but rather the reception of the other as other" requiring a willingness on the part of the host "to undergo a form of *alienation* . . . [presuming] *expropriation* . . . [and] becoming *oneself another*."[128]

The final inter-religious hermeneutic appropriates particular skills and hermeneutical tools used in one tradition for use in another. Such an approach can be seen in the practice of applying the Jewish tradition of midrash to non-Jewish texts, or applying the hermeneutical tools of Christian political theology to assist in interpretation of Jewish and Muslim sources as they pertain to the practice of hospitality.

Nevertheless, of the approaches explored here, the third inter-religious hermeneutic, which seeks to gain understanding of other traditions while using that understanding to sharpen and enrich one's own, has the greatest resonance with the approach adopted here. While elements from the other approaches will be utilized, as has been noted, the majority of the work presented here seeks to rediscover the tradition of hospitality in the Christian tradition while utilizing the traditions of Judaism and Islam to identify the gaps that need to be addressed. This particular approach will, however, inevitably lead to further identification of complementarity present in the three traditions that provides material for meaningful dialogue, cooperative theological development, and faithful social action.[129]

May helpfully sheds light on the cooperative nature of shared religious life together by exploring the language used. Borrowed from the language of science, inter-religious concepts of "complementarity" and "symbiosis" are

125. Cornille, "On Hermeneutics in Dialogue," xviii.

126. Ibid., xix.

127. This will be discussed later in this chapter in the context of a hermeneutic of hospitality.

128. Moyaert, "Absorption or Hospitality," 85. See also Moyaert, "The (Un-)translatability of Religions?," 337–64.

129. I do, however, admit that the more orthodox or fundamentalist/conservative branches of Christianity, Judaism, and Islam may take issue with some approaches and assumptions found here. As there is no monolithic expression of religious adherence, this is unavoidable. Nevertheless, all three traditions have theological traditions related to liberation and feminist theology that have more in common with one another than difference.

necessary as they emphasize the role of imagining, theorizing, and building models where "two organisms need to engage in an exchange of life-giving substances with one another in order that both may survive."[130] Building upon this, May asserts two other ideas for inter-religious life borrow from science: "synthesis" in which "elements combine to create a substance which contains the old elements in a new form"[131] and, what May calls, a corresponding "osmosis of discourse"[132] in which religious ideas maintain individual identity but move through their self-identifying boundaries in order to borrow and use language, theological formulations, and ethics of other traditions that can provide new ideas and ways of being faithful.

Furthermore, May highlights the "danger of dualism" that can often be found in inter-religious dialogue where distinct entities enter into relationship under the auspices of "us" and "them."[133] To counteract this, May suggests dialogue not be "merely the reciprocal presentation of proposals for belief, but the profoundly religious act of making oneself able to welcome the stranger by facing the alien in oneself," as difference "becomes an agent of self-discovery and a source of mutual enrichment."[134] Indeed, May says, "[o]ur own spirituality is neither fully real nor genuinely autonomous until we acknowledge that other people's can be too" and, therefore, we "must be strong enough not only for the dialogue of like with like, but for the encounter of unlike with unlike."[135]

No religious tradition is monolithic and unchanging. Every religious tradition including Christianity's claim to *ecclesia semper reformando* undergoes reformation as it encounters new questions, challenges and contexts.[136] Furthermore, inter-religious scholar James Heft concludes it "is the *responsibility* of each religion to correct itself, to perform the sacred task of self-criticism."[137] For this to happen, dialogue needs to take place and new ideas need to be disseminated, allowing for a "new consensus of authorities that will not tolerate" inherited claims to be developed.[138] As a result of this

130. May, *After Pluralism*, 57.

131. May explains this further by giving examples: "Zen Christianity pioneered by Hugo Enomiya-Lasalle SJ . . . the universalist and peaceable Baha'i faith as a transmutation of Islam; the incorporation of traditional and Christian rituals in the African Independent Churches" (*After Pluralism*, 57).

132. Ibid., 58–59.

133. Ibid., 70–71.

134. Ibid., 80.

135. Ibid.

136. Reynolds, "Improvising Together," 62.

137. Heft, "Resources for Social Transformation," 7 (italics mine).

138. Greenberg, "Religion as a Force for Reconciliation and Peace," 101.

reformation in each tradition, a natural outcome will be that those adherents who move toward justice-oriented theologies feel as if they have more in common with believers from other religious traditions "than they have with members of their own communities" who are not concerned with the same issues.[139] Such realities require further encounter with the religious other and dialogue in order to build stronger frameworks for shared action.

Welcoming the religious other is an essential premise of this research. On a theoretical level, some will find this welcome difficult, particularly in relation to exclusivist truth claims. Nevertheless, welcome should not be dependent upon these claims. Instead, the welcome of religious others acts as "subversive presences" where traditions "embark [with one another] on a dialogue of life and of thought, a theological and philosophical negotiation."[140] In light of this, Catholic inter-religious scholar Joseph Stephen O'Leary speaks of the unavoidability of complementary theological dialogue by stating:

> Radically to separate the religions is impossible. Their roots intertwine. Their lights are always ready to blend, even across thick veils of language . . . Thus any attempt to judge, or reject, the other religions in the light of a single one elevated to normative status comes undone. A religious tradition is not a cathedral which contains everything, but a crossroads open to everything. Every religion . . . has a police which guards its frontiers; this theological vigilance is a necessary precaution, but of uncertain effect, for spiritual movements are characterised by great permeability, so that [each religion] is incessantly transforming itself in response to the pressure of all the currents of the surrounding culture and of newly encountered foreign cultures.[141]

Likewise, the differences between each religious tradition are changing. Each generation sees what differentiates one faith from another in disparate ways. Those changes, in turn, then have the potential to "challenge even our most treasured assumptions about interreligious hermeneutical methods and possibilities."[142] As such, I seek to voice some of those challenges and highlight new possibilities.

139. Gross, "Religious Pluralism in Struggles for Justice," 1.

140. O'Leary, *Religious Pluralism and Christian Truth*, 1.

141. Ibid., 14–15.

142. Jeanrond, "Toward an Interreligious Hermeneutics of Love," 45.

Towards an Abrahamic Approach

The use of the term "Abrahamic" is widespread, most often applying to the traditions of Judaism, Christianity, and Islam.[143] It refers to the religions that look to a common spiritual ancestor in the person of Abraham, whose narrative is found in the Torah, the Bible, and the Qur'an, and that claim to worship the God of Abraham and follow his spiritual tradition of monotheism also referenced in these texts.[144]

There are several practical reasons why I choose to use the term "Abrahamic." Firstly, using "Abrahamic" is a stylistic convenience. To refer each time to the traditions discussed here as "Judaism, Christianity, and Islam" is unwieldy. The only other shorter term used to refer to these three traditions is the blandly generic "monotheist traditions," which lacks the convenient and applicable emphasis upon Abraham and the impression of common roots and heritage. Secondly, to embrace all religions would be too broad. Furthermore, by using the term, there is recognition of a level of debate that already exists as to what *Abrahamic* entails and a decision to follow the common usage, which refers to Judaism, Christianity, and Islam as the primary Abrahamic family of faith.[145] Thirdly, the person of Abraham in these three traditions is emphasized and is a "point of reference" by which each community "can and must be measured critically,"[146] particularly in relation to conversations about hospitality.

In the vein of O'Leary's statement about the intertwined roots of religious traditions, the intertwined relationship between the three monotheistic Abrahamic traditions has been chosen for three reasons. First, to concentrate solely on Christianity would give a myopic view of a rich tradition—that is, hospitality—found in a variety of religious cultures that has transformative potential worldwide. Second, ecumenical and Abrahamic scholar Lewis Mudge points to the Abrahamic traditions as being "among the worst religious troublemakers through the centuries" despite the fact that "these three faiths are historically interrelated and look to overlapping scriptures . . . [suggesting] that there is potential . . . among them for something

143. There are other traditions that also see themselves as Abrahamic, such as Ba'hai, Druze and Rastafarianism. However, usage restricts itself to (what so far is) the more widely-used categorical definition which restricts "Abrahamic" to Judaism, Christianity, and Islam, as found in works such as those comprising Burrell's Abrahamic Dialogues series; Ochs and Johnson (developers of the Scriptural Reasoning movement), *Crisis, Call and Leadership in the Abrahamic Traditions;* and Fitzgerald, "Relations among the Abrahamic Religions."

144. See also Goodman et al., *Abraham, the Nations, and the Hagarites.*

145. See also Mudge, *The Gift of Responsibility;* and Swidler, "Trialogue," 493–509.

146. Kuschel, *Abraham*, 204.

new."[147] Last, to focus on the specific commonalities of the Abrahamic traditions have regarding hospitality—especially when the common patriarch of Abraham is held up as an example of one who gives hospitality—provides a good test case for the development of an Abrahamic theology and ethic of protective hospitality that will hopefully be a model for further values and practices in religious traditions for common social benefit.

The role these Abrahamic traditions play in the public, globalized sphere have tremendous importance in the societies in which they are found. Unfortunately, the impression the traditions and their respective adherents have created has been largely negative.[148] Since the Abrahamic traditions are, to reiterate Mudge's assertion, "among the worst religious troublemakers through the centuries,"[149] it seems only right these three traditions also cooperate with one another in order to address particular grievances. Much needs to be done to heal the wounds that have been inflicted over the centuries; yet, one must start somewhere constructive. Cooperating with one another, particularly in areas that have the potential to heal and reconcile such as the practice of protective hospitality, has tremendous power to provide an alternative vision of religious life together.

Conflict and competition are not the sole means of relating to one another. The following chapters work to examine complementarity, collaboration, and cooperation as transformative and effective methods for the Abrahamic traditions. This complementarity, collaboration, and cooperation has the positive potential to enable the Abrahamic traditions to be in relationship with one another, seeking the welfare of the other through welcome, sustenance, dialogue and the provision of safe space.

Judaism, Christianity, and Islam each consider Abraham to have been a friend of God[150] who embraced his identity as a "stranger and sojourner, a displaced person whose homeland lay elsewhere."[151] The friendship between God and Abraham was not characterized as one of exclusion, but as one rooted in Abraham's identity as a stranger wherein he was "impelled by

147. Mudge, *The Gift of Responsibility*, 4, quoting Arendt, *The Human Condition*, 10–11, 157–58. While the Abrahamic traditions are very similar in many ways, Judaism, Christianity, and Islam are still very different religions. Therefore, this work treads a fine line as it seeks to highlight common belief and practice while honoring each tradition's particularity.

148. Particularly in light of current events as seen in global terrorism, the liberal vs. conservative religion wars in US culture and politics, and issues related to Israel/Palestine, all of which are arguably caught up in one another.

149. Mudge, *The Gift of Responsibility*, 4.

150. 2 Chr 20:7; Isa 41:8; Jas 2:23; Qur'an 4:125.

151. Kuschel, *Abraham*, 14.

his trusting relationship with God to intercede for those who are in need . . . someone who is open to the needs of his brothers and sisters."[152] To be called the children of Abraham implies the same devotion to caring for others.[153]

In Islam, the Arabic name for Abraham is *Ibrahim* and later tradition interpreted the name to mean *ab Rahim,* which translates to "compassionate father."[154] This interpretative tradition sees Abraham and his wife Sarah as the parents of those in need of parents in paradise.[155] Abraham is the "father to those who have no father . . . [and] is the embodiment of the Qur'anic injunction to care for the orphans and the needy."[156]

As such, the Abrahamic traditions require its adherents be their brothers' and sisters' keepers. One is bound to another and religious practice is made more relevant when attention is given to "the insights, symbols, ethical demands and religious practices of other religions and alternative movements," not in an effort to replace one's own but to complement, enrich and challenge it.[157] Given the inter-relatedness of these traditions, Mudge noted "there is potential, some of it already beginning to be realized, among them for something new, for what Hannah Arendt calls 'natality,' to arise on the stage of history."[158] I wish to build upon that natality, to offer a possible model from which other complementary theologies and cooperative ethics from these traditions can be born.

Towards a Hospitable Approach

A distinctive aim of this book is to explore the traditions of Judaism, Christianity, and Islam and their theology and practice of protective hospitality; but it also is an endeavor in hospitality in itself. The work here is rooted in a self-consciously Christian theological tradition. Yet, to be hospitable in

152. Fitzgerald, "Relations among the Abrahamic Religions," 75.

153. Ibid.

154. Ayoub, "Abraham and His Children," 122.

155. The Qur'an version of the story of Hagar does not depict Abraham turning his back on her and casting her off as the Torah does. Instead, he leaves, trusting God to take care of her and she acknowledged that if what he was doing was because of the bidding of God, that would happen. She has more agency in the Islamic tradition than in the Jewish and Christian versions.

156. Ibid.

157. Küng, *Islam*, 651–52.

158. Arendt describes natality as the state where each birth represents a new beginning, and as such, the potential for newness and novelty to enter the world with each birth. Mudge, *The Gift of Responsibility*, 4, quoting Arendt, *Human Condition*, 10–11, 157–58.

its approach, this work also requires a certain level of openness, accessibility, and welcome in one's method, structure, and language. This is particularly necessary here where belief and practices of other traditions beyond Christianity are addressed, while seeking to give a voice to the needs of the threatened stranger, and generate shared interest in growing alongside others through cooperative efforts of protective hospitality. Therefore, this work will be an exercise in Christian hospitality in the spirit of philosopher Paul Ricoeur's idea of linguistic hospitality as discussed by inter-religious scholar Marianne Moyaert, where the foreign is welcomed and aims of perfection in translation and interpretation are set aside for greater meaning and context.[159]

One could proceed along the different route whereby religious identity is protected and preserved,[160] and inter-religious contact is for the benefit of strengthening one's own identity.[161] Ricoeur referred to this need to protect identities, namely by withdrawal into one's own linguistic tradition, as the "theological exemplification of a resurgence of sectarianism and tribalism . . . [wherein the] protective withdrawal is prompted by a fear of otherness."[162] In contrast, a theology of hospitality can reach out to other traditions by means of mutual encouragement, challenge, and integration as an act of hospitality.

Ricoeur looks to hospitality as "a model for integrating identity and otherness," recognizing the practice of hospitality is embedded in the recognition that "we all belong to the human family" and is encapsulated by "showing concern for a concrete other because she or he is human."[163] As such, hospitality is antithetical to sectarianism or tribalism.[164] Furthermore, Moyaert claims that where "tribalism locks the community safely into a given tradition, the praxis of . . . hospitality calls for another approach: 'that of taking responsibility *in imagination* and *sympathy*, for the story of the other.'"[165]

In the context of the inter-religious nature of this research, the applicability of Ricoeur's idea of "linguistic hospitality" is appropriate. As one considers examining the traditions of the religious other, such approaches

159. See also Ricoeur, *On Translation*.

160. Moyaert, "Absorption or Hospitality," 64.

161. Ibid., 67, referring to Lindbeck, *The Nature of Doctrine*, 54–55, 61–62.

162. Moyaert, "Absorption or Hospitality," referring to Ricoeur, "Universality and the Power of Difference," 146.

163. Moyaert, "Absorption or Hospitality," 83. Moyaert says this in the context of discussing Ricoeur, "New Ethos for Europe," 4–6.

164. Moyaert, "Absorption or Hospitality," 83.

165. Ricoeur, "New Ethos for Europe," 7.

are, in essence, "translating the untranslatable, commensurating the incommensurable, and comparing the incomparable."[166] Ricoeur's idea of linguistic hospitality accepts the need for the other in development of religious traditions and that the "denial of translation equals the refusal to recognize what is foreign as a challenge and a source of nourishment for one's own 'religious identity.'"[167]

Instead of being "one more form of colonizing the other," I hope that this work will hold to Ricoeur's argument that the "model of hospitality implies a reciprocal process: 'it is really a matter of living with the other in order to take that other into one's home as a guest.'"[168] For Ricoeur, linguistic hospitality "is the act of inhabiting the word of the Other paralleled by the act of receiving the word of the other into one's own home, one's own dwelling."[169] As such, the hope is that a prevailing hermeneutic of hospitality is visible here. Rather than absorption or colonization,[170] where ideas, texts or traditions are taken without regard for their original context or meaning to its followers, I seek to take the texts and traditions of Judaism and Islam pertaining to protective hospitality into my Christian "home"; to treat them as guests; to question, find complementarity with, recognize the humanity in, and accept gifts from them as they challenge and add to my own as a result of this interaction.

166. Moyaert, "Absorption or Hospitality," 84.

167. Ibid., referring to Ricoeur's ideas presented in both "New Ethos for Europe," 4, and *On Translation*, 4.

168. Ricoeur, "New Ethos for Europe," 5.

169. Ricoeur, *On Translation*, 10.

170. For significant work on the issue of colonization, see Said, *A Critical Reader*.

2

Extending Hospitality

Hospitality as Ethical Practice

. . . to be moral is to be hospitable to the stranger.

—Thomas Ogletree[1]

INTRODUCTION

Before undertaking theological analysis and reflection of protective hospitality, there needs to be an examination of what hospitality is and is not. This chapter explores the various understandings and discussions about hospitality and details the contributing factors that inform ideas and convictions regarding its practice. The first section of this chapter will investigate the meanings of hospitality. More specifically, it will analyze the linguistic roots and etymological dimensions of hospitality and then consider the various tensions found in it that lend further meaning to the practice of hospitality.

The second section will identify overarching themes—from the more obvious themes of food and drink, to the lesser-identified but equally important themes around intellectual welcome and provision of protection—found in the practice of hospitality. This section will draw the links between

1. Ogletree, *Hospitality to the Stranger*, 1.

hospitality in general and the particular issues of protection that will be examined later.

The third section will make connections with regards to corresponding relationships and values in hospitality that inform its understanding and practice, particularly as this will set the stage for the Abrahamic traditions and their understanding of hospitality. Specifically, the relationship between hospitality and politics, tolerance, solidarity, and honor will be identified, building an analytic foundation for subsequent chapters.

THE MEANING OF HOSPITALITY

The literature on the subject of "hospitality" offers no single definition. The discussions within the literature do, however, offer some commonalities in that all seem to use terms such as "stranger," "other," and "welcome." Exactly how those terms, in turn, are defined and connected together with some form of action makes defining hospitality all the more difficult. Meanwhile, there are consequences to the fact that there is no single definition, mainly found in the variety of ways in which hospitality is discussed while lacking a cohesive sense of authority and practice in communities. Therefore, instead of looking for a definition of hospitality, it is more beneficial to explore the meaning of hospitality.[2]

In general, hospitality connotes ideas of welcome and openness to others. However, the full extent of this welcome and openness is difficult to define. Is hospitality simply the act of welcoming or is it welcoming *in* of others? Of what does "openness" consist and how does one practice it? Furthermore, there are questions related to the issue of space and mastery over that space, as well as factors to be determined in order to differentiate genuine hospitality from superficial hospitality. Lastly, to whom should hospitality be extended and what boundaries, if any, are necessary? Questions such as these would be helpful to consider in order to understand the meaning of hospitality.

Deconstructionist philosopher John Caputo problematizes the understanding of the word "hospitality." He describes it as one of those "words

2. In contemporary understandings, "hospitality" carries ideas of entertainment, reception, generosity, and friendliness. Out of these understandings arise the current uses that bring to mind what is known as the "hospitality industry," referring to hotels, restaurants, and other similar customer-service based businesses where food, drink, or accommodation is provided. Hospitable establishments greet guests (i.e., customers) with a smile and friendly service. Nevertheless, hospitality has a much wider meaning that does not necessarily involve business transactions or industrial standards.

that promise something that they do not quite deliver."[3] He states that "[w]hat hospitality means seems simple enough: welcoming the other, welcoming the coming of the other into the same," but he remarks that when most try to be hospitable, one usually invites friends and those "whose company we enjoy and from whom we can expect reciprocity . . . or else people whose favor we are currying."[4] Caputo argues that when hospitality is practiced in this manner "there is a good deal of inhospitality built into our hospitality" as it tightens the "circle of the same" and only welcomes those "who are welcome to begin with, not those who are unwelcome."[5]

Secondly, it can be ascertained from a variety of sources that interaction with the "other"[6] is the hinge upon which hospitality swings. Welcome is irrelevant if there is no one to whom it is extended. But who, then, is the other in this context? Furthermore, in light of Caputo's observations above, is hospitality or one's imperfect, limited, and short-sighted practice of it being defined? Liberation theologian Leonardo Boff asserts hospitality is "always defined by the other," and gives the following outline as to who the other is:

> 1) the other who is unknown, and who knocks at the door; (2) the other who is a foreigner, who comes from another country, speaks another language, has different habits and culture; (3) the other who belongs to a different social class and lives in poverty; (4) the other who has been snubbed by society, who is in need, tired, and starving; (5) the other who is the radical Other, who is God hidden behind the figure of two wandering people.[7]

For Boff, hospitality "applies to all kinds of the other."[8] Furthermore, Boff asserts that hospitality implies "overcoming certain attitudes, which are loaded with reserve and fear, that are present in people who are extremely cautious and suspicious."[9] Constantly questioning if people can be trusted

3. Caputo, *What Would Jesus Deconstruct?*, 75.

4. Ibid., 75–76.

5. Ibid., 76.

6. In the literature, the use of the word "other" refers to anyone other than oneself, usually connoting a sense of strangeness or something that is not completely known. It can be understood as simple or as complex as one chooses as it is a very broad term. At times, it is capitalized—"Other"—and many refer back to Emmanuel Levinas as the one who has informed their understanding of what "Other/other" means. For simplicity and consistency's sake, I will use the lowercase version. For more information, see Levinas, *Time and the Other;* or Levinas, *Humanism of the Other.*

7. Boff, *Virtues*, 48–49.

8. Ibid.

9. Ibid., 49.

and suspecting threat upon an encounter with the unknown stranger does not embody the practice of hospitality according to Boff.[10]

To further complicate matters, Caputo expands his earlier question by asking "if hospitality is what we say it is—that is, welcoming the other—then ought it not be a matter of welcoming those who are unwelcome . . . [and] extended beyond our friends to our enemies?"[11] This inclusion of enemies as the other is an important and overlooked factor in the consideration of hospitality. Caputo's admonition that one should extend welcome to those who are unwelcomed is a demanding prospect for most, and rightly so. Questions related to risk and violence are appropriate and the harsh realities of welcoming the unwelcomed and uninvited will be explored later.[12] Nevertheless, the definition of hospitality calls one to consider the extent to which one welcomes those outside of one's comfort zone, those who are not the same and are among those who make one uncomfortable.[13]

Thirdly, a continued exploration of the definition of hospitality leads to the consideration of space.[14] The practice of hospitality involves inextricable links to the space in which it is expressed; to practice hospitality is to welcome others into what will become a shared space with the presence of another. The limits on such space are few, however. It can be real or imagined, public or private, permanent or temporary, and yet common space is necessary in that it creates an environment where welcome and freedom can dwell.[15]

Tending to space that is potentially shared in order to encounter others is part of the essence of hospitality.[16] With it comes a need for intentionality and responsibility with regards to practicing hospitality, creating

10. Ibid.

11. Caputo, *What Would Jesus Deconstruct?*, 76.

12. This will be analyzed in more detail in chapter 4.

13. Boff refers to the understood others, particularly during the Crusades (i.e. Muslims) and the colonial era (i.e. indigenous peoples), but he also refers to the Earth as being a "new other" in our current context. Where peoples were once exploited, in the last few centuries, humanity has moved to the Earth as the resource to be exploited, making it the new other, He states "[t]his understanding of the Earth as the other who should be subjugated broke up the natural alliance between the human being and nature and the Earth. By breaking up this natural pact we placed ourselves above nature and the Earth and as such we are no longer with and within nature and the Earth. We have exiled ourselves from the Earth and we have separated ourselves from the community of life, of which we are but a link and a representative among others" (*Virtues*, 77).

14. This will also be given more detailed analysis in chapter 4 in the context of place, home, and boundaries.

15. Sutherland, *I Was a Stranger*, x.

16. Ibid.

spaces where the other—the stranger, foreigner, enemy, the oppressed and marginalized, the unwelcome—is welcomed.[17] In this response to the other, "one's ultimate calling and obligation . . . is to provide the space and hope for that Other to unfold and reveal his or her naked identities—while still remaining an Other—a distinct, autonomous being."[18] Similarly, one might say hospitality is "primarily the creation of a free space where the stranger can enter and become a friend instead of an enemy . . . not to change people, but to offer them space where change can take place."[19] Similarly, Boff argues that hospitality "is to welcome the stranger just as the stranger presents itself . . . without need to place the stranger within the acceptable framework of the community."[20] Such an assertion echoes Henri Nouwen's claim that hospitality is not about changing the other, but securing space where "openness, courage to face and overcome strangeness" is allowed to transform "fear, suspicion, disconnection, and even rejection of the other."[21] In this way, it appears true hospitality is then contingent upon space and the possibility of transformation, as well as the other and welcome.

Likewise, the relationship to justice, truthfulness, and courage in the practice of hospitality is essential if there is to be space for transformation. In order for the other to feel safe to reveal one's true identity and to be heard, justice in the form of being given the status of a valuable "equal partner," as well as truth-telling and courage to submit oneself to another, are required.[22] Adherence to these values "indicates a receptivity and generosity of spirit that 'welcomes' the different'" and "embodies an openness or availability to the other that lies at the core of . . . genuine communal solidarity."[23] As such, Christian theologian Thomas Reynolds notes hospitality is "an ethical prescription built into the fabric of dwelling together" as it "acknowledges another as one's neighbor, a potential brother or sister."[24]

The Linguistic Roots of Hospitality

While Caputo's explorations of what hospitality means are valuable, it is also necessary to consider the linguistic roots of hospitality and how it has

17. Ibid., xiii.
18. Admirand, "Healing the Distorted Face," 303.
19. Nouwen, *Reaching Out*, 51.
20. Boff, *Virtues*, 68.
21. Ibid.
22. Reynolds, "Improvising Together," 54–55.
23. Ibid., 55.
24. Ibid.

evolved in both perception and interpretation over the centuries. Oddly, it is only in the scholarship of French linguist Emile Benveniste, and its corresponding dissemination by literature scholar Tracy McNulty that the most detailed exploration of the linguistic roots of hospitality can be found.[25] Therefore, this section will focus upon their arguments, and will call on other sources where appropriate.

Benveniste begins by delineating the two original strands of contributing roots that make up "hospitality." The first, *hostis*, implies "guest" or "host"[26] and, the second, identified as *pet-* or *pot-*, implies "master" and carries with it connotations of identity. The Latin *hospes* is formed from these two roots, put together as "*hosti-pet-s*." It is from this construction that modern usage arises.[27] Consequently, this later Latin root is where most scholars begin without considering what contributed to its development.

One implication McNulty points out in her own research is that "before [a master] had any subjects, the master was his own subject, a subject properly speaking: the roots *-pet-*, *-pot-*, and *-pt-*, (Latin *-pte*, *i-pse*), originally signified 'personal identity.'"[28] Therefore, in order to extend welcome to a guest, McNulty contends that one must have an identity, and, in ancient connotations, be linked in with a concept of home, the place from which "the master makes the law" or where the master "resides within an identity . . . [and] gathers together and disposes of what is proper to him."[29] As a result, the "master is eminently himself [and] offers hospitality from the place where he is 'at home.'"[30] In the spirit of McNulty's argument, one could make a similar argument that if *hostis* is also used for "guest," then in order to receive welcome, one must also have an identity that is linked to one's home.

Yet, addressing the former primary root—*hostis*—is more complex than just "guest" and "host." According to McNulty and Benveniste, the original idea of *hostis* "is that of reciprocity, or equality by compensation;

25. These two sources are the most significant places where this information has been found. Jacques Derrida refers to Benveniste's work in *Deconstruction in a Nutshell*, 110–12, but McNulty's exploration is much more thorough. Unfortunately, Benveniste's work is only available in French, and, therefore, I am reliant upon McNulty's references to it in *The Hostess*. Other sources, such as Newland, *Hospitable God*, 29, mention the linguistic roots, but do not go into as much detail as Benveniste, Derrida, or McNulty.

26. As does the French term *hôte*.

27. Benveniste, "L'hospitaite,'" 87–101, quoted in McNulty, *The Hostess*, viii–ix.

28. McNulty, *The Hostess*, ix. While it goes beyond the remit of this book, McNulty's related discussion of *ipseity* has been discussed more widely in the work of Paul Ricoeur. See Van Den Hengel, "Paul Ricoeur's Oneself as Another and Practical Theology," 458–80; Ricoeur, *Oneself as Another*; and Hand, "Working out Interiority," 422–34.

29. McNulty, *The Hostess*, x.

30. Ibid.

hostis is he who compensates a gift with a counter-gift."[31] Because of this reciprocity, *hostis* "comes to designate both the host and the guest, who become identified as reciprocal positions by virtue of the obligation to counter the initial act of hospitality with gifts or later compensatory deeds."[32] Similarly, the French term *hôte* indicates "one who gives, *donne*, and the one who receives, *reçoit*, hospitality" and to forget the dual nature of the term "would be to erase the demand made by hospitality."[33]

Furthermore, McNulty asserts that when *hostis* and *potis* are linked, what is found is a "union of two somewhat contradictory notions: a social or legal relationship defined by reciprocity and exchange, and despotic power, mastery and personal identity."[34] She further argues that it "implies not only the power of mastery, but power *over* the guest, by virtue of his debt or obligation to the host."[35] With this linkage, further tensions are identified within hospitality wherein "notions of reciprocity or exchange and mastery or power" are explored which have the possibility of provoking instances of "anxiety, rivalry, or hostility, in which the host's power over the guest is conceived in a threatening manner, or in which the guest threatens to overtake the host's place as master by usurping his home, personal property, or social position."[36]

An evolution of definition and usage is visible from this point as one explores *hostis* in more recent contexts. Under Roman law, *hostis* was used to refer to "a resident foreigner invested with the same rights as Roman citizens, 'equal' under the law," and whereby "it no longer names the stranger in general . . . [it does identify the] resident alien who has been recognized by and inscribed within the state . . . as having certain rights."[37]

31. Ibid.

32. Ibid. This practice of compensating one for hospitality seems, however, to contradict an earlier assertion by McNulty where she states, "in religious myth, the hospitality act was forbidden to have any economic dimension" (ibid., viii). How one can compensate for hospitality and yet hospitality was forbidden to have an economic dimension is unclear. Perhaps it is somehow related to when the guest is known to the host (as opposed to the unknown/divine stranger, beyond the initial aspect of hospitality there is no relationship)?

33. Anidjar, "A Note on 'Hostipitality,'" in Derrida, *Acts of Religion*, 356. Anidjar writes the forward to Derrida's *Acts of Religion* where Derrida coins the term "hostipitality," which is meant to capture this juxtapositional nature of hospitality as will be explored later and raise "in a radically new way the question of the subject of hospitality."

34 McNulty, *The Hostess*, xi.

35. Ibid.

36. Ibid. This possibility of anxiety or hostility is particularly of interest if the host/hostess is providing protection for his/her guests.

37. Benveniste, "L'hospitaite,'" 93, quoted in McNulty, *The Hostess*, xi.

But with this codification of Roman law related to strangers, McNulty details how *hostis* began to take on more negative meanings. Whereby previously *hostis* implied "an unlimited obligation" on the part of the host to extend welcome to the guest who was "upheld by sacred rites and protected by the vigilance of potent divinities,"[38] its usage evolved and later began to be "applied exclusively to 'enemy' and no longer names the guest."[39] Concurrently, McNulty points out that the Greek term *xenos* came to be more popularly used "to mean 'stranger' to the exclusion of 'guest.'"[40] Signaling a change in "civic or national attitude toward the stranger," McNulty asserts, "explains how *hostis* became the linguistic root of 'hostility,' an affect that otherwise seems at odds with the institution of hospitality."[41]

In light of this evolution and eventual contradiction in meaning, the practice of hospitality as the conversion from "*hostis* to *hospes*" holds more weight if one sees it as the act whereby one cultivates safe spaces in which people can live lives free from fear and where transformation from enemy to guest can take place.[42]

The Tensions within Hospitality

When exploring the various understandings of hospitality, the seemingly contradictory nature of it and its practice begin to attract one's attention. These understandings, however, are not contradictions as such, but more like juxtapositions that hold hospitality in tension with other related aspects of its practice. For example, the above exploration identifies links between hospitality and hostility, calling into question the balance of welcome and unwelcome, shaping identity and highlighting universality, inclusion and exclusion, embrace and coercion, protection and violence. How do the positive and negative co-exist within this realm of hospitality? It is this tension that makes hospitality so difficult to define, and yet so powerful in its potential.

38. McNulty, *The Hostess*, xi.

39. Benveniste, "L'hospitaite,'" 95, quoted in McNulty, *The Hostess*, xii.

40. McNulty, *The Hostess*, xii.

41. Ibid. To further complicate things, McNulty also notes that from this, the "modern word 'hostess' is not a feminine form" of *hostis* in its original form. Instead, it is a "corrupted form of 'hostility.'" From this, she uses the biblical examples of Jael (Judg 4:17—5:27) and Judith (Jdt 10–15) to illustrate the hostility of the feminine in a guest/host position (ibid., xliii).

42. Nouwen, *Reaching Out*, 46. Such concepts are fascinating and will be explored in further detail in the following sections and in chapter 4 as the themes of violence and protection are given more specific attention.

As conflicts related to identity formation are waged on both small and large scales throughout the world, McNulty's presentation of hospitality as "an act that constitutes identity"[43] is informative. When home is being threatened, home can also the place where the conflict can either be perpetuated or diminished. This contrasting idea of home is found in McNulty's research when she writes:

> [Hospitality] is the act through which the home—and the homeland—constitutes itself in the gesture of turning to address its outside. But as an accidental encounter with what can be neither foreseen nor named, hospitality also insists on the primacy of immanent relations over identity. Hence, it both allows for the constitution of identity and challenges it, by suggesting that the home can also become unhomely, *unheimlich*, estranged by the introduction of something foreign that threatens to contaminate or dissolve its identity.[44]

In the end, it is how the foreign is considered and welcomed or unwelcomed that highlights some of the tensions within hospitality.

Similarly, McNulty explores the Israelite traditions of hospitality, based in the tent of Abraham and evolving to more exclusivist tendencies found in the development of Temple Judaism and some prophetic texts. The fact that both radical welcome and radical exclusivity are found in the Hebrew scriptures points to the duality that exists in the practice of hospitality. The tension "between the hospitable tent and the exclusive temple" is where the transformative power of hospitality lies, as "the tent persists and insists within the temple,"[45] always present and yet demanding change while continuing to define an individual or community through its practice.

The separation barriers (called "peace walls") along the Catholic and Protestant interfaces in Northern Ireland are a prime example of the duality of inclusivity and exclusivity in hospitality. Security and peace in Northern Ireland can never be ensured until they are broken down; and yet, for those who live near them, the walls ensure their security (either real or perceived) each day they remain. Furthermore, the walls, for now, ensure enough separation to enable actors to take a step back and assess the conflict safely. The walls "persist and insist" within the peace—and, simultaneously, the ongoing conflict—in Northern Ireland. They are a constant reminder of the past while pointing out through their existence the work that still needs to be done in the present and future. The same might be said for similar walls

43. McNulty, *The Hostess*, viii.

44. Ibid.

45. Ibid., 35.

built in Israel/Palestine or other areas of conflict. The reasons and uses for the walls coexist, equally true yet seemingly contradictory.[46]

Such boundaries in the context of exclusivity and welcome not only form identity, but serve to illuminate universality through the practice of hospitality. The reversal of roles in the practice highlight the identities of those who participate while reflecting the universal needs, desires, and nature of those same participants. It may be counterintuitive, but as "the host gives to the guest, the host paradoxically receives something previously unexpected, becoming more than he or she was before."[47] As such, the one who welcomes "becomes honored and enhanced by sharing space," and "the vulnerable stranger who allegedly has nothing to offer becomes a source of enrichment to the household, reconfiguring and transforming it" as the boundaries between guest and host become more permeable.[48] The stories shared by a guest have the ability to gift the host with a new perspective, spark the imagination, and enrich the world one inhabits. As such, this reality illustrates "the theological root of hospitality: God blesses through the stranger."[49]

Similarly, there is tension between hospitality's timing and intentionality. Jacques Derrida considers this when he writes:

> Hospitality must wait *and* not wait. It is what must await *and still* [*et cependant*] not await, extend and stretch itself [*se tender*] and still stand and hold itself [*se tenir*] in the awaiting and the non-awaiting. Intentionality *and* non-intentionality, attention *and* inattention. Tending and stretching itself between the tending [*le tendre*] *and* the not-tending or the not-tending-itself [*ne pas se tendre*], not to extend this or that, or oneself to the other . . . Indeed, if we gather [*nous recueillons*] all these words, all these values, all these significations (to tend and extend, to extend oneself, attention, intention, holding [*tenue*], withholding [*retenue*]), the entire semantic family of *tenere* or of the *tendere* (Gr. *teinô*), we see this same contradictory tension at once working, worrying, disrupting the concept and experience of hospitality while also making them possible . . .[50]

46. See Jarman, *Building a Peaceline*; Jarman, "Security and Segregation"; Hamilton, Bell, and Hansson, "Sectarianism and Segregation"; and Community Relations Council, "Towards Sustainable Security."

47. Reynolds, "Improvising Together," 59.

48. Ibid.

49. Ibid.

50. Derrida, *Acts of Religion*, 360.

Tension is inherent in the practice of hospitality, as Derrida has illuminated. That tension is, perhaps, the core reason hospitality is so difficult to define and practice. Is it intentional or unintentional? Is it risky or safe? Is it about drawing in or reaching out? Is it about anticipation or spontaneity? In hospitality, these tensions coexist, albeit precariously.

Furthermore, Derrida explores the intentionality of meditated invitation coupled with the element of surprise and welcoming the unexpected when he writes:

> . . . "to extend an invitation": to tend or extend [*tendre ou etendré*] an invitation—and we will see or recall in a moment that if hospitality seems linked to invitation, an invitation offered, extended, presented, sent; if it seems linked to the act of invitation, to the inviting of invitation, one also make a note [*prendre acte*] of this: that radical hospitality consists, *would have* to consist, in *receiving without invitation*, beyond or before the invitation . . .[51]

Such possibility of welcome without invitation carries with it substantial risk. The act of invitation itself is a sign of disarmament or approval, that the host acknowledges her or his position and welcomes the other who, while still possibly a threat, will abide by the rules laid down as part of the cultural practice of hospitality. To welcome without invitation opens one up to the unexpected.

This risk found in hospitality understandably hampers its practice. If *hostis* is perceived as negative in the form of "enemy," the practice of hospitality becomes more difficult as the *hostis* is considered to be "someone who threatens to overtake the host, who must be excluded by reason of his potential similarity to the host and capacity for usurpation of his power."[52] The threat manifests itself in the "possibility of homelessness . . . [p]recisely because the home . . . is a figure for identity . . . [and] the failure to repossess this home or clear it of strangers can also result in a loss of identity," resulting in the home becoming "unhomely, *unheimlich*, estranged by the introduction of something foreign that threatens to dispossess it of its self-identity; whence the continuum between hospitality and hostility."[53]

51. Ibid. I am intrigued by Derrida's use of the term "radical hospitality" in this section. It is unclear if Derrida wishes to differentiate "hospitality" from "radical hospitality" through this willingness to "receive without invitation" or if Derrida is merely commenting on the radical nature of hospitality itself.

52. McNulty, *The Hostess*, xii.

53. Ibid., xiv.

Nevertheless, opening one's home to the other is the foundation of hospitality's ethics.[54] The contrasts inherent in such ethics can be seen in the "challenge of sustaining relation as 'impossible,'" and where there exists a "double bind" in which "the host must both take in the stranger and respect for its foreignness, name the stranger and acknowledge its unnameability, welcome the stranger there where he is at home and risk homelessness or dispossession at his hands."[55]

Ethics are formed in this seeming contradiction. McNulty also asserts "[o]ne might even argue that every ethics is fundamentally an ethics of hospitality, since the original meaning of *ethos* is 'abode' or 'dwelling place.'"[56] It is the concept of the "home" or "abode" where the basis of ethics is formed, according to the philosopher and ethicist Martin Heidegger.[57] As the home is where one is best equipped to encounter strangeness, ethics is, in turn, "the opening of what is familiar to man to the unfamiliar."[58] The Jewish thinker Emmanuel Levinas placed home as essential to hospitality as it is "what makes the ethical possible."[59] Similarly, Derrida builds on Levinas by likening home to culture and stating "hospitality is not merely one ethics among others, but the ethics par excellence."[60]

Derrida's statements regarding culture and hospitality reflect the final juxtaposition to be explored here. He writes:

> *on the one hand*, hospitality must wait, extend itself toward the other, extend to the other the gifts, the site, the shelter and the cover; it must be ready to welcome [*accueillir*], to host and shelter, to give shelter and cover; it prepare itself and adorn itself [*se préparer et se parer*] for the coming of the hôte; it even

54. Ibid.

55. Ibid., xv.

56. Ibid.

57. Heidegger, "Letter on Humanism," 234.

58. Ibid.

59. Katz, *Levinas, Judaism, and the Feminine*, 59.

60. Derrida, "Hospitality and Hostility," a seminar given at UC Irvine, April 3, 1996, quoted in McNulty, xvii. Derrida has written and spoken extensively on the subject of hospitality, particularly in relation to aspects such as politics, law and ethics from a philosophical perspective as well as critically engaging with Emmanuel Levinas' ideas on hospitality as well. While both men profess to be secular Jews, their religious tradition does seem to have significant impact on their ideas regarding hospitality. Unfortunately, to address their work more systematically would be worthy of a PhD dissertation and, therefore, will not be dealt with in depth here, but will only be referenced in relation to specific points. For more information, see Derrida, *Of Hospitality*; Derrida, *On Cosmopolitanism and Forgiveness*; Derrida, *Acts of Religion*; Levinas, *Totality and Infinity;* or Levinas, *Humanism of the Other.*

> develop itself into a culture of hospitality, multiply the signs of anticipation, construct and institute what one calls structures of welcoming . . . [as] there is no culture that is not also a culture of hospitality . . . Hospitality—this is culture itself.[61]

While Derrida and many cultures view the practice of hospitality as central to culture, Christian ethicist Christine Pohl argues the practice of hospitality is countercultural.[62] This dichotomy could be confusing unless one either looks at ancient versus contemporary contexts or frames it in the same tension found in defining hospitality in the first place, namely in the recognition that there are both impersonally superficial and intentionally meaningful ways in which hospitality is practiced. Is the countercultural practice of hospitality *true* hospitality and cultural tradition a false one? Perhaps the aspects of culture and countercultural practice of hospitality are found more in a spectrum, where the extremes on each side form more inauthentic, or dangerous, expressions of hospitality.

The extremes on each side of the spectrum of hospitality point to the demarcation and implementation of boundaries. Appropriate boundaries must be present and maintained, as either their absence or, on the other side, inappropriate boundaries are formed through excessive hardening. Either option has the potential to complicate and contaminate the practice of hospitality. Any activity, be it hospitality or some other identity-forming enterprise, has the potential to serve "to harden boundaries [but] can also be in other circumstances a legitimate and necessary means of building, nurturing, or maintaining identity."[63] Therefore, when home and its corresponding hospitality becomes synonymous with one's own identity to the exclusion of others, when walls no longer provide protection but serve to keep people separate, or when so much is given that gifts of hospitality no longer hold any value, then boundaries have been hardened or diminished and, in conjunction, hospitality is extinguished.

While this potential is inherent in the practice of hospitality, it is not a weakness necessarily; *the fluidity of and tension within hospitality is its genius*. Its adaptive nature to culture, identity, and context is what enables it to be a tool, particularly in times of conflict, for the common good. In hospitality's mystery and tensions lies its power to transform.

61. Derrida, *Acts of Religion*, 360–61.

62. Pohl, "Building a Place for Hospitality," 35.

63. Liechty and Clegg, *Moving Beyond Sectarianism*, 247.

PRACTICES OF HOSPITALITY

As a further attempt to define and describe hospitality, an exploration of what it entails is useful. Pohl describes hospitality's components as "[w]elcoming strangers . . . and offering them food, shelter, and protection."[64] Further instances of hospitality include the welcome of and sharing in different ideas, and encountering one another in an environment of safety and mutual respect.

In light of these descriptions, the next section will explore the three main practices through which hospitality is offered. The first, table fellowship, is the most obvious as it entails the offering and/or sharing of food and drink. This aspect of hospitality is the first that most people think of when hospitality is mentioned. The second, intellectual welcome, is perhaps the most obscure and yet, in the historic practice of hospitality by the Abrahamic traditions, equally important. Seen in the centuries of collaborative dialogue and debate, intellectual welcome between scholars provides an additional vision for the practice of hospitality beyond the norm of table fellowship. The third aspect, the provision of protection or sanctuary, is more accepted than intellectual welcome. Yet protective hospitality is perhaps the most difficult to document as there is little research on the topic, and what is written is dispersed in a variety of disciplines. Accounts of atrocities committed are numerous; accounts of those who provided sanctuary for the threatened and protected them from violence or annihilation are harder to come by. Linking their motivations to the practice of hospitality or their religious belief is even more difficult, and yet, it is there. Hospitality makes its presence known in even the most dangerous of places.

Table Fellowship

The sacramental nature of sharing food and drink is the first example of hospitality most consider when the topic arises. There is a mysterious, but tremendous, power in the role of food and drink among people and the recognition of that power and its accompanying rituals signal its significance in the exploration of hospitality.

On a personal level, sharing a meal or a cup of coffee invites a level of encounter that is difficult to induce without it.[65] There is something very basic, very human, very egalitarian to the act of eating or drinking together.

64. Pohl, *Making Room*, 4.

65. See Watson and Caldwell, *Cultural Politics of Food and Eating*; Counihan and Van Esterick, *Food and Culture*; and Dietler and Hayden, *Feasts*.

To sit at the same table—on the same level with and next to another person—invites a particular level of intimacy that is difficult to replicate in other contexts. On a more communal scale, the examples and exhortations in the Abrahamic traditions and their sacred texts to sit at a table together, to provide guests with food and drink, and to welcome the stranger into one's home and community are shockingly prolific, as will be explored in more detail in the next chapter.

Furthermore, there is a common value in these traditions of sharing and abundance. Primarily as a metaphor for God's own abundance toward God's people and by extension, the abundance of the people of God toward others is expressed through hospitality. The obligation to provide more food than is necessary is common in cultural traditions married to the Abrahamic faiths; and these traditions are inextricably linked to values of honor, dignity, and generosity. Furthermore, the ritual of eating and drinking together is documented throughout the Abrahamic traditions as a reconciling and remembering activity, encouraging the adherents to live in peace and cooperation with their neighbors. The process of *sulh* or feasts of the *Eid* in the Islamic tradition; the observance of the Eucharist and feast days in the Christian tradition; and the Passover Seder, Shabbat, and other holy days in the Jewish tradition all illustrate the importance of hospitality—with particular emphasis upon food and drink—in religious observance.

Miroslav Volf, a Christian theologian, recounts a true story of a Bosnian man whose three-year-old daughter was shot by a sniper while playing outside of her home during the siege of Sarajevo in the 1990s. Recorded by a television camera as he brought his daughter into the hospital, the crying father stated he would like to invite the man who shot his daughter "to have a cup of coffee with him so that [the sniper] can tell him, like a human being, what has brought him to do such a thing."[66] Instead of seeking revenge, the Bosnian father invites the man who shot his daughter to "participate in a ritual of friendship,"[67] and to reaffirm each other's humanity by sitting together over a cup of coffee and hearing what each other has to say. This vision Volf provides is hospitality at its messiest and most profound.[68] One cannot expect to walk away from such an encounter unchanged.

66. Volf, "A Cup of Coffee," 917.

67. Ibid.

68. It is important to make note of those who would be inhospitable to this idea as well. For many, the father's invitation might be inappropriate given issues surrounding justice, guilt and forgiveness. Similarly, the expression of inhospitality on the part of the sniper by targeting a child raises questions related to invitation and force. To highlight this scenario is not to hold up an ethical ideal for others in similar circumstances, but to give attention to how some people perceive the power of hospitality. The relationship

There is something almost indescribable about the effect a cup of coffee or a meal has on those who share it and yet it is something ingrained in Abrahamic tradition and culture. The fact that this man made an immediate connection to such an act is telling. Eating or drinking together, inviting others into personal space, is an intimate act with sacred connotations. It is not always comfortable or entertaining; sometimes it is very difficult or contentious as Volf's scenario suggests. Yet, this practice of hospitality requires one to face the other, to see the other's humanity staring back, and to invite the divine into this sacred space.

Intellectual Welcome

Intellectual welcome is, perhaps, not what someone would consider a practice of hospitality, but discussions in scholarship address the importance of creating spaces where a variety of opinions can be expressed. The diversity of opinion, as well as the ritual of coming together to discuss and to disagree, point to a further practice of hospitality. The ritual of dialogue carries with it connotations of spiritual practice. Within the Abrahamic inter-religious dialogue that is often marked by such divergent opinions, the fact that a variety of ideas are allowed to exist and are treasured as part of the theological spectrum is remarkable.

Historically, the Abrahamic traditions took pride in the practice of discussion, debate, and dissent in such a way as to honor it as a religious discipline. As such, I prefer to give it a name—"a holy rite of disagreement." Those considered most faithful and authoritative were those who engaged in dialogue with others—not as an attempt to convert but in the deep belief that God was so great that merely one person could not grasp the entire truth. There was the recognition that one needed the other to test one's ideas, and welcoming the other into one's space was part of this desire to know God more fully. To disagree was not to reject but to engage with the other, and in that engagement there is the recognition that one could not walk away unaffected.

The Jewish rabbinic tradition is particularly well-known in this regard. The spirituality of debate and disagreement has been honed in Judaism over centuries. Examples given of Maimonides participating in this rabbinic

between hospitality and violence and the corresponding boundaries of protective hospitality will be considered in greater detail in chapter 4. Furthermore, the issue of hospitality being "messy" is explored in more detail in the same chapter 4 in the sections related to purity and risk. See Douglas, *Purity and Danger;* and Beck, *Unclean.*

tradition debating how God created the world illustrate this point.[69] This concept stands in Islam as well, although it may not be as well known. The importance of education and knowledge of the methodology of theological thinking was highly emphasized, teaching its foundational thinkers such as Abu Hamid Muhammad Al-Ghazali to offer an opinion that takes into consideration the ideas that have gone before them. Omid Safi, a contemporary Muslim theologian, details this process as comparing a variety of schools of thought and then situating oneself within a tradition. It seems elementary but Safi points out that it is refreshing to see intellectual honesty practiced by summarizing "the perspectives of various schools of thought, to legitimize a range of opinions and to acknowledge a spectrum of interpretations!"[70]

Henri Nouwen details a similar process, making overt links to hospitality. In his detailing of hospitality as seen in the relationship between a teacher and a student, he says "hospitality can be seen as a model for a creative interchange between people [and i]f there is any area that needs new spirit, a redemptive and liberating spirituality, it is the area of education."[71] Moreover, Nouwen equates teaching with "the commitment to provide the fearless space where . . . questions can come to consciousness and be responded to, not by prefabricated answers, but by an articulate encouragement to enter into them seriously and personally."[72] He continues, stating "[w]hen we look at teaching in terms of hospitality, we can say that the teacher is called upon to create for his [or her] students a free and fearless space where mental and emotional development can take place."[73]

These three traditions come together when one considers the cooperation of scholars from each of the three Abrahamic traditions and their reliance upon one another in the development of one's own theology. At various points over the centuries, the Abrahamic traditions have utilized cooperation in theological exploration. One account of such encounters is as follows:

> On countless evenings, the court [of Harun al-Rashid who ruled the Abbasid caliphate from Baghdad] was transformed into an arena for theological debate. Muslim men of learning, schooled in sharia, the law derived from the Quran, offered their wisdom and drew on the philosophical tradition of the ancient Greeks. The works of Aristotle and Plato were translated into Arabic and

69. Fox, *Interpreting Maimonides*, 262.

70. Safi, "The Times They Are A-Changin'," 19.

71. Nouwen, *Reaching Out*, 58.

72. Ibid., 60.

73. Ibid.

> used not only to enrich Islam but to create new science and new philosophy. And the caliph was not content simply to take the world of his learned men. He wanted to see how their ideas met opposing theologies, and he invited scholars and preachers of other faiths to his court. Jews, Christians, Buddhists, and Muslims engaged in spiritual and spirited jousts, and each tradition was enriched by knowledge of the others.[74]

The same can be said for the intellectual hospitality found in medieval Iberia "where the Jewish polymath Maimonides, the Sufi mystic Ibn 'Arabi, and a phalanx of Christian monks helped one another unravel the meaning of God and the universe."[75] This practice of welcome accompanied by holy debate and disagreement has been largely forgotten.

While the much of the theological debate in the early and medieval periods was intra-religious, it and the corresponding inter-religious discussions still provide an authoritative basis upon which this holy rite can be reclaimed. In the contemporary context, this discipline of welcoming others of different opinions and beliefs has become threatening. In many Abrahamic communities, certainty is valued and there is little desire to be affected by the other. The practice of hospitality in welcoming others who disagree has been lost in the larger context of religious life.

Yet, welcoming the ideas of traditions other than one's own in order to enhance one's understanding is an act of hospitality. Efforts to recover the medieval traditions are being made in a variety of inter-Abrahamic relationships, not least of which is the rise in the discipline of scriptural reasoning under the influence of Jewish scholar Peter Ochs. While Lewis Mudge argues the actual practice of scriptural reasoning is a particularly Jewish tradition, it has been made available and encouraged as "an act of hospitality" to the other Abrahamic traditions in order "to form pragmatic hypotheses for guiding shared action toward the 'repair' of the 'failed logic of modernity.'"[76]

Responding to the need for shared action that arises from shared understanding and conviction is where relationships between the Abrahamic traditions will flourish, transform society, and help to create a more peaceful future. Furthermore, it is this capacity for intellectual welcome of the religious other that I wish embody in these pages as it uses the practice as the basis for illustrating the positive potential for a cooperative theology of protective hospitality.

74. Karabell, *Peace Be Upon You*, 4.

75. Ibid., 6. See also Menocal, *The Ornament of the World*.

76. Mudge, *The Gift of Responsibility*, 123.

Protection

The final theme of hospitality to be noted is the theme upon which the majority of this work will concentrate. It is the practice of hospitality exhibited through the taking in of others, not only in simply providing accommodation but also in providing protection, sanctuary or safe haven.

Providing accommodation is simple enough. As with the theme of table fellowship, providing a warm bed for a tired guest is thought of as a common expression of hospitality and, for the most part, is not debated. All three Abrahamic traditions agree on this value. It carries with it some risk—as any expression of hospitality usually does—but most Abrahamic adherents do not argue about the ethical value of taking in a guest for a night or two, or even providing shelter for the homeless in most cases.

Instead, the riskier and more debatable expression of hospitality would be the taking in of guests who are in need of safe shelter. Creating safe places, whether for ideas to be shared without judgment or condemnation, or for physical safety such as in the case of Le Chambon or the Sanctuary Movement mentioned previously, has also been an exhortation from the Abrahamic traditions. In these sanctuaries, in whatever form they take, a dedicated space where witness can be borne to truth is important. A sense of safety is difficult, if not impossible, to sustain without truth. Deception and silence as a means of differentiation do nothing but destroy any attempt to welcome others and create a sense of safety and community. Instead, an environment that fosters hospitality must be one that supports openness and honesty and affirms values that contribute to life for all. In this way, "truth-telling has to be a spiritual practice"[77] and becomes important to the wider practice of hospitality which encompasses it.[78]

While not explicitly considered in the literature, the inclusion of hospitality as provision of space—particularly safe space—appears in several sources. Christine Pohl echoes Nouwen by implying that giving people "a safe place" is synonymous with hospitality. As Pohl discussed what hospitality means with a particular practitioner, the gentleman emphasized the safe place he provides for his guests as an important factor. Pohl uses Nouwen's argument regarding space to affirm such actions are, indeed, hospitality.[79] For Pohl, the inclusion of protection is automatic, and she states "hospitality involves sharing food, shelter, protection, recognition, and conversation."[80]

77. hooks, *Remembered Rapture*, 120–21.

78. Reinhold Hütter wrote an excellent essay on hospitality and its relationship to truth—"Hospitality and Truth: The Disclosure of Practices in Worship and Doctrine."

79. Pohl, *Making Room*, 3, referring to Nouwen, *Reaching Out*, 66.

80. Pohl, "Building a Place for Hospitality," 27.

Pohl also echoes the Jewish tradition's understanding of inclusion, and she cites the laws that provide protection to strangers and resident aliens[81] referring to "the stranger, the widow, and orphan" as "not simply metaphorical . . . [but instead are those] individuals [who] require our attention because of their very real circumstances—they lack protection and support of any kind."[82] Extending welcome to those who are in need of protection is rife in the sacred texts of the Abrahamic traditions.

Christian feminist theologian Letty Russell takes a similar route. Russell begins with a discussion of the term "hot-house," which arises from the context of Japan where mothers with children affected by deformities caused by industrial pollution gathered together and set up "special place[s] of safety, comfort and care."[83] From this example, Russell builds her ecclesiology of sanctuary and makes vital links to hospitality. She articulates that "the vision women have for the church is that it could be a sanctuary [a hot-house], a place of safety for all who enter, and especially for those who are the most marginal, weak or despised of any community."[84] Yet, not only is this applicable to the Christian Church, but could also be said by scholars from the other two traditions as well. There is nothing distinctly Christian about this vision; it is only Christian when worked out in a particularly Christian theological manner—and even then there is still much room for agreement and cooperation between the Abrahamic traditions.

Russell declares that both the Jewish and Christian traditions have "acknowledged the need for sanctuary and protection of the one seeking a refuge or home . . . [and this idea] is rooted in the tradition of the 'cities of refuge' . . . [which] were a holy or sanctified place, often a temple, where God and the people of Israel protected those who seek refuge."[85] Such concepts of refuge are not the property only of Judaism and Christianity, however. Islam has this value as well, albeit with different historical precedents and exhortations. Yet, the underlying concept is the same and is applicable to all

81. Ibid., 28.

82. Katz, *Levinas, Judaism, and the Feminine*, 58.

83. Russell, "Hot-House Ecclesiology," 48.

84. Ibid. (brackets are Russell's).

85. Ibid., 49. The issue of the "cities of refuge" per se is not part of the Islam tradition. However, there is emphasis placed upon refuge in the tradition due to the historic significance of the early followers of Prophet Muhammad's flight from Mecca to Medina, where they found refuge from persecution for a period of time in Abyssinia under the protection of the Christian king (alternately known as Ashama Ibn Abjar, Negus, or al-Najashi) in 615 CE / 7 BH. This narrative is particularly reflected upon in inter-religious circles as evidence of inter-religious understanding and cooperation and is held up as an ethical and religious ideal. This narrative will be explored later in chapter 3.

three traditions when Russell goes on to say "[t]his right of protection of all persons is derived from God's holiness and provides the basic theological understanding of hospitality . . . [that h]uman beings are created by God and are to be holy, and to be treated as holy or sacred."[86]

While chapter 4 explains protective hospitality in more detail, it will be helpful to consider the aspects of hospitality that inform it as an ethical practice first. Therefore, the following sections will explore hospitality as ethics by considering factors such as political practice, tolerance, solidarity, and honor.

HOSPITALITY AS ETHICAL PRACTICE

Historically, hospitality as the practice of welcoming the stranger is connected to an overarching religious belief found in Mediterranean traditions that equated welcoming the other to welcoming the divine. As seen in "classic hospitality legends," as McNulty calls them, common stories are found in Greek and Roman mythology as well as regional religious traditions where "a deity or its emissaries appear to human beings in the guise of an unknown stranger, challenging the host to prove his character by offering food and shelter."[87] Therefore, "hospitality is motivated by the potentially sacred nature of the guest," since the host is, in these cases, unaware of the identity of the guest.[88] As the principal divinity depicted in the narratives holds hospitality as its "special domain," that same divine character "evaluates the character of human hosts by appealing for hospitality disguised as a supplicant."[89] Not surprisingly, ancient Greece considered one's religion to be the practice of hospitality as it was the "defining social ethics of *Zeus Xenios*, Zeus god of strangers."[90]

Therefore, there are implications that hospitality's importance as a spiritual discipline is part of its original meaning, and yet it seems to be rarely stressed in current religious circles, or when it is practiced it generally lacks deeper elements of intentionality. This reality coincides with the increasing privatization of faithful life and a seemingly unrelated socio-political reality. The tension between these two aspects when one is to relate to others both within and without one's religious community in a way that is reflective of one's beliefs and religious adherence, and yet it is rarely taught or emphasized

86. Ibid., 50.
87. McNulty, *The Hostess*, 8.
88. Ibid., 8–9.
89. Ibid., vii.
90. Ibid.

in the current context.[91] Nevertheless, it has many implications for life today as it speaks to concepts of political life and cultural diversity.

Just as Derrida stated that hospitality is "ethics par excellence," Christian ethics scholar Thomas Ogletree similarly notes that "to be moral is to be hospitable to the stranger."[92] This emphasis upon morality fuels the practice of hospitality in times where the stranger is in need and is unable to reciprocate. When one looks to the gifts of guests and hosts, there is an assumed equality in many cases. However, there are instances when "the stranger stands before me in his vulnerability, there is . . . an inequality of power in our relationship" as the stranger "has need of . . . recognition and service" and the potential host has at her/his disposal "support systems which already suffice for [her/his] needs."[93] In such cases, the ethical choice comes to bear. Boff writes that hospitality "is connected to minimum human needs: to be welcomed with no reluctance, to be given shelter, food and drink; and to be able to rest" as he acknowledges "[w]ithout the bare minimum nobody lives or survives."[94] Boff likens this physical and material minimum to a "spiritual bare minimum," and declares it is "that which makes us human, which is that capacity of unconditional welcome of the other, of being charitable, cooperative, and communal."[95]

The morality of hospitality is based upon the concept of home, in that "to be oppressed is to be virtually without a home" where one's self definition is oftentimes "determined by definitions, priorities, and interests of the oppressor;"[96] and, therefore, to provide hospitality is to provide a space where one can define oneself as one chooses and be at home. The morality of hospitality requires both guest and host to "take into account another center of meaning and valuation, another orientation onto the world, in making [one's] own decisions and in carrying out [one's] own actions,"[97] and in so

91. This dichotomy can be found, most alarmingly, in a recent survey conducted by the Pew Forum on Religion and the Public Life in the United States, where 54% of Americans who attend church at least once per week feel torture is "often" or "sometimes" justified, in comparison to 44% of those feel that is "rarely" or "never" justified. The Pew Forum survey indicates that more frequent church attendance corresponds with an attitude of acceptance with torture, with the concentration of acceptance highest (62%) among white evangelical Protestants. Pew Forum, "The Religious Dimensions of Torture Debate."

92. Ogletree, *Hospitality to the Stranger*, 1.

93. Ibid., 3.

94. Boff, *Virtues*, 50.

95. Ibid.

96. Ogletree, *Hospitality to the Stranger*, 4–5.

97. Ibid., 35.

doing, create a home where both can exist.[98] As such, these ideas regarding hospitality have connections with political practice as well as with concepts related to tolerance, solidarity, and honor that require closer exploration and analysis.

Hospitality as a Political Practice

Hospitality as a political practice begins to gain meaning when one considers how a community should function and what comprises the common good, particularly in relation to how the community treats those who are outside of its defining boundaries.

According to biblical scholar Andrew Arterbury, the stranger in the ancient world "did not always find a hospitable reception."[99] Travelers through foreign lands were extremely vulnerable to criminals who laid in wait along the sparsely populated transit routes. There was also the idea in the ancient world (and continues in the contemporary world as well, albeit in different forms) that "mysterious strangers" were a potential threat and, in turn, the community "sought to shun, abuse, or eliminate these outsiders before they could harm the community."[100]

In the Greco-Roman world, hosts who took in strangers were thought to be more likely to be "motivated by fear of an ominous stranger, by fear of Zeus, the god of hospitality, or by a desire to create politically advantageous alliances with powerful counterparts."[101] But later, communities marked by Abrahamic traditions were more likely to have different motivations; the impetus to provide hospitality in these communities "more often grew out of the desire to please God."[102] Nevertheless, in many cases of earlier eras, key members of the community "often bore the primary responsibility for hosting strangers"[103] since it had such political potential in relation to forming alliances or providing for the health of the community by absorbing the threat

98. This concept in hospitality reminds me of Archbishop Desmond Tutu's *ubuntu* theology wherein he asserts "My humanity is caught up, is inextricably bound up, in yours" and that "a person is a person through other persons" as detailed in his book *No Future Without Forgiveness*, 31. See also Gathogo, "African Philosophy as Expressed in the Concepts of Hospitality and Ubuntu," 39–53; Mzamane, "Building a New Society Using the Building Blocks of Ubuntu/Botho/Vhuthu," 236–48; and Lewis, "Forging an Understanding of Black Humanity through Relationship," 69–85.

99. Arterbury, "Entertaining Angels," 20.

100. Ibid.

101. Ibid., 21.

102. Ibid.

103. Ibid.

of the stranger. Furthermore, out of this expression of hospitality a principle of reciprocity was established. When someone was hosted in another's home, it became customary to vow "to provide protection and provisions for their counterpart whenever the other was traveling in one's region."[104]

According to Boff, hospitality, "by its own nature, presupposes reciprocity" as it is "a *duty* that must be practiced by all, and a *right* that all must enjoy."[105] Similarly, Volf asserts the role reversal between guest and host that takes place in the practice of hospitality, when "in an embrace a host is a guest and a guest is a host," highlights that reciprocity is required. He goes on to argue that while "one self may receive or give more than the other . . . each enter the space of the other, feel the presence of the other in the self, and make its own presence felt."[106] As such, Volf concludes, "there is no embrace," there is no hospitality, "[w]ithout such reciprocity."[107]

Yet, because of this principle of reciprocity, the political dimensions of hospitality start to take form. With reciprocity comes recognition; and it is the desire for recognition that many political and ethnic conflicts take place in our current global context. Nouwen speaks of hospitality as the provision of safe spaces and gives particular reference to the need for space for strangers to express their culture and language, to "sing their own songs, speak their own languages, [and] dance their own dances."[108]

In a similar way, Pohl echoes Nouwen's sentiments, but builds upon the work of philosopher Charles Taylor and others on the issue of multiculturalism and the politics of recognition.[109] Since recognition entails "respecting the dignity and equal worth of every person and valuing their contributions,"[110] discussions related to equality and human rights are a natural by-product. Furthermore, Pohl asserts some religious adherents are suspicious of issues related to human rights, equality, and recognition since they assume that these notions "have been imported from secular philosophies, political theory, and sociology."[111] Instead, Pohl insists such ideas are instead deeply rooted in the practice of hospitality as exhibited in historic Abrahamic convictions.[112]

104. Ibid.
105. Boff, *Virtues*, 59.
106. Volf, *Exclusion and Embrace*, 143.
107. Ibid.
108. Nouwen, *Reaching Out*, 51.
109. See also Taylor, *Multiculturalism.*
110. Pohl, *Making Room*, 61.
111. Ibid., 63.
112. Ibid. Pohl focuses upon the Judeo-Christian traditions, rather than being

Perhaps more controversially, Pohl looks at hospitality's power of recognition as an act of resistance. Rather than being a "tame and pleasant practice," Pohl asserts it has a "subversive, countercultural dimension."[113] Citing ideas from a Catholic Worker perspective, Pohl points to hospitality as "a different system of valuing and an alternate model of relationships."[114] The subversive power, according to Pohl, resides in the act of welcoming those who are "socially undervalued" and in understanding that the recognition of "their equal value can be an act of resistance and defiance, a challenge to the values and expectations of the larger community."[115]

For example, the northern Bosnian village of Gunja, situated on the border with Croatia, is known for its hospitable resistance during the years of the war.[116] Comprised of a Croat Catholic priest, a Serb Orthodox priest, and a Bošnjak imam, the religious leaders of the village made a point to be seen together throughout the conflict. As the war waged around them, the clerics publicly walked together through the streets and sat together over coffee to show their adherents a political and religious alternative. To welcome one another, ensure each other's safety, and show solidarity to a splintering world beyond them was, indeed, an act of defiant hospitality. In the same way, Boff argues that to live hospitably is "to subscribe to the political cause of . . . [those] who have been humiliated and ignored, so that they can be heard and included."[117] Likewise, theologian Amos Yong contends "interpersonal and international hospitality are important components that can contribute to a just and peaceful world."[118]

Hospitality as resistance is applicable in societies where exclusion and denigration are systematized. Therefore, to consider hospitality as a political practice, philosopher and ethicist Immanuel Kant relies upon a belief that hospitality makes possible a world where "people from different cultures 'can enter into mutual relations which may eventually be regulated by public laws, thus bringing the human race nearer and nearer to a cosmopolitan

---

inclusive of Islam in her writings. However, her statement regarding human rights and hospitality is equally true for Islam as well as for Judaism and Christianity.

113. Ibid., 61.

114. Ibid.

115. Ibid., 62.

116. As far as I am aware, this case is not documented anywhere, but while I resided in eastern Croatia, I had a chance to speak with the imam and hear his telling of these events and encountered others who were aware of them.

117. Boff, *Virtues*, 67. It is here where one can particularly see liberation theology at work in the context of hospitality.

118. Yong, *Hospitality and the Other*, 146.

constitution.'"[119] Kant's explorations of hospitality were written in the context of building or sustaining "peace between states,"[120] building upon concepts that are equated with modern conceptions of human rights.

Lastly, the work of theologian and ethicist Elizabeth Newman explores other political implications of hospitality. Describing hospitality as both "*ecclesial* and *public*," Newman asserts its practice embodies "a politics, economics, and ethics at odds with dominant cultural assumptions . . . [highlighting our temptation] to resist living out the conviction that our Host will provide."[121] For Newman, the classical understanding of politics as "how a community, a *polis*, is ordered to produce a common good" is used in order to say that hospitality uses this framework since "[t]he politics of Christian hospitality looks to the good of the Body of Christ."[122]

However, such an assertion should be broadened. Understandably, Newman writes as a Christian theologian and ethicist who seeks to revitalize the Christian community through the practice of hospitality. Yet, the practice of hospitality is neither the property of nor unique to the Christian tradition, nor can it be used solely by Christianity for theological purposes. To articulate it as such is to do a disservice to the common theological values and ethical imperatives found in many of the world's religions and, more specifically, in the Abrahamic traditions.[123] Instead, it would be appropriate to say the politics of hospitality, in general, looks to the good of humanity, or, in a more specific context, the good of one's neighbors. In this way, being one another's keeper is a political act.

Hospitality and Tolerance

In addition to the idea of hospitality as politics, Newman's work also asserts that "hospitality as inclusivity" is a distortion.[124] One might say the practice of hospitality is synonymous with popular negative views of tolerance, sometimes depicted as a lack of conviction, mere coexistence, or a failure

119. Kant, "Perpetual Peace," 106. Kant's "Perpetual Peace" will be explored more in chapter 4's discussion related to hospitality's relationship to violence.

120. Yong, *Hospitality and the Other*, 118, quoting Kant's "Perpetual Peace," 105–6.

121. Newman, *Untamed Hospitality*, 14.

122. Newman, "Untamed Hospitality," 17–18.

123. However, it is acknowledged that the majority of the literature regarding hospitality does, indeed, come from the Christian tradition, so it can easily appear to the unfamiliar that Christianity is the only tradition familiar with hospitality. One desired outcome of my research is to show this is not the case.

124. Newman, *Untamed Hospitality*, 31.

to draw limits or highlight expectations. Yet, I would contend that this does not encapsulate the practice of true hospitality. Simiarly, Newman asserts in her Christian understanding of hospitality that "Jesus's inclusivity is not without expectations" and in the Johannine story of the woman about to be stoned (8:1–11), "[h]e loves and accepts her but also calls her to a different way of life."[125] Newman argues that to celebrate diversity as an "internal good of hospitality is to distort it" since the "'good' of hospitality as diversity ends up underwriting a consumeristic and aesthetic way of life" which is basically noncommittal.[126] According to Newman, diversity for diversity's sake is not a mark of genuine hospitality, but instead turns guests into decoration or a consumable product.

Similarly, theologian and ethicist Luke Bretherton contrasts hospitality and tolerance. For Bretherton, "tolerance is the most common way of conceptualizing relations with an 'other' with whom one disagrees"[127] and, therefore, it is not congruent with the aims of genuine hospitality. Instead, Bretherton asserts hospitality "constitutes a better way of framing relations with strangers than tolerance."[128] He defines tolerance as involving "the willingness to accept differences (whether religious, moral, ethnic or economic) for which, at whatever level, one might, as an individual or as a community, disapprove."[129] Furthermore, Bretherton details three conditions that need to be met in order for a group or individual to be tolerant:

> First, there must be some conduct about which one disapproves, even if only minimally or potentially. Second, although such a person or group has power to act coercively against, or interfere to prevent, that of which they disapprove, they do not. Third, not interfering coercively must result from more than acquiescence, resignation, indifference or a balance of power. One does not tolerate that which one is not concerned about; nor is it tolerance simply to accept what one cannot, or is not willing to, change (either because one lacks power to effect change or because, for whatever reason, one fears to use one's power) . . . toleration is particularly important and problematic when it involves a principled refusal to prohibit conduct believed to be wrong.[130]

125. Ibid.
126. Ibid.
127. Bretherton, *Hospitality as Holiness*, 5.
128. Ibid.
129. Ibid., 122.
130. Ibid.

Bretherton identifies tolerance as an "early modern period" phenomenon that "overshadowed the notion and practice of hospitality,"[131] and asserts hospitality is "founded on more explicitly biblical and theological imperatives" than tolerance.[132] Moreover, Bretherton appropriates the argument by philosopher John Gray, stating that "[l]iberal toleration presupposed a cultural consensus on values even as it allowed for differences in beliefs . . . [making tolerance] an inadequate ideal in societies in which deep moral diversity has become an established fact of life."[133]

Hospitality's influence has heavier potential than tolerance in shaping society and social interaction, and has significant political implications as it can often mean the giver of hospitality finds oneself "actively opposed by those who would be . . . inhospitable to the vulnerable stranger."[134] Here explorations of the boundaries of hospitality are necessary in light of the realities that accompany the need to protect those who are vulnerable. As opposed to toleration, the host cannot be "uncritically welcoming of everyone . . . [as] a proper evaluation must be made of who, in any particular instance, is the stranger to be welcomed."[135] This requirement, of course, leads to an unavoidable tension. Bretherton identifies this tension as being torn

> between greeting every stranger . . . and discerning who would genuinely benefit from care, the tension of establishing institutional . . . forms of hospitality and the need for hospitality to be personal . . . and the tension between provision and the capacity to provide wherein the integrity and resources of the community can be overwhelmed by the abuse of, or extensive need for, hospitality.[136]

Compared to tolerance, hospitality provides a much more meaningful framework as it has a greater capacity to enact and ensure social peace and security. Yet, both are needed. Hospitality cannot and should not replace tolerance, but instead should be recognized as something greater, a next step, and take tolerance further into actual engagement with the concrete other. Tolerance is limited because it does not encourage "active engagement and concern in the life of others" and does not foster as much of an impetus "to dialogue [and commit] to collaborative truth-seeking and the enrichment of

131. Ibid., 125.

132. Ibid.

133. Gray, "Pluralism and Toleration in Contemporary Political Philosophy."

134. Bretherton, *Hospitality as Holiness*, 141.

135. Ibid.

136. Ibid., 142.

life through the insights of others" as does hospitality.[137] In contrast, hospitality seeks "to welcome those with the least status," actively working to support and address the needs of "the suffering-dying . . . who are likely to be neglected or oppressed because they lack the means to protect themselves."[138] Since tolerance does not include a command "to attend to and actively help those without a place or a voice in society," a tolerant society can [still], in some ways, "be deeply oppressive for many of its members."[139]

Hospitality and Solidarity

As one considers hospitality's political dimensions, it is appropriate for its relationship with solidarity to be explored. The practice of hospitality, particularly on behalf of the threatened or oppressed other, and acts of solidarity certainly overlap.

The French term *solidarité* was first recorded in 1841 with the birth of communism, socialism, and anarchism as political ideologies, and, therefore, seems to have arisen out of a political and sociological context. In contemporary English usage, it connotes a "unity (as of a group or class) that produces or is based on community of interests, objectives, and standards"[140] and carries with it ideas of mutual responsibility and interdependence.

The relationship between hospitality and solidarity is somewhat ambiguous, but is present nonetheless. Christian theologian Thomas Reynolds writes about both as if they are music being made, different notes that form a song. He views solidarity as an interactive praxis that is "hybrid, boundary-transgressive, and self-differentiating . . . unstable and opens outward from the inside" and is brought into the fabric of a community by hospitality.[141] He describes the relationship between hospitality and solidarity further by stating:

> Hospitality nourishes a community precisely because it is disposed . . . toward what lies beyond the conventional margins of a group's identity . . . [and] recognizes solidarity and kinship

137. Markham, *Plurality and Christian Ethics*, 188. Bretherton remarks in a footnote that Markham provides no justification for why there is a need to move beyond tolerance (*Hospitality as Holiness*, 147).

138. Ibid., 148.

139. Ibid.

140. Its root is the Latin term *solidum* connoting entirety and from which the English term "solid" arises. See Merriam-Webster Dictionary Online, http://www.merriam-webster.com/dictionary/solidarity.

141. Reynolds, "Improvising Together," 54.

> with what is unconventional and other. Put succinctly, hospitality acknowledges another as one's neighbor, a potential brother or sister. It is, thus, generous and courageously uncalculating, willingly granting by credit a solidarity with what comes unexpectedly and unannounced—the stranger, one who does not belong and who comes from "outside" the zone of the familiar and expected. This requires both courage and justice: the former because one cannot forecast the outcome of the encounter, and the latter because one presumes the worth and dignity of the stranger. In fact, it is the presumption of worth that ennobles the risk of welcoming another. It willingly grants that another also possesses the moral characteristics of justice, humility, courage, and truthfulness, an assumption that could urn out in the end to be wrong. Thus, welcoming the stranger could mark one's undoing, but such welcoming is a risk that communal solidarity cannot avoid taking.[142]

Therefore, to welcome another is to be open and available to the needs of the other and this welcome "lies at the core of genuine communal solidarity."[143] And through hospitality, the identities of the guest and host become "transposed through the encounter, each becoming an other for one another . . . [which creates an] enlarged sense of solidarity . . . [or] being at home with others—having a shared identity."[144] As such, Reynolds asserts hospitality "is the fulcrum for cultivating solidarity, the moral fabric of a community's ongoing sense of itself."[145]

While the term solidarity is not present in the sacred texts, according to Golden and McConnell it is a "sacred act" that "captures the essence" of the Abrahamic traditions in their struggle to "maintain solidarity with their God and with the poor."[146] Similarly, Reynolds contends that solidarity "is the modern equivalent of [the] covenant bond made with God."[147] Therefore, if solidarity is the bond, is hospitality then the action that honors the bond? If solidarity is the contract, perhaps hospitality is the actions and attitude that bring the contract of solidarity to life. While further research needs to be conducted on the connection between hospitality and solidarity, there appears to something similar to a chemical catalytic relationship whereby their interaction causes a reaction and transformation into some-

142. Ibid., 54–55.

143. Ibid., 54.

144. Ibid., 56.

145. Ibid.

146. Golden and McConnell, *Sanctuary*, 188.

147. Ibid.

thing new. In this case, that something new is the willingness to put oneself at risk to seek the benefit of the other.

In contexts of oppression and marginalization where solidarity is the most appropriate response, the "challenge is to secure social space within which an alternative world of meaning can be established and nurtured, generating resistance to oppression."[148] The creation and maintenance of that space is an act of hospitality. Yet, hospitality on its own cannot be the sole moral response in this context. Ogletree asserts hospitality practiced by those who benefit from structures of inequality sets in motion "a movement of awareness which leads to repentance," or "a deep turning of mind away from the familiar world toward the possibility of a new order of the world," which in turn informs and feeds solidarity and enables a reciprocal relationship to be formed.[149] In some cases, to show hospitality and solidarity to those who are under threat is to "surrender altogether the location which gives [one] power and privilege" that most likely will cause oneself to then be counted among the threatened as well.[150] As such, hospitality and solidarity come at a price.

Hospitality and Honor

As will be explored further in chapter 4, a central contention of this argument is that the practice of hospitality is inextricably linked to concepts of honor. While there has not been any significant research conducted specifically on the relationship between hospitality and honor, there is enough in the research that exists on each independently to suggest the connection is of importance to what is being explored here.[151]

Honor, as considered by philosopher Kwame Anthony Appiah, is closely connected with other key concepts such as identity and recognition.[152]

148. Ogletree, *Hospitality to the Stranger*, 5.

149. Ibid., 6.

150. Ibid.

151. On concepts of honor as it informs this discussion on hospitality, see Benedict, *The Chrysanthemum and the Sword*; Peristiany, *Honour and Shame*; Friedrich, "Sanity and the Myth of Honor"; Pitt-Rivers, *Fate of Shechem*; Herzfeld, "Honour and Shame"; Gilmore, *Honour and Shame and the Unity of the Mediterranean*; Peristiany and Pitt-Rivers, *Honor and Grace in Anthropology*; Cairns, *Aidos*; Miller, *Humiliation*; Williams, *Shame and Necessity*; Nisbett and Cohen, *Culture of Honor*; Stone, *Sex, Honor, and Power*; Blok, *Honour and Violence*; and Lawrence, *An Ethnography of the Gospel of Matthew*.

152. Appiah, *The Honor Code*, xiii. Appiah's connections between honor, identity, and recognition seem similar to Ricoeur's idea of politics of recognition in *The Course of Recognition*. Appiah also refers to Hegel's ideas of *Anerkennung* (recognition), which are compiled and explored more fully in Williams, *Hegel's Ethics of Recognition*. See also

As such, Appiah asserts honor is given when "others . . . respond appropriately to who we are and to what we do" and, therefore, it must have "a crucial place . . . in our thinking about what it is to live a successful human life."[153] In turn, Appiah makes the connection between the role of honor in a successful human life and the role of flourishing in Aristotle's concept of *eudaimonia*, upon which the study of ethics is based.[154] Therefore, according to Appiah, honor is integral to ethical behavior and accordingly honor plays "a central role" in moral revolutions,[155] as morality "is an important dimension of ethics."[156] Furthermore, he asserts honor is "an engine . . . that can drive us to take seriously our responsibilities in a world we share" and, as such, honor makes integrity, or "caring to do the right thing," public.[157]

However, Appiah differentiates honor and morality in an important way. He states:

> A grasp of morality will keep soldiers from abusing the human dignity of their prisoners. It will make them disapprove of the acts of those who don't. And it will allow women who have been vilely abused to know that their abusers deserve punishment. But it takes a sense of honor to drive a soldier beyond doing

Frantzen, *Bloody Good*, for an exploration of the relationship between chivalry (which reads remarkably similar to honor) and concepts of sacrifice for a greater good as an expression of heroic masculinity through a context of violence. Protective hospitality has the potential to provide an alternative vision of honor, which embraces risk (instead of heroism), egalitarian practice, and nonviolence as a means of honoring all life.

153. Appiah, *The Honor Code*, xiii–xiv. Similarly, the pursuit towards justice in liberation and feminist theologies could be construed as primarily a pursuit for recognition and honor, shown by allowing those who are often left out to be heard, valued, protected and given hospitality. Appiah notes the psychology and physicality of honor by noting it is "deeply connected with walking tall and looking the world in the eye . . . when able-bodied people with a sense of honor remember they are entitled to respect, they literally walk with their heads held high . . . Humiliation, on the other hand, curves the spine, lowers the eyes . . . shame's face is the face of a person with eyes cast down . . ." (xvii–xviii).

154. Ibid. This connection to flourishing, honor, and ethics complements Jacques Derrida's assertions related to ethics and hospitality as discussed earlier in this chapter.

155. Ibid., xii, xiii. Moral revolutions for Appiah are dramatic shifts in cultural values that move toward honor and respect for the flourishing of human life. In his book, he focuses upon the stigmatization of what were at one time acceptable cultural practices, such as foot binding, slavery, and "honor" killings.

156. Ibid., xiv. Appiah differentiates ethics from morality by stating "morality . . . is an important dimension of ethics: doing what I should for others is part of living well." Appiah sees ethics as that concept of living well, and therefore, morality appears to be that which is done to enable one to live well.

157. Ibid., 179. This public aspect of honor will be a necessary element in the formation of protection as a form of hospitality in later chapters.

> what is right and condemning what is wrong to insisting that something is done when others on his side do wicked things. It takes a sense of honor to feel implicated by the acts of others.[158]

Conversely, honor without morality leads to practices of honor codes that encourage its adherents to "do things that are actually immoral."[159] It cannot be ignored that honor has been used as a means to sustain oppressive power and authority, and provided justification for horrific abuse throughout the centuries on both interpersonal and systemic levels. To counteract this, Appiah argues that honor and morality must be partners if a more just and inclusive society is to be developed.[160]

Appiah also discusses the outward manifestations of honor and respect by stating that when one loses respect, others are inclined to treat that person more poorly.[161] Conversely, when honor is gained and enacted, it "powers the global movement for human rights" and also "allows communities both large and small to reward and encourage people who excel . . . [and] motivate citizens in the unending struggle to discipline the acts of their governments."[162]

So what about hospitality, and where does it meet honor? Writer and theologian G. K. Chesterton wrote "the most obvious expression of honour [is] hospitality."[163] How then do they relate to one another? One way in which one can ascertain the relationship between honor and hospitality is to consider it anthropologically. Tone Bringa, an anthropologist who studied villages in central Bosnia, noted hospitality "is a form of social exchange" where actions such as "ceremonial gift-giving, voluntary work, ritualized hospitality and institutionalized visiting patterns" illustrate the strong relationship between honor and hospitality as a cultural ethos.[164] She noted that the provision of hospitality is "closely related to the reputation of individual

158. Ibid., 204.

159. Ibid., 177. Appiah gives the example of honor killings, but his arguments would apply to all manner of actions that were once acceptable but have now been stigmatized in many circles as immoral such as torture, blood feuds, and child labor, among others.

160. Ibid., 175–204.

161. Ibid., 180–95. This is not a neutral state, however. Such an exhibition of "losing honor" is found in so-called "honor killings," which Appiah addresses. In truth, however, David Tombs notes honor in the South Asian context (where honor killings are carried out) usually "reflects mainly male interests" and that of the family, instead of specifically the woman's honor ("'Shame' as a Neglected Value in Schooling," 24). See also Jasam, *Honour, Shame and Resistance;* and Jafri, *Honour Killing*, 18–33.

162. Ibid., 195.

163. Chesterton, *The Collected Works*, 381.

164. Bringa, *Being Muslim the Bosnian Way*, 68.

households" and illustrates the connection in Bosnian for "the verb for offering hospitality (častiti) [as having] the same etymology as the word for honor (*čast*)."[165] She also noted that "a household, which outsiders always see as a unit and therefore reflecting on men and women equally, gains social standing ("honor") from the way it receives a guest."[166] As a result, the economic struggles of the 1980s in then-Yugoslavia" often made it difficult (or of lower priority) for people to honor (*častiti*) guests as they believed they should" as there was "a sense of shame and inadequacy in not being able to offer guests much in the way of food" in a context where "lavish hospitality is . . . an expression of both the moral superiority of the host and the political potential of the guest."[167]

Anthropologist Anne Meneley noted similar findings in the context of Yemen.[168] The Islamic idea of *adab*, translated as manners or "correct comportment," refers to one's "social personhood,"[169] carries within it connotations of honor and hospitality. According to Meneley, in order for the elite to maintain their position in society (i.e. their honor), they "must display, consume and distribute their wealth in a way that indicates a willingness to engage with others in the community, through acts of generosity and hospitality" as the values of "generosity, hospitality and charity are . . . shared by all."[170] Those values are perpetuated throughout society, however, by the "daily negotiation, contestation and competition" of hospitality where "neglecting a guest in one's own home only hurts one's own reputation" and "honour accrues to those who are visited, who are thereby acknowledged as socially significant and morally sound, and those who are allowed to give (or give back) rather than receive."[171]

When considering honor and hospitality historically, one finds further evidence of their relationship in the context of ancient Greece. *Aidos*

165. Ibid., 69.

166. Ibid. Bringa also refers to the work of Michael Herzfeld, who pointed out the link between hospitality and honor in Cretan society. Herzfeld notes that "social worth [*filotimo*, 'sometimes glossed as honour'] is hospitality" ("As in Your Own House," 75–78).

167. Bringa, *Being Muslim the Bosnian Way*, Bringa refers again to the work of Herzfeld in relation to the moral and political implications of "lavish hospitality."

168. Meneley, "Living Hierarchy in Yemen," 61–74.

169. Ibid., 67.

170. Ibid.

171. Ibid., 68. The importance of the value of hospitality and honor within Arab societies has been documented elsewhere. One example is the work of Sammy Smooha, who looks at the cultural difference in perception of hospitality between Israeli Jews and Arab Palestinians that serve to feed stereotypes and ongoing conflict. See Smooha, *Israel*, 199–200, 380.

was the Greek goddess or personification of modesty, humility and shame, and as such *aidos* was a value and emotion in Greek culture that kept one from doing wrong through the power of reverence or shame, enabling one to abide by accepted ethical codes of behavior.[172] As a result, *aidos* dictated that "abuse of another's hospitality . . . [was] disgraceful" and "both abuse of hospitality and failure to protect a guest . . . as inappropriate and unseemly"[173] as "protection of strangers was . . . [in the context of ancient Greek literature] a Homeric ideal."[174]

Likewise, New Testament scholars Carolyn Osiek and David Balch assert the context of the early Christian church points to the relationship between honor and hospitality by noting that "receiving a stranger as a guest . . . creates a bond . . . whereby the stranger is welcomed as fictive kin."[175] Furthermore, honor plays a role in this expression of hospitality in that "the host violates the rules of hospitality by allowing the guest to be dishonored or harmed . . . [and] the guest violates the rules by dishonoring the host or anyone in his household."[176]

Another historical example of honor and hospitality that continues to be applied in the current day is seen in The Kanun of Lekë Dukagjini, a fifteenth century codified collection of laws related to honor and hospitality often referred to as *besa*, in Albanian culture. As an ethical code, it relies upon the fictive kin relationship as well as calling upon its adherents to "treat strangers as if they were family . . . and guard them with their lives."[177] Accordingly, abiding by the code of *besa* brings honor to the family, and those who do are described as being "full of besa."[178]

172. *Aidos* could be considered as similar to conscience as it is a self-regulating ethical mechanism. See Williams' book on *Shame and Necessity* for a discussion of honor and shame as determiners of modern moral categories.

173. Cairns, *Aidos*, 110, referring to Homer's *Odyssey* 20.294–95.

174. Cairns, *Aidos*, 113.

175. Osiek and Balch, *Families in the New Testament World*, 39.

176. Ibid. This concept of dishonor as a result of the guest being harmed will be important in the development of the practice of protective hospitality in the following chapters.

177. CBS News, "The Righteous." The code of besa would be attributed as the reason why so many Jews found refuge in Albania during World War II. See also Gershman, *Besa*.

178. David Tombs explores the concept of *izzat* (honor) in Hindi/Urdu-speaking South Asian communities in England in his article "'Shame' as a Neglected Value in Schooling." The usage of the word *izzat* and its corresponding *bei'izzat* (shame/dishonor—sometimes shortened to *behzti*) in the context of discussion of honor sounds remarkably similar to the Albanian *besa*, albeit one is negative and the other is positive. Yet, one could see how a code of dishonor/shame could easily morph into a code of honor as culture, geography, and language changed.

The relationship between hospitality and honor is not a one-to-one relationship, but as evidenced thus far, it does illustrate that each has an impact upon the other. How this relationship plays out in the practice of protective hospitality has been alluded to here, but will be presented in much greater detail in chapter 4.

Ogletree asserts that "[t]o offer hospitality to a stranger is to welcome something new, unfamiliar, and unknown into our life-world" and requires "a recognition of the stranger's vulnerability in an alien world . . . [where they are in need of] shelter and sustenance."[179] This assertion—that hospitality requires showing welcome to the unknown other and a sensitivity and willingness to meet the needs of that other in a hostile world—will be explored in more detail in the following chapter, as it pertains to the Abrahamic traditions in particular.

179. Ogletree, *Hospitality to Strangers*, 2.

3

Hospitality and the Abrahamic Traditions

> *Real religion teaches us that we must assume responsibility for helping the weakest, most damaged people around us. We must stand up for them inside our own communities. If we don't, we become partners in the evil . . .*
>
> —Rusmir Mahmutčehajić[1]

INTRODUCTION

This chapter will build upon the preceding chapter, which extended hospitality and analyzed its contributing factors, to focus upon hospitality in the theology and practices of the Abrahamic traditions of Judaism, Christianity and Islam. Foundations of the Abrahamic traditions that inform the practice of hospitality will be explored, namely in the original geography and cultures in the traditions' development, as detailed in the first section that addresses shared origins. This exploration will be made with an acknowledgment that "universal truth is worth more than local particularisms."[2] The

1. Mahmutčehajić is a scholar and Muslim theologian who works for International Forum, Bosnia. Quote from Shriver and Shriver, "Open Wounds," 5.

2. Levinas, *Difficult Freedom*, 179. See also Derrida, *Acts of Religion*, 367. Levinas makes this statement in reference to Islam and how he thinks it understands this principle better than any other religious tradition.

universality in this case is found in the commonalities that exist within the traditions, that upon which hospitable life has been built.

In addition, as each tradition is considered in turn in the following sections, their common history of exile and persecution in formational periods; the role of prophets and models as examples of personified hospitality; common values such as dignity, generosity and honor, and other particular factors that inform hospitality as an ethic will also be analyzed. In addition to these commonalities, specific understandings and resources available in each tradition—that which makes them particular—will be highlighted and considered. Each section will conclude with an analysis of challenges in the contemporary context of each tradition as it relates to the practice of hospitality.

The final section of this chapter will highlight emphases that are currently missing in the contemporary Western Christian scholarship.[3] Through consideration of the practice of hospitality in Judaism and Islam and the particular resources available within the tradition, Christianity will be examined in order to identify aspects that have perhaps been forgotten over the centuries. This section will serve as a means of reflection and exercise of the dialogical method utilized within the body of this research.

SHARED ORIGINS: THE ABRAHAMIC TRADITIONS AND THE PRACTICE OF HOSPITALITY

In order to provide an overview of resources in the Abrahamic traditions of Judaism, Christianity, and Islam that contribute to a theology and ethic of hospitality, it is first important to consider some common themes in each tradition that inform hospitable practice.

Over the last century, the relationship between Judaism and Christianity has been increasingly accepted and the term "Judeo-Christian" has been used quite frequently to describe certain theological and ethical similarities between the two religious traditions. The use of this term refers to an acceptance that these traditions are similar enough as they have common bonds, common heritage, common scripture and common understandings. Nevertheless, Islam's inclusion is necessary, particularly as it also finds its root in Abraham, is increasingly acknowledged in global relations, shares common values, geography and reverence for religious figures such as Moses and

3. Again, because of the limitations of this research, the emphasis here (unless noted otherwise) is upon English-speaking, western Christian scholarship, while also noting that western Christian thought is not all there is to Christianity, and at the same time acknowledging western Christianity does not equal contemporary Christianity.

Jesus, as well as its strong tradition in the practice of hospitality. Moreover, Jewish philosopher Jacques Derrida advocated the inclusion of Islam in the discussion of what has been called "Judeo-Christian spirituality," as Islam presents itself "as a religion, an ethics, and a culture of hospitality."[4] As such, in each instance Derrida discusses religion in his work, his focus is "always on the Abrahamic."[5]

To refer to the traditions as *Abrahamic* implies an overarching common theme in that each tradition finds its spiritual roots in the person and narrative of Abraham.[6] The term "Abrahamic" has been widely adopted to refer generally to the three traditions that look to Abraham as a founding patriarch and over the years has been appropriated as a term that originated from language used in primarily Islamic religious discourse.[7] Nevertheless, it is how the three traditions perceive this person of Abraham and the respective narratives attributed to him that lend authority to commonality and practice of hospitality.

Lewis Mudge found importance in the gift of responsibility that God gave to Abraham as a result of God's promise that Abraham and his descendents would be a "blessing to the nations" as that which binds the traditions together.[8] Mudge asserts Abraham "comes to know that true obedience to God requires him responsibly to exercise the gift of discernment of what obedience requires . . . [and t]his . . . gift of responsibility . . . [is] at the origin of all three Abrahamic faiths."[9] Furthermore, Mudge contends that as a result of this promise, adherents to Abrahamic traditions are to "do those things that make [them] free to be instruments of the promise of 'blessing' extended to all human beings . . . [and] this 'blessing' is both an act of giving

4. Derrida, *Acts of Religion*, 365.

5. Anidjar, "Once More, Once More," 3.

6. The use of the term "Abrahamic" can be construed in two different ways: Either it can be considered a marker of the "original and gathering root of the three major monotheistic faiths or, more pervasively, as the (three) branches of one single faith. It suggests the reclaiming of territorialized roots, the reoccupation and gathering of a site of welcoming togetherness, where old fallen branches can come back to life: as Paul writes, 'God is perfectly able to graft them back again' (Romans 11:23) . . . it also institutes the possibility of comparison under the allegedly unified figure of Abraham, whose name appears in the three scriptural traditions." Anidjar, "Once More, Once More," 3.

7. Anidjar, "Once More, Once More," 3; Smith, "Religion, Religions, Religious," 276.

8. Genesis 17:16, 18:18, 22:18, 26:4; Qur'an 2:124, 3:33, 14:36. The Qur'anic interpretation of the covenant of blessing with Abraham is most often interpreted as conditional and based upon whether or not Abraham's descendents obey God and live righteous lives.

9. Mudge, *The Gift of Responsibility*, 8–9.

and a gift that conveys the responsibility to be what we will be, in [oneself] and for others."[10]

Model: Abraham

Since the traditions of Judaism, Christianity and Islam are collectively known as "Abrahamic" traditions, the person of Abraham is a foundational character to each tradition's formation. The perception of him as a model whereupon the traditions find authority and inspiration for the practice of hospitality is no coincidence.

Judaism, Christianity, and Islam considers Abraham a patriarch who "came to this earth as a 'stranger, a hôte, *gêr*,' and a kind of saint of hospitality" and a pilgrim who "left his own"[11] to go where God directed him for the purpose God had in mind. Each tradition looks to Abraham and his descendents as the "center of the paradigmatic hospitality narratives"[12] for the foundation of their faith and hospitable practice. Abraham is the archetype for both the practice of hospitality as well as "nomadic, national, and exilic experiences"[13] which marked "'the first time in human history in which the divine world was seen to side with 'outlaws, fugitives and immigrants' rather than with the political structures whose policies and use of power made such social types inevitable.'"[14]

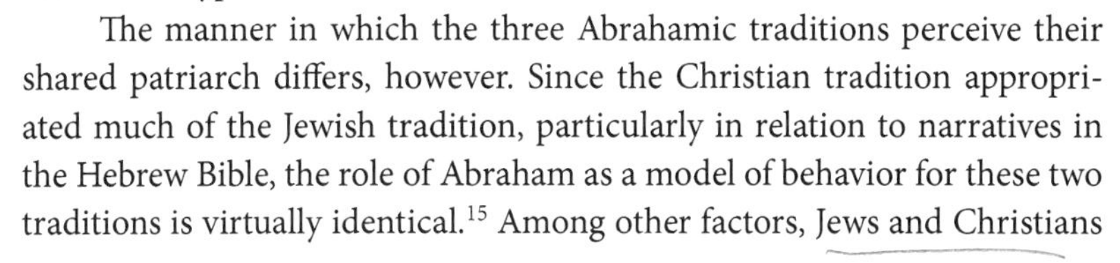

The manner in which the three Abrahamic traditions perceive their shared patriarch differs, however. Since the Christian tradition appropriated much of the Jewish tradition, particularly in relation to narratives in the Hebrew Bible, the role of Abraham as a model of behavior for these two traditions is virtually identical.[15] Among other factors, Jews and Christians

10. Ibid., 9.

11. Derrida, *Acts of Religion*, 369, quoting and referring to Massignon's work, "The Three Prayers of Abraham" 3–20. See also Peters, *Children of Abraham*; Kushchel, *Abraham*; Hinze and Omar, *Heirs of Abraham*; and Chittister et al., *The Tent of Abraham*.

12. Yong, *Hospitality and the Other*, 109. Cf. Gen 18, 19, 24, 29; Acts 7; Heb 11; Qur'an 11, 15, 51.

13. Yong, *Hospitality and the Other*, 109. Yong refers to the work of Bolin, "'A Stranger and an Alien Among You,'" 57–76.

14. Ibid., 109–10, quoting Spina, "Israelites as *gerîm*," 332.

15. The obvious exception to the Abraham narrative in the Hebrew Bible as told in Judaism and in Christianity is the identity and, therefore, the importance of the guests Abraham entertains. In the Jewish tradition, the guests are angels or messengers of God. In Christianity, there are some who interpret the three guests as a theophany but also physical manifestations of the Trinity, primarily based upon a Trinitarian interpretation of the Hebrews 7 text as well as Gen 18; 19:24; and John 8:56. It is also depicted in Orthodox iconography as Trinitarian, with famous icons such as Andrei Rublev's

see Abraham as the first wanderer, the first sojourner. As such, the power of Abraham in this context lies in his narrative highlighting the idea "that no one, neither people nor individual, really has a home in world history, that no one is finally secure, that we are all pushed about, that we are all-eternal strangers, since it is only in God that we are finally at home and secure."[16] Yet, in contrast to Judaism and Christianity's additional and heretofore unmentioned interpretations of Abraham as the "father of nations," Muslim theology related to Abraham does not carry the connotations of "a special history of revelation for a particular people" as is present in Judaism and Christianity.[17] Instead, Muhammad understood Abraham "a priori as the model of true faith, which anyone can practise, quite independently of belonging to a people or having a place in salvation history."[18]

As a model of behavior regarding the practice of hospitality, Abraham's narrative is powerful. Referred to by the sacred texts of all three traditions, the account of Abraham's (and his wife Sarah's) hospitality to the three strangers carries fundamental weight.[19] From the originating text found in Genesis 18, the Abrahamic traditions develop their particular theologies and ethic related to hospitality[20] in light of Abraham's response to the unexpected visit from what were considered to be messengers from God. Arterbury notes other texts, such as the Septuagint,[21] Philo's *De Abrahamo*,[22] Josephus' *Antiquities of the Jews*[23] and other later texts by Clement (75–110

1410 icon that is called a variety of names, including "The Old Testament Trinity" or simply "The Trinity."

16. Barth, *Church Dogmatics* III/3, 224–25.

17. Kuschel, *Abraham*, 163. In the interest of Gentiles (in Muhammad's case, Arabs), the issue of God's covenant with Abraham and blessing of a particular group of people is unhelpful.

18. Ibid. The apostle Paul argues similarly in Rom 4 and Gal 3.

19. Gen 18:1–33; Acts 7; Heb 11; Qur'an 11:72; 15:51; 51:24.

20. Derrida, *Acts of Religion*, 371. Derrida also asserts that "it is indeed the hospitality of the hôte Abraham that is placed at the center of Islam and that makes of Islam the most faithful heir" since within the Qur'an the Genesis text is referenced and shows "that Islam has deduced the principle of *Iqra* (*dakhalk, jiwar*), right of hospitality, *ikram al dayf*, respect of the human person, of the *hôte*, sent by God" (*Acts of Religion*, 371, quoting from Pierre Roclav, *Louis Massignon et l'islam*, 33).

21. Arterbury, *Entertaining Angels*, 61, references the work of Samuel Sandmel, *Philo's Place in Judaism*, 181, wherein he notes the differences between the Masoretic text and the Greek Septuagint text of Genesis 18, which seem to cater to the hospitality preferences and rituals of a Greek audience rather than a Hebrew one.

22. Borgen, "Philo of Alexandria." See also Sandmel, *Philo's Place in Judaism*.

23. Josephus, *Jewish Antiquities*. See also Feldman, *Flavius Josephus*.

CE),[24] Rabbi Nathan (later 3rd century CE),[25] and the *Genesis Rabbah* (c. 400 CE)[26] that also make reference to the hospitality narrative of Abraham, establishing a paradigm in the development of the merits of welcoming the other in religious thought and practice, as well as in social duty, over the centuries.[27]

Ethics Based in Culture

The contribution of geography and cultures prevalent in the region of the Mediterranean and Near East are a common factor in the development of a theology and ethic of hospitality in Judaism, Christianity and Islam. Although these respective traditions have spread throughout the world over the centuries and continue to be shaped by a variety of local contexts even today, they all arose from a particular place and cultural milieu that necessitated hospitality as a social, religious, and political practice.[28]

When considering hospitality in the Abrahamic sacred texts, it is helpful if one understands the cultural approach to hospitality in antiquity instead of importing contemporary concepts that may or may not be relevant to the original context. Therefore, the following two sections will deal with two specific cultural aspects of the practice of hospitality that inform the Abrahamic traditions: Mediterranean/Near Eastern and desert contexts.

Mediterranean/Near Eastern Societies

The majority of academic writing on hospitality in antiquity has been in the area of Greco-Roman practices of hospitality found in the Mediterranean

24. Lake, "The First Epistle of Clement to the Corinthians." For later Christian interpretations of the hospitality of Abraham, see *Apocalypse of Paul,* 27; Origen's fourth homily on Genesis; and John Chrysostom's forty-first homily on Genesis.

25. Goldin, *The Fathers according to Rabbi Nathan.* See also Neusner, *The Fathers according to Rabbi Nathan.*

26. Neusner, *Genesis Rabbah.* Arterbury references each of these texts as noted above, comparing and contrasting the Jewish traditions with the Greco-Roman traditions of hospitality and the language used to describe them (*Entertaining Angels,* 61–70).

27. Arterbury, *Entertaining Angels,* 70. See also Van Seters, *Abraham in History and Tradition.*

28. It is a generally accepted anthropological truism that the greatest influence upon the shaping and practice of religion and social ethics is local culture. For more information on how this works, the work of anthropologist Clifford Geertz is useful. For general anthropological work in this area, see Geertz, *Interpretation of Cultures;* or Geertz, *Local Knowledge.* For his work in comparing Islam as "a single creed . . . in contrasting civilizations," see Geertz, *Islam Observed.*

and the Near East.[29] Although hospitable practice existed long before Greco-Roman culture became prevalent in these areas, the practices were undoubtedly appropriated, assimilated, and developed further into the colonized context and were recorded for posterity into the literature and social practices still being analyzed today. Examples such as Ovid's myth of Baucis and Philemon, Homer's *Odyssey*, or Heliodorus' *An Ethiopian Story* along with several other works give significant insight into the practice of hospitality in the region of the Mediterranean and the Near East in antiquity.

In general, however, when hospitality is considered in antiquity in this context, it is usually defined "as the kind treatment of travelers or strangers, which included welcoming, feeding, lodging, protecting, and aiding the traveler . . . [but also] hinges upon the identity of the persons involved."[30] How and why that hospitality is expressed, however, is varied.

Arterbury refers to the work of antiquities scholar Ladislaus Bolchazy who delineates five motives for hospitality according to the customs found in Mediterranean and Near Eastern antiquity:

1. "Medea" hospitality (based on Euripides' *Medea*) finds its motivation through "'magico-religious xenophobia'" which required kindness to strangers in order that they might be disarmed of any ill will or occult powers that could be used against the host or his/her community.[31]
2. Theoxenic hospitality is the expression of hospitality whereby the motivation derives from the conviction that "gods or their representatives often visited humans in the form of beggars or strangers."[32] Because of the ability to hide their divinity under the guise of human form, the gods or their emissaries were able to test their human subjects regarding their character and capacity for hospitality, determining if they were morally upstanding. Understandably, cultures that adhered to this particular belief were then motivated to treat the other with kindness and hospitality because to welcome the other was to possibly

29. See also Herzfeld, "As in Your Own House," 75–89; and Peristiany, *Honour and Shame*.

30. Arterbury, *Entertaining Angels*, 16. Arterbury alludes to the work of Herman, who notes that hospitality is a reciprocal relationship "between individuals originating from separate social units" (Herman, *Ritualised Friendship*, 10). Therefore, Arterbury states, "the recipient of hospitality in antiquity was a person who was traveling outside of his or, more rarely, her home territory" (*Entertaining Angels*, 16).

31. Bolchazy, *Hospitality in Antiquity*, 8–10.

32. See ibid., 11–14. This same justification is seen in the motive found in Christianity, particularly in reference to the idea that to entertain strangers would be to entertain Christ himself or angels unaware.

welcome the divine.[33] Such an idea—that the gods test humanity on the merits of their provision of hospitality—then makes it reasonable to ascertain that "hospitality is the attribute or special domain of the principal divinity (YHWH, Zeus, Jupiter Capitolinus, the Holy Trinity," and that in ancient Greece "one [may] even argue that hospitality *is* religion, the defining social ethics of *Zeus Xenios*, Zeus god of strangers."[34]

3. *Ius hospitii, ius dei* is translated as "right of the guest, right of god" manifests itself in the motivation to provide hospitality to strangers because "the host believed hospitality was in accordance with the desires of the gods."[35] This motivation for hospitality is very simple in that a host welcomed others because that is what he/she felt was what was expected in order to please the gods.

4. Contractual hospitality is based on the principle of reciprocity and is motivated by "personal advantages that [are] accrued to both parties" as part of a reciprocal relationship.[36] For this reason, hosts desired to develop new relationships and therefore offered hospitality to guests in order that during future travels, the host "could expect the same kind of blessings, provisions, and protection from their guests."[37] Arterbury clarifies this elsewhere in his work by noting hospitality in this context depends upon "the foreignness of the two parties" involved and that

33. McNulty, *The Hostess*, 8.

34. Ibid., vii, xiv–xv.

35. See Bolchazy, *Hospitality in Antiquity*, 14–16.

36. Ibid., 16–18.

37. See ibid., and cf. Arterbury, *Entertaining Angels*, 27. Interestingly, Arterbury claims the principle of reciprocity was stronger in Greco-Roman contexts than in Jewish and Christian expressions of hospitality in antiquity. He compares the two by stating Greco-Roman culture endorsed the practice of selecting guests and/or hosts "whom they anticipated would create a personal benefit for them through the exchange of gifts and the like," whereas Jewish travelers "avoided accepting hospitality from non-Jews . . . [by seeking] out a distant family member or tribesman if possible," and Christians acted similarly by offering hospitality "only to Christian travelers" (Matt 25:31–46; 1 Pet 4:9; 2 John 10–11; 3 John 5–8) despite exhortations from the apostle Paul and the author of Hebrews (Rom 12:13b; Heb 13:2) to do otherwise (ibid., 132). There are some problems with these claims Arterbury makes, however, as the proofs he gives are based on pericopes in the sacred texts of the traditions that were most likely not set out to give an account of the full sociological phenomenon of hospitality. While he may be identifying trends, such sweeping statements seem unfounded given the proof he cites. He does not critically interact in the context of narrative purpose, if those seeking hospitality were avoiding others out of fear or religious exclusion, if they simply did not expect others to extend them hospitality, or if there are underlying issues of religious purity.

it is "a reciprocal relationship 'between individuals originating from separate social units.'"[38]

5. Altruistic hospitality is the final motivation to provide hospitality wherein one welcomed others not out of "fear of strangers, the fear of gods, the desire to please the gods, nor the desire for personal gain . . . [but instead it is] primarily motivated by one's love for one's fellow human being."[39]

Such a breakdown of classic motivations for the provision of hospitality is helpful in that it assists in delineating underlying issues, fears, risks and beliefs both in antiquity and in current contexts as several still apply. The final three motivations—*Ius hospitii, ius dei*; contractual hospitality; and altruistic hospitality—are the most relevant in the current context of Abrahamic protective hospitality. Despite the various monastic orders in the Christian tradition that exhort followers to welcome strangers *as* Christ, the primary motivation is closer to *Ius hospitii, ius dei* rather than actually believing that the stranger *is* Christ.[40] Furthermore, Ovid's myth of *Baucis and Philemon* places an additional emphasis on the idea that while "whoever welcomes a pilgrim, a foreigner, a poor person, welcomes God . . . [also w]hoever welcomes God turns himself or herself into a temple of God."[41]

Love of God and love of humanity are the most obvious Abrahamic motivators for providing hospitality. Based in ethical practice at its most elemental state, loving God and neighbor should be inseparable according to the Abrahamic traditions.[42] Yet, the importance of contractual hospitality should not be underestimated. This principle of reciprocity has tremendous power in both the ancient and modern context. While Arterbury portrays this type of hospitality, particularly as practiced by the Greco-Romans, as a way of getting a return on one's hospitable investment, the development of relationships as a result of contractual hospitality should be taken seriously for through these developments hospitality can go beyond the simple "love

38. Arterbury, *Entertaining Angels*, 16, referring to Herman, *Ritualised Friendship*, 10.

39. See Bolchazy, *Hospitality in Antiquity*, 18–20.

40. In our contemporary context, it seems as if we no longer expect God to appear in human form, but instead our religious practice and textual interpretation has changed in that the adherent is expected to treat the stranger *as if* he/she were God but, rationally speaking or out of concerns regarding monotheism and idolatry, are not expected to believe that the stranger could be or is, indeed, divine.

41. It is a similar connection, but also distinctly different, which requires pointing out. See Boff, *Virtues*, 42, referring to Ovid, *Metamorphoses*, 190–93.

42. Lev 19:18, 34; Deut 6:5; Matt 22:37–40; Luke 10:27; Qur'an 4:36; *Sahih Bukhari* 8:73:160.

of God and love of neighbor" justification to a more accountable practice calling upon the contracted parties to be responsible to one another. In some ways, contractual motivation is more compelling and carries more ethical weight in its requirement that the adherent act on behalf of the other than the more ambiguous "love of God, love of neighbor" motif.

Simultaneously, contractual hospitality carries political weight. Either on an individual or communal basis, if one goes out of one's way, risking oneself, for the other, it then becomes more than just a single occurrence. Therefore, contractual hospitality has the potential for a social movement and for cooperative action, as it is closely bound with understandings of honor where one is honor-bound to repay debts, particularly if they are incurred on one's behalf.[43] This potential also extends to highlight obligations to identify with, increase solidarity among, and stand up for each other among the three Abrahamic communities. Such obligations would help to develop a partnership that begins to look out for the interests of the other, building an ever-strengthening relationship of respect, dignity and social justice.

Desert Climates and Cultures

There is a variety of deserts found on Earth and if there is human community that resides in them, their cultures often seem to be particularly known for hospitality. Desert people, by necessity, are often nomads.[44] Therefore, concepts of home, place, and stranger carry different connotations than in cultures where communities remain fixed. In a desert climate, prevalent cultures are reminded daily of the inhospitality of the land that surrounds them—the baking sun, the dry earth, the lack of shelter, the scarcity of water and vegetation—and how these conditions make the division between life and death much more immediate.[45]

43. Ken Stone notes that some anthropologists who have looked into the role of honor in Mediterranean and Near Eastern societies "suggest that the early analysts of honor and shame stressed the sexual aspects . . . of 'honor' in a one-sided manner and neglected thereby other important components of honor such as honesty, cooperation, and especially hospitality" (*Sex, Honor, and Power*, 74).

44. An exception to this would be the Pueblo people indigenous to the southwest of North America, who built houses, water storage and irrigation systems that fostered an agricultural culture rather than a nomadic culture. The geology of the area (a mid-latitude desert) in which they settled most likely lent itself to their permanent establishment, whereas shifting sand dunes on the Arabian peninsula and elsewhere make erecting and maintaining permanent structures virtually impossible without a significant amount of civil engineering.

45. Leonardo Boff spends some time in his book, *Virtues For Another Possible*

Without romanticizing the life of desert nomads, it is important to note the cultural proclivity nomadic communities have to fold up tents and move on to another location. Whereas settled agricultural communities "give up part of their freedom, whether to the group as a whole or to . . . a ruler, in exchange for peace, security and the prosperity which order brings,"[46] desert cultures find security and prosperity in the tribe or clan and the community created in their particular non-geographical boundaries. Furthermore, life within this context is determined by "the principles of honor and integrity demanded by the free life of the desert . . . [and as such i]t was these very conditions of desert living which led to the cultivation and growth of the virtues of hospitality, bravery, mutual assistance, neighbor protection, and magnanimity."[47]

The virtues held dear by desert cultures reflect these foundational principles of hospitality and protection. In a hostile desert environment, a dependency is built between individuals and the tribe or clan. In sparsely populated environments, the sight of another human being is cause for celebration because fellow travelers often brought news, resources, and long-awaited company beyond the confines of one's own tribe. As a result, hospitality is ritualized and guests are accepted into the households of clans, and protected as if they are family.

Within Bedouin practices, which became absorbed into Islam at a later date, it was customary to take complete strangers into one's tent, feed and protect them for up to three days before being asked where the stranger has come from or who he/she was.[48] There have also been observations that Muslim historians and poets have great similarity with pre-Islamic literature, particularly in relation to hospitality, noting "it is inevitable that the

World, extolling the unconditional hospitality of Mother Earth—"We exist because we were welcomed without hesitation by the Mother Earth, of whom we are sons and daughters; by nature, who was so good to us . . ."(50). To be sure, Boff's emphasis upon the ecological aspects and practices of hospitality are needed, but Boff is unquestioningly positivist in his depiction of nature. However, Boff's optimistic depiction of nature does not take into account inhospitable climates which have developed and informed human practices of hospitality in order to ensure survival as detailed here.

46. Hayka, *The Life of Muhammad*, 13.

47. Ibid. While one can debate whether or not Judaism and Christianity arose out of the same desert culture as Islam, there remains the experience of the Israelites wandering in the desert having been liberated as slaves from Egypt on which many of their motivations for ethical behavior are based, as seen in the deuteronomic code to care for the widow, orphan and stranger because God brought them up out of Egypt and into the land of Israel, as will be detailed in the next section.

48. See also Bailey, *A Culture of Desert;* Bailey, *Bedouin Law*; Zeid, "Honour and Shame" 245–59; Fluehr-Lobban, *Islamic Societies in Practice*; and *Sahih Bukhari* 8:73:156.

themes of Arab verse should recur constantly . . . [as] Beduin [sic] life varied little from generation to generation."[49] The literature arising from this region reflected the reality that the Bedouins' "horizon was bounded by deserts, and consequently camels and horses . . . [and] hospitality and tribal pride were constantly mentioned in song."[50] To trace the origin of this imagery and influence of hospitality would be next to impossible, but the themes present in pre-Islamic and Islamic literature appear in the visions of "the generous man who slaughters camels for the hungry guest in winter when the famine deprives even the rich of wealth, even when kinsmen refuse their help; the man who entertains when camels' udders are dry; the cauldron full of the hump and fat of the camel" and so on.[51]

Similar practices in the desert of the Australian outback among the Aboriginal people reflect the virtue of hospitality, at least in the beginning. In the period of the 1850–1860 Victorian gold rush, there were many initial accounts of hospitality and generosity by the Aborigines, who were "'proud of their country' and happy to establish friendly contact with [the white] strangers" while also affording "significant assistance and hospitality."[52]

Traditional proverbs and greetings in these cultures also reflect the virtue of hospitality. Throughout the Near and Middle East, the traditional greeting of "*ahlan wa sahlan*" in Arabic, meaning "may you be part of the family and may your path be easy," reflects this cultural value of welcome to the guest or stranger. Likewise, there is a similar proverb attributed to the Mongols in the Gobi Desert: "Happy is the one who has guests; merry is the home boasting a tethering rail full of visitors' horses."[53]

The collection of proverbs and greetings, as well as values that exist as a part of the geographical terrain of desert climates all contribute to the development of an ethic of hospitality in particular cultures. As a result, such common practices and values have a great deal to lend to a complementary theology and ethic of hospitality in the Abrahamic traditions.

49. Guillame, introduction to *Life of Muhammad*, xxvi–xxvii n. 2.

50. Ibid.

51. Ibid. See also Abu-Lughod, *Veiled Sentiments*.

52. Clark and Cahir, "The Comfort of Strangers," 8. This was, of course, prior to the exploitation and inhospitality shown by the goldminers and missionaries that upset the balance. The authors also cite there was the possibility of other motivations for aboriginal hospitality (i.e., "access to the possessions of white people, hastening the departure of potentially dangerous sojourners, and ensuring that travelers avoided sites of spiritual significance"), but still maintain that the Aboriginal people "were generally highly regarded for their hospitality" (ibid.).

53. This proverb is unverifiable as to its origin, but is cited in several locations as a colloquial proverb in reference to the Mongol peoples inhabiting the Gobi desert.

CHRISTIANITY

Unlike Judaism and Islam as will be discussed later, the practice of hospitality has had a renaissance in recent Christian theological scholarship. Therefore, what is covered in the next section is much more detailed since there has been more specific scholarship made available with regards to the Christian tradition and its theology and practice of hospitality.

This section on Christianity is divided into six different sub-sections. The first will consider the impact of the early experiences of persecution upon the prioritization of hospitality as a religious value while the second will look at the role of Jesus as a model of hospitable practice. The third section will explore hospitality as it was expressed in Christian antiquity, moving into the fourth section which will address the particular theological concept of "welcome others, welcome Christ" as practiced by the monastic communities. Finally, the fifth section will analyze the discussions related to hospitality in contemporary Christian thought making way for the sixth section that will highlight the challenges to the theology and practice of hospitality present in contemporary Christianity.

Early Christian Persecution

Development of the Christian tradition in its early days was rooted in the use of house churches, wherein hosts gave the fledging community protection from the persecution of the Roman Empire and safety in order to worship together.[54] The experience of persecution was valuable in the formation of Christianity and its practice of hospitality, both in its theology and ethical practice, as it rooted the identity of adherents as aliens or strangers.[55]

According to theologian Amos Yong, it was "precisely because of [their] . . . precarious situation that they took hospitality seriously."[56] Furthermore,

54. Those who are documented in the New Testament as house church hosts include the mother of John Mark (Acts 12:12), Priscilla and Aquilla (Rom 16:5; 1 Cor 16:19); Nympha (Col 4:15); Philemon (Phlm 2); and Lydia (Acts 16:15, 40). See Osiek and Balch, *Families in the New Testament World*, 97. See also Eusebius, *The History of the Church*.

55. Yong, *Hospitality and the Other*, 115. Of course, there was already a religious understanding among those who came from a Jewish background regarding an identity that was rooted in the experience of being a stranger, foreigner, or outsider and such an understanding would undoubtedly be used in the development of similar Christian ideas.

56. Ibid. Yong refers to 1 Pet 4:9; 1 Tim 5:10. He also notes it was important in this context of house churches for "guests . . . to conduct themselves in an honorable and blameless manner midst their hosts (e.g., 1 Pet 2:12)." Perhaps it was precisely because of this precarious situation that they took hospitality seriously.

the experience of persecution and self-identification with the powerless in society caused Christian hospitality not only to be "directed . . . to fellow believers but also to strangers" as commanded by the apostle Paul in Rom 12:13, which lies within the context of "blessing one's persecutors and doing good to one's enemies (12:14–21)."[57]

In the periods of persecution for early Christians, many relied upon hospitality for survival. In the practice of hospitality as seen in the Mediterranean and Near East cultures at the time, a guest, either fellow Christian or not, becomes "fictive kin" and while under a host's roof, a quasi-familial bond is created whereby the host ensures protection at risk to his/her own reputation and honor if a guest is harmed.[58] Out of this practice, house churches grew and became stronger communities, mobilizing themselves in order to care for one another as a family unit and extending charity to many who were in need.

Model: Jesus

In Christianity, the preeminent role model who shifted the paradigm relating to hospitality is the person of Jesus of Nazareth.[59] Despite the debates regarding Jesus' nature, relationship to God, and his intercessory abilities both in Christian theology and in inter-religious conversations, Jesus' words and actions as depicted in the New Testament portray a person who welcomed the other and counted the other as one who mattered. In the life and work of Jesus as understood by adherents of Christianity, "the other has absolute precedence"[60] since the other's opinions, care and well-being was thought to have direct impact upon one's own righteousness.[61]

The paradigm of hospitality seen in the person of Jesus is radical and pervasive. His presence and work in the world as described in the New

57. Yong, *Hospitality and the Other*, 115.

58. Osiek and Balch, *Families in the New Testament World*, 39.

59. It is worth noting that Jesus is a model in Islam as well. In Arabic, Jesus is called *'Isa*. Additionally, the Gospels wherein Jesus' life is given the most attention in Christianity is referred to as the *Injil* in Islam and is considered one of the four holy books, in addition to *Zabur* (the Psalms), *Tawrat* (Torah) along with the most holy and uncorrupted, the Qur'an. Many Muslims regard the *Injil*/Gospels as corrupted, particularly in reference to statements about Jesus being the Son of God or the account of his crucifixion, death and resurrection, which are incongruous with how Muslims perceive Jesus and his purpose. The issue of corruption does affect the implications of authority in many Muslims' eyes, but nevertheless, the holiness of the *Injil* is not really disputed.

60. Boff, *Virtues*, 81.

61. Matt 5:23–24; Qur'an 2:177, 3:2–4.

Testament, according to Yong, "represents and embodies the hospitality of God . . . [as he was] the exemplary recipient of hospitality" by being continually "dependent upon the welcome of others" and relying upon "the goodwill of many,"[62] particularly as documented in the Gospel of Luke but also found throughout the Jesus narratives.[63]

The Gospel of Luke, however, has a special focus upon the practice of hospitality.[64] From the earliest chapters of the gospel accounting the lack of hospitality given to Mary and Joseph in Bethlehem to the final chapters detailing the activity of the community on the road to Emmaus and in the upper room before Jesus' ascension, the Gospel of Luke's emphasis upon hospitality is profound. Particularly found in the parable of the Good Samaritan in 10:30–37, Jesus' call to protective hospitality illustrates the sacrifice, risks, and unexpected nature of caring for the threatened other.[65]

Additionally, the fluid movement between guest and host is seen in the stories of Jesus recorded in the New Testament through his exemplification of "the redemptive hospitality of God," who is welcomed as a guest into a variety of homes but who ushers his hosts into the redemptive "banquet of God for all those who are willing to receive it . . . [as t]hose who welcome Jesus into their homes, in turn, become guests of . . . God."[66]

Of the Gospels, the Gospel of Luke mentions and emphasizes the aspect of hospitality in the life and ministry of Jesus most often. Throughout the Gospel of Luke, Jesus is continually a guest in someone's home, sitting

62. Yong, *Hospitality and the Other*, 101. That dependency Yong sees in his conception and inhabitation of Mary's womb, his birth in a manger, and his burial in a tomb owned by Joseph of Arimathea as basic, yet perhaps forgotten, elements of Jesus' receipt of hospitality. Yong then connects this state of being for Jesus to his statement "the Son of Man has nowhere to lay his head" found in Luke 9:58.

63. Yong points out the hospitality thread pervasive in the Lukan narratives, giving examples of where Jesus partakes of hospitality (either as guest or host), such as being a guest of Simon Peter (Luke 4:38–39), Levi (Luke 5:29), Martha (Luke 10:38), Zacchaeus (Luke 19:5), and various Pharisees and other unnamed individuals (Luke 5:17; 7:36; 10:5–7; 11:37; 14:1; 22:10–14). Nevertheless, Yong also notes the Lukan hospitality narratives "can be supplemented by details in other Gospels—e.g., Mark 3:20; 7:17, 24; 9:28; 10:10; 14:3; and Matt 9:10; 17:25; 26:6, 18" (*Hospitality and the Other*, 101). Amy Oden also notes Jesus as host and the hospitality intrinsic in the stories where Jesus feeds thousands (Matt 14:13; 15:29; Mark 6:30; 8:1; Luke 9:10; John 6:1). See Oden, *And You Welcomed Me*, 13–15.

64. See Byrne, *The Hospitality of God*.

65. This text is particularly applicable to the practice of protective hospitality in that it highlights the assumed norm of risk one should take on behalf of the other in contrast to the high risk the Good Samaritan took in stopping in his travels, subjecting himself to a possible ambush and robbery by being lured in through fake injury, in order to care for an unknown stranger.

66. Yong, *Hospitality and the Other*, 102.

around a table eating a meal with followers, Pharisees and a range of others. Yet, throughout the book, it is also intriguing to note, as Yong asserts, that "the most eager recipients of the divine hospitality [of Jesus] were not the religious leaders but the poor and the oppressed."[67] Their affinity for his hospitality could be contributed to the fact that in their presence

> Jesus frequently breaks the rules of hospitality, upsets the social conventions of meal fellowship (e.g., Jesus does not wash before dinner), and even goes so far as to rebuke his hosts. Luke thus shows that it is Jesus, not the religious leaders, who is the broker of God's authority, and it is on this basis that Jesus establishes . . . the inclusive hospitality of the kingdom [of God].[68]

While Jesus relied upon the hospitality of others, there is also an element whereby he is portrayed in the Gospels as a stranger, even among his own family. Having left his home,[69] he took up the vocation of itinerant preacher that, in turn, shamed some among his family who attempted to dissuade him from his endeavors or rejected him outright.[70] Therefore, as a result of Jesus' model, rejection and strangeness even among those who would be most familiar is intrinsic in the Christian understanding of life and functionality in the world, making the role of hospitality all the more necessary.

Hospitality in Christian Antiquity

The foundation of hospitality in the Christian tradition shares a common heritage with Judaism and some of the texts explored above.[71] For non-Jews, hospitality as practiced by Greco-Roman society would have been the accepted cultural norm. Therefore, the practice of hospitality already existed and was developed within the religious and cultural consciousness of the new adherents of Christianity.

67. Ibid.

68. Ibid.

69. One would be correct to read in allusion to Abraham who was also commanded by God to leave his home and "go to the land which [God] would show him" (Gen 12:1). Such a call to leave homeland and be a sojourner and stranger is a running theme in both the Hebrew Bible and New Testament.

70. Boff, *Virtues*, 68. Cf. Matt 10:35–38, 19:28–30; Mark 3:20–25; Luke 2:47–49, 14:25–27; John 1:11.

71. The Christian tradition on the whole, however, does not find authoritative the rabbinic tradition upon which much of the systematization of the practice of hospitality in Judaism is based. Instead, its focus would be more on scripture and the established traditions of various parts of the Church, such as the Benedictine Rule or hospitality as seen in Trinitarian theology as expressed most fully by the Eastern Orthodox.

However, Christian practice of hospitality takes on its own characteristics in the New Testament. The previous section noted the role of Jesus of Nazareth as modeling the importance and practice of hospitality. However, other factors outside of Jesus' example point to its evolution in thought and practice.

One factor that makes Christianity unique among the Abrahamic traditions is its focus upon love.[72] As such, the two commandments to love God and to love one's neighbor reiterated from Jewish tradition[73] in Matt 22:34–40 and echoed in Luke 10:26–28 are consolidated into one commandment by Jesus and is the one law upon which Christian life should rest. Therefore, to love one's neighbor is to love God; to love God is to love one's neighbor. In turn, the practice of hospitality encompasses both; to welcome the stranger is to show love for God and for one's neighbor.

This duality was practically expressed in the use of space by the early church, where the home became "'a new sort of sacred space, where the reign of God produces the community of grace, the house of God, *Beth-El*, where God dwells.'"[74] Love for God and love for neighbor were demonstrated through the shared meals and worship that took place in host homes where, in the book of Acts, "they enact and realize the meal fellowship of God that marks the reconciliation of the Jew, Samaritan, and Gentile, male and female, young and old, slave and free in the present life of the church."[75] Each took responsibility for the other, sharing resources, and the new

72. This is not to say that Judaism and Islam do not emphasize love, but it is to say that the overarching story in Christianity (compared to Judaism and Islam) is based upon the repeated allusions to God's love and the commandment for followers to reflect that same love: that God "so loved the world" (John 3:16), God is love (1 John 4:16); love your enemies (Matt 5:43–45; Luke 6:26–26; Rom 12:9–21), the greatest thing is love (1 Cor 13: 1–13), love fulfills the law (Rom 13:8; Gal 5:14, Jas 2:8). See also Augustine, *De Trinitate* 8.10; Boff, *Virtues*, 80–81. However, there is debate within Christianity about just how love is expressed, seen particularly in debates about God's judgment and in the furor over the recent publication of Rob Bell's *Love Wins: A Book about Heaven and Hell and the Fate of Every Person Who Ever Lived*, where more universalist teachings about love rather than judgment and punishment were espoused. Nevertheless, there are strands in both Judaism and Islam that do emphasize love, particularly in the mystic traditions. In Islam, Sufism's strong emphasis upon love is analyzed in Mahmutcehajić's book, *On Love*. For Judaism, see Heschel's work, *God in Search of Man*. See also Strhan, "And Who Is My Neighbour?," 145–66.

73. Interestingly, the law to love one's neighbor is in the levitical/priestly code (Lev 19:18, 34). However, the commandment to love God, usually worded as "Love your God with all your heart and soul" (and in Deut 6:5, "strength" is added) is found primarily in the deuteronomic texts, as seen in Deut 6:5, 10:12, 11:13, 13:3, 30:6; and Josh 22:5.

74. Berryhill, "From Dreaded Guest to Welcoming Host," 85.

75. Yong, *Hospitality and the Other*, 105. Cf. Acts 2:17–18, 44, 46; 4:32–37; and 5:42. This eradication of social divisions is also referred to by the apostle Paul in Gal 3:26–29.

Christian community distributed food daily in order to maintain equality.[76] As a result, the emphasis upon love and mutual responsibility built up an ethical framework of hospitality and mutual responsibility in the Christian tradition that provided the ideal example to which many communities over the coming centuries would aspire.[77]

Moreover, the most obvious practice of hospitality in Christianity is found in the sharing of Eucharist, whereby followers are invited to God's table, to partake of God's generous abundance and welcome through the work of Christ, and to share table fellowship with other members of the community.[78] According to theologian Michelle Hershberger, the apostle Paul in his first letter to the church in Corinth emphasizes hospitality and community as such "important elements" of the Eucharist and that "if hospitality was not practiced and community not nurtured, their gathering with the bread and wine [would not be considered] the Lord's Supper at all."[79] Hershberger asserts three things happen in the practice of the Eucharist: "socioeconomic barriers [come] tumbling down, discernment about the true nature of the believers [takes] place, and Christ [comes] as a guest bringing either grace or judgment."[80]

Therefore, at its best, hospitality became "a feature of Christian life, [wherein it] is not so much a singular act of welcome as it is a way, an orientation that attends to otherness, listening and learning, valuing and honoring."[81] Similarly, Christian historian Amy Oden argues hospitality plays an important role in moral development in the Christian tradition by stating:

76. Acts 6:1. Cf. Yong, *Hospitality and the Other*, 105.

77. The role of women—in particular Lydia—in hospitality as expressed in the early Christian church era is beyond the scope of this work but is important and worthwhile nonetheless. Sutherland briefly explores it in his book, *I Was a Stranger*, 41–56.

78. The hospitable aspect of the Eucharist often gets pushed aside as theological debates about who can administer as well as receive communion are had in the Christian community. Some more conservative elements of Christianity restrict Eucharist to only professed and devout Christians, others to only members of that specific denomination, and other still to only members of that specific local church community. Obvously, there is little hospitality in a closed communion as it invites and accepts only those who are similar as an identity-affirming activity, rather than being extended to the person or community who is other.

79. Hershberger, *A Christian View of Hospitality*, 223, referring to 1 Cor 11:17–22.

80. Hershberger, *A Christian View of Hospitality*, 223.

81. Oden, *And You Welcomed Me*, 14. This development can be seen, among others, in the development of hospitals, hospitable support of pilgrimages, and growth of intra-communal as well as inter-religious scholarship and debate as noted in chapter 2.

> Hospitality is characterized by a particular moral stance in the world that can best be described as readiness. Early Christian voices tell us again and again that whether we are guest or host we must be ready, ready to welcome, ready to enter another's world, ready to be vulnerable. This readiness is expectant. It may be akin to moral nerve . . . Such readiness takes courage, gratitude, and radical openness. This moral orientation to life relinquishes to God both the practice of hospitality and its consequences.[82]

There is some debate, however, about whom exactly the early Christian was to be ready to welcome. On the whole, Arterbury notes Christians most often offered hospitality "only to Christian travelers"[83] despite exhortations from the apostle Paul and the author of Hebrews[84] to do otherwise.[85] Yong differs from this assertion, noting that "in the New Testament, the love of neighbor is never confined only to believers" and he credits Christianity with the influence that "extended the ancient Roman conception of hospitality so as to include the hospitable treatment of strangers."[86] Yong continues this argument by noting the "ancient Hellenist xenophobia was gradually overcome by the indiscriminate application of the Golden Rule [to love God and neighbor] and the conviction regarding the common [humanity] of all."[87]

Welcome Others, Welcome Christ

As hospitality developed over the earlier centuries of Christianity, the theme of Christ coming as a guest became a primary motivator for hospitality in the Christian tradition. Jesus' assertion in Matt 25:35–36 claims that on the day of judgment, Christians will be found wanting if they did not welcome the stranger (along with feeding the hungry, clothing the naked, visiting those in prison) as if that stranger were Christ.[88] Out of this challenge made by Jesus, there arose expressions of Christianity that saw hospitality as a

82. Ibid., 15.

83. Matt 25.31–46; 1 Pet 4.9; 2 John 10–11; 3 John 5–8.

84. Rom 12:13b; Heb 13:2.

85. Arterbury, *Entertaining Angels*, 132.

86. Yong, *Hospitality and the Other*, 107.

87. Ibid., 107 n. 32. Yong recommends Bolchazy, *Hospitality in Early Rome*, especially ch. 3 for the argument. It is acknowledged, however, that this is a very idealized depiction of Christian origins and ethical practice.

88. This is an example of theoxenic hospitality.

core ethic, namely found in monastic communities.[89] Again, love of God was found in the love (expressed in welcome and care) of the neighbor or stranger.

This theoxenic motivation for hospitality emerged as a result of Jesus' commandment being taken to heart. Within formational theological bodies and their corresponding edicts and texts, monastic communities took root and spread as the reach of Christianity extended. The first instance where this motivation for hospitality became more systemic appeared in the publication of the Rule of St. Benedict (ca. 529 CE) which reads:

> Let all guests that come be received like Christ Himself, for He will say 'I was a stranger and ye took Me in.' And let fitting honour be shown to all, especially such as are of the household of the faith and to wayfarers. When, therefore, a guest is announced, let him be met (*occurratur ei*) by the superior or the brethren, with all due charity. Let them first pray together, and thus associate with one another in peace . . . In the greeting let all humility be shown to the guests, whether coming or going; with the head bowed down or the whole body prostrate on the ground, let Christ be adored in them as He is also received. When the guests have been received, let them be accompanied to prayer, and after that let the Superior, or whom he shall bid, sit down with them. Let the divine law be read to the guest that he may be edified, after which let every kindness be shown him. Let the fast be broken by the Superior in deference to the guest . . . Let the abbot pour water on the hands of the guests, and himself as well as the whole community wash their feet . . . Let the greatest care be taken, especially in the reception of the poor and travelers, because Christ is received more specially in them; whereas regard for the wealthy itself procureth them respect.[90]

This motivation for the practice of hospitality became further codified with a decree from the twenty-fifth Council of Trent (1563) that declares:

89. While not monastic per se, the role of the Beguines and their beguinages established primarily in northwestern Europe from the thirteenth century, which were communities of lay women who did not take formal vows or separate themselves from society, also enacted the ethics of hospitality, taking in strangers, caring for the sick and hungry, and providing an example of faithful life for laypersons, particularly during the Middle Ages. While their contribution is less known, one would be remiss to not give them mention. For more information on the Beguines, see Bowie and Davies, *Beguine Spirituality*; Murk-Jansen, *Brides in the Desert*; Simons, *Cities of Ladies*; and Richard Woodward, "A Lost World Made by Women."

90. *The Holy Rule of St. Benedict*, chap. 53.

> all who hold any ecclesiastical benefices, whether secular or regular, to accustom themselves, as far as their revenues will allow, to exercise with alacrity and kindness the office of hospitality, so frequently commended by the holy Fathers; being mindful that those who cherish hospitality receive Christ in the person of their guests.[91]

As such, the understanding continues among many even in the contemporary context that to welcome others is to, indeed, welcome Christ into their midst.[92]

Hospitality in Contemporary Western Christian Thought

An influential exploration on the importance of hospitality in contemporary Christian theology and spiritual practice was Henri Nouwen's 1975 book, *Reaching Out: The Three Movements of the Spiritual Life*. Based on the three dimensions of life—one's relationships to oneself, others, and God—Nouwen links the discipline of hospitality with one's relationship to others, noting there should be conscious movement "from hostility to hospitality."[93] He assumes the development of hospitality as a spiritual practice is based on the other two corresponding movements of hospitality toward oneself and to God. Therefore, hospitality toward others is not a practice in isolation, but is an outward reflection of the "ever-changing relationship" of welcome and openness one has to oneself and to God.[94] Believing it is "one of the richest biblical terms that can deepen and broaden our insight into our relationships to our fellow human beings,"[95] Nouwen calls for the practice of hospitality to be explored and renewed in our contemporary context. Nouwen goes on to define the concept of hospitality as follows:

> Hospitality, therefore, means primarily the creation of a free space where the stranger can enter and become a friend instead

91. From the twenty-fifth session (Dec. 4, 1563), chapter 8, in *The Canons and Decrees of the Sacred and Ecumenical Council of Trent*, 232–89.

92. Yet, a critique in this context may be that although Jesus, as well as Benedict and other influential leaders in the Christian tradition encouraged (or commanded) the practice of hospitality does not mean that their followers practice it. Throughout this book, a tension between the ideals set forth for hospitable practice and the reality that it is often neglected despite the religious imperatives has been highlighted. If it were carried out systematically, there would be no need for hospitality research that seeks to recover its practice.

93. Nouwen, *Reaching Out*, 45.

94. Ibid., 46.

95. Ibid., 47.

> of an enemy. Hospitality is not to change people, but to offer them space where change can take place. It is not to bring men and women over to our side, but to offer freedom not disturbed by dividing lines. It is not to lead our neighbor into a corner where there are no alternatives left, but to open a wide spectrum of options for choice and commitment. It is not an educated intimidation with good books, good stories and good works, but the liberation of fearful hearts so that words can find roots and bear ample fruit.[96]

Theologian Elizabeth Newman argues hospitality is not about "generic friendliness or private service" because to describe it as such is "to domesticate it."[97] Furthermore, domestication "distorts how extraordinary and strange . . . hospitality really is . . . [as it] names our participation in the life of God, a participation that might well be as terrifying as it is consoling."[98] In this vein, she refers to the story of the burning bush in Exodus 3 wherein Moses becomes a stranger removing his shoes and crossing the threshold onto holy ground, and notes "in this instance, hospitality involves not our usual pleasantries but rather command, terror, and, not least of all, a puzzling call from God, a political calling through which God works to create and sustain the nation of Israel."[99]

Newman's contribution to the discussion of hospitality is helpful in that she refers to some "dominant cultural assumptions" that distort the practice of hospitality:

> 1) that Christianity (and religion more broadly) is primarily about personal beliefs, 2) that ethics is primarily about private choices and values, 3) that politics is primarily the work of government and the nation-state, 4) that economics is only about money and ultimately defined by the market, and 5) that the church is basically a collection of like-minded individuals.[100]

As has been noted previously, the practice of hospitality stands contrary to these assumptions. The practice of hospitality implies both public

96. Ibid., 51.

97. Newman, *Untamed Hospitality*, 13.

98. Ibid. Newman qualifies many of her statements regarding hospitality as being "Christian hospitality." However, for the purposes of an Abrahamic tradition of hospitality, many of the explorations she designates as "Christian" are not antithetical to a Jewish or Muslim understanding of hospitality.

99. Ibid.

100. Ibid., 14.

and private, political and subversive, communal and individual, diversity and commonality, life and risk.

Newman also looks at how hospitality takes shape in the Christian tradition. First, she makes connections between hospitality and Christian worship, stating that "worship is the primary ritualized place where we learn to be guests and hosts in the kingdom of God."[101] Second, Newman discusses what it means to call hospitality a "practice," pointing to concepts related to tradition, culture, communal action, internal good[102], and truth-telling.[103] Third, referring to the work of philosopher William H. Poteat, Newman explores the distinctions between "theory and practice," while linking it with the literary work of author Flannery O'Connor and her narratives that set in the American South that emphasize the differentiation between thought and action.[104] Particularly in the case of O'Connor's short stories, Newman points out that when hospitality exists only in theory, as shown in superficial manners and niceness, it "collapse[s] in the face of truly monstrous evil" and "fail[s] to produce true goodness."[105] On the contrary, hospitality practiced in conjunction with theory, according to Newman, may not necessarily thwart evil but bears witness to courage and profound good.[106]

Another contemporary theologian, Hans Boersma, also describes hospitality as a virtue. He goes further to detail hospitality as "sharing something of our lives with others" since both sides are to be edified in the experience.[107] Yet, for Boersma, hospitality, in a theological sense, is primarily "God's work of reconciliation in Jesus Christ" exhibited in God's "hospitality toward us in giving [God's self] in Christ."[108] Boersma refers to the traditional Christian understanding of Jesus' death and resurrection as a salvific act, whereby Christians are able to enter into God's presence and "see the face of the divine host . . . the face of God" because of the sacrifice

101. Ibid., 17. While Newman takes a very Trinitarian approach, wherein worship imitates the hospitality of God to God's self as seen in (using classic language) the divine expressions of Father, Son and Holy Spirit, I would assert that this reality of ritual "where we learn to be guests and hosts" in God's world is not just a Christian understanding but would be understood as such, albeit in a different manner, by Jews and Muslims as well.

102. Newman refers to the work of the ethicist Alasdair MacIntyre and his book, *After Virtue*, 188, in this discussion of internal versus external good.

103. Newman, *Untamed Hospitality*, 19–24.

104. Ibid., 21–24.

105. Ibid., 25.

106. Ibid. This aspect of bearing witness to courage and profound good will be of benefit as protective hospitality is considered in the next two chapters.

107. Boersma, *Violence, Hospitality and the Cross*, 15.

108. Ibid., 15–16.

that was made on their behalf.[109] This issue of sacrifice and related violence in relation to hospitality will be explored later.

Contemporary Christianity and Challenges to Hospitality

Until the third century of the Common Era, hospitality had been primarily private, practiced by individuals, families, and early church communities reflected in the New Testament references.[110] However, as mentioned previously, with the adoption of hospitality in the monastic communities and codified by religious leadership as was done in the Council of Trent, the paradigm of private hospitality, according to Arterbury, shifted toward public or corporate hospitality. As a result, the practice was "placed under the authority of the bishop, and hospitality primarily became a charitable service for travelers collectively performed by entire congregations and supported with the corporate funds that were available to these congregations."[111]

While the formalization of hospitality can be seen as helpful in setting up systemic practice in the wider Christian community, it did have its drawbacks. Arterbury and Oden note that John Chrysostom exhorted his congregation not to neglect acts of private hospitality in lieu of corporate hospitality, believing both expressions are necessary.[112] Nevertheless, this movement shows a shift in the practice of hospitality from personal, private, individual expressions of hospitality to a more industrialized concept of hospitality, perhaps leading to the practice being lost on a personal level over the centuries. Through this shift, hospitality began to be considered as the responsibility of the local congregation, monastery or, in current day, a non-profit charity instead of individuals or private households.

Both private and public practice of hospitality is necessary; but with current systems in place, if a stranger were to appear at one's doorstep and hospitality were to be extended, it would more than likely be civil or charitable authorities who would be called upon to address the stranger's needs rather than an individual or household. Therefore, with the movement

109. Ibid. Because of this understanding, the majority of Boersma's work is centered on the traditions of atonement theories and hospitality's relationship to violence, which will be explored in more detail later.

110. Arterbury, *Entertaining Angels*, 128.

111. Ibid. See also Oden, *And You Welcomed Me*, 215–79, for a collection of sources that point to the institutionalization of hospitality through Christian services under the authority of the state.

112. Arterbury, *Entertaining Angels*, 129; Oden, *And You Welcomed Me*, 248.

toward more public and industrial concepts of hospitality, the meaning and responsibility of private hospitality has been diminished or lost.

JUDAISM

Jewish religious and cultural tradition takes hospitality quite seriously understanding hospitality is not "simply a matter of good manners," but is instead a "moral institution."[113] Furthermore, the sense of obligation to practice hospitality is strong in Judaism, both historically and in the contemporary context, as hospitality is one of the *mitzvoth*, or acts that are sacred obligations as expression of religious devotion, and those who practice hospitality embody *chesed*, a quality in Hebrew that embodies mercy, compassion, and a willingness to go above and beyond the call of obligation. The practice of hospitality is itself called *hachnasat orchim* in Hebrew, meaning literally "the bringing in of guests."[114]

In order to explore the role of hospitality in Judaism, however, certain themes need to be addressed. Therefore, this section will be divided into four sub-sections that emphasize the following factors: the role of exile, slavery and exodus in Jewish thought and practice related to hospitality; the realities of hospitality as practiced in Jewish antiquity; the role of honor as it applies to hospitality in Judaism; and the challenges to hospitality present in contemporary Judaism that make its practice more difficult.

Jewish Exile, Slavery and Exodus

When one considers the contribution of persecution and exile to religious formation, the most obvious tradition where such a contribution is present is in Judaism. The experiences of exile, slavery, and persecution are foundational to Jewish identity and theological formation.[115]

The Jewish narrative tradition begins with exile as the first humans—Adam and Eve—experienced exile from the Garden of Eden because of sin.[116] Later, due to a famine in the land, the descendents of Abraham, Isaac, and Jacob migrated to Egypt in search of food and were, over the course of time,

113. Diamant, *Living a Jewish Life*, 25.

114. Ibid.

115. For more information on the formational experience of exile in Judaism, see Scott, *Exile*; Wettstein, *Diasporas and Exiles*; and Keen, *Exile and Restoration in Jewish Thought*.

116. Gen 3:22–24.

bonded into slavery by the Egyptians.[117] In this experience—as well as the experience of being liberated from slavery and taken out of Egypt[118]—the levitical and deuteronomic ideas of hospitality to the stranger take form. Repeatedly throughout the Torah, God admonishes the Israelites to be hospitable to the stranger for they also were "once strangers in Egypt."[119]

This experience in Egypt and the subsequent liberation that left the Israelites wandering in the desert for forty years[120] embedded in their self-understanding a deep sense of being outsiders, strangers in a foreign land, inhabiting somewhere that was not their own, but given to them by God in the Torah as a result of a promise made through the covenants made by God to Abraham,[121] Jacob,[122] and Moses.[123]

Therefore, it is no surprise the levitical and deuteronomic legal codes exhibit significant sensitivity to the vulnerability and experience of those who may be strangers and sojourners among the Israelites, providing specific protections and assurances for their fair treatment. Once the nation of Israel inhabited the promised land of Canaan, there were "responsibilities to the aliens and strangers in her midst: Israel is now no longer merely a guest but host to others."[124]

This paradigm changes, however, when the monarchical system of Israel and Judah disintegrates, invading armies conquer the land and its inhabitants are driven into exile. Assyria defeated the northern kingdom of Israel and many tribes of Israel were deported in 740 BCE. Similarly, the Babylonian Empire defeated Assyria and the southern kingdom of Judah around 586 BCE, enacting similar deportations to Babylon.[125] Theologi-

117. Gen 47; Exod 1.

118. Exod 6:7; 12–13.

119. Exod 22:21, 23:9; Lev 19:34; Deut 10:19, 23:7.

120. Exod 16:35.

121. Gen 15–17.

122. Gen 28:12–15.

123. Exod 19–24 is where the covenant is specifically given to Moses. However, another covenant is documented in Deut 29:1–29, 30:1–10, which is considered an expansion of the Mosaic covenant given to the people of Israel. Later, a covenant is made with David (the Davidic covenant) in 2 Sam 7 wherein the establishment and reign of the kingdom and dynasty of David are promised, which has substantial importance in relation to the experience of the Jews in the context of the Assyrian and Babylonian exiles as well as oppression at the hand of the Roman Empire.

124. Yong, *Hospitality and the Other*, 110.

125. It is generally thought there was no return from the Assyrian exile. The Jews exiled by the Babylonians, however, were released by Cyrus the Great in 538 BCE after the defeat of Babylon by the Persian Empire. For more information on this period of history, see Shanks, *Ancient Israel;* and Albertz, *Israel in Exile.*

cally, this experience of exile revised Jewish identity and belief, as noted in the prophetic exilic and post-exilic literature in the Tanakh and in later thought.[126]

Hospitality in Jewish Antiquity

When Judaism is discussed as a tradition, particularly in a context such as this, it is important to note the locus of authority has shifted over the course of the centuries in relation to the practice of hospitality. As a Christian, this author is more familiar with the Hebrew scriptures, the *Tanakh*, but it is important to note that with the emergence of Second Temple Judaism and the development of an expansive corpus of rabbinic literature over the last two millennia, the center of authority has shifted.[127] Judaism as practiced today is referred to as "*rabbinic* Judaism—the Judaism of the rabbis."[128] Nevertheless, as it relates to building a culture and tradition of hospitality in Judaism, the Hebrew Scriptures, the Septuagint, various apocryphal writings, and earlier rabbinic literature established a foundation that has continued in rabbinic Judaism.[129]

Hospitality in Judaism is regarded as the "kind reception of a stranger or traveler."[130] A host was expected, first and foremost, to supply "both provisions and protection."[131] As has been noted previously, Abraham served

126. There is a great deal of overlap, however, related to the composition of deuteronomic law and histories and prophetic literature during this period of exile. During the Babylonian exile, the deuteronomistic literature is thought to have been redacted and codified, which, therefore, could have caused the theme of being hospitable to the stranger more pronounced as the Jews were, once again, in a foreign land. Unfortunately, there is no foolproof way to date and verify the evolution of thought regarding hospitality to the stranger without original texts. See Knoppers and McConville, *Reconsidering Israel and Judah,* for more information on textual issues in this period.

127. Gopin, "Judaism and Peacebuilding," 111.

128. Firestone, "Judaism as a Force for Reconciliation," 77.

129. This period (2nd century CE) marks the point where Judaism began to shift its self-identification from Hellenistic Judaism to rabbinic Judaism, and Christianity began to systematically define itself independent from Judaism, making them "other" to each other. Additionally, one might assert that hospitality's decline in practice in Judaism reflects hospitality's decline in practice throughout Western society and in Christianity as well. Furthermore, I would also suggest Judaism's experience over the centuries with anti-Semitism on small and large scales has influenced Judaism's practice of hospitality today in relation to how the faithful welcome the potentially threatening stranger.

130 Arterbury, *Entertaining Angels*, 57.

131. Ibid. Arterbury refers to Gen 19:1–23 and Judg 19:14–28, which will be dealt with in more detail in chapter 4.

in Judaism as the ideal role model for this practice of hospitality[132] based primarily upon the Genesis 18:1–33 passage where he and Sarah welcome three strangers, who in turn, give them news of the imminent birth of a son and heir according to Jewish tradition.

In his research on hospitality as expressed in antiquity, Arterbury details a few unique characteristics related to the Jewish practices of hospitality at that time. First, he asserts that when one wanted to find hospitality, one would often look to a "distant relative or kinsman . . . or fellow Israelite,"[133] and if needing to partake of the hospitality of strangers, it would be typical to "find a host at a well or source of water while in a rural area,[134] or at the city gate or the city-square in an urban area."[135]

Second, in order to ensure the reciprocity of hospitality through kinsmen, it was not uncommon for hosts to give their sister or daughter as a bride to a male guest.[136] Such an act formed a permanent bond between the guest and host that served to build a network of hospitality in the ancient community and marked a "code of reciprocity" whereby the men of households were obliged to treat guests well in order that when the householder himself traveled and needed hospitality, he would in turn be treated well. This code, however, did not serve only an interpersonal purpose; it was also "a village's most important form of foreign policy."[137]

Yet it is noted that although the giving of daughters or sisters as brides may be a valuable gift between a host and guest, such a gift also signals the expendability of women in this ancient world and its codes of hospitality.

132. Ibid., 58.

133. Gen 24:15–27; Judg 19:12; Tob 5:6; 6:11; 9:5; Philo, *On the Life of Abraham*, 116; Josephus, *Jewish Antiquities* 5.144. Cf. Arterbury, *Entertaining Angels*, 91.

134. Gen 24:17; Exod 2:15; 1 Sam 9:11–13.

135. Gen 19:1; 24:1–58; 29:1–14; Judg 19:14–15; 1 Kgs 17:10. Cf. Arterbury, *Entertaining Angels*, 91.

136. Gen 24:50–51; Exod 2:21; Tob 7:11; John Chrysostom, *Joseph and Aseneth* 4:8, 21:1–3. Cf. Arterbury, *Entertaining Angels*, 92. Arterbury explains the giving of gifts is quite common with Greco-Roman hospitality traditions, but they did not usually give this type of gift. Conversely, giving gifts in the Hebrew/Israelite/Jewish tradition was not common, but when it did happen, the giving of women as wives was notable.

137. Matthews and Benjamin, *Social World of Ancient Israel*, 82–83. This text also notes villages "used hospitality to acknowledge their status on the land as guests of their divine patron. As hosts they did for others what their divine patron was doing for them . . . [as t]he Hebrews understood themselves as strangers . . ." Additionally, when it comes to foreign policy and the exchange of daughters, the narrative of Dinah and Shechem in Gen 34 illustrates a variety of factors at play related to power, hospitality, role of women, honor and fear of the other.

One can hypothesize such a gift was given in order to create filial bonds, neutralize threats, or to satiate a guest's physical and sexual needs.[138]

An exception to this is the story of Rahab in Joshua 2–6 where 1) a woman is the primary provider of hospitality, namely in the form of protection;[139] 2) she comes to no harm despite being labeled a "harlot";[140] and 3) she remains with her family, under the reciprocal protection of the Israelites after the destruction of Jericho.[141] Jewish tradition goes further to state that after the events in Jericho, Rahab converted to Judaism, was labeled *hasidot* ("the pious"), married Joshua, the leader of the military campaign against Jericho, and contributed to Jewish culture by becoming a forebearer of eight priest-prophets, including Jeremiah, and the prophetess Huldah.[142]

Interestingly, as seen in the hospitality of Rahab, the Hebrew scriptures and some related Apocryphal writings often praised subversion in the practice of hospitality. The subversive hospitality narratives almost exclusively highlight the actions of women, as seen in the examples of Sarah laughing at her guests' proclamation in Genesis 18:10–12; the murder of Sisera while a guest in Jael's tent in Judges 4:17–22; Abigail overriding her husband Nabal's lack of hospitality in 1 Samuel 25; and the murder of Holofernes in his own tent by his guest Judith to save her people in Judith 13:1–10.[143] Intrinsic to these texts are the assumed codes of hospitality turned on their heads in

138. Particularly problematic, however, are the two cases recorded in Gen 19 and Judg 19 in which women are given over to people who threaten male guests to ensure protection for the host and his male guest(s). As there is not a proliferation of stories such as these, we cannot speculate as to whether or not this was common practice. Yet, since the stories do, indeed, exist, one does have the permission to consider the role of women in this particular type of hospitality, namely in providing protection. These texts will be considered more closely in chapter 5.

139. Josh 2:3–21.

140. Josh 2:1; 6:25.

141. Josh 6:26. Interestingly, the fate of Rahab is contested between the Jewish and Christian traditions. According to Christian interpretation, Rahab's hospitality is lauded and held up as an exemplary model (Heb 11:31; Jas 2:25; *1 Clem.* 12:1–3), but unlike other similar scenarios explored here she is neither taken as a bride nor as spoils of war after the events at Jericho. If she did get married later, the text makes no mention of it being due to an exchange or reward as a result of her act of hospitality.

142. *b. Meg.* 14b and *Midr. Tadshe*, in Epstein, "Mi-kadmoniyyot ha-Yehudim," Supplement, xliii. Cf. Hirsch and Seligsohn, "Rahab."

143. The book of Judith was not canonized by the rabbis and is, therefore, not officially included in Jewish sacred texts although the narrative is still referred to and present in literature. The reasons why it was not canonized are fascinating, but unfortunately are beyond the scope here. See LaCocque, *The Feminine Unconventional,* for an exploration.

order to defend and protect the survival of the tribe, family, or the women themselves. These narratives are rife with irony and sexual innuendo involving both consensual and forced relations, implying the authors as well as the readers know hospitality carries with it political machinations, certain dangers, and substantial potential for intrigue.

Honor

The golden rule found in the Torah (Lev 19:18) requires one to love others as one loves oneself. This concept of self-love in classical Judaism enables the devout to direct love toward others.[144] Rabbinic development of this levitical imperative to self-love was taught by Rabbi Akiva (c. 110–135 CE) as "the preeminent principle of Judaism." Yet, Akiva and his contemporary Rabbi Ben Azzai debated that the self-love principle would allow for someone to make the assertion "since I have been abused, let my fellow human being be abused, since I have been cursed let my fellow human being be cursed."[145] In turn, Azzai asserted the highest principle was, instead, the belief "that every human being is created in the image of God, and is therefore invaluable."[146]

Whether it arises from self-love, conviction of the divine image in each person, or a combination of both, honor plays an important role in Judaism. The concept of honor, the Hebrew root *kabed*,[147] is found throughout

144. Gopin, "Judaism and Peacebuilding," 116. Gopin notes, however, that this imperative to love others as one loves oneself is "one of the hardest things for members of a hated minority [such as Jews] to truly feel."

145. Ibid., 125 n. 10, quoting *Genesis Rabbah*, 24.

146. Ibid. Gopin uses this opportunity to shed light on the Jewish psyche in relation to the other and persecution endured, by stating:

> R. Tanhuma adds [to the debate between Azzai and Akiva], ad loc., "If [God] made him" [Gen 5:1]. We have here, in a nutshell, what might be the thought patterns of abused people the world over who, despite a good conscience, feel that, from the point of view of justice, if they have been unloved and abused, why should they treat others any differently? This statement by Ben Azzai is meant to contradict that tendency of feeling within the Jewish people of his time. It means that the only way a Jewish person could devalue another human being would be to consider him or her not really created in the image of God, not really human, which manifestly contradicts the sacred text.

147. David Freedman notes that "[t]he word translated in most English translations as 'honor' comes from the Hebrew root *kabed*, which means 'to be heavy.' This word appears throughout the Hebrew Bible, though it is obscured in most of its occurrences because of translation" (*The Nine Commandments*, 68). Freedman also notes that it is a complex term as it is translated differently according to context, including references to severity (as in "the famine was heavy upon the land" found throughout Genesis), wealth ("Abram was very heavy in cattle, in silver and in gold" in Gen 13:2), sorrow

the Tanakh, not only in the levitical and deuteronomic codes of the Torah but also in priestly and deuteronomic ideology and theology present in the major prophets.[148] Yet, the Talmudic Rabbis articulated the idea of honor further as it related to hospitality and the guest/host relationship as Judaism evolved in the beginning of the rabbinic period. One honored oneself and others by abiding by the rabbinic mandate to "greet everyone with a loving, or literally 'beautiful,' face, '*sever panim yafot*.'"[149] Honoring the other was exhorted as one of the highest *mitzvoth*, whereas shaming another was equated to murder that happens when "language and actions . . . make the face turn white with embarrassment . . . [or] literally the shedding of blood of the face."[150]

As it applies in current contexts, rabbi and conflict analyst Marc Gopin notes this emphasis upon honor and importance of face and draws a connection between acts of honor and the practice of hospitality as it relates to violence and conflict. Gopin understands that "[f]ace is a critical category in conflict analysis . . . [as c]ollective humiliation is one of the main reasons for the self-perpetuating cycles of numerous international and inter-ethnic conflicts."[151] As a Jew, Gopin asserts honor is an "underutilized strategy of conflict prevention and conflict resolution" and as such, "[a]ny Jewish

(Gen 50:10) or even Pharaoh's heart (translated as "hardened" in Exod 7:14). Furthermore, Freedman asserts that a derivative of the root *kabed* is *kabod*, which is most often translated as "glory," and is "used to express God's presence among [God's] people . . . God's 'heaviness' or 'weightiness,' that is, [God's] importance or . . . significance" (ibid., 69). The concept of honor as it applies to rituals of hospitality is also *kabod*, but in these instances it implies "heavy" with regards to respect, high regard, importance, and/or recognition rather than divine glory (see Prov 3:35). Regardless, the antithesis of honor (i.e. dishonor/shame) in the Hebrew context seems to connote something important (one might say "heavy with import") which has been ignored, neglected, cast aside, or made light of with thoughtlessness.

148. See Olyan, "Honor, Shame, and Covenant Relations," 201–18, and compare Hobbs, "Reflections on Honor, Shame, and Covenant Relations," 501–3; Doorly, *Laws of Yahweh*; Stiebert, *Construction of Shame*; and Avrahami, "בוש in the Psalms," 295–313. In short, while honor is found in both levitical and deuteronomic schools of theology and ideology, the motivation for honor is different between the two. Levitical ideology sees honor and its expression in social ethics as it relates to holiness particularly as it relates to cultic ritual, God or God's presence in the world (see Lev 19:2; Exod 14:4, 17). The deuteronomic ideology of honor is more humanity-centric in its social ethics and moral code and is particularly prevalent in the prophecies of Isaiah and Jeremiah.

149. Gopin, "Judaism and Peacebuilding," 116. The phrase *sever panim yafot* is still in common usage, referring to a pleasant demeanor, kind greeting, or manner by which one is greeted. It is commonly attributed to the Mishnah (*Pirkei Avot* 1:15).

150. Gopin, "Judaism and Peacebuilding," 116; and Odenheimer, "Honor or Death," 25.

151. Gopin, "Judaism and Peacebuilding," 116.

methodology of conflict resolution would have to focus on honor and the necessary engagement with the face of the enemy."[152] Moreover, encounter with the other, be they enemy or stranger, is a moral gesture that should be marked by honor and hospitality, risking oneself by entering into the other's domain, providing food and drink, and truly encountering each other in order for transformation to take place. In this way, Gopin emphasizes honor becomes "contagious" and relationships increase in hospitality and cordiality as a result.[153]

The contagion of honor and hospitality in Judaism are made known in both the home and the public sphere, according to Gopin, as the two contexts inform the practice of hospitality in each. Additionally, Gopin states there is a "strong sense of responsibility" to connect the two by "making one's home and family open to some degree as a refuge from the inevitable harshness of the public sphere."[154]

To be welcomed into a home is to receive haven and protection from the dangers of the outside world. According to the Rabbis, one is commanded to show honor to guests by providing an escort as they depart one's home. Commentator Micha Odenheimer writes "[e]scorting a departing guest . . . is an essential part of the commandment of hospitality . . . [and] the Torah holds [the host] responsible [for the guest's safety] if there was no escort."[155] Odenheimer notes Rabbi Yehuda Loew, a 17th century mystic often known as the Maharal of Prague, commanded escort as it is "a tangible sign of honor, and honor provides protection" wherein the "divine image as a sort of aura that surrounds each human being . . . can be either strengthened or diminished" by acts of honor and hospitality.[156]

Contemporary Judaism and Challenges to Hospitality

Related to the practice of hospitality and welcoming the other in the Jewish tradition, certain factors need to be taken into consideration. First, welcoming the other is inherently risky. Therefore, populations of Jews who were

152. Ibid., 117.

153. Ibid.

154. Ibid., 118. This concept of refuge and its connection to hospitality will be explored more fully in chapter 4.

155. Odenheimer, "Honor or Death," 25.

156. Ibid. According to Odenheimer, Rabbi Loew likened the divine image in each person to a cloak given to each other through acts of honor and compared it to "the garments of the high priest [in Exodus 28:35] . . . [and] our protection from death."

subjected to more severe anti-Semitism[157] are more reticent to welcome the potentially threatening other. Instead, these Jewish communities tended to keep to themselves and look out for the interests of their own.[158]

Second, the relationship between religious tradition, national identity, and mainstream culture is such that [a community that welcomes in many cases is the one that perceives itself as safe and perhaps holding power within a society. If a community feels under threat, it can be assumed it will be less likely to express itself in a hospitable manner.[159] As Jews have "lived mostly unempowered and quietist for nearly two thousand years,"[160] perhaps the practice of hospitality gave way to making room for ensuring survival.

These two factors can be seen at play in Gopin's claim that "the prevailing focus of attention [in Judaism] has been increasingly on those rituals and laws[161] . . . that would buttress cultural and physical survival, which

157. On the whole, it is generally accepted that Ashkenazi (Central and Eastern European) Jews suffered a longer and more severe history of anti-Semitism than Sephardic (Spanish and Portugese) or Mizrahi (North African, Middle East, Central Asia region, and who are often lumped in with Sephardim) Jews who were not subjected to pogroms as frequently but did often endure forced conversion under Christian rule and second-class citizen status where they resided under Islamic rule. As a result, Ashkenazi Jews are stereotyped as being more culturally reticent, wary of strangers and less assimilated with non-Jews than their counterparts. Therefore, it is understandable that history and cultures of their residing country had an impact upon how particular communities of Jews perceived and welcomed the other. See Fast, *The Jews*; Zohar, *Sephardic and Mizrahi Jewry*; and Ehrlich, *Encyclopedia of the Jewish Diaspora*.

158. There is substantial scholarship related to Jewish assimilation that would be important to mention but goes beyond the remit of this book. Assimilation and hospitality toward the threatening other are very different matters and while there is substantial evidence documenting both movements toward assimilation and tendencies toward segregation, there appears to not be as much debate related to who was allowed into Jewish inner circles. See Jacobs, *Hidden Heritage*; Frankel and Zipperstein, *Assimilation and Community*; and Weeks, *From Assimilation to Antisemitism*.

159. This reality is applicable to any community, not just those within the Jewish tradition, but such an argument does seem to be quite particular to the Jewish community given their history as an ethno-religious group.

160. Firestone, "Judaism as a Force for Reconciliation," 81–82. Firestone qualifies this earlier by noting the quietist character of Judaism began around the second century CE. He also asserts that "without a this-worldly protective power, the deepest piety could not protect the Jews from the will and willfulness of the powers under which they lived" and that the only "time that a community of Jews attained actual self-rule since the Roman destruction of the Jerusalem Temple is the present time in the Jewish state of Israel" (ibid.). Firestone also makes the link between violence and religious development, noting Islam and biblical Judaism "emerged out of an environment in which it was required to fight in order to survive" whereas Rabbinic Judaism and Christianity "emerged out of an environment in which they were required to *refrain* from fighting in order to survive" (ibid., 81).

161. By "rituals and laws," Gopin refers to "rituals that make the Jew different," such

would be specifically aimed against annihilation."[162] Gopin goes on to say that this definition of focus particularly emphasizes

> [the] minutiae of practice that make a clear boundary between who is in and who is out of the group, who can be trusted and who cannot be trusted, rituals that become, in their modern incarnation, markers of ethnic and national trust, markers of distinction, markers of insulation from a dangerous world.[163]

As a result, such an emphasis strengthens and defines *who is the other*, i.e. anyone who does not participate in these activities.

Gopin proposes an intriguing idea that the key toward moving Judaism out of this more blinkered approach is in the practice of mourning, which is "a close cousin to and healthy evolution out of rage over the past" and has the capacity to speak to a "group's sense of threat to its future, its fear of annihilation" out of which eventually a relationship with the potentially threatening other can be built.[164] This need for mourning speaks to the disconnect between the need for security for the Jewish people and their reluctance to provide it to threatened others. The community expends valuable energy to ensure its own survival and, understandably, very little is left over to provide protected and safe spaces for others, particularly if others may have been complicit in Jewish destruction in decades or centuries past.

As a result, mourning is a metaphorical key to unlock the revival of more active other-centered actions he perceives to be essential to the Jewish tradition.[165] Enabling and sharing mourning of loss with the similarly mournful other, which requires acts of hospitality in the process, has the

---

as "obligations of protecting *Jewish* life, education to the uniqueness of Jewish life and practice, inculcating radical levels of defense of any Jew whose life is in danger, and ritual practices that are particularist by definition, such as dietary and purity laws" ("Judaism and Peacebuilding," 112. Italics mine).

162. Ibid. As a result, one would think adherents to Judaism should be particularly sensitive to the importance of hospitality and needs of those being threatened and in need of protection in order to ensure their safety and survival. Yet for cultures that perceive themselves as under threat of annihilation, outward-looking ethics are usually less emphasized in favor of survival.

163. Ibid.

164. Ibid., 114.

165. Ibid., 114–115. Gopin gives practical examples of how this could be done: "to visit the dead together, to bury them together in symbolic ways, to memorialize lost lives and lost homes . . . to talk about the losses for as long as it is necessary, to thoroughly indulge the past rather than suppress it, for fear that it would disrupt rational dialogue and conversation" (ibid., 115). None of those actions can take place effectively without hospitality being brought into the interaction.

potential to illuminate the reality that what is being mourned is the failure to act out the tradition of hospitality for the other in the first place.[166]

ISLAM

As stated previously, Derrida asserts Islam is "perhaps even more than Judaism and Christianity . . . a religion, an ethics, and a culture of hospitality."[167] Moreover, Derrida reflects Abrahamic scholar Louis Massignon's assertion that "the hospitality of the hôte Abraham that is placed at the center of Islam . . . makes Islam the most faithful heir, the exemplary heir of the Abrahamic tradition."[168]

In the research, however, the sources that address the issue of hospitality and welcome tend to be sources that are invested in the benefits of such practice, those considered the more progressive, marginal, or feminist voices in the Islamic tradition. This is not to say that mainstream Islam does not consider hospitality; it is to say that within the scholarship, hospitality and welcome are of particular interest to certain voices in Islam. Nevertheless, such a perspective appears to be the case in Judaism and Christianity as well considering the prior two sections, so this issue is not unique to Islam by any means.

In order to analyze the role of hospitality in Islam, this section is divided into four sub-sections. The first two sections will mirror others conducted in the Christian and Jewish section, considering the impact of the first Muslim migration (*hjira*) to Abyssinia and the experience of persecution upon the practice of hospitality in Islam, followed by consideration of Muhammad as a model of hospitality. The third sub-section will divide further, analyzing foundational values of *tawhid*, *ummah*, *adab*, and *sulh* that contribute to the practice of hospitality. Lastly, the fourth sub-section will, like those before it, address the challenges to the practice of hospitality that are present in contemporary Islam.

First Muslim Migration (hijra) to Abyssinia

Texts recounting the experience of persecution in Islam are where the first instances of the term *jihad* are used in the Qur'an in order to exhort

166. This would apply for both Arab and Jew in the context of Israel/Palestine. Inhospitality has been committed by both sides, and what is mourned could be interpreted as essentially a lack of hospitality as commanded by both Judaism and Islam.

167. Derrida, *Acts of Religion*, 365.

168. Ibid., 370.

adherents to strive toward faithfulness, to resist persecution, and not to let detractors of Islam cause adherents to stumble.[169] It is in the early experiences of persecution that faith is formed and takes root, developing into something of its own and growing in maturity. In Islam, the persecution that resulted in the first migration (*hijra*) into Abyssinia in 615 CE was a formational experience.[170] The Qur'an does not record the event itself, but its earliest source is found in Ibn Ishaq's eighth century biographical collection of the Prophet Muhammad, *Sīrat Rasūl Allah*, or "Life of the Messenger of God."[171]

Abuse and punishment for converting to Islam was growing in its early days. It is generally thought Muhammad started receiving his revelations in the year 610 CE and began to have a following of fellow believers soon thereafter. As this group of followers grew, to outsiders it may have seemed as if "Muhammad was forming a new kind of clan composed in the main of young dissidents who had thrown aside their old family loyalties," that had both political and economic implications within the tribal/clan system of the Arabian peninsula.[172] Yet, those who were opposed to these new religious developments as a result of Muhammad's revelations had to be careful. Certain converts, including Muhammad himself, were higher up in society and were part of powerful clans, which, under a vendetta cultural system, protected them. Nevertheless, the opposition "could attack slaves and the weaker Muslims with impunity" and such adherents were at significantly more risk.[173]

Muhammad was from the clan of Hashim, whose patriarch had already developed a good economic and trading relationship with the Negus, the Christian king of Abyssinia.[174] When the persecution became too much

169. See Ramadan, *In the Footsteps of the Prophet*, 51–62, where he discusses the themes of "Resistance, Humility and Exile." There is a great deal of literature that considers the meaning and limitations of *jihad*. For examples, see Marranci, *Jihad Beyond Islam*; and Heck, "Jihad Revised," 95–128.

170. In this period, there were other examples of persecution beyond the first *hijra*, but this particular event in Islamic history encapsulates the experience of persecution and exile.

171. Ibn Isḥāq, *Life of Muhammad*. This text is divided into *sira* (sections) that are numbered and will be referenced in addition to page numbers, as the *sira* appear to be consistent across the various editions available.

172. Armstrong, *Muhammad*, 121.

173. Ibid.

174. Ibid., 74. Abyssinia is now known as Ethiopia. 'The Negus" is a title; this king of Abyssinia is also known in other Islamic historical sources as Ashama Ibn Abjar or al-Najashi. Whether the trading relationship had been built with this particular Negus or one of his predecessors is unclear as there is no date for when the relationship began or the age of the Negus at the time of the first migration.

to bear for his followers, Muhammad realized he could not protect them all, including some members of his own family, and sought a refuge for them by asking the Negus to provide sanctuary for them.[175] In total, approximately one hundred Muslims crossed the Persian Gulf into the safety of Christian Abyssinia.[176]

Once it was discovered that a number of Muslims had fled, leaders of the ruling tribe in the area of Mecca, the Quraysh, sent two delegates to the Negus to request the emigrants be returned to Mecca. They informed the Negus the emigrants should be returned because the Muslims "had blasphemed against the faith of the people of Mecca and had disrupted society . . . [and] were therefore extremely dangerous and should not be trusted."[177] The Negus then gave the emigrants the opportunity to affirm their faith and the revelations to which they adhered, including corresponding beliefs regarding Jesus and Mary to address concerns that the Negus was harboring heretics. Satisfied with their response, the Negus refused to give them over to the Quraysh delegates and affirmed the Muslim refugees would be welcome and free to worship and stated he would "protect them and see that they receive proper hospitality while under [his] protection.[178] Therein they remained for about fifteen years, by which time Islam had taken further root in the Arabian peninsula and Muhammad had gained control of Yathrib/Medina, making it safe to return.[179]

The importance of this story in Islam's history as it relates to the practice of protective hospitality should not be underestimated. In inter-religious

175. Ibn Isḥāq, *Life of Muhammad*, sira 208 (p. 146).

176. Ibid. Ibn Isḥāq gives a list of the men who went, from which eighty-three arise. Armstrong also gives this number, saying eighty-three individuals and their families (*Muhammad*, 122). Tariq Ramadan says about 100 people—83 men and about 20 women (*In the Footsteps of the Prophet*, 59). Also, Armstrong notes there are some scholars (although she does not identify who they are) who question the motivation for seeking asylum, saying it may not have been to escape persecution but so that Muhammad could"establish an independent trade route to the south for . . . Muslims who were suffering under . . . trade sanctions" or that there may "have been some disagreement in the Muslim community" (*Muhammad*, 122). Nevertheless, Armstrong also asserts that while "Muhammad may have had an economic or political plan that did not work out so that, by the time historians like Ibn Ishaq started to write, these plans had been forgotten" (ibid., 123).

177. Armstrong, *Muhammad*, 122; and Ibn Isḥāq, *Life of Muhammad*, sira 218–219 (pp. 150–151).

178. Ibn Isḥāq, *Life of Muhammad*, sira 219 (p. 151). See also Armstrong, *Muhammad*, 122–123.

179. Ramadan, *In the Footsteps of the Prophet*, 62. Muhammad's control of Yathrib/Medina is noted in the foundation of the Constitution of Medina in 622 CE, which will be explored in more detail in chapter 5.

contexts, the story is told to illustrate the actions of a Christian king who recognized the truth in the belief of a fledgling Muslim community and acted to protect them from their abusers. In hospitality contexts, the narrative illustrates the provision of sanctuary and protection to a threatened and strange other, setting a precedent for "dangerous memories" that inform action and attitude centuries later when the need arises.[180]

Model: Muhammad

In Islamic texts, Muhammad's hospitality is well-documented. As someone who was an inhabitant of the Arabian Peninsula, hospitality was a way of life. Life in the desert necessitated "the cultivation and growth of the virtues of hospitality, bravery, mutual assistance, neighbor protection, and magnanimity"[181] for which Muhammad was known.[182]

Muhammad's family was also known for its hospitality. His ancestor Hashim, who had been the leader of the clan to which Muhammad belonged, was reputed to have been a prosperous and hospitable man, calling upon members of his tribe to provide food for pilgrims to Mecca[183] who were considered to be "God's guests, and, therefore, worthy of their hospitality."[184]

Having been orphaned three times in his childhood, Muhammad finally came under the protection of his uncle Abu Talib, who was considered "the noblest and the most hospitable and, therefore, the most respected among the Quraysh."[185] Because of his orphan status, Muhammad knew all too well the necessity of hospitality and such experiences may well have honed his sensitivity toward hospitality all the more.

There are numerous teachings and sayings attributed to Muhammad, particularly in the Hadith, that emphasize the need for and details the practice of hospitality. For example, Muhammad is said to have taught:

> The period of the entertainment of a guest is three days, and utmost kindness and courtesy is for a day and a night. It is not permissible for a Muslim to stay with his brother until he makes him sinful. They said: Messenger of Allah, how he would make

180. The term "dangerous memories" was explored in chapter 1 briefly and will be discussed further in the conclusion.

181. Hayka, *The Life of Muhammad*, 13.

182. See also Armstrong, *Muhammad*, 59, 105.

183. As it was a holy shrine even before the advent of Islam.

184. Hayka, *Life of Muhammad*, 2. Hashim also set up a treaty of trade with the Negus of Abyssinia, which developed the relationship that would be useful later on.

185. Ibid., 50. See also Armstrong, *Muhammad*, 76–79.

> him sinful? He (the Holy Prophet) said: He stays with him (so long) that nothing is left with him to entertain him.[186]

Muhammad understood hospitality could become a burden and guests carried a responsibility to honor their hosts by not overstaying their welcome. Such behavior might cause resentment in the heart of the host, which Muhammad likened to sin.

Moreover, Muhammad taught the ethical responsibility of the Muslim was to do no harm to one's neighbors, to provide good meals for guests, to be charitable, and to give hospitality generously.[187] To be prepared for hospitality, a bed should always be made and ready for a guest.[188] And like the admonition Jesus gave in Luke 14, Muhammad also shunned "ostentatious hospitality that had become . . . a display of power and confidence" rather than inviting those who were in need of hospitality such as the poor, the orphan, and the powerless.[189]

Foundational Values of Hospitality in Islam

The practice of hospitality is firmly rooted in values found and encouraged in Islamic thought. Scholars identify the virtues that contribute to the practice of hospitality in the Islamic tradition as: *sharaf* (honor), *karamuh* (saving face/dignity), *muru'ah* (valor), *hikmah* (wisdom), *karim* (generosity), *ihtiram* (respect), and *'afu* (forgiveness).[190]

In the Islamic tradition, the particular virtue of *karim* (generosity) cannot be overemphasized. As one of the ninety-nine names of God, *Al-Karim* ("The Bountiful, The Generous") illustrates that *karim* is an important factor in how the Muslim is taught to perceive God, and, in turn, to abide by the standard of *karim* in one's own life and interaction with others. *Karim* is considered a "quality of the spirit or soul," and its importance in Muslim culture and tradition has remained intact throughout the centuries.[191]

186. *Sahih Muslim* 18:4287. However, this teaching is found in many other places in a variety of forms as the Hadith is comprised of sayings people remembered and attributed to the Prophet.

187. *Sahih Bukhari* 1:10:576; 3:43:641; 5:58:142 (repeated in 6:60:411); 8:73:47–48, 155–156; *Sahih Muslim* 1:75.

188. *Sahih Muslim* 24:5190.

189. Armstrong, *Muhammad*, 105. See also Sira 612–613, Ibn Isḥāq, *Life of Muhammad*, 405.

190. Abu-Nimer, *Reconciliation, Justice and Coexistence*, 98; Fluehr-Lobban, *Islamic Societies in Practice*, 64.

191. Fluehr-Lobban, *Islamic Societies in Practice*, 62.

Upon consideration of the importance of *karim*, it is useful to remember survival in an inhospitable desert climate depends upon the hospitality of those who dwell in it. Survival in this sort of environment depends upon an "intricate web of relationships . . . and reciprocity between individuals and groups that . . . enable[s] desert families not only to survive but also to reproduce and flourish in their challenging environment."[192] The giving of water, bread, or meat to a guest, even if it means the host family must do without, is an act of solidarity and survival. Those who dwell in the desert know that to turn away guests is to consign them to their death.[193] Moreover, in the Islamic tradition considers it a duty to be generous and gracious to guests by providing sustenance, honor, and entertainment to them.[194]

Nevertheless, the guest also has responsibility in this hospitable relationship. The law of hospitality, *al-diyafah*, details this relationship. The host is called upon to provide without complaint, but the guest is not to stay so long that he or she becomes a burden upon the host.[195] Such regulation of hospitality illustrates a principle of mutuality found in Islam; to allow both to express generosity by either providing for the guest or by limiting how much one will take from the host are both marks of one's submission to others and to Allah. Concurrently, this illustrates the principle that hospitality is not one-sided; it is not something done *to* guests without requiring the guests to do something in return.

A reputation for *karim* is a virtue in Islamic tradition as one cannot practice true hospitality if one is not willing to be generous to one's guests. Frugality has no place in Islamic hospitality. Providing generously to guests is a mark of dignity (*karamah*). This link between *karim* and *karamah* is extremely important in the relationship between a guest and a host.[196] As both arise from the same root in Arabic, the implication is that an act of *karim* enables both the giver and the receiver to restore or maintain their *karamah*.[197]

192. Ibid.

193. Ibid.; and Schulman and Barkouki-Winter, "The Extra Mile."

194. Abu-Nimer, *Reconciliation, Justice and Coexistence*, 54; Al-Kaysi, *Morals and Manners in Islam*, 156; and Schulman and Barkouki-Winter, "The Extra Mile."

195. *Sahih Bukhari* 8:73:156.

196. Fluehr-Lobban, *Islamic Societies in Practice*, 64.

197. It is important to note here the underlying basis for *karamah* (dignity) in Islamic thought. As Islam, unlike Western Christianity, does not have a concept of original sin, the foundation for *karamah* lies in the dignity to exist and be a good steward of creation. "In contrast to the Western idea of free choice and freedom from constraint, Islam accentuates existential freedom—freedom to *be*—and locates the fulfillment of the human being in service. The dignity of the individual is underscored, in a broader context of social solidarity" (Said, introduction to *Peace and Conflict Resolution in Islam*, 8).

This principle of reciprocity manifests itself in other traditions or concepts in Islamic thought and practice. Similar to the Jewish understanding, *barakah* (blessing) connotes an idea of both giving and receiving, for it carries the meaning of both "blessed" as well as "blessing." The implication of *barakah* is this: To be blessed is to bless others; to receive blessing requires giving blessing. Found in the Abraham narrative, a blessing given by Allah requires the descendents of Abraham to be a blessing to the nations.[198] Likewise, reciprocity appears in the traditional greeting of the Muslim culture. "*Al-salam 'alaikum*" ("May peace be upon you") is said in greeting with the reply being "*'alaykum al-salam*" returning the peace to one's greeter. In this tradition, a host bearing peace becomes a guest of peace as well.

Additionally, Islamic theology of food informs the practice of hospitality. In Islamic thought, food is holy and deserves respect, and is therefore elevated on a table or stand and is rarely placed on the floor or other undignified surfaces. As a result, the sharing of food has a higher meaning than simple sustenance. Some Muslim cultures[199] refer to *halil ibrahim sofrasi* ("the table of Abraham"), which carries connotations of a bountiful table and describes a host or home whose table is always overflowing with food and welcome.[200]

Moreover, there are several concepts in Islamic thought that can be connected to a broader understanding of the practice of hospitality, providing a theological basis beyond what has already been explored above. These concepts are namely *tawhid* (unity), the *ummah* (community), *adab* (etiquette/interpersonal ethics), and *sulh* (the process of reconciliation) and will be explored in closer detail below.

198. Qur'an 37:108

199. It appears in areas where there was a strong Turkish influence, probably spread as a result of the Ottoman Empire, and is seen in Southeast Europe and Turkey.

200. A popular Turkish song performed by Barış Mançο (*Hal Hal*, Mu-Yap Records, 1989) titled "Halil Ibrahim Sofrasi" is translated as: "When human beings had known their limits / And hadn't yet spoken maliciously / Hadn't yet looked at other's honour venomously / What a table was set in the name of Abraham / A saucepan in the middle / . . . / Friends, please sit down at the table of Abraham / Blameless and perfectly happy people / Please to the seat of honour / Those who serve other humankinds slavishly / . . . / If you get your desires under control / You will sit on your throne comfortably / . . . / Those who have strong fists and are lionhearted / Support a family and don't know what's earning illegitimately / You're also welcome with us . . . / Join us friends . . . / . . . An empty saucepan doesn't have its place on this table . . ." The video is available in Turkish at http://youtu.be/Tvsi2ghrZz0.

Tawhid

One of the most foundational and socially radical principles in Islam involves the concept of *tawhid* (unity). *Tawhid* refers not only to the unity of Allah but also to a "fundamental unity of all things," humanity included.[201] The unity of humanity to God's own unity is based in the transformative focus from "self to one on the Self, the ultimate reality, the source of all other selves."[202] Islamic scholar Abdulaziz Sachedina recognizes this by noting the Qur'anic call to "compete with one another in good works," which is a call, according to Sachedina, founded upon "a universally recognizable moral good,"[203] as seen in Surah 5:48:

> And We have sent down to thee the Book with the truth, confirming the Book that was before it, and assuring it. So judge between them according to what God has sent down, and do not follow their caprices, to forsake the truth that has come to thee. To every one of you We have appointed a right way and an open road. If God had willed, He would have made you one nation; but that He may try you in what has come to you. So be you forward in good works; unto God shall you return, all together; and He will tell you of that whereon you were at variance.[204]

Additionally, *tawhid*'s social implications are visible in terms of unity exhibited through equality in the eyes of God and each other.[205] Under this principle, even "mortal enemies are fellow human beings, the creation of

201. Noor, "What is the Victory of Islam?," 324.

202. Sachedina, *The Islamic Roots*, 30.

203. Qur'an 5:48. However, Sachedina notes: "What is not clear, however, is whether the Koran acknowledge a variable cultural or historical understanding of what constitutes good. Since K. 5:48 is addressed to all religious communities, it is consistent to maintain that the good in the passage is applicable across religious traditions. But such an interpretation has not been universally accepted by scholars of Islamic ethics." (*Islamic Roots*, 70). In reference to the claim Sachedina makes regarding 5:48 being for "all religious communities," he refers to Ibn Kathir, *Tafsir*, 2:589, which "mentions another opinion that regards the audience of the passage to be the Muslim community. However, the subsequent subjunctive clause beginning 'Had God willed' clearly makes its audience communities under different prophets" (Sachedina, *Islamic Roots*, 151 n. 20).

204. Translation according to Arberry, *The Koran Interpreted*. Nevertheless, the debate Sachedina refers to is seen even in the English interpretations of the Qur'anic text, as the Hilali-Khan refers to "you" as Muhammad and the Book as the Qur'an, while the Khalifa interpretation notes the book was given to "confirm previous scriptures, and *supersede* them" (again, assuming it speaks of the Qur'an) and gives an impression of competition for who is better or more right than how Sachedina and other interpretations, such as this one, interpret the text.

205. Engineer, *Islam and Liberation Theology*, 8.

the same God."[206] As a basis for an ethic of hospitality in Islam, *tawhid* has immense power as it implies that whatever dehumanizes one dehumanizes all.[207] Feminist Islamic theologian Amina Wadud argues this point as follows:

> If [*tawhid* is] experienced as a reality in everyday Islamic terms, humanity would be a single global community without distinction for reasons of race, class, gender, religious tradition, national origin, sexual orientation or other arbitrary, voluntary or involuntary aspects of human distinction.[208]

Therefore, as all of humanity is one, being inhospitable and inflicting violence or perpetuating injustice is seen as anti-*tawhid*.[209]

Likewise, seeking justice for the sake of *tawhid* is rooted in the practice of hospitality. As hospitality is based upon the value of fellow human beings and in the belief the other has something to offer in reciprocal relationship, working for justice to benefit members of the human community and to create a space for humanity to thrive is an act of hospitality. The *Sahih al-Bukhari* illustrates these values of justice and generosity by sharing this message from Muhammad given to leaders of his conquest of Yemen:

> That his father said, "The Prophet sent Mu'adh and Abu Musa to Yemen telling them. 'Treat the people with ease and don't be hard on them; give them glad tidings and don't fill them with aversion; and love each other, and don't differ.[210]

In the same vein, the Mu'tazilites, whose thoughts in turn contributed to the development of Shi'ism, valued the work of justice to such an extent that "they identified themselves as the folk of 'Divine Unity and Justice' (*ahl al-tawhid wa 'l-'adl*)."[211] Furthermore, the Sunni community remembers the Prophet reminded his followers frequently "a real believer is one whose neighbor does not go to bed hungry."[212]

206. This understanding of *tawhid*, however, is marginal. For many in the Muslim community, *tawhid* may only refer to the unity of the Muslim community itself and not wider as Wadud or Noor interprets. Noor qualifies this interpretation of *tawhid* as to being found primarily with those in the Muslim community who seek peace and social justice. Noor, "What is the Victory of Islam?," 324.

207. Qur'an 5:32.

208. Wadud, *Inside the Gender Jihad*, 28.

209. Noor, "What is the Victory of Islam?," 324–25.

210. *Sahih Bukhari* 4:52:275.

211. Safi, "The Times They Are A-Changin'," 9.

212. Ibid.

To provide space for rest or safety, to feed the hungry, to address the needs of one's neighbor—these are all acts of *tawhid* and of *'adl* (justice), and, in turn, also acts of honor and hospitality in the Islamic tradition. Even the simple act of eating together carries tremendous weight, for sharing a meal together strengthens "social ties . . . between members of a community irrespective of social status."[213] In this way, table fellowship and acts of solidarity have capacity to strengthen *tawhid.*

Since in the tradition of *tawhid* all of humanity is the Muslim's neighbor, a concept which is similar to the understanding of neighbor in the Christian and Jewish traditions, the idea of being one another's keepers is then also an extension of *tawhid.*[214] Under this concept, the differences between people are an illusion as are the seeming dualities of Allah's nature. Instead, humanity's mutuality and the unity of the character of God, along with the virtue of reciprocity as articulated in every religion's "golden rules," gives life meaning.[215] Moreover, the denial of *tawhid* is the greatest sin as it implies the denial of the meaning of life itself since life and its meaning "originates in the unity of existence which is essentially the manifestation of the unity of God" as spoken in the *shahadah.*[216]

Ummah

Related closely to the concept of *tawhid* is the idea of the *ummah* (community), where the issue of pluralism and welcoming the religious other into the community in Islam is most visible. While *tawhid* is an overarching, foundational concept related to the nature of God and God's creation, *ummah* is the reality of that unity as exhibited and enacted in everyday life in the here and now. The *ummah* exists because of *tawhid*; it addresses issues of identity and otherness in more concrete terms, such as detailing who is in the *ummah* and who is not.

Muslim communities debate the definition of *ummah.* For Muslims who hold to an inclusive definition of *tawhid*, an inclusive *ummah* is a natural assumption; yet, the more common contemporary understanding is that *ummah* refers to the Muslim community only. The debate centers around how one interprets the inclusive example of the *ummah* provided by Muhammad in the Constitution of Medina[217] versus the more exclusive

213. Al-Kaysi, *Morals and Manners in Islam*, 26.

214. Safi, "The Times They Are A-Changin'," 9.

215. Wadud, *Gender Jihad*, 28–29.

216. Khan, "Islam as an Ethical Tradition of International Relations," 79–80.

217. The Constitution of Medina and its impact upon the concept of the *ummah*

examples used in the post-Muhammad years of early Islam, the usage that has primarily prevailed in mainstream contemporary Islam.

Nevertheless, if one adheres to the more inclusive definition, understanding all are unified with God and to each other through *tawhid*, the worldwide community is the *ummah*, regardless of whether it professes Islam as a religious identity or not. Moreover, the plurality in the Muslim community itself is proof enough that multiplicity does not threaten the *ummah* but it is instead built upon "the common threads that bind" them together as a community.[218] Through this inclusive view of the *ummah* Muslims in progressive communities "call for the rejection of a dialectical approach to the Other which can only frame the other in negative terms as the enemy (or potential enemy) that has to be greeted with suspicion and fear."[219] Understanding that welcome and inclusion are markers of Islam, those who hold to this interpretation of *ummah* are self-critical of the idea that it is pure or monolithic and are, therefore, committed to the ideal of plurality and hospitality since room for the guest should be made.[220]

Those who embrace an inclusive *ummah* take very seriously the words of the Qur'an which state that God created everyone and the differences are apparent in order that "you may know one another."[221] "All those who believe in God are members of this community too," writes Mohammed Abu-Nimer,[222] and it is here that the foundation for pluralism in Islam can be found. The inclusion of the *dhimmi*, "protected people" including other People of the Book (i.e., Jews and Christians or *ahl al-kitab*), is instrumental in this vision of the *ummah*.[223] As believers who have received divine revelation, those who seek to make the *dhimmi* welcome hearken back to the words of God who said "surely this, your community (*Ummah*), is a single community."[224]

The relationship between Christians and Muslims during the time of the Prophet bears witness to the practice of hospitality as the Christians gave safe harbor and protection from persecution to the Muslim Diaspora.

---

and the legal obligations to protect the *dhimmi* will be more closely explored in chapter 5. For now, let us note there are some scholars who argue an exclusive definition of the *ummah* is in contradiction to Muhammad's early teaching.

218. Noor, "What is the Victory of Islam?," 327.

219. Ibid., 332.

220. Ibid.

221. Qur'an 49:13.

222. Abu-Nimer, *Reconciliation, Justice and Coexistence*, 74.

223. Again, these concepts will be explored more fully in chapter 5.

224. Qur'an 23:52, quoted in Abu-Nimer, *Reconciliation, Justice and Coexistence*, 74 (italics mine).

Expelled from Mecca because of their conversions from polytheism to Islam, the Prophet encouraged his followers to seek refuge in Abyssinia under the Christian emperor as was explored in the previous section. While no formal pacts were made regarding this relationship and its implications for the concept of *ummah*, this act represents "the first time that Muslims, as Muslims, dealt with Christians as a community."[225] No animosity was present in this relationship; instead, this episode in Islamic history "is a very early example in Islam of the importance of pluralism and interfaith dialogue" and the commonalities the People of the Book shared.[226]

The Prophet would continue to speak favorably of Christians because of their hospitable acts towards the young Muslim community. In the words of the Prophet, one can see the further development of the concept of the *ummah* in relation to the Christian and Jewish communities. When speaking of the value of plurality in light of these historical realities, the hadith *Sahih al-Bukhari* states:

> The Prophet instructed his followers on many occasions on the importance of solidarity between the believers and Muslims. He compared their relationship to the organs of the body, which communicate pain if one part is ill, or to a building, which is strengthened by the coherence of its parts. 'The believer to another believer is like a building whose different parts enforce each other.' The Prophet then clasped his hands with fingers interlaced (while saying that).[227]

When considering the importance of plurality in the *ummah*, one must be clear to define what pluralism is and how it contributes to this idea of hospitality. As religious scholar Diana Eck points out, pluralism and diversity are not the same. She notes one "may have people from different religious and ethnic backgrounds . . . in one place, but unless they are involved in active engagement with one another, there is no pluralism . . . pluralism is not and cannot be a non-participant sport."[228] Likewise, hospitality is not and cannot be a non-participant sport. To practice genuine hospitality implies engagement, interaction, willingness to be affected by those who share one's space. To embrace pluralism and to practice hospitality is to try actively to understand—not just tolerate—the other.[229] It is the active attempt

225. Hussain, "Muslims, Pluralism, and Interfaith Dialogue," 254.

226. Ibid.

227. *Sahih Bukhari* 3:43:626, quoted in Abu-Nimer, 74. The similarities between this exposition on a community of believers and that of the image of the Body of Christ (typically interpreted as strictly Christian) by the apostle Paul in 1 Cor 12 is remarkable.

228. Eck, *A New Religious America*, 70–71..

229. Ibid.

to understand and engage those who are different that should characterize the *ummah* and it is important to remember that, as *tawhid* is sought in the reality of pluralism, unity and uniformity are not one in the same either.

Adab

Moving from the general and theoretical to the more concrete and practical in the principles that support the practice of hospitality in Islam, the concept of *adab* is important because it is the most obvious link to hospitality. Encompassing connotations of etiquette, social manners, and interpersonal ethics, *adab* is an elaborate framework for the code of Muslim behavior, which is bound up in values of honor, kindness, humaneness, civility, generosity, and courtesy. *Adab* addresses the simplest to the most complex of social situations: from sneezing or yawning, to how to conduct occasions such as weddings, or to operate within wider social relationships in a way that honors all involved.[230]

Sharaf (honor), *karamah* (dignity), *karim* (generosity), and *ihtiram* (respect) are the virtues of *adab*; one cannot adhere to the code of *adab* without its companion virtues, with honor playing the most important role. Simply feeding hungry people is not the fullest expression of hospitality and fulfillment of *adab*. In order to practice hospitality in its most meaningful way, it must be honorable and generous as well. How Muslims conduct themselves socially relies heavily upon honor. Proper adornment when accepting or giving hospitality is important, as is providing a comfortable and clean entertaining space, an abundance of food, and an attentive attitude toward one's guests and host. Furthermore, refusal to accept invitations or to visit another's home carries significant weight in relation to one's honor and reputation as a hospitable host.[231] Therefore, *adab* is, in its essence, an ethic of hospitality to be practiced in the religious tradition in order to remind the observer of one's connection to God and the divine directive to live a just, honorable, and compassionate life.[232]

230. Al-Kaysi, *Morals and Manners in Islam*, 17; Safi, "The Times They Are A-Changin'," 13.

231. Anne Meneley, "Living Hierarchy in Yemen," 67–68. Meneley also notes this emphasis upon honor in hospitality causes honor to be accrued "to those who are visited, who are thereby acknowledged as socially significant and morally sound, and those who are allowed to give (or give back) rather than receive." Meneley writes from the context of Yemen, but this behavior is found throughout the Near and Middle East, if not to some extent in most Islamic contexts.

232. Al-Kaysi, *Morals and Manners in Islam*, 17. It is of little wonder then that Islamic scholar Omid Safi writes of an interaction with another scholar specializing in

One of the Muslim communities that seems to be growing, particularly among those who are coming to Islam from other faiths, is Sufism; and it is this same branch that takes *adab* very seriously. "All of Sufism is *adab*," writes one author detailing that Sufis have cultivated *adab* from not just an interpersonal but to a communal code of conduct and ethic.[233] Believing *adab* forms and sustains the context where humaneness is developed, every relationship and situation, in fact "every level of being," in the practice of Sufism is suffused with *adab*.[234] Similar to Buddhism's eightfold path, Sufism's practice of *adab* is rooted in the belief that right action leads to right speech, which in turn leads to right hearts and, finally, to right faith. Committed to fellowship and to the idea that each relationship is a chance to grow in self-discovery and purification, *adab* dictates the welcome and treatment of others as family.[235]

Included in the practice of *adab* for this community is the discipline of being "straightforward with sincerity and truthfulness."[236] Honesty and keeping commitments are symbols of authentic faith; lying, breaking promises, or acting insultingly in a quarrel are, concurrently, signs of hypocrisy according to the Prophet.[237] To practice *adab* is to understand "the value of one's word."[238] Similarly, the practice of hospitality is not something one can fake. For hospitality to be genuine, it welcomes and encourages truth and honesty since one cannot accommodate and welcome others if one is unwilling to be truthful "about distinct persons, the state of the world and society, and even [oneself] in new and challenging ways."[239] Furthermore,

fundamentalism, Gilles Kepel, who noted that all of the Abrahamic fundamentalists had something in common. When pressed to what that commonality might be, Kepel replied, "They all have such bad *adab*!" Believing Kepel spoke the truth, Safi goes on to note it is the loss or bad practice of *adab*, this lack of humaneness, courtesy, honor, welcome and genuine hospitality that has been so detrimental to the Muslim community, both in its relationship to outsiders as well as to those within its own ranks ("The Times They Are A-Changin'," 13). Concurrently, how Muslims perceive the other is caught up in their expectations of the other to also practice *adab*. Research done in the context of the Israel/Palestine conflict notes "Arabs . . . feel themselves to be distant from Jews, and they are observed to stereotype Jews as haughty, materialistic and lacking certain traditional Arab social graces such as honour, hospitality and neighborliness" (Smooha, *Israel: Pluralism and Conflict*, 199–200).

233. Safi, "The Times They Are A-Changin'," 14 (italics mine).

234. Helminski, "Adab."

235. Ibid.

236. Ibid.

237. *Sahih Bukhari*, 1:2:33.

238. Keller, "Adab of Islam."

239. Hütter, "Hospitality and Truth," 216. Although this text was written for a Christian context, its application in the practice of *adab* as it relates to hospitality is congruent with Muslim understandings.

to practice hospitality—to treat others with *adab*—is to open oneself up to challenge and growth as encounter with the other inevitably brings change.

Sulh

One of the most ritualized practices of hospitality found in Islam, called *sulh*, is particularly valuable to those who are interested in the work of peace and reconciliation. Although hospitality does not consist entirely of sharing of food or drink together, Islam, through its marriage of religion and culture, has maintained the practice of hospitality in the context of reconciliation efforts more visibly than, perhaps, more Westernized versions of Christianity and Judaism. While the actual practice may not be the same throughout the Muslim world, the function it has in Islamic tradition and culture is widespread.

Sulh is most documented in areas around Jordan, Lebanon, and Palestine.[240] Because it is the final step in a three-part approach toward community restorative justice, *sulh* is a process of reconciliation after a wrong has been committed and its practice could be seen as a microcosm of the role hospitality plays in Islamic life.

Two steps precede *sulh* in this movement toward reconciliation. In the first step, *atwah*, the perpetrator or his/her family provide some form of temporary economic compensation (i.e. goods, money, animals, food, etc.) to the family of the victim. If the receiving family accepts the compensation, it "indicates an agreement that revenge will not take place for the period of the dispute resolution."[241] Related to virtues of *karamah* (dignity) and *sharaf* (honor), this economic exchange is important as it symbolizes the honor and dignity shown to the victim's family as well as humility and gratitude for benevolence and forbearance of revenge on behalf of the family of the perpetrator.[242] Following *atwah*, the second step called *hudnah* refers to a period of time, similar to a truce, that begins after *atwah* is accepted. It is during this period that the two parties begin talks or, if necessary, conduct investigations.[243]

After the time of *hudnah* is complete, *sulh* begins.[244] During *sulh* parties or families involved in the dispute are brought together again to either

240. Irani and Funk, "Rituals of Reconciliation," 180–82.

241. Ibid., 184.

242. Ibid.

243. Ibid.

244. While some regions may use the term *sulhah* for the process of reconciliation, the term actually refers to the actual event or hospitality ritual of reconciliation rather than the process. See Abu-Nimer, *Reconciliation, Justice and Coexistence*, 98–99.

publicly accept or reject the results of the mediation effort and the terms offered.[245] If the terms are accepted in a public display, then the process of reconciliation moves into the personal sphere when the family of the perpetrator visits the family of the victim's home. During this visit, the victim's family serves coffee, and in turn the ritual reverses when the family of the perpetrator hosts and shares a meal, called *mumalaha* ("partaking of salt and bread").[246]

The public and private dimensions of *sulh* are equally important. The values that operate within this very real example of hospitality, and the outward expressions of the values of honor and generosity are part of *sulh*. The parties involved in the process have the right to refuse to accept terms or to refuse to drink coffee together or share a meal, indicating they may feel they have not been treated with enough honor, dignity, or generosity. This right to refusal, both in the public and private spheres, is "a form of pressure, a tactic to gain concessions, since the failure to produce an outcome may humiliate or disappoint . . . [and therefore] damaging the disputants and their clans' social status."[247]

Contemporary Islam and Challenges to Hospitality

Without question, the practice of hospitality is well-fixed in the Islamic religious and cultural traditions. There are questions, however, whether hospitality as it is practiced by Muslims makes a real difference to the non-Muslim other, particularly in cases where that other is threatened or threatening.[248]

245. Abu-Nimer, *Reconciliation, Justice and Coexistence*, 98–99.

246. Irani and Funk, "Rituals of Reconciliation," 185.

247. Abu-Nimer, *Reconciliation, Justice and Coexistence*, 95. Once again, one can see the economic power of hospitality—practice of hospitality as currency—and the use of reciprocity to indicate honor and respect, as previous chapters have explored.

248. This question takes particular shape in the 2011 news related to Muamar Qaddafi's family finding refuge in neighboring Algeria after he had been overthrown by the National Transitional Council (NTC) of Libya. While the NTC condemned Algeria for offering shelter, referring to it as "an act of aggression," the Algerian ambassador to the United Nations, Mourad Benmehidi, declared that "in desert regions there was a 'holy rule of hospitality' and his country had accepted the family on humanitarian grounds" (BBC News, "Libya interim leaders give ultimatum to Gaddafi forces," Aug. 30, 2011). Such a situation highlights several factors worth noting. First, Algeria does not have a reputation for taking in non-Muslims on humanitarian grounds, so it is appropriate to question the full extent of this declared "holy rule of hospitality" as it is applied to Muslims and non-Muslims alike. Second, if the practice of hospitality in Islam were monolithic, the Muslims of Libya would recognize the protective hospitality the Muslims of Algeria have given and would respect it since it is a "holy rule" after all. Third, and related to this, if ever an example were needed that illustrated how a

There are obvious impediments to the arguments presented thus far regarding the practice of hospitality in Islam. First and foremost, much of the argument stated here is based upon a very inclusive interpretation of the Qur'an and the Hadith as well as theological concepts foundational to Islam. Undoubtedly, some Muslims would disagree with the discussion of *tawhid* (unity) and the *ummah* (community) as some traditional understandings limit them to including only to those who profess Islam. Nevertheless, the reality that these inclusive interpretations have originated from Muslim scholars and theologians bears witness to the fact that there is great plurality in the Muslim community as well. The fear among those who do not hold such a view is that, if the *ummah* is opened up to everyone, it will dissolve into something without meaning. Nevertheless, this "presupposes the unity and fixity of the *umma[h]* in the first place."[249]

Furthermore, for those who might interpret *tawhid* and *ummah* as specific to the Muslim community, there is an even greater temptation to restrict them to only Muslims in one's specific community to the exclusion of other Muslims with whom one may not agree. Primarily these are issues related to how Muslim communities view plurality and diversity, and how these same communities embrace the other. Some argue "Western values and cultures underlie pluralism," and are therefore resistant to it.[250] Yet, there is sufficient evidence that the Prophet embraced plurality (as opposed to relativism). For those who are willing and open to embrace and engage the other, there is more flexibility in considering who is part of the *ummah* and to whom one should show solidarity through the concept of *tawhid*.

There is substantial evidence in the Qur'an, the Hadith, and other writings to support this flexibility. In those same texts, however, there is room for legitimate interpretation to go against this flexibility. Therefore, as with any other religious tradition, interpretation becomes the pivot point whereby one can justify actions on either end of the spectrum.

---

religious imperative gets subverted by political interest or gain, this would be it. While sometimes subversion is a positive development, in certain cases it can be negative and one can see how a "holy rule of hospitality" can be adopted or neglected depending upon the situation at hand. Finally, this scenario and this research as a whole highlights that "holy rules" are rarely, if ever, interpreted purely or in the same manner in the current context as they had been in the past, and imperatives understood by one generation are often further complicated or forgotten altogether in future generations.

249. Noor, "What is the Victory of Islam?," 328.

250. Abu-Nimer, *Reconciliation, Justice and Coexistence*, 82.

OBSERVATIONS FOR CHRISTIANITY'S PRACTICE OF HOSPITALITY IN THE ABRAHAMIC CONTEXT

> *...she listened for the holes—the things [they] did not say; the questions they did not ask...*
>
> —Toni Morrison, *Beloved*

As this research is an exercise in liberation and feminist theology, re-assessing the Christian tradition's theology and ethic of hospitality in light of other authoritative sources that speak to gaps in belief and practice is appropriate. Black liberation theologian James Cone argues for utilizing this method when he notes the black Christian community "listened to the white theological rhetoric about justice of God and the unity of the church and then related it to white passivity regarding the transformation of ecclesiastical and social structures of oppression."[251] From that listening exercise, he notes the black community concluded "white church people talk about love and reconciliation," and one could add hospitality, "but seldom with the practical intention of translating theological doctrines into political realities."[252] Therefore, inconsistencies and gaps that practice need to be identified and addressed in order to have an effectual theology.

Moreover, being in dialogue—and practicing hospitality—allows for observation of other traditions that enhance and highlight what is missing in one's own, where the blind spots and holes are, what one may not see without the other's presence and witness. Cone does this in a different context by noting Christianity "does not possess in its nature the means for analyzing the structure of capitalism" and, therefore, the adoption of Marxism "as a tool of social analysis can disclose the gap between appearance and reality, and thereby help Christians to see how things really are."[253] The utilization of a dialogical inter-religious hermeneutic as part of the methodology used here lends further expectations that the other Abrahamic traditions of Judaism and Islam have something to contribute to Christianity in this context. It is understandable the theology and ethic of hospitality in each of the Abrahamic traditions should have elements that are particular to one tradition in contrast to another. Yet, the absence of certain aspects in

251. Cone, *Speaking the Truth*, 147.

252. Ibid.

253. Cone, *For My People*, 187.

one tradition should give reason for pause, as it may point to something that has been lost, forgotten, ignored, or overwritten through the course of the tradition's development.

As such, the crucial observation to be made is there is practically no discussion in contemporary Western Christian theological and ethical scholarship related to honor outside of antiquated contexts.[254] Furthermore, there are no discussions related to the role of honor in the life of the faithful today. It seems as if the concept of honor disappeared into the realm of chivalry in Western culture; and the concept of honor is perceived as premodern and irrelevant to the current context. Yet, honor is not a monolithic concept, and perversions of honor, as a means to abusively sustain power over another or commit violence and violation, may have also contributed to its decline. Nevertheless, the absence of discussion related to honor in Western Christian scholarship and faithful life illuminates the disconnect one often senses in inter-religious dialogue, particularly with Jewish and Muslim counterparts.

Nevertheless, honor does exist and plays a role in Christian thought, albeit primarily explored in historical contexts rather than present day. Throughout the New Testament, one notices the existence and sensitivity to an honor/shame code, and yet its impact upon current thought has lessened extensively.

Unsurprisingly, the expression of honor in the New Testament is primarily linked with issues of social justice and hospitality. Jesus' Sermon on the Mount found in Matthew 5–7 carries in it understandings of honor and shame, particularly in 5:38–42 where Jesus exhorts followers to maintain honor and dignity when others seek to shame. Similarly, the hospitality narratives of Jesus found in the Gospel of Luke illustrate the importance of honor. In Luke 14:8–13, Jesus shares a parable that emphasizes the role of honor in the invitation of guests as well as where those guests are placed at the table in relation to the host. As a result, as Hershberger notes, "honor was at the heart of . . . hospitality" in these texts.[255]

Similarly, Jesus' teachings contradicted the cultural convention of advantageous reciprocity as it applies to hospitality, which, in turn, carries with it acts and attitudes of honor and shame according to Hershberger. In the later part of the Lukan passage above, Jesus calls upon his listeners to

254. There are some explorations regarding dignity, integrity and keeping promises that could be interpreted as honor, but the use of the word "honor" to describe them is practically non-existent in Western Christian scholarship, as is the connection between honor and current Christian theological and ethical scholarship in the area of hospitality.

255. Hershberger, *A Christian View of Hospitality*, 125.

invite those who are in need of hospitality—the poor, crippled, lame, and blind, among others—rather than simply inviting one's friends, family and wealthy colleagues. Instead, Jesus calls for the attendance of those in need who have nothing to give in return other than themselves. In this way, hospitality according to Jesus is about honoring the individual, not accruing honor by way of reciprocity for oneself.[256] Hershberger notes Jesus' teaching here refers to a "downward mobility" that is antithetical to how hospitality was practiced at this time. She notes his admonition for "bringing unclean people into your house, people who would defile you . . . [was about] seeing everyone as your equal and demonstrating that with your hospitality," which contributes to the political implications of hospitality as such acts would be considered quite subversive.[257] In the end, Jesus appears to imply God grants honor through acts of hospitality and that this relationship between the two is not a mechanism in a reciprocity system given by one's peers, guests, or hosts.

The link between hospitality and social justice is also apparent in these texts and in the later epistles that outlined hospitable practices of the early church. As early Christians saw themselves as strangers and aliens who inhabited "marginal situations of shame, unrest, and even persecution," it was expected for them "to conduct themselves in an honorable and blameless manner midst their hosts."[258] Concurrently, the apostle Paul admonishes adherents to strive to out-do each other with regards to honor while practicing hospitality, effectively linking honor and hospitality in a more direct way.[259]

On the whole, hospitality in Christianity as it is practiced today does not emphasize honor as such. Yet, if one considers the practice of hospitality in the Christian tradition, it is not difficult to imply honor as part of the equation. The concept of honor carries with it a certain aspect of moral authority and practice, which is certainly present in the Christian practice of hospitality in the current context. Pohl describes hospitality as a "way of life [that is] fundamental to Christian identity"[260] and that "[w]elcoming strangers into a home and offering them food, shelter, and protection" are its "key components."[261] Regarded as a "highly valued moral practice," Pohl asserts hospitality is "an important expression of kindness, mutual aid,

256. Ibid., 126.

257. Ibid.

258. Yong, *Hospitality and the Other*, 115, with reference to 1 Pet 2:12.

259. Rom 12:9–13

260. Pohl, *Making Room*, x.

261. Ibid., 4.

neighborliness, and response to the life of faith"[262] and it stands as "one of the pillars of morality on which society [is] built."[263] In Judaism and Islam, those values and actions are inextricably linked to concepts and etiquettes of honor.

Furthermore, the absence of understanding and discussion in scholarship related to honor in Western Christianity illuminates a gap that undoubtedly contributes to the decline in the practice of hospitality. As has been explored in the above section related to Islam, one can assert that there appears to be a correlative relationship between honor and hospitality in that when honor is strongly emphasized in a tradition, the practice of hospitality is taken more seriously as well. As a result, there are two possible ways this can be interpreted: either hospitality is best understood and practiced when honor is taken seriously, or traditions and individuals who practice hospitality best are those who understand honor.[264]

The inability to understand the importance of honor and the ritual of hospitality illuminates a possible reason why inter-religious dialogue, cooperation, and collaboration can sometimes be ineffectual or superficial. Cooperative theology and practice on behalf of the marginalized and threatened other is also a hospitable and honorable theology and practice. A cooperative theology characterized by honor and hospitality that is shared between the cooperating traditions is the ideal. Thus, a recovery of a vocabulary and understanding of honor in the Christian tradition is needed if hospitable theological and ethical relationships between the Abrahamic traditions are to be propagated further.

262. Ibid.

263. Pohl, "Building a Place for Hospitality," 27.

264. This could be seen as a bit of a chicken/egg scenario. Is honor an internal attitude of hospitality? Or is hospitality an outward expression of honor? Or, perhaps, both?

PART TWO

Protective Hospitality

4

Hospitality and Protection

To leave one's country in search of refuge, to save one's family, one's community, meant facing the unknown, and not knowing what would happen tomorrow or whether the place one had chosen as temporary refuge would open its doors and warmly welcome those fleeing terror and death.

—Rigoberta Menchú Tum[1]

INTRODUCTION

Heretofore, I have explored the complexity of hospitality as ethical practice (Chapter Two) and the religious dimension that the Abrahamic traditions offer towards this (Chapter Three). Throughout there has been a movement toward considering a particular aspect of hospitality: the provision of protection. Chapter Two highlighted three main strands of hospitality—table fellowship, intellectual welcome, and protection. In Chapters Four and Five, protective hospitality for the threatened other will be given specific focus, analyzing theory and contributing factors that both encourage and hamper the practice of providing sanctuary for the endangered other, particularly in contexts of conflict or serious threat.

1. Rigoberta Menchú Tum, foreword to *Presencia de los refugiados guatemaltecos en Méxica* (Mexico City: COMAR and UNHCR, 1999), 17, in García, *Seeking Refuge*, 1.

As this chapter is first time hospitality will have been considered through the particular lens of protection, the sources considered in this chapter are from a variety of disciplines. When considering the practice of protective hospitality during the course of this research, it became quite clear early on that contextual orientation was necessary. If formulations were going to be presented that were realistic and reflective of belief and practice within the Abrahamic communities, representatives of the faiths needed to be consulted on what they understood hospitality, and more specifically protective hospitality, to be. Therefore, I conducted informal group and individual conversations with a number of religious leadership and laity from Jewish, Christian, and Muslim traditions in both Northern Ireland and Bosnia between 2007 and 2011.

As a result of those conversations, it became clear early on that the religious leadership, laity, and their communities were fairly limited in their capacity to identify or "do theology" related to protective hospitality. For example, in 2009–2010 I conducted focus group conversations in Northern Ireland, situated around a table including a meal that was accompanied by tea and coffee, to discuss the role of hospitality within their respective religious traditions. Over the course of four weeks, the group discussed hospitality centered around four different emphases: welcoming the other, the role of food & drink, risk and refuge, and hospitality as peacemaking.

These conversations were enlightening in that they indicated the level of engagement present within the communities related to hospitality. By the end, it was obvious that those who participated tended to think of hospitality in very conventional ways. Discourse regarding the theology of hospitality has been primarily restricted to conversations about tea and coffee, table fellowship or possibly as far as immigration or inter-religious dialogue, but it rarely goes wider. However, when faced with questions of "Who do you welcome?," "For whom do you put yourself at risk?," and "What does your faith say about providing safe space?," the focus group participants—religious leadership and lay persons alike—were often hard pressed to come up with well-articulated, confident, and authoritative answers. Instead, there was speculation, exploration, and furrowed brows. Despite hopes for theology to be a "practical discipline, emerging from concrete human situations, informing patterns of faithful living,"[2] these conversations illuminated a disconnect between religious thought and religious practice around the topic of hospitality. Furthermore, when protective hospitality was discussed, the

2. Graham, *Theological Reflection*, 9.

conversation automatically turned to risk, violence, and, somewhat surprisingly, concerns related to the purity of communal identity.[3]

This disconnect between religious thought and religious practice is perhaps understandable. My own background illuminates the contextual nature of theological construction and the disconnect between stated religious belief and practiced religious ethics. I am a product of the "Christ-haunted"[4] and racially-divided American South. Religion and its influences upon culture and ethical practice contribute to who I am. I grew up in a white, lower middle class culture that prided itself on its Southern hospitality and yet was often antagonistic, fearful, hateful, or simply dismissive toward black community members who lived on the other side of town and went to different schools.

Moreover, in a specifically religious context, I grew up immersed in a Protestant evangelical context that taught its followers to seek and follow God's will in one's life and reach one's highest potential, but as a woman I was unwelcome to study theology, teach men, or be a pastor. These embedded ironies were unresolved. As such, places such as Bosnia, Croatia and Northern Ireland where I have lived and worked over the last two decades have felt familiar in their the mixture of religion and social constructs which serve to undergird both the imperatives for hospitality and protection as well as acts of profound inhospitality.

While theology can open the door to new perspectives and horizons, oftentimes the process of theological reflection evokes bemusement in some while taking root and providing illumination in others.[5] There are some communities who are exceptions, but my experience agrees that "few congregations [are] given the resources to think intelligently about their faith . . . [d]espite references to theology as 'the work of the people of God.'"[6]

This disconnect between thought and practice and the limitations present in religious communities and mainstream culture to conceive of and clearly articulate their understandings of hospitality and protection, therefore, affects how this research is presented. This chapter will be more exploratory than empirical, more a prescription of issues and possibility

3. Both on social and religious communal levels.

4. A term used to describe the South by southern writer Flannery O'Connor, where she says, "While the South is hardly Christ-centered, it is most certainly Christ-haunted," referring to the religion ever-present in American Southern culture. From a paper read by O'Connor at Wesleyan College for Women, Autumn 1960 in Macon, Georgia and is reprinted in *Mystery and Manners*, 44.

5. Graham, *Theological Reflection*, 6.

6. Ibid., referring to Mudge and Poling, introduction to *Formation and Reflection*, xiv.

than a description of a current state of affairs. What will be presented in this chapter seeks to examine protective hospitality in such a way as to encourage dialogue and cooperative responsible action for the other.

To address what is present in the literature and the issues that were highlighted by the conversations mentioned above, this chapter is comprised of two parts. The first part will begin with three sections that lay the groundwork for the rest of the chapter, articulating the mechanics and conceptions of protective hospitality. The first section will detail the stages of protective hospitality based on the work of scholar Amy Oden. This will set the stage for an understanding that protective hospitality is not a singular, static event but is a nuanced and multi-staged movement. Furthermore, Oden helpfully illuminates the reality that protective hospitality, in and of itself, provides no guarantees for a positive outcome. The second section will consider the meaning and limitations of protection, with its particular emphasis upon preserving dignity and supporting human rights as an explicit act of social justice. The third section will identify several motivations in literature that arose out of Holocaust research as to why people practice protective hospitality by giving sanctuary to the threatened other. Such an understanding of motivation is important as it enables Abrahamic communities to emphasize and further develop the values and skills identified in order to inform the future practice of protective hospitality.

The second part of the chapter seeks to address the obstacles that hamper the practice of hospitality which were identified in the conversations held. This second part is also divided into three sections. The first section will address the issue of risk. It will begin with an analysis related to the formation and enforcement of boundaries as elements of protection as well as control and isolation, marking where boundaries are healthy and where they are a hindrance to the practice of protective hospitality. This examination of risk will continue by considering the elements of protective hospitality that require one to be open to encounters with the uninvited where there are no guarantees for a particular outcome. It will conclude with an assessment of an "ethic of risk" that informs responsible action, enabling one to enter into the practice of protective hospitality with awareness and a sense of empowerment. The second section will address the issue of purity and argues that concerns for individual, communal or moral purity are most often concerns about unity and control, whereas protective hospitality requires one to be open to outside "contaminants" in order to preserve life. The third and final section of this chapter will consider the intersection between protective hospitality and violence, emphasizing hospitality's concern for life, freedom from cruel relationship, openness to the influence of others, and affinity to the principles of nonviolence over the destructive elements of violence.

THE MECHANICS OF PROTECTIVE HOSPITALITY

There are three sections in the first half of this chapter that examine the mechanics of protective hospitality. The first analyzes Oden's definition of the stages of hospitality, considering specifically the provision of protection. The second examines the meaning and limitations of protection. Finally, the third section identifies motivations present within literature that explain why practitioners of protective hospitality acted as they did. As a result, this section seeks to provide a foundation for the construction of the remainder of the chapter as it considers the mechanics and conceptions of protective hospitality.

Stages of Protective Hospitality

Hospitality is often depicted as a singular, static, and often one-dimensional act, but as argued in Chapter Two it is much more nuanced and complex. Protective hospitality, like general hospitality, is practiced in stages. Christian historian and specialist in hospitality scholarship Amy Oden contends there are four stages in the practice of hospitality that help shape the process by which hospitality is extended, and these stages are particularly helpful in formulating the specific process of providing protective hospitality.[7]

Oden suggests the first stage is one that "encompasses a set of practices that welcome the guest," seen in the simple acts of "a warm greeting, words of welcome or an embrace, [or] even going out to greet the guest."[8] In light of the need for protective hospitality, Oden includes the "*offer* of sanctuary to an exile or fugitive" in this first stage of hospitality.[9]

The second stage of hospitality, according to Oden, involves acts of restoration whereby the host seeks to "restore the guest, usually by addressing the most immediate needs whether physical or spiritual or both" which might include "foot washing, bathing, feeding, clothing, and prayer."[10] Acts

7. Oden, *And You Welcomed Me*, 146–47. Oden references the *Didache* and early Christian writers such as Tertullian, Dionysius, Eusebius, Ambrose, Basil, Gregory of Nyssa, and John Chrysostom and Bede as examples of how the various stages of hospitality take shape and are practiced.

8. Oden, *And You Welcomed Me*, 146.

9. Ibid. Oden qualifies the first stage, however, by stating "the first movement of hospitality that initiates contact is not always an act of receiving. It may be expressed in the practice of visiting another, such as the sick or the hungry. In this case, hospitality is initiated by going to the other and, in a sense, receiving them, though it may be in their own homes or place of refuge, even the street . . ."

10. Ibid.

of restoration primarily concern the health and well-being of the guest.[11] In the practice of protective hospitality, the bringing or taking in of the threatened other to establish safety would be part of the second stage.

Oden identifies the third stage as the act of "dwelling together." This stage is a step further than the previous in that it is no longer the establishment of protection, but a sustained effort over the course of an amount of time. Oden emphasizes that in this stage there should be a "willingness to share one's life with the other" and acts in this stage could include "sharing lodging or shelter of some kind, providing protection or sanctuary, and sharing resources such as food, clothing, medical care, and alms."[12] Oden notes this stage may comprise of "practices that reframe social relations away from exploitation and toward dwelling together" in a different way than before.[13] As such, Oden calls this third stage "a hospitality of presence."[14]

The fourth and final stage is letting go or "sending forth" the guest,[15] when the need for protection is recognized by the host and guest as coming to an end. Oden describes this stage as entailing "release, letting go of the stranger or guest with whom one has dwelt" and includes the act of "burying the dead as an hospitable practice that can be categorized . . . as sending forth."[16] From a justice perspective, this stage implies the practice of hospitality "does not create systems of dependence, but empowers the other to move on" as hospitality is to be "offered with open hands, so one does not hang on to the other in order to justify one's continued hospitality."[17] In

11. It is here where the resonance between the practice of genuine hospitality and the practicality of life as seen in Maslow's hierarchy of needs is the most visible. Being hospitable requires sensitivity to the most pressing and basic, yet unfulfilled, needs of the stranger. However, in the context of threat, Maslow's physiological and safety needs may be interchangeable. In some cases, the need for safety will be paramount and will override even the basic need for food and drink. Another approach could be found in Judith Lewis Herman's *Trauma and Recovery*, chapter 8 (pp. 155–74), where she details the necessity for safety to be ensured before recovery from trauma can be considered: "Recovery unfolds in three stages . . . [and] the central task of the first stage is the establishment of safety" (ibid., 155).

12. Oden, *And You Welcomed Me*, 146–47.

13. Ibid., 147. Oden explains this by giving the following example: "the relationship of master to slave may be reoriented toward living in the awareness of a shared *imago dei*, or a wealthy person may divest themselves, reframing their social location so that they no longer help the poor but are the poor, dwelling together."

14. Ibid.

15. Ibid.

16. Ibid.

17. Ibid.

this final stage, Oden notes "blessing, giving food or other supplies for the journey, or giving companions for escort" would be offered.[18]

However, Oden identifies further significance to this final stage of hospitality by stating:

> The act of release includes letting go of the outcome of the practices of hospitality . . . [as] the practices of hospitality are independent of their outcomes. One lives hospitably without any guarantee of a payoff. The sick person may die, the stranger may misuse the resources shared, the hospitality offered may not be honored. Desire for a particular consequence of hospitality must be released.[19]

In light of Oden's assertion that the means of hospitality should be differentiated from its end, a positive outcome from hospitality cannot be guaranteed. It is this lack of guarantee, this possibility for risk, failure, or endangerment that dissuades many from extending protective hospitality to the threatened other in favor of one's own safety, control and, ultimately, isolation in what might be particularly hostile times. Nevertheless, in the ensuing discussion related to protective hospitality, a realistic awareness of this absence of guarantee for a positive outcome is necessary.

Protection: Meaning and Limitations

While chapter two focused on the various meanings and limitations of hospitality, attention should also be paid as well to the meaning and limitations of protection as the focus shifts toward protective hospitality. The origin of the word is Latin, *protegere*, which means "to cover in front" or "to cover over."[20] As a transitive verb, it is defined as "to shield from injury or harm," or "to secure or preserve against encroachment, infringement, restriction, or violation; maintain the status or integrity of" and carries with it heavy usage within legal vocabularies.[21]

18. Ibid. In the provision of escort, the continued provision of protection or assurance of safety is still being given. Ancient expressions of hospitality took this stage seriously, as guests would be escorted to the city gate to ensure that they were safe as possible within the realm of the host's domain. See Gen 18:16 as an example where Abraham escorted the divine messengers from his home and to the boundaries of his domain.

19. Oden, *And You Welcomed Me*, 146–47.

20. From *pro-* (front) and *tegere* (to cover). See "Protect," Merriam-Webster's Dictionary of Law, http://www.merriam-webster.com/dictionary/protect.

21. "Protect," Merriam-Webster's Dictionary of Law. Merriam-Webster's also notes its usage in other contexts: "In a gangster sense, 'freedom from molestation in exchange

"To shield" or "to secure or preserve" from violation and to "maintain . . . integrity" all point to protection as being an inherently exclusive action in that something (a person, place, species, etc.) is set aside, blocked off, guarded, or placed somewhere where it cannot be corrupted, injured, or harmed. Meanwhile, hospitality has been popularly portrayed, as examined in previous chapters, as an action that is inherently inclusive. Therefore, would not these seemingly opposed ideas make the term "protective hospitality" an oxymoron?

On the surface level, perhaps, it is. But as has also been discussed in previous chapters and will be explored here more fully, the meaning and practice of hospitality is full of tensions. One of those tensions is the idea that hospitality is only hospitality within a particular set of defining boundaries, such as via place given, actions taken, manners shown, people present, or a myriad of other factors. The same is true for protective hospitality, with simply more overt emphasis placed upon those boundaries and, as being put forward here, the ethical obligations that those within the Abrahamic traditions have to shield and secure the threatened other.

Pohl's inclusion of the provision of protection and shelter in the discussion of hospitality is useful to this discussion. The inclusion of protection is automatic, in that her definition of hospitality "involves sharing food, shelter, protection, recognition, and conversation."[22] She mentions the Israelite laws regarding providing protection for strangers and resident aliens,[23] but also brings attention to the practices in the early church protecting the community's hospitality from abuse, detailing parameters set into place in order to make its long-term practice sustainable.[24] Additionally, Pohl later connects the practice of hospitality with the changes in language from the Reformation era, noting "concerns about respecting and protecting strangers that had originally been articulated in the language of hospitality were recast as concerns about human rights."[25]

---

for money' . . . is attested from 1860. Ecological sense of 'attempted preservation by laws' is from 1880 (originally of wild birds in Britain). Protectionist in the economics sense is first recorded in 1844, from French *protectionniste* (in political economy sense, protection is attested from 1789)."

22. Pohl, "Building a Place for Hospitality," 27.

23. Ibid., 28. The laws that deal with the cities of refuge will be discussed in more detail later in this chapter.

24. Ibid., 29.

25. Ibid., 32. Perhaps the shift in language of hospitality which precipitated the movement away from honor as noted in the chapter previous is in some way connected to this shift toward human rights language. In human rights discourse, it is much more common to hear the word "dignity" rather than honor.

It is this evolution toward human rights language that, perhaps, makes those who are more unfamiliar with theological language see the practical aspects of hospitality, particularly when one considers its role in contexts of conflict. The implications of hospitality for protecting the threatened other are seen in a statement by Darrell Guder, a Christian theologian who focuses on the role of the church in contemporary society. He asserts the practice of hospitality by the faithful is a participation in the peaceable kindom of God and such a practice "indicates the crossing of boundaries (ethnic origin, economic condition, political orientation, gender status, social experience, educational background) by being open and welcoming of the other."[26] Without this example of crossing boundaries through the practice of hospitality, Guder continues, "the world will have no way of knowing that all God's creation is meant to live in peace."[27] Such an assertion is particularly true in the provision of protective hospitality.

Similarly, Leonardo Boff claims those who are concerned about and work for justice for the poor and excluded are practicing a modernization of the Abrahamic "legacy of covenant and hospitality" which is not meant to be a "paternalistic attitude of being there *for* the other; it rather . . . [is] being *with* the other, and whenever possible . . . living *as* the other."[28] Moreover, in focusing upon the needs of others, the practice of hospitality will inevitably bring one into contact with social injustices and challenge the practitioner to look for ways to work towards the good of all creation, including the good of one's guest.[29] It is in this aspect of placing oneself in another's shoes, living in solidarity with the other, and committing oneself to the practice of crossing boundaries and welcoming the threatened other that protective hospitality resides.

Nouwen highlights the connection between hospitality and sanctuary by emphasizing the Latin roots depicting a movement from "*hostis* to *hospes*," noting there is desperate need for safe, nurturing spaces where people can live lives free from fear and hostility, and where transformation from enemy to guest can take place.[30] While he does limit the discussion of hospitality and creating space around more spiritual, mental, and emotional realms and does not include the physical dimension as well, he does make important links between the need of space for cultural and language recog-

26. Guder, *Missional Church*, 177.

27. Ibid.

28. Boff, *Virtues*, 83. Boff specifies Judeo-Christian rather than Abrahamic in his assertion, yet there is no reason why Islam cannot be included in his idea.

29. Bass, "A Guide to Exploring Christian Practices."

30. Nouwen, *Reaching Out*, 46. The discussion of *hostis* vs. *hospes* is dealt with more thoroughly in chapter 2.

nition, where freedom is given to strangers to "sing their own songs, speak their own languages, [and] dance their own dances."[31]

Furthermore, in the practice of protective hospitality, particularly among Abrahamic traditions, the one who is welcomed "is consistently defined as someone who lacks any resources to support themselves . . . who lacks a 'place' in society because they are detached or excluded from the basic means of supporting and sustaining life—family, work, polity, land and so on—and are thus vulnerable."[32] Similar to Nouwen's emphasis upon recognition, this emphasis upon supporting the place of the vulnerable and excluded in a society carries significant political weight and, therefore, highlights the political potential of protective hospitality.

Yet, ethicist Alasdair MacIntyre adds another dimension to protective hospitality that combines both its political nature and its capacity to contribute to communal health. While MacIntyre sees hospitality "as a universal practice . . . central to the proper functioning of any society,"[33] he argues it is grounded in the "virtue of *misericordia*," defined as "the capacity for grief or sorrow over someone else's distress just insofar as one understands the other's distress as one's own . . . [or] an aspect of charity whereby we supply what is needed by our neighbour."[34] Bretherton takes this further and considers the implications of *misericordia*, acknowledging its practice in conjunction with hospitality "directs one to include the stranger within one's communal relationships" which extends "the bounds of one's communal obligations, and thereby including the other in one's relations of giving and receiving characterized by just generosity."[35] Such understandings provide the foundations for the practice and provision of protective hospitality.

In all of these ways in which hospitality is discussed, it is clear that provision of safety, refuge or space in which the threatened other can live, and hopefully thrive, is an act of justice but also an act of hospitality. As a result, protective hospitality is uniquely placed, with this particular emphasis upon dignity and human rights, as an act of social justice.

31. Ibid., 51. It is unclear by this text if Nouwen is aware of Paul Ricoeur's work on the politics of recognition, yet this statement would resonate with Ricoeur's assertions that recognition is a moral exercise. See Ricoeur, *Course of Recognition*. Ricoeur's work is explored more closely in chapter 2.

32. Bretherton, *Hospitality as Holiness*, 139. Bretherton uses this definition of stranger to explain who is a stranger in the Christian tradition because he has limited his research to this particular community. Nevertheless, his concept of a stranger would not be foreign to the Jewish and Islamic understandings either and, therefore, I have taken the liberty to broaden it. See also Gopin, "The Heart of the Stranger," 3–21.

33. MacIntyre, *Dependent Rational Animals*, 123.

34. Ibid., 125.

35. Bretherton, *Hospitality as Holiness*, 127.

Motivations for Protective Hospitality

Chapter Three considered the variety of motivations for providing hospitality based upon the work of Andrew Arterbury and Ladislaus Bolchazy. Similarly, this chapter considers the variety of motivations that lead people to put themselves at risk and provide protective hospitality for the threatened other.

Are some more prone to provide protective hospitality than others? While I wish to highlight the theological and ethical resources in the Abrahamic traditions that can inform the practice of protective hospitality, wider inclusion of research in the area of altruism and the typology of rescuers is useful. Understanding what motivates people to act in solidarity with the threatened other can help Abrahamic communities emphasize and further develop the values and skills to inform the practice of protective hospitality.

David Gushee, a Christian ethicist, considered the motivations of rescuers during the Holocaust, surveying the work of altruism researchers, sociologists, and others who were interested in the actions of those who risked their lives to give safe harbor to Jews during World War II.[36]

In his research, Gushee collated the various motivations found in the sociological studies done upon rescuers, and identified seven main motivations as to why some people decided to risk themselves for the other. He lists them as follows: moral obligation, inclination toward inclusivity, religious affiliation, social responsibility and empathy, resistance and solidarity, special kinship with other Abrahamic peoples, and remembered experiences of persecution.

1. *Moral Obligation*: This motivation for protection and rescue assumes that those threatened are "within the boundaries of moral obligation" wherein the host acts on "the conviction that it [is] morally obligatory to invite the stranger within the reach of human care, even though doing so might cost . . . everything."[37] Furthermore, those who act with this motivation refuse to allow government bodies or abusive systems to define the threatened other "as outside the boundaries of moral obligation."[38]
2. *Inclined toward Inclusivity*: For those who are willing to put themselves in harm's way to protect the other, "*tolerance* appears steadily, though

36. See especially Gushee, *Righteous Gentiles*. Gushee's findings are relevant here because they are also applicable in the more contemporary setting of protective hospitality among the Abrahamic traditions, despite his own research parameters.

37. Gushee, *Righteous Gentiles*, 113.

38. Ibid., 134.

not universally . . . [as] values learned in childhood" by those who provide protective hospitality.[39] They may have been taught altruism and inclusion, assessing people "as individuals rather than as group members" and having "'a predisposition to regard all people as equals and to apply similar standards of right and wrong to them without regard to their social status or ethnicity.'"[40]

3. *Religious Affiliation*: In the research on those who were rescuers, there does not appear to be any differentiation between those who were religious and those who were not.[41] Additionally, religious commitment in those who provided hospitality as opposed to those who did not were similar, as approximately "70% of both groups described themselves as 'very' or 'somewhat' religious."[42] Gushee notes, however, that the majority of those who professed to be religious were rescuers, while a majority of those who professed to be "not at all religious" were also found to be rescuers, indicating "rescuers may have had stronger convictions about religion, positive or negative, than nonrescuers did."[43]

4. *Social Responsibility and Empathy*: Gushee refers to tests conducted by Oliner and Oliner that "offered stronger and more systematic evidence concerning rescuer personality traits," and found rescuers "scored higher than nonrescuers on the Social Responsibility Scale, a measure assessing the individual's sense of responsibility toward other people and sense of duty to contribute to the well-being of others and the

39. Ibid., 120.

40. Ibid., quoting and referring to the work of Oliner and Oliner, *The Altruistic Personality*, 149–51. Gushee also references Fogelman's *Conscience and Courage*, 259–60, noting her statement that tolerance was "taught to 88 percent of her sample of rescuers," and cites Fleischner, who noted "some rescuers 'reacted against their [intolerant] family background,' drawing upon other resources." See also Fleischner, "Can Few Become the Many?," 242.

41. Gushee, *Righteous Gentiles*, 126.

42. Ibid., 126–27.

43. Ibid. This point is extremely important. Detractors of religion and religiously motivated ethics would point to the lack of differentiation between rescuers and nonrescuers by religious factor as evidence that religion plays no role in the decision to provide protective hospitality. As protective hospitality is not the domain of only religious individuals or communities, such a statement might be true in some cases. However, the findings Gushee notes imply the strength of conviction for or against religion still plays a role in a majority of the findings' samples, and, therefore, should not be dismissed.

community."[44] The individuals also scored higher "on the Empathy Scale . . . [which measures one's] responsiveness to other's *pain*."[45]

5. *Resistance and Solidarity*: Similar to concepts of moral obligation, those who were motivated toward protective hospitality in the studies refused to allow others to define for them who was in and who was out.[46] Instead they were more practiced in the "habits of political resistance and solidarity" wherein those "with relatively more power and freedom stand with those who are most threatened, working in partnership . . . for survival and ultimately in liberation."[47]

6. *Special kinship with other Abrahamic peoples*: The research to which Gushee refers found the motivation for protective hospitality among many Christians was their "strong sense of religious kinship with Jews as a people."[48] Nevertheless, such kinship should not be restricted to the Judeo-Christian relationship, but broadened to the Abrahamic family as a whole. While the research on Muslim rescuers may not be present in Gushee's work, such a restriction is short-sighted as it does not take into account the Muslims who protected Jews during that period as well.[49] Furthermore, to date there has not been any significant research conducted in contexts such as Israel/Palestine where the situation is somewhat reversed and Jewish individuals are now working to protect Palestinian Muslims, and often refer to this idea of kinship.[50]

7. *Remembered Experience of Persecution*: Lastly, the experience of minority communities who remembered their own experiences of discrimination historically was also a motivator for protective hospitality. The French Huguenot community of Le Chambon relied heavily on its past experiences of persecution. Similarly, the small

44. Ibid., 132, referencing Oliner and Oliner, *The Altruistic Personality*, 173–74.

45. Ibid., referencing Oliner and Oliner, *The Altruistic Personality*, 173–74.

46. Gushee, *Righteous Gentiles*, 134.

47. Ibid., 141–42.

48. Ibid., 152.

49. The emergence of the activities of Muslims during the Holocaust seems to have only really become present in mainstream Holocaust scholarship in the last decade. For more information on these stories and motivations, see Hellman, *When Courage Was Stronger Than Fear*; and Satloff, *Among the Righteous*.

50. However, various organizations operating in Israel/Palestine began on the Israeli side and find their work based in ideas of kinship and shared humanity. See Women in Black (http://www.womeninblack.org/), Rabbis for Human Rights (http://rhr.org.il/eng/), and Israeli Committee Against Housing Demolition (http://icahd.org/), among others.

Baptist community in Lithuania and Western Ukraine likewise utilized their history of persecution to identify with and provide protection for the threatened other in the context of the Holocaust.[51]

From Gushee's research, one can see that religious belief is not the sole determiner of decisions to provide protective hospitality for the threatened other. A variety of factors inform the practice, and Gushee's work shows there were a significant number of religious individuals who *did not* protect. Rather than interpret this negatively toward religion, however, it presents adherents of the Abrahamic traditions with an opportunity. This work highlights each of these motivations—moral obligation, inclusive values, religious affiliation, social responsibility and empathy, resistance and solidarity, special kinship, and remembered experiences of persecution—as part and parcel of the Abrahamic theology and practice of protective hospitality. Some motivations have been already mentioned and others will be considered in more detail in the following chapters. Each of these motivations are present in the Abrahamic traditions and might be able to contribute to a cooperative theology which supports the practice of protective hospitality among the Abrahamic communities in response to situations where the threatened other is in need of refuge.

EMBRACING RISK: BOUNDARIES, PURITY, AND VIOLENCE IN THE PRACTICE OF PROTECTIVE HOSPITALITY

In the following sections, an analysis of risk as it pertains to the provision of protective hospitality will be considered. Within the area of risk, more focused analyses on the issues of place and boundaries and the tension between the invited and uninvited aspects of hospitality will be considered. Building upon those considerations, an examination of purity and its role in serving to discourage encounter with the other will be conducted, followed by an assessment of the relationship between protective hospitality and violence. This section on violence will specifically consider the contribution of Christian theologian Hans Boersma and the arguments related to nonviolence in the provision of protective hospitality.

51. Gushee, *Righteous Gentiles*, 159–60.

Risk

The fact that risk is involved in the provision of protective hospitality is undisputed. When protective hospitality is discussed, risks including harm to oneself, family, home or community and/or a perceived or real negative impact upon one's reputation, social or political standing, or economic well-being are usually also considered. Understandably, the fear of these risks, along with the risks to purity to be discussed in more detail later, is the primary impediment to the practice of protective hospitality. Therefore, if the practice is to be examined in detail, an analysis of the risk involved and how it can be dealt with is necessary.

When faced with any decision, most individuals or communities analyze the risk of acting upon that decision.[52] Risk is defined as "the possibility of incurring misfortune or loss,"[53] and when faced with the decision to provide protective hospitality for a threatened—or "at risk"—other, there is an understanding that the threats which endanger the other may also threaten the one who gives her/him safe harbor. Pohl notes an awareness of such risks:

> Hospitable households, cities of refuge, the underground railroad, and the sanctuary tradition have sometimes made the difference between life and death for those fleeing danger. In its resistance to the dominant powers, this kind of hospitality has cost some hosts their lives.[54]

As mentioned previously, it is impossible to practice genuine hospitality and avoid all risk, or as one author puts it, when it comes to hospitality, "[t]here are no guarantees."[55] Nevertheless, it is natural to avert risk whenever possible. It is natural to want to reduce or eliminate risk altogether, often with the understanding that "the loss of anything of value is loss that [one]

52. See Douglas, *Risk Acceptability*. Primarily comprised of literature review, Douglas analyzes the relationship between risk perception, risk analysis, risk acceptability, social justice, and morality, looking at a variety of risks found in life including gambling, insurance, building property within the reach of natural disaster potential, health decisions, and so on. It becomes obvious that every aspect of life carries with it some sort of risk, and therefore, life itself is risk management. Furthermore, even Jesus talked about counting the cost, particularly in relation to becoming his follower. See Matt 8:18–22; Luke 9:57–62; 14:25–34.

53. "Risk," *Collins English Dictionary—Complete and Unabridged 10th Edition*. http://dictionary.reference.com/browse/risk.

54. Pohl, *Making Room*, 64.

55. Reynolds, "Improvising Together," 59.

cannot accept."[56] Theologian Miroslav Volf argues "security is important . . . because of our vulnerability."[57] As hospitality is practiced, boundaries become more transparent and "the host is made vulnerable and dependent"[58] upon the goodwill of the stranger he/she protects and, in many ways, the systems or actors under whose threat the guest flees.

Nevertheless, life consists of a series of risks, and according to Volf, "[t]o be human is to be vulnerable" and "[v]ulnerability is the essential condition of human life."[59] Life with others—in effect, a society—is equally full of risks. To avoid risk and vulnerability is to avoid life, and to vigilantly assess risk and vulnerability at the cost of the threatened other is to create an idol of one's own false sense of security. In light of the risks involved in the provision of protective hospitality and its various implications with regards to politics and solidarity, scholar Charles Fried declares that rather than "asking how much risk is acceptable . . . the general question would be what kind of society do you want?"[60]

Place and Boundaries

As hospitality is always given in a specific context—in a home, a community, a city, a nation—the issue of place and its role in the provision of hospitality, particularly protective hospitality, should be analyzed. Since place is defined by boundaries, as in what is *here* and what is *there*, the concepts of place and boundaries are inextricably linked.

Philosopher Claire Elise Katz notes "it is the home that makes the ethical possible."[61] With such a provocative statement, defining what home means and how it determines ethical behavior and morality is necessary. "House" implies a physical structure, a tactile arrangement of materials that provides at least a modicum of shelter from the natural elements. Comparatively, "home" can refer to that same physical structure, or a particular community, a nation, but the defining factor is its impact on the emotions and self-identification of the one who calls the particular place "home."

56. Volf, "How safe can we be?," 66.

57. Ibid.

58. Reynolds, "Improvising Together," 59.

59. Volf, "How Safe Can We Be?," 66.

60. Douglas, *Risk Acceptability*, 14–15, quoting the Kantian "moral theory based on risk" work of Charles Fried, *Anatomy of Values*.

61. Katz, *Levinas, Judaism and the Feminine*, 59. Her statement is given in the context of thoughts from the Talmud and interpretations by Emmanuel Levinas, who asserts that the final chapter of Proverbs, wherein the ideal woman and her home is described, is "a moral paradigm."

Additionally, Derrida asserts that to welcome "is perhaps to insinuate that one is at home here, that one knows what it means to be at home, and that at home one receives, invites, or offers hospitality."[62] Obviously, Derrida argues, one welcomes others into a place where one feels at home, a place that affirms one's identity.

Therefore, since home plays a defining role in the development and definition of one's self-identification, a return to the concept of the practice of hospitality as "an act that constitutes identity"[63] is necessary in order to help address issues that arise in the consideration of home. While it has been noted previously, this particular emphasis upon home is enhanced by McNulty's discussion of home as it relates to identity and place:

> [Hospitality] is the act through which the home—and the homeland—constitutes itself in the gesture of turning to address its outside. But as an accidental encounter with what can be neither foreseen nor named, hospitality also insists on the primacy of immanent relations over identity. Hence, it both allows for the constitution of identity and challenges it, by suggesting that the home can also become unhomely, *unheimlich*, estranged by the introduction of something foreign that threatens to contaminate or dissolve its identity.[64]

McNulty's assertion that the home is the place where hospitality is given and identity is constructed, and, as a result, where hospitality carries with it risks to the home's purity, is revealing.[65] However, the issue of place and home as the hub of hospitality first requires expansion. Pohl defines hospitable places as "comfortable and lived in . . . settings in which people are flourishing . . . [where] the people that inhabit them [are given] shelter and sanctuary in the deepest sense of these words," and, therefore, she notes shelter and protective hospitality are not limited to physical place but also present in people and "the shelter of relationships."[66]

62. Derrida, *Adieu to Emmanuel Levinas*, 15.

63. McNulty, *The Hostess*, viii.

64. Ibid.

65. The issue of purity will be discussed in a following section.

66. Pohl, *Making Room*, 152. Elie Wiesel makes a similar statement, related to refuge being found in persons, saying each person is a sanctuary that no one has the right to invade ("The Refugee," 387). This sentiment of protective hospitality based in persons and relationships rather than in specific locales can be seen in the work of Christian Peacemaker Teams (CPT), the Ecumenical Accompaniment Programme in Palestine and Israel (EAPPI), and others who do not work out of physical locations, but who work to be centers of hospitality in inhospitable contexts (border crossings, checkpoints, and other locations where the threatened other is at risk), bearing witness

Yet, since a physical home, in the sense of a house, community, or nation is defined by what is within its boundaries, it stands to reason that boundaries are, therefore, important.[67] Boundaries provide the criteria by which identity is formed, belonging is established, and health and safety are maintained. They are the realm in which normative aspects of life are conducted. Boundaries are also necessary if one seeks to provide protective hospitality to the threatened other, as those under threat often "come from living in chronic states of fear" and are in need of a safe place "to relax, heal, and reconstruct their lives."[68]

Furthermore, if hospitality is to be considered "an utter openness," then the concept of home becomes empty, lacking commitment and without identity.[69] When practiced unreservedly by "allowing itself to be 'swept by the coming of the wholly other, the absolutely unforeseeable stranger'"[70] and without boundaries, it allows the other the potential to become "so radically overpowering and incommensurate that it ruptures all . . . mediation, receding into an indiscernible and anonymous horizon, making [one] in principle responsible for all, even for the one who would destroy."[71] In such a context, there is no common space for reciprocity, and "the result is an evaporation of . . . vitality."[72] In turn, this form of hospitality lacks protection for those who are under threat. Likewise, without boundaries, there is simply "nothing to which we can invite or welcome anyone else."[73]

On a theological level, rabbi and conflict transformation scholar Marc Gopin argues Abraham's model in monotheistic religion illustrates that the love of God, who is "the quintessential stranger to this world," requires adherents to understand boundaries that perpetuate the Otherness of God.[74] Gopin contends that if the boundary to God's otherness is transgressed, and God is invited "too far inside," one ends up "worshipping something else—not God, but ourselves quite often, or a piece of land"; however, if one does

to injustice and attempting to provide safety through the use of their own bodies and physical presence. For more information on the work of the these groups, see Boardman, *Taking a Stand*; Brown, *Getting in the Way*; Müller, *The Balkan Peace Team*; Clark, *People Power*; Kern, *In Harm's Way;* and Kern, *As Resident Aliens.*

67. For a more focused but less academic discussion of boundaries and hospitality, see Westerhoff, *Good Fences,* which addresses the issue for Christian churches as they negotiate issues of inclusivity, identity and hospitality.

68. Pohl, *Making Room*, 140.

69. Reynolds, "Improvising Together," 63.

70. Derrida, *Acts of Religion*, 362–63.

71. Reynolds, "Improvising Together," 63.

72. Ibid.

73. Westerhoff, *Good Fences*, 7.

74. Gopin, "The Heart of the Stranger," 8.

not "open the door to this extraordinary Stranger then we risk an existence bereft of meaning, [and] of spiritual and emotional depth."[75]

Yet, Reynolds notes boundaries that establish "too much rigidity in communal formation can suffocate grace and undermine protective hospitality, negating difference by creating constrictive mechanisms of exclusion and violence."[76] The issue of communal identity formation and preservation through the enforcement of strict boundaries has, at times, caused the respective Abrahamic communities to choose "self-protective and inwardly turned solidarity over care and concern for others not shaped in its own image."[77] Such actions to preserve identity, particularly when motivated by fear of the unknown,[78] "tempts a community to feign security by claiming certainty over and against others who are seen as threats" and if these temptations are succumbed to, hospitality is traded "for an alleged possession of 'the' truth" which, in turn, "obstructs the cultivation of moral characteristics, such as humility, justice, courage, and, ironically, truthfulness."[79]

Richard Beck, a Christian professor of psychology, argues the psychotherapeutic community has "fetishized" the concept of interpersonal boundaries, which has exhibited itself in unhealthy ways in relation to hospitality.[80] More specifically, Beck asserts the concept of boundaries arise in a psychotherapeutic sense from "concerns about unhealthy boundaries, enmeshment, victimhood, and dependency" which are rooted in "a morbid situation" where "relationships are often found to be diseased, dysfunctional, or maladaptive."[81] Boundaries, for Beck, are indications that the

75. Ibid.

76. Reynolds, "Improvising Together," 63.

77. Ibid.

78. Fear of the unknown could also be a motivation, considering how Abrahamic communities remember what has been done to each other over the centuries.

79. Ibid.

80. Beck, *Unclean*, 126–28. Beck notes:

> The psychotherapeutic community has tended to fetishize the notion of boundaries. And in this fetishization of boundaries, the psychotherapeutic community has, perhaps unwittingly . . . incorporated some of the most toxic aspects of modernity into their views of mental and spiritual health . . . The modern view of the self . . . is characterized by what Charles Taylor has called the 'buffered self.' [referencing Taylor's book, *A Secular Age*] . . . the modern notion of selfhood became introverted and individualistic, the self as isolated and distinct ('buffered') from the world. The notion of a self-determined, isolated, autonomous ego is a ubiquitous feature in modernity. The buffered self is a critical feature in how we moderns view our social contract, politically and economically.

81. Ibid., 127.

"mutuality of love has been lost" and are necessary for those with a "morbid self-concept [wherein] the individual allows the other to 'use and abuse' them."[82] Beck goes further by noting when boundaries are necessary, love has failed in some way as one is "actively hurting" another.[83] As a result, when boundaries are used, they are used "as a form of *protection*" from further harm.[84]

In Beck's opinion, the issue with boundaries as it relates to the general practice of hospitality is that boundaries are being discussed and applied when there is no real reason for them to be put in place.[85] Beck understands that in cases of abuse or danger, boundaries that ensure safety are essential. Yet, within the realm of hospitable life, which Beck asserts should be characterized by love, boundaries often keep one disengaged from others and can be poisonous and antithetical to the practice of hospitality. Interestingly, Beck compares acts of what could be considered "protective hospitality"[86] to the love in healthy family relationships, by detailing how "love [of] the self and the other become so identified, emotionally and symbolically, that the two form a union, an identification, a fusion."[87] While such a relationship "might seem like the very definition of enmeshment," in actuality, he asserts, "this description of love describes how most of us . . . experience love."[88] He goes on to state:

> What parent, if faced with the choice, wouldn't sacrifice the use of his or her right arm to save their child? Or even give their very life? The point is that the safety and well-being of the child is more important than the parent's own physical body. This, after all, is what we mean by sacrificial love: the loss of the self (e.g., one's own life or situation in the world) for the sake of the other . . . . In all of this we see how our notions of selfhood become intertwined and fused with the other to the point where *the well-being of the other is how I define my selfhood*![89]

82. Ibid.

83. Ibid.

84. Ibid. (italics are in the original text).

85. In a situation where protective hospitality is being given, boundaries to protect the threatened other from the abuser, however, would be an exception to Beck's assertion. Beck is challenging the status quo of those communities who find themselves safe and comfortable, unchallenged by the other or the need to act on behalf of justice for the other because of self-protective boundaries.

86. Beck never names it as such.

87. Beck, *Unclean*, 126.

88. Ibid.

89. Ibid.

Archbishop Desmond Tutu's ubuntu theology of South Africa concurs with the idea that one's identity is defined by the well-being of others:

> A person is a person through other persons . . . A person with *ubuntu* is open and available to others, affirming of others, does not feel threatened that others are able and good, for he or she has a proper self-assurance that comes from knowing that he or she belongs in a greater whole and is diminished when others are humiliated or diminished, when others are tortured or oppressed, or treated as if they were less than who they are.[90]

In this way, we, as members of the human race, have the "responsibility to welcome endangered persons into [our] lives . . . and communities" when their "basic well-being is under attack by the larger society."[91] Those attacks, related to the definition and violation of boundaries, are borne out of "dynamics of disgust and dehumanization [which] foster exclusion and expulsion."[92] Conversely, the practice of protective hospitality welcomes into safety "the outcast and stranger as a full member of the human community . . . expand[ing] the moral circle, to push back against the innate impulse" in human communities that assumes "humanity ends at the border of the tribe."[93]

While self-identification is a natural part of human existence, Pohl asserts "when, by acknowledging difference, we only endanger," we are obligated to forgo boundaries and "only acknowledge our common human identity."[94] To address this, Pohl calls for "a constant, complex interaction between identity-defining, bounded communities and a larger community with minimal boundaries that offers basic protection for individuals."[95]

90. Tutu, *No Future without Forgiveness*, 31. See also Battle, *Reconciliation;* and Paul, *The Ubuntu God.*

91. Pohl, *Making Room*, 82–83.

92. Beck, *Unclean*, 124.

93. Ibid. André Trocmé of Le Chambon was asked by the police to turn over the Jews they were hiding, and he was noted to have said, "We do not know what a Jew is. We only know men" (Pohl, *Making Room*, 82–83). Additionally Gopin notes the portrayal of God's "singling out" Abraham as well as Abraham's petition on behalf of Sodom in Gen 18, noting the "act of singling out and making promises to a particular clan are clear evidence of the valuation of boundaries" as it details that "out of a place of *particularity*, of being a sojourner who nevertheless crosses boundaries with a universal concern . . . Abraham presents an ideal model of engagement with the world, without consuming that world or allowing it to consume him." Gopin argues further that relation "becomes possible without violence, while the spiritual mission of interrelationship is not only maintained but is realised on a far deeper level than would be thought possible" ("The Heart of the Stranger," 13).

94. Pohl, *Making Room*, 82–83.

95. Ibid.

Invited and Uninvited

In popular terms, hospitality is often spoken of as always being ready for a guest. Yet philosopher Jacques Derrida questions this assumption. He asserts that while hospitality is certainly about catering to the needs of the invited guest, it conversely requires an aspect of the unexpected or uninvited as well. In fact, Derrida describes hospitality as something that "consists in welcoming the other that does not warn me of his coming."[96] John Caputo adds to Derrida's argument by declaring that if an invitation "is a selection process whereby one puts in place in advance a set of prior conditions under which the hospitality will be exercised," then "the most radical or unconditional hospitality [would] be a hospitality without invitation" of the other.[97] Such a discussion of the invited guest as opposed to the uninvited guest is appropriate since the experience of protective hospitality is very often accompanied by this reality of surprise and a call for immediate action.

Caputo relies upon the work of Derrida and states Derrida draws distinctions "between invitation and visitation" of the other in that "hospitality by invitation is always conditional, a compromised and programmed operation, as opposed to hospitality to the uninvited other—who pays us an unexpected visit—which is unconditional and unprogrammed."[98] For Derrida, hospitality "presupposes waiting, the horizon of awaiting and the preparation of welcoming."[99] Nevertheless, hospitality's relationship with risk comes with Derrida's assertion that it also presupposes letting "oneself to be overtaken, *to be ready to not be ready*, if such is possible, to let oneself be overtaken, to not even *let* oneself be overtaken, to be surprised, in a fashion almost violent, violated and raped [*violée*], stolen [*volée*] . . . precisely where one is not ready to receive."[100] Particularly in the context of protective hospitality, this tension exists between being prepared to act on behalf of the threatened other and never truly being prepared for whatever situations may arise that require the provision of sanctuary. Derrida illuminates the

96. Derrida, *Acts of Religion*, 381.

97. Caputo, *What Would Jesus Deconstruct?*, 76.

98. Ibid. Yet, one must ask, without invitation or some other general public declaration that hospitality is available, how will the "uninvited" know to come, that such a place to come is even available? Does there need to be a culture of invitation rather than an explicit "please come to my house" invitation? Furthermore, such a discussion begs the questions: Does the practice of hospitality assume a total eradication of social convention? Are there not still some behaviors common to all that express both need for hospitality and an invitation to hospitality?

99. Derrida, *Acts of Religion*, 361.

100. Ibid. Derrida goes further by saying it is "not only *not yet ready* but *not ready, unprepared* in a mode that is not even that of the 'not yet.'"

potential for danger in the practice of protective hospitality, and he explains it by noting that "[i]f I welcome only what I welcome, what I am ready to welcome, and that I recognize in advance because I expect the coming of the hôte as invited, there is no hospitality."[101] While this potential for danger exists in the general practice of hospitality, its potential is all the greater in the provision of protective hospitality since its practice is often conducted at great risk to the practioners as well as the threatened other.

Nevertheless, Derrida differentiates between "absolute hospitality" and "conditional hospitality."[102] Absolute hospitality "cannot depend on the 'invitation,' over which 'we' regain control . . . but must be beholden to the 'visitation'" of the unexpected guest, where the host must be "prepared to be unprepared, for the unexpected arrival of *any* other."[103] In comparison, conditional hospitality is "structured by the economy of exchange," of reciprocity and "the logic of gratitude," depending in many ways on the conventions of place and time."[104]

Given the risk involved, Derrida's dichotomy between absolute hospitality and conditional hospitality has implications for the Abrahamic traditions. Derrida contends absolute hospitality is veritably "impracticable" as it would require the host to "submit to . . . dispossession, [and] to realize [one's] identity as a host at the cost of risking everything that defines one as master" of one's own self.[105] Nevertheless, this willingness to submit to dispossession is often considered a marker of devout religious life and experience as one is continually called upon in the Abrahamic texts to submit to God. Therefore, "the privileged representative of . . . absolute hospitality—the patriarch Abraham,"[106] after whom the Abrahamic tradition follows, lends authority to and provides a model for protective hospitality.[107]

101. Ibid., 362. The assessment of risk in relation to the threats Derrida mentions will be dealt with in the following section.

102. Kearney and Dooley, *Questioning Ethics*, 70, in Yong, *Hospitality and the Other*, 120–21.

103. Ibid. (italics in original).

104. Ibid.

105. McNulty, *The Hostess*, xx.

106. Ibid., xx–xxi.

107. Abraham's own dispossession of homeland and life as he knew it as claimed in Genesis 12 is referenced in the Abrahamic traditions that dispossession and submission in service or obedience to God is part and parcel of the faithful life. However, as with anything, the nature of the dispossession and to whom it is credited, as opposed to who actually does the dispossessing, requires identification. I would argue a relationship characterized by religious and emotional abuse that dispossesses the abused in the name of God is not of God. Therefore, wisdom and discernment must be utilized.

Caputo also asks a few important questions, in the spirit of Derrida and his definition of absolute hospitality, particularly in relation to this issue of danger and tension between hospitality for the invited versus the uninvited:

> But what is to say that I will not be murdered in my bed by all this hospitality? How am I to distinguish between the guest and the outright enemy, who will do me and mine the worst violence? Am I not duty bound to protect myself and my family from such violence?[108]

Caputo notes his answer to these questions is found in Derrida's validation and surmises "there would never be any way in principle to eliminate all the risk and still preserve the ideal of hospitality."[109]

The practice of protective hospitality is situated not in the avoidance of risk, but instead in considering how risks should be encountered and managed with and on behalf of the threatened other. In the context of protective hospitality, avoidance of risk is rooted in an "ethic of control" wherein "agency, responsibility and goodness . . . [are] a particular construction of *responsibility*" on the assumption that "it is possible to guarantee the efficacy of one's actions."[110] An "ethic of risk," on the other hand, is "an alternative construction of *responsible action*"[111] wherein risk is understood as a matter of course. The ethic of risk is rooted in the belief and practice that, in essence, protective hospitality should be provided in solidarity with those who are the "most vulnerable and least able to help themselves."[112]

Ethicist Sharon Welch identifies the ethic of risk with a corresponding factor—maturity. She describes maturity in this context as a "recognition that the language of 'causes' and 'issues' is profoundly misleading," that "evil

108. Caputo, *What Would Jesus Deconstruct*, 76. Such a question about duty to protect family elucidates a follow-up question: what constitutes family?

109. Ibid. Caputo refers to a conversation had with Richard Kearney, Jacques Derrida, and himself in *God, the Gift, and Postmodernism*, 130–36, which informed this statement. Elsewhere, Derrida asserts: "Hospitality, therefore—if there is any—would have to open itself to an other that is not mine, my hôte, my other, not even my neighbor or my brother, perhaps an 'animal'—I do say animal, for we would have to return to what one calls the animal, first of all with regards to Noah who, on God's order and until the day of peace's return, extended hospitality to animals sheltered and saved on the ark, and also with regards to Jonah's whale, and to *Julien l'hospitalier* in Gustave Flaubert's narrative . . ." (Derrida, *Acts of Religion*, 363). Derrida's play on words in reference to the invitation of animals obviously also alludes to the dehumanization often applied toward enemies, threatening others, the most-often uninvited.

110. Welch, *The Feminist Ethic of Risk*, 14 (italics mine).

111. Ibid. (italics mine).

112. Love, "The Ethics of Risk."

is deep-seated . . . [as] barriers to fairness will not be removed easily by a single group or by a single generation" and that "the creation of fairness is the task of generations, . . . [since] work for justice is not incidental to one's life but is an essential aspect of affirming the delight and wonder of being alive."[113]

Conversely, without maturity in an ethic of risk and its correlated responsible action, the idea prevails "that work for justice is somehow optional, something of a hobby or a short-term project, a mere tying up of loose ends in an otherwise satisfactory social system."[114] For Welch, responsible action comes as a result of an ethic of risk and

> does not mean one individual resolving the problem of others. It is, rather, participation in a communal work, laying the groundwork for the creative response of people in the present and in the future. Responsible action means changing what can be altered in the present even though a problem is not completely resolved. Responsible action provides partial resolutions and the inspiration and conditions for further partial solutions by others. It is sustained and enabled by participation in a community of resistance.[115]

The resistance to which Welch refers, borne out of an ethic of risk, is "far from naïve," but is characterized by a "full awareness" of the risks one must take as well as "the different costs faced by others."[116]

According to Welch, the ethic of risk and the real risk of losing everything including oneself, as is possible in the provision of protective hospitality, hinges upon love.[117] Because of love for and from others, and not simply because of self-sacrifice, people "are empowered to work for justice . . . [which] often entails grave risks and dangerous consequences."[118] She continues:

> The concept of self-sacrifice is faulty in two fundamental ways . . . To those resisting, the primary feelings are those of integrity and community, not sacrifice . . . [and] what is lost in resistance

113. Welch, *Feminist Ethic of Risk*, 70.

114. Ibid.

115. Ibid., 74–75.

116. Ibid., 78. In this section, Welch is analyzing the risks taken by the Logon family in Mildred Taylor's *Roll of Thunder, Hear My Cry* as a case study in how an ethic of risk is practiced.

117. Welch's ideas regarding love echo Beck's argument about love in the context of boundaries in the previous section.

118. Welch, *Feminist Ethic of Risk*, 165.

> is precisely *not* the self. One may be deprived of the accoutrements of a successful self—wealth, prestige, and job security [or even life, maybe]—but another self, one constituted by relationships with others [or with God], is found and maintained in acts of resistance. When we begin from a self created by love for nature and for other people, choosing *not* to resist injustice would be the ultimate loss of self.[119]

As such, the failure to practice protective hospitality and act with an ethic of risk endangers the self to a greater extent than whatever risks one might face otherwise.

To place these realities within a narrative, post-modern philosopher Peter Rollins tells a modern parable entitled "Salvation for a Demon" where this issue of invitation and potentiality for risk, through extending hospitality to "monsters,"[120] takes on challenging form.[121] The parable introduces the reader to a "kindly old priest" who was famous for his hospitality as he "welcomed all who came to his door and gave completely without prejudice or restraint . . . [as e]ach stranger was, to the priest, a neighbor in need and thus an incoming of Christ."[122] The reader's concept of hospitality and risk, however, is challenged when, in the middle of a cold winter's night, a demon, "with large dead eyes and rotting flesh,"[123] knocks on the door of the church and asks the priest, "I have traveled many miles to seek your shelter. Will you welcome me in?"[124] The priest welcomes the demon in "without hesitation," and once inside, the demon proceeds to spit venom, curses, and blasphemy while destroying icons and other holy decoration in

119. Ibid. There would be critiques to Welch's dependence upon love as a defining factor of an ethic of risk. Marxism, in particular, would take issue with this reliance upon love, seeing it as sentimentality and "brotherly sympathy" upon which people become "intoxicated" (See Bober, *Karl Marx's Interpretation of History*, 146). Welch responds to the Marxist critique by agreeing that "love for individuals is not enough . . . Yet, if the motive of love for all people is lost, programs for social change become idealized as ends in themselves, and groups of people are oppressed in the name of the greater good" (*Feminist Ethic of Risk*, 166).

120. "Monsters" in the sense of "the nadir of sociomoral disgust, the final outworking of its logic in which people are dehumanized to the point of being ontologically Other . . . subhuman *and* malevolent, a source of social threat and danger." Beck, *Unclean*, 92–93.

121. Rollins, *The Orthodox Heretic*, 24–29. This parable is also referred to in Beck, *Unclean*, 132–33

122. Rollins, *The Orthodox Heretic*, 24.

123. Ibid., 25.

124. Ibid.

the sanctuary.[125] The priest does nothing in response, but continues his devotions until it was time to go home. Upon the priest's departure, the demon asks the priest where he is going and asks if he can come since he is tired and needs a place to sleep. Again, the priest welcomes the demon to stay in his home, saying he will prepare the demon a meal. Once inside the home, the demon mocks the priest and destroys the religious artifacts decorating the home. The priest does nothing in retaliation or to protect his property. Then the demon makes one final request:

> "Old man, you welcomed me first into your church and then into your house. I have one more request for you: will you now welcome me into your heart?"
>
> "Why, of course," said the priest, "what I have is yours and what I am is yours."
>
> This heartfelt response brought the demon to a standstill, for by giving everything the priest had retained the very thing the demon sought to take. For the demon was unable to rob him of his kindness and his hospitality, his love and his compassion. And so the great demon left in defeat, never to return.
>
> . . . And the priest? He simply ascended the stairs, got into bed and drifted off to sleep, all the time wondering what guise his Christ would take next.[126]

Fantastical as it seems, Rollins' parable challenges his reader to consider for whom one would open the doors to one's home and sacred places, and to whom will one provide sanctuary and protection. How would the parable seem to the reader if the demon had killed the priest's family or burned his house down, or was the other upon whom all blame of suffering and injustice in one's own community was laid? Such an outcome is not outside of the realm of possibility, and makes real the risk that is placed upon the safety and purity of one's home, life, and self-identification as a result of providing protective hospitality. Yet, Rollins' reflects on his own parable by noting:

> To welcome the demon, in whatever form the demon takes, is all but impossible. But through our trying to show hospitality to the demon at our door, the demon may well be transformed by the grace that is shown. Or, we may come to realize that it was not really a demon at all, but just a broken, damaged person like ourselves.[127]

125. Ibid.

126. Ibid., 26–27.

127. Ibid., 29

By inviting in the demon, or the stranger, and providing shelter, one is given the opportunity to determine his or her true nature, and as Beck notes, realize the possibility "the monster might not really be a monster at all."[128]

Purity

The fear of the loss of self in Welch's argument detailed in the previous section is often constructed in terms related to loss of purity. Contamination, tainting, dilution, ruination or stain either in the areas of morality and ethics, belief and orthodoxy, or self-identification either on an individual or communal level are risks taken when one practices protective hospitality.[129]

According to Mary Douglas, an anthropologist specializing in issues of purity and defilement, risks to purity emerge when something is out of its normal place.[130] In this way, Douglas asserts, "where there is no differentiation there is no defilement,"[131] and, as a result, "ideas about separating, purifying, demarcating and punishing transgressions have as their main function to impose system on an inherently untidy experience."[132]

If purity is of concern, then the "messiness" or untidiness of life experiences, particularly where others are concerned, is a constant struggle. Douglas' identified system of differentiation, according to Beck, "creates the attribution of *dirt*" whereby life becomes "'messy' and disordered, where aspects of life—physical or, more often, moral—have come into illicit *contact*, been *blended* or dissolved into an undifferentiated *mixture*."[133] Furthermore,

128. Beck, *Unclean*, 133.

129. Such risks to purity are greater if the one being given refuge is from a different ethnic, religious, ethical or moral background or as a result of perceived or real crime or sin was committed which necessitated the need for protection. Furthermore, while it will not be explored here, the role of fear as it relates to purity is worth noting. In relation to cultic practice and identity formation—both now and in biblical era—threats to purity are usually responded to with fear—fear of being cut off, rejected, stained or tainted as noted above. As will be explored, there appears to be an oppositional relationship between purity and mercy. Is there a similar oppositional relationship between purity and love, related to the admonition in the New Testament epistle of 1 John, "Perfect love casts out fear" (4:18)?

130. Douglas, *Purity and Danger*. According to this reasoning, Douglas would argue dirt (as in soil), in and of itself, is not *dirty*, per se, but is only dirty when it is somewhere it should not be in accordance with boundaries that have been set up in relation to it. Similarly, Martha Nussbaum states "one's own bodily products are not viewed as disgusting so long as they are inside one's own body, although they become disgusting after they leave it" (*Hiding from Humanity*, 88).

131. Douglas, *Purity and Danger*, 161.

132. Ibid., 4.

133. Beck, *Unclean*, 130–31.

"[d]irt . . . defines (negatively so) the normative core of the community, the shared assumptions about what is licit and illicit, about what is proper versus transgressive" and "signals a normative failure" through transgression over boundaries designed to keep it contained.[134] In the end, these normative failures signaled by the presence of "dirt, pollution, and contagion" create a "powerful psychological system" where the "norms of the community" are then imposed upon those who have disregarded the boundaries of purity.[135]

In religious life, a concern for purity is interrelated with concerns about holiness. Douglas notes "[t]o be holy is to be whole, to be one; holiness is unity, integrity, perfection of the individual and of the kind."[136] This integrity, as a result of holiness, is "intimately associated" with purity, particularly in relation to "normative integrity" where the individual or community eventually has to "make distinctions, to draw lines in the sand to define its normative existence."[137]

In the Jewish tradition, concepts of purity and impurity are primarily rooted in the priestly, levitical sources of the Torah, and the socio-moral classifications of purity developed later in rabbinic Judaism.[138] Jewish scholar Jacob Neusner notes in the "early days of Biblical Judaism the terms 'pure' and 'impure' originally had no ethical value."[139] Nevertheless, as time went on and socio-cultural development evolved, "the employment of purity and impurity as value-judgments" began to distinguish the pure as "the equivalent of the good or morally right" while the impure became equated with "evil or . . . immorality."[140] When the Second Temple was destroyed in 70 CE, the emphasis upon *ritual* purity waned, the influence of morality in purity grew, and the issue of purity, in general, became more conceptual than concrete as evidenced in the Talmud, whose "purity laws comprise and create a wholly abstract set of relationships"[141] in comparison to the earlier priestly literature.[142] Similar to a familiar example of impurity seen in the

134. Ibid.

135. Ibid.

136. Douglas, *Purity and Danger*, 55.

137. Beck, *Unclean*, 131.

138. Neusner, *The Idea of Purity*, 26–27.

139. Ibid., 11. Neusner also notes that, as a result, the earlier texts reflect this as well.

140. Ibid., 11–12.

141. Ibid., 16.

142. It bears noting, however, that Neusner claims "Christians (to the end of New Testament times) reverted to the prophetic and sapiential contrast between ethical and cultic purity, but developed nothing in the already-available interpretative legacy. Only with rabbinic Judaism do we see a sustained and original effort to renew the inquiry into the meaning and potentialities of the details of purity both as law and as

condition of leprosy, it is understandable the concept of impurity arose from objects of "loathing—reptiles, dead bodies, menses and other excretions, birds of prey that eat dead bodies, eels, octopus, insects and the like."[143] As these objects were the "primary sources of impurity," the ideas of impurity associated with them were later "extended to other objects by analogy and pseudosystematic reasoning."[144]

On the other hand, cleanliness and purity became associated with "doing good, without explicit reference to the cultic terms" from which it originally arose.[145] Later texts such as Trito-Isaiah (64:5), Neusner argues, allude "to the incongruity of one who, while ritually pure, does impure deeds."[146] The connection is then made between moral or ethical impurity as uncleanness, which, in turn, leads to rejection by God into whose holy and pure presence one cannot enter.[147]

To draw boundaries in order to define purity from impurity is part of human nature as "all communities . . . establish notions of dirt and pollution."[148] Like the issue of boundaries explored previously, purity

metaphor" (ibid., 31). David deSilva, in *Honor, Patronage, Kinship and Purity,* would dispute Neusner's claim, articulating the ways in which Gentile influence shaped and re-formed the concepts of purity and impurity in the new Christian tradition during the time which Neusner mentions. Neusner also claims "Christians, who did not care to see the Temple rebuilt, ultimately gave up on the purity-laws" (*The Idea of Purity*, 129). While Christians did give up on the dietary laws, the issue of rebuilding the Temple and its impact on the abandonment of the purity laws is up for debate. I would argue it was not abandonment per se, but a shift in understanding from cultic/ritual purity—"be holy for I am holy" (Lev 19:2)—to moral purity—"be perfect as your Heavenly Father is perfect" (Matt 5:48). For the inclusion of Islam in the discussion of purity and impurity, particularly in the case of dietary laws, see Dawes, "The Sense of the Past," 9–31 (see specifically pp. 20–23).

143. Neusner, *The Idea of Purity*, 11–12. The evolution of purity as a socio-moral indicator is seen in the example of "leprosy of a person or of a house," which, according to Neusner was traced in later rabbinic Judaism "to a wide variety of sinful acts" including "murder, selfishness, idolatry, pride, false swearing, incest, arrogance, robbery, envy, and, especially, slander" (ibid. 115). See also Beck, *Unclean*, 13–32, 143–64, for a particularly helpful description of the role of disgust and aversion as determiners of purity boundaries.

144. Neusner, *The Idea of Purity*, 11–12.

145. Ibid., 13. Cf. Ps 18:21, 25; 24:3–5; Isa 1:16.

146. Neusner, *The Idea of Purity*, 13. Neusner also gives the example of Ecc 9:2, which "equates the righteous and wicked with the clean and unclean."

147. Ibid. Neusner describes Isa 35:8 as outlining "a holy highway, over which God will not permit the unclean or the fool to pass." See Jer 33:8; Lam 4:15; Ezek 14:11, 20:26; Hag 2:11–14; Zech 3:5. Neusner also asserts, "uncleanness also serves as an allegory for exile" (*The Idea of Purity*, 115).

148. Beck, *Unclean*, 131.

serves a positive function by defining identity, belonging, safety, health, and normative behavior. Humanity is programmed with a "psychology of disgust and contamination," which, in turn, "regulates social boundaries."[149] Helpfully, Martha Nussbaum notes that as the psychology of disgust "concerns the borders of the body," it assists in health by focusing "on the prospect that a problematic substance may be incorporated into the self" and, therefore, the "disgusting has to be seen as alien."[150]

Nevertheless, in the context of hospitality, concern about purity appears to be primarily a concern for unity and control. To sustain that unity and control, formulations regarding purity enable the development of classifications and "[c]ommunal integrity is maintained by monitoring and preserving . . . [these] classifications, keeping aspects of life distinct and separate."[151] Yet, this idea of a "pure" religion or community is a fallacy. Religious violence is often justified as a response to a threat to purity, often hinging upon the idea that a particular set of believers are the sole proprietors of truth and are, therefore, responsible for the purity of those around them, and have been appointed by God to rid the area of "contaminants."[152] A refusal to risk purity is a refusal to allow the contamination of the other or commit any perceived or real transgression that may, rationally or irrationally, be equated with the actions of those seen as impure or immoral.

Magda Trocmé, a woman renowned for her own efforts alongside those of her husband and fellow villagers in providing protective hospitality to Jews in Le Chambon during World War II, noted that "the righteous often pay a price for their righteousness; their own ethical purity."[153] This becomes a real possibility when one blurs boundaries and endangers the purity of one's community, home, or life by allowing someone or something different to enter into one's space. Lies, subversion, and concealment are all possible realities to ensure the safety of the threatened other in the provision of protective hospitality and, yet they are, in equal measure, also possible threats to communal, ethical, and theological or spiritual purity.

149. Ibid., 4.

150. Nussbaum, *Hiding from Humanity*, 88, in Beck, *Unclean*, 84–85. The same could be said for the communal body and that which is outside it.

151. Beck, *Unclean*, 130–31.

152. See Almond et al., *Strong Religion;* and Kimball, *When Religion Becomes Lethal.* While she does not use the term "purity," this issue is considered in Marshall's book *Christians in the Public Square,* particularly in her chapter on "theological humility" (pp. 73–106).

153. Attributed to Magda Trocmé, wife of protestant pastor André Trocmé, who led the effort in Le Chambon (Russell, "Hot-House Ecclesiology," 50). Dietrich Bonhoeffer also argued something similar in his books *Ethics* and *Letters and Papers from Prison*, 212.

In classic literature from my native American South, this issue is played out successfully in Mark Twain's *Adventures of Tom Sawyer and Huckleberry Finn*, where Huckleberry Finn contemplates his friend and traveling companion, Jim, who is a runaway slave. Finn has been told in Sunday School that those who allow slaves to go free will go to hell and decides to notify Jim's "owner," Miss Watson, of Jim's whereabouts in order to redeem himself. Then Finn remembers Jim, the times they have had, and the friendship they have shared, imagining Jim not as a slave but as a fellow human being. At that point, Finn says to himself, "Alright, then, I'll go to hell," deciding he would risk whatever moral and spiritual purity he thought he had in order to ensure Jim's freedom.[154]

Yet, in the context of Christian theology, the model of Jesus of Nazareth provides an obvious resource in addressing the purity question. In Matt 9:10–13, Jesus defends his practice of hospitality in the company of "tax collectors and sinners" to the established religious leadership by highlighting the tension between "mercy" and "sacrifice."[155] Beck notes the paradigm of sacrifice, "the purity impulse," sets up boundaries of holiness, differentiating between what is clean and unclean. "Mercy, by contrast, crosses those purity boundaries," he argues, by blurring "the distinction, bringing clean and unclean into contact."[156] Beck applies this further, noting "holiness and purity" are concerned with building walls and erecting division, whereas "mercy and hospitality" transgress and disregard those same boundaries.[157] In turn, this reaction against purity highlights the "politically subversive" potential of protective hospitality as it is "an attack upon the status quo" and "the antithesis of sociomoral disgust,"[158] through the provision of sanctuary to an other who has been labeled undesirable.

Similarly, Jesus' discussion with the religious leadership regarding his healing miracles and meeting desperate need on the Sabbath in Matt 12:9–11 and Luke 14:4–6 illustrates that for a greater, higher good, one must be willing to risk one's moral purity and transgress even those boundaries

154. Twain, *The Adventures of Tom Sawyer and Huckleberry Finn*, 281–83. An interesting discussion in Newlands, *Hospitable God*, 139–68, considers hospitality as salvation. According to Newlands premise, Finn's action to provide hospitality to and protect Jim was potentially a salvific act, despite Finn's concerns about "going to hell" for not turning Jim in.

155. Beck, *Unclean*, 1.

156. Ibid., 2–3.

157. Ibid.

158. Ibid., 123–24. Beck references, as an example, the Eucharist and "the hospitality associated with it . . . [as] a deeply countercultural act in the life of the early church," wherein "[s]ociomoral borders, often associated with socioeconomic disparities, were challenged and dismantled" (123).

that may have been put into place for a good reason. As Jesus notes later in Matt 22:38–40, all of religious law is encompassed in the dual-obligation of loving God and loving one's neighbor. To follow the letter of the law and not abide by these greater boundaries of responsible action is to make an idol of the law or one's own purity.

In an ethical framework of risk as noted previously, the reliance upon mercy and hospitality as a counterbalance to the pursuit of holiness and purity is valuable. Yet, one must be careful as holiness is still an important aspect of Abrahamic religious life. Bretherton is helpful here in his research, aptly titled *Hospitality as Holiness*, wherein he notes that in the Christian tradition, "Jesus does not resolve the tension between hospitality and holiness."[159] Instead, Bretherton contends Jesus inverts the relationship between hospitality and holiness, as "hospitality becomes the means of holiness."[160] He continues:

> Instead of having to be set apart from or exclude pagans in order to maintain holiness, it is in Jesus' hospitality to pagans, the unclean, and sinners that his own holiness is shown forth. Instead of sin and impurity infecting him, it seems Jesus' purity and righteousness somehow 'infects' the impure, sinners, and the Gentiles . . . Instead of Jesus having to undergo purity rituals because of contact, it is the [impure] who [are] "cleansed" by contact with him.[161]

Bretherton asserts that in the context of Jesus' life and ministry, his "speech and action announces a form of hospitality that, to some of his contemporaries, is shocking in relation to certain Old Testament precedents," and as a result, "his hospitality brings him into contact with the custodians of Israel's purity."[162] Yet, Jesus preserved holiness in that he rejected "co-option by, and assimilation to, the pagan hegemony, and capitulation to sin."[163] Instead, Bretherton concludes, the balance between hospitality and holiness through the witness of Jesus is seen in his "participation in the kingdom of God as enacted in his table-fellowship."[164]

Ethicist Philip Hallie's work on what he calls the "yeasaying" and "naysaying" ethics are applicable here. Hallie notes "yeasaying," or positive, ethics are well documented, such as the biblical imperative to be one another's

159. Bretherton, *Hospitality as Holiness*, 130.
160. Ibid.
161. Ibid.
162. Ibid.
163. Ibid., 130–31.
164. Ibid., 131.

keeper, and are named as such because they "say yes to the protection and spreading of life" and urge their adherents "to help those whose lives are diminished or threatened."[165] Hallie asserts, however, that to abide by a positive ethic is "less hygienic" as one gets dirty hands in the process as it requires one to act, to get involved, to take risks.[166] Conversely, to follow the "naysaying," or negative, ethic requires one to have "clean hands" and is an "ethic of decency, of restraint,"[167] or as perhaps Welch might have described it as an ethic of responsibility where one is responsible to one's purity and the powers that be.[168] Hallie argues one can obey the negative ethic by remaining silent, and still do evil by allowing injustice and threat to life to prevail. Alternatively, Hallie's formulation of the positive ethic "demands action,"[169] or again in Welch's terms, responsible action or an ethic of risk, as one must "be alive . . . [to] meet its demands," being prepared to perhaps go far out of one's way, and even be willing to risk one's own life.[170]

Beck addresses the tension between purity and hospitality in religious terms by noting the ethical call to provide hospitality is "a call to remake the heart" since the faithful life does not hinge upon "moral and spiritual 'purity,'" but upon one's "fundamental stance toward the other."[171] That fundamental stance toward the other is found in what Volf calls "the will to embrace," which is described as a "default stance . . . prior to any judgment of the other" and the position from which any judgments arise in the future.[172] Volf further articulates the will to embrace by describing it as

> the will to give ourselves to others and 'welcome' them, to readjust our identities to make space for them, is prior to any judgment about others, except that of identifying them in their humanity. The will to embrace precedes any 'truth' about others

165. Hallie, *Eye of the Hurricane*, 26–27.

166. Ibid.

167. Ibid.

168. One could interpret this in the Abrahamic traditions as idolatry, as it prizes purity above the moral and ethical obligations God places upon followers.

169. Hallie, *Eye of the Hurricane*, 26–27.

170. Ibid.

171. Beck, *Unclean*, 136–37. Beck couches his argument in a discussion about Paul's regulations regarding church discipline set out in 1 Cor 5:1–11, where followers were enjoined to "not associate with sexually immoral people." Beck argues, and I think he is right, that 1 Corinthians 5 "cannot be understood without understanding 1 Corinthians 13," where Paul declares the greatest of all things is love. Beck applies the requirement for love by noting that without it, "acts of charity can be dehumanizing," "church discipline can be dehumanizing," and "calls for holiness can be dehumanizing."

172. Volf, *Exclusion and Embrace*, 29. Cf. Beck, *Unclean*, 138.

> and any construction of their 'justice.' This will is absolutely indiscriminate and strictly immutable; it transcends the moral mapping of the social world into 'good' and 'evil.'[173]

In light of Volf's assertion, Beck declares "no conversation about sin, purity, or holiness can begin until human dignity has been secured beyond all question of doubt."[174] He adds:

> Discussions of purity and sin cannot be *primary* discussions. For when the "will to purity" trumps the "will to embrace" (when sacrifice precedes mercy), the gears of sociomoral disgust begin to turn, poisoning the well of hospitality by activating the emotions of otherness. In the desire to secure purity the faith community will begin to turn *inward*. The moral circle *shrinks* . . . Walls—ritual, physical, and psychological—are erected to protect and quarantine the faith community.[175]

Therefore, while purity and boundaries are a necessary and natural part of human existence and behavior, the implication in relation to protective hospitality is that purity should rarely, if ever, be used as a reason for inaction or exclusion of the threatened other.

Violence

The relationship between hospitality and violence is a complex one. Generally, the literature depicts hospitality as nonviolent and non-coercive. Yet, protective hospitality's proximity to violence, as well as its response to the reality or potential of violence cannot be ignored, especially as both hospitality and hostility arise from the same root as was explored in Chapter Two. Furthermore, the place of violence in the provision of protection is potentially problematic and should be explored.

In an attempt to set some parameters around this exploration and respond to certain definitions and categories of violence that arise within the context of conversations related to protective hospitality, I want first want to focus upon the work of Christian theologian Hans Boersma.[176] Boersma's theological constructions provide an interesting foil for the dissemination of opposing views related to the relationship between hospitality and violence, primarily because, thus far, his 2004 work is the only theological

173. Volf, *Exclusion and Embrace*, 29. Cf. Beck, *Unclean*, 139.

174. Beck, *Unclean*, 139.

175. Ibid.

176. Boersma, *Violence, Hospitality, and the Cross.*

source that specifically addresses the particular intersection of hospitality and violence.[177] After addressing Boersma, this section will then consider the issues that arise from his argument, other concepts of violence, the disparity between cruelty and hospitality, and finally widen the lens briefly to consider questions raised by broader ideas related to peacekeeping and intervention on national and international levels based on Immanuel Kant's *Perpetual Peace*.

Boersma's argument arises from a Dutch Reformed tradition in South Africa,[178] and is centered upon a very broad definition of violence and a corresponding vision of God's election[179] and limited hospitality. Each of these aspects play an important role in his formulation of the relationship between hospitality and violence. Emanating from his interpretations of an Augustinian understanding of violence, Boersma defines violence broadly as "any use of coercion that causes injury, whether that coercion is positive or negative."[180] Boersma expounds on this by noting "the Christian Church has hardly shown a consensus on the inherent negativity of violence," and, as a result, uses the term on a much broader and neutral way than many would assume is possible.[181] For Boersma, violence can include "properly

177. Derrida has briefly addressed the issue of hospitality and violence but not in a systematic way and from a philosophical rather than theological point of view (see "Violence and Metaphysics," 79–153). However, despite the isolation of Boersma's work, the potential scope for research into the relationship between violence and hospitality is enough for a book of its own. Therefore, what will be covered here is simply a selection and critique of Boersma's work as it applies to the broader topic of protective hospitality rather than an exhaustive analysis.

178. While Boersma would understandably debate with this assessment, one cannot help but note some of the more problematic theological foundations of the Dutch Reformed church and its corresponding views of violence presented here provided the ideological and spiritual underpinnings for South Africa's apartheid system.

179. Referring to the idea that only a chosen few—as opposed to everyone—will be able to enter into God's presence/paradise/heaven upon death or in an eschatological sense.

180. Boersma, *Violence, Hospitality, and the Cross*, 17, 43–51. For example, Boersma refers to monotheistic religions as violent in that they exclude other concepts of God, beliefs outside of their own faith constructions, etc. He also refers to conditional hospitality as violent in that it has conditions (i.e. limits which make it exclusive). Boersma bases his understandings of violence on Augustine's *Confessions*, 1.9.14; and *Reply to Faustus the Manichaean*, 22.74.

181. Boersma, *Violence, Hospitality, and the Cross*, 43. He backs up his argument by asserting this claim is evident by the fact that "none of the traditional atonement models have felt the need to absolve God from all violence" and that "by far the majority of theologians have argued that human violence also can, under certain circumstances, be justified and even regarded as an act of love" (43), referring to the theologies of Augustine, Thomas Aquinas, and John Calvin as supporting this stance. Boersma refers to Cole, "Good Wars," 27–31 for a discussion of these.

administered punishment,"[182] physically restraining someone in danger (from an outside force or themselves), economic boycotts or strikes which intentionally cause harm to the one(s) against whom they are directed,[183] or *any* other force, coercion or act "of damage or injury (including morally acceptable ones)," whether they be "physical or nonphysical."[184] Such acts or forces would also include boundaries and limitations, mechanisms by which exclusion are applied. He then asserts that, as a result, "the practice of hospitality does not exclude all violence" and, therefore, it is "impossible to extend hospitality without at the same time also engaging in some violence" as all acts of hospitality are limited in some way.[185] Furthermore, in the vein of Augustine, Boersma refers to "morally acceptable" actions as acts of "ordered love,"[186] and, accordingly, declares "justified violence . . . can be an act of love."[187]

For Boersma, hospitality requires coercion and is, therefore, violent as seen through some of the Christian theological traditions of the atonement.[188]

182. Boersma, *Violence, Hospitality, and the Cross*, 45.

183. Ibid., 46–47.

184. Ibid., 47.

185. Ibid., 48. He parallels this with God and God's hospitality by saying "God's hospitality requires violence, just as [God's] love necessitates wrath," although he clarifies by noting "God *is* love, not wrath; [God] *is* a God of hospitality, not a God of violence," noting an "absolute primacy of hospitality over violence" (49).

186. Ibid., 47, referring to Augustine's *Reply to Faustus the Manichaean* 22.74; and also to Burt, *Friendship and Society*. Boersma clarifies Augustine's stance by noting "[e]ven if the use of violence is necessary, it is, of course, still possible that people use with the wrong motivation or in the wrong fashion" and, therefore, "the *love* of violence—not every act of violence as such—[is] . . . something that must be opposed."

187. Boersma, *Violence, Hospitality, and the Cross*, 48.

188. Boersma follows the traditional Reformed perspective on the death of Jesus Christ, seen through the lens of substitutionary atonement, necessitating his torture and death for the salvation of mankind as a perfect sacrifice was required in order for the elect (or, perhaps one should say, God's chosen people) to be covered by Christ's sacrificial blood and enter into God's presence unblemished by sin. Therefore, because there are those who are elected to enter into God's presence and will encounter the "divine face of hospitality in [God's] electing love," Boersma sees this going "hand in hand with the violent exclusion of others." Moreover, Boersma sees the act of Jesus being crucified as an act of hospitality in that it enables us to be invited into God's presence, leading to his assertion that "[v]iolence does not destroy hospitality." Since such a sacrifice was required according to Boersma's theological interpretation, violence was necessary in order for hospitality to be practiced by God for the benefit of those who accept it, yet hospitality maintains its integrity despite this (*Violence, Hospitality, and the Cross*, 16–17). There is substantial disagreement over this particular facet of Christian theology, however, primarily based in feminist theology. For discussions on alternative atonement theories and arguments related to redemptive suffering, see Brock and Parker, *Proverbs of Ashes*; Heim, *Saved from Sacrifice*; and Weaver, *The Nonviolent Atonement*.

According to his argument, God's hospitality is conditional upon two kinds of violence. First, it depends upon a redemptive violence found in the torture and crucifixion of Jesus and, second, God's hospitality is violent in that it is exclusive to those who accept it.[189] Yet, Boersma argues, this violence makes possible God's "vision of eschatological unconditional hospitality."[190]

Curiously, Boersma seeks to answer postmodern philosophers such as Derrida and Levinas who, according to Boersma's interpretation, assert humanity is "always engaged in an inescapable web of violence, which makes hospitality . . . impossible."[191] Boersma interprets Derrida especially as being negative toward conditional hospitality, which is an unfair interpretation and lacking in a complete understanding of Derrida's full arguments regarding hospitality. Naturally, Boersma broadens the concept of where and by what means hospitality can be practiced and asks: "[i]s hospitality without violence even possible?"[192] For Boersma, when one decides whom one lets into one's home and whom one chooses to keep on the other side of one's doors, one has chosen to exclude and therefore act with violence, making the "violence of exclusion a necessary counterpart to the practice of hospitality."[193] Boersma argues further, noting one should "practice hospitality with an eye to the future of God's pure hospitality in which violence will no longer have a place" but for now, "[s]uch a practice necessarily involves violence."[194] Additionally, Boersma asks the question: "do we as hu-

189. Boersma, *Violence, Hospitality, and the Cross*, 17.

190. Ibid.

191. Ibid., 16. However, Boersma designs what he calls "limited hospitality" in opposition to Derrida and Levinas, which is ironically in many ways similar (in relation to the conditionality of hospitality) to ideas presented by Derrida in his book *Acts of Religion* or in *Adieu to Emmanuel Levinas*, which Boersma never mentions or acknowledges exists, and thereby negating much of his argument. Boersma only interacts with Derrida's discussion of unconditional/impossible, or eschatological, hospitality, which Derrida admits is impossible on human terms in *Acts of Religion*, 363–67. See also Derrida, "Violence and Metaphysics," 79–153; Kearney and Dooley, "Hospitality, Justice and Responsibility"; and Derrida, "Hospitality," 110–12. However, unlike Boersma, my interpretation of Derrida is that he never seems content to consign unconditional hospitality as impossible, but encourages the reader to wrestle with the tension inherent in the practice of hospitality, all the while pushing to welcome as much as possible.

192. Boersma, *Violence, Hospitality, and the Cross*, 27.

193. See Boersma's footnotes on pp. 27–28 of *Violence, Hospitality, and the Cross*, in which he discusses the guarding of boundaries in relation to hospitality with reference to Westerhoff, *Good Fences*; Oden, *The Rebirth of Orthodoxy*, 131; and Volf, *Exclusion and Embrace*, 63–64.

194. Ibid., 50. Later Boersma responds to Rene Girard, arguing Girard's depiction of violence and his corresponding politics of hospitality are flawed by his assertion that violence is pervasive in human culture and that the work of Christ on the cross was a scapegoat mechanism in order to release and detract itself from the grasp of

man beings have the right, and perhaps even the duty, to protect ourselves and others against strangers who might want to abuse our hospitality?"[195] Such a question, again, invites an exploration of boundaries and protection of both host and guest in the practice of protective hospitality that has been explored previously.

Boersma's argument differs from others regarding the relationship between hospitality and violence around some fundamental issues: the broad definition of violence, the meaning of hospitality, God's limited versus universal embrace, and the necessity of violence as a means of redemption or love. Boersma is correct in his understanding of hospitality as practiced in this world as being a limited and imperfect practice. As has been noted elsewhere, Derrida differentiates between conditional and unconditional hospitality. Such realities are a matter of course in the context of an imperfect, free-willed humanity. Liberation theologian Leonardo Boff reflects Derrida's ideas on the relationship between conditional and unconditional hospitality much more succinctly when he states:

> There ought always to be a dynamic articulation between conditional and unconditional hospitality so that one is not sacrificed in the name of the other. The ideal of hospitality must help with the formulation of good laws and to inspire generous public policies that welcome foreigners, immigrants, refugees, and those who are different . . . [U]nconditional hospitality needs conditional hospitality so that it becomes effective. And conditional hospitality needs unconditional hospitality so that it does not become bureaucratic, and does not lose its openness, which is something essential when welcoming someone.[196]

For Boff, the tension between conditional and unconditional hospitality is both natural and necessary. Furthermore, Boff contends "the ideal of hospitality becomes a utopia without concrete content," requiring both the unconditional and conditional aspects of hospitality to temper one another in the confines of present reality.[197] Again, Boff declares

---

violence through a new model of nonviolence provided by Jesus (*Violence, Hospitality, and the Other*, 133–51). Boersma, on the other hand, is informed by his conviction that violence "can be a positive expression of love" (ibid., 144–45) and, therefore, rescuing culture from violence is unnecessary. For Boersma, the end of violence will only be an eschatological reality (ibid., 257–61).

195. Ibid., 27–28. Derrida would call this type of hospitality "hostipitality." See *Acts of Religion*, 356–420.

196. Boff, *Virtues*, 57.

197. Ibid.

> Hospitality is simultaneously a utopia and a practice. As utopia it stands for one of the greatest yearnings in the history of humanity, the yearning to always be welcome, independent of social and moral conditions; and to be treated humanely. As practice it creates policies that make it possible for and provide guidance for welcoming. But because it is concrete, it suffers from the hindrances and the limitations of given situations.[198]

However, Boersma's definition of violence and its role in hospitality has a weakness. Whilst there is a need for boundaries between that which is deemed safe and unsafe and what constitutes identity and otherness, Boersma's definition of violence has the potential to relegate violence into the realm of the absurd. This lessens the impact of "real," traumatic violence from which the threatened other seeks protective hospitality in order to escape, live, and thrive.[199] Therefore, one particular critique is that Boersma does not take violence and the trauma it causes seriously.

Additionally, where is human agency and personal judgment in Boersma's construction of violence in relation to protective hospitality? If violence is defined so broadly that it can be labeled as an "act of ordered love," then so must love be defined as broadly. At what point does one decide that one act of violence is justified and another is not if both arise from a place of "love"? If love is defined as broadly as violence, one can imagine the abuses, intentional or unintentional, that are committed under the umbrella of misguided love.[200] Boersma's formulations leave no room for the

198. Ibid., 108–9.

199. Is the fact that I am not encouraged to receive gifts in honor of Father's Day celebrations because I am neither male nor a father an inherently violent act? I do not believe it is. If I were to undergo gender reassignment and become a man and was still excluded, then I could concede an injustice may exist that would need to be addressed, but much of it would depend upon how I perceived the exclusion, my feelings about being a father, and the motives and actions of those who sought to exclude me. But that is precisely where Boersma's argument fails: the role of human agency and personal judgment in the use of violence. Yet, I can also understand Boersma's point, particularly in relation to the protection question. Can one provide hospitality in the form of protection in a nonviolent manner, without coercion or exclusion in its more aggressive forms toward either the host, guest or those still on the outside who seek to do the guest harm?

200. It is already common to hear of violence being committed against individuals (such as children and women in contexts of domestic abuse or clerical abuse) in the name of love and protection. But in the Augustinian tradition, such acts of "ordered love" as seen in cases of "just war," which was used by the Bush and Blair administrations in the US and UK respectively to justify the Iraq war as an exercise in protecting powerless people from an evil regime, are equally problematic.

fallibility of personal judgment within the inherent violence of protective hospitality as Boersma would understand it, which is deeply problematic.

Moreover, since Boersma asserts hospitality is defined ultimately as God's actions through Jesus' torture, murder and resurrection, it leaves little, if any, room for others (non-Christians, for example) who are not a part of that particular paradigm.[201] One anticipates that Boersma would most likely assert that their exclusion is part of the violent aspect of God's hospitality. Yet, such a stance toward the issue of election and limited hospitality on a soteriological level is problematic, particularly in the context of the Abrahamic traditions being explored here. What is the point of hospitality in Judaism and Islam if the ultimate, eschatological purpose of hospitality is in God's hospitality through Jesus?

Lastly, inherent in Boersma's argument is a concept of God common in the reformed Christian traditions who is omniscient and, more importantly, omnipotent, who has an overarching plan to which everyone abides. This perception sees God as "the all-powerful determiner of every event in life, and every event is part of a bigger picture—a plan that will end in triumph,"[202] a plan that will inevitably end in the culmination of extension of God's hospitality to the chosen few. Yet, when such an idea is taken seriously, it implies God has a purpose in the death of twelve million people during the Holocaust, or in the rape and mutilation of a woman held in a Serbian rape camp during the 1990s war in Bosnia.[203] According to feminist theologians Joanne Carlson Brown and Carole Bohn, these types of scenarios illustrate the "travesty of this theology" which relies upon a deterministic universe under the capricious control of an omnipotent God.[204] In light of what has been presented here, such a position appears arrogant and short-sighted, particularly given the practice of protective hospitality and the realities faced by others who are often traumatized by violence and are seeking meaning for their experiences.

In opposition to Boersma's definition of violence, consideration of Rabbi Irving Greenberg's concept of violence in the context of protective hospitality is valuable. Greenberg asserts there is a "crucial distinction"

201. To be fair, Boersma's work is an exercise in Christian theology. He never implies an inter-faith or ecumenical understanding in his argument.

202. Brown and Bohn, *Christianity, Patriarchy and Abuse*, 7. There are, however, problematic elements of this deterministic thought in Islam as well.

203. Ibid., and Robeson, "Weapons of War."

204. It could also be argued that such theological claims serve to hamper the practice of protective hospitality in that, at its worst, it would claim those who are suffering are getting what God wants them to receive or what they deserve, which serves a higher purpose negating any obligation to intervene.

between "exercising power and force" and violence.[205] According to Greenberg, violence is defined "as an unjustified use of power and force," and as such, "not all use of force is violent or wrong."[206] He goes on to note "[m]easured force . . . is legitimate" as evil with "access to unlimited aggressive force and power would triumph unopposed . . . [and d]eath [would win] out if good people are unable or unwilling to take up arms in defense of life."[207]

Such a stance is not comfortable for those who adhere to the principle of nonviolence, but it is less problematic than Boersma's definition. Nonviolent force is possible in Greenberg's definition. However, the key terms here in Greenberg's definition are *unjustified*, *measured*, *legitimate* and, most importantly, *defense of life*. As has been examined previously, the necessity for boundaries exists, as hospitality without boundaries "offers no protective mechanisms to counter violence, in effect surrendering all categorical leverage to name and resist evil."[208] Yet, the use of violence (as Greenberg sees it) still negates the life of those who do evil, willingly or unwillingly.

Alternatively, combining the practice of protective hospitality with the principles of nonviolence would, in effect, offer "protective mechanisms to counter violence" without resorting to violence itself. The case of rescuers of Jews in Le Chambon highlights the practicality of nonviolence in a context that is often used to negate the effectiveness of nonviolence.[209] The rescue efforts led by André Trocmé and Edouard Theis in Le Chambon adhered to the practice of nonviolence and still succeeded in saving the lives of thousands of Jews who sought refuge there. Hallie notes a discussion he had with Edouard Theis years later about the events in Le Chambon. Theis declared he had never hated or advocated violence against the Germans and other authorities who sought to destroy the Jewish population. Instead, he stated: "You see, we weren't only trying to save the children; we were trying to keep the Germans from staining their lives with more evil."[210]

Classic concepts of nonviolence are much more conducive to the practice of protective hospitality than Boersma's argument. While Boersma allows that the *love* of violence is not condoned, the lack of discussion related

205. Greenberg, "Religion as a Force for Reconciliation," 104.

206. Ibid.

207. Ibid.

208. Reynolds, ""Improvising Together," 63.

209. See Brimlow, *What About Hitler?* for a helpful discussion of the common use of the context of World War II, Hitler, and the Holocaust when the topic of violence and nonviolence arise. See also Stassen, *Just Peacemaking*.

210. Hallie, *In the Eye of the Hurricane*, 34.

to human agency and personal judgment highlights the fact that enforcing a "pure" use of violence is impossible.

Related to this, Boersma neglects to explain the absence of love and the presence of cruelty in his exploration of the relationship between protective hospitality and violence. Can protective hospitality be given without love or with cruelty? Some say no. Beck argues the provision of hospitality is not simply charity but something much more inward, an act of love:

> There is a vast difference in receiving welcome, refuge, or table fellowship from chilly, hostile, and begrudging hosts versus the embrace of warm, affectionate, and big-hearted hosts . . . The call to hospitality is not simply a call to charity but is, rather, a call to remake the heart . . . The critical issue concerns the fundamental stance toward the other . . . Acts of charity can be dehumanizing . . . Calls for holiness can be dehumanizing. The outcome of these actions pivot off the status of the heart.[211]

Similarly, according to Hallie,[212] the link between cruelty and hospitality is oppositional. He asserts "the opposite of cruelty is not simply freedom from the cruel relationship; it is *hospitality*."[213] To explain his point, Hallie contrasts the difference between liberation from cruelty and protective hospitality by focusing upon a testimony from a Jewish woman who received protective hospitality from the people of Le Chambon during the Holocaust:

> It was indeed a very different attitude from the one in Switzerland, which while saving us also resented us so much. If today we are not bitter people like most survivors it can only be due to the fact that we met people like the people of Le Chambon, who showed to us simply that life can be different, that there are people who care, that people can live together and even risk their own lives for their fellow man.[214]

Hallie explains this testimony by noting that "the Swiss liberated refugees and removed [those who were threatened] from the cruel relationship" through charity, whereas the people who provided protective hospitality to

211. Beck, *Unclean*, 136–37.

212. Hallie specialized in research on cruelty, particularly in relation to research that was conducted on Jewish and Roma children by the Nazis, and then was compelled to do research on goodness as evidenced by the community of Le Chambon, which was discussed in chapter 1. The intersection between the two strands of research is found in his various works; see Hallie *Cruelty*; Hallie, *Lest Innocent Blood be Shed*; and Hallie, *In the Eye of the Hurricane*.

213. Hallie, "From Cruelty to Goodness," 26.

214. Ibid., 26–27.

the threatened other in Le Chambon went further by teaching those they provided refuge to "that goodness could conquer cruelty, that loving hospitality could remove them from the cruel relationship."[215] Hallie argues:

> The opposite of the cruelties of the camps was not the liberation of the camps, the cleaning out of the barracks and the cessation of the horrors. All of this was the *end* of the cruelty relationship, not the opposite of that relationship . . . No, the opposite of cruelty was not the liberation of the camps, not freedom; it was the hospitality of the people of Chambon, and of very few others during the Holocaust. The opposite of cruelty was the kind of goodness that happened in Chambon.[216]

Hospitality without love is not real hospitality but, is instead, merely charity; and protective hospitality without love is not protective hospitality but, instead, merely rescue or liberation in the most basic sense. The key component is hospitality's power to provide space for transformation.

According to Boersma, "violence does not destroy hospitality,"[217] but, is instead, a part of hospitality. Yet, if hospitality's emphasis is upon life, freedom from cruel relationship, and openness to the other's influence, then the relationship between hospitality and violence becomes extremely tenuous. Feminist theologians Rita Nakashima Brock and Rebecca Ann Parker noted, in their exploration of violence and redemption, that violence "denies presence and suffocates spirit," robs its victims and perpetrators of "knowledge of life and its intrinsic value," stealing one's "awareness of beauty, of complexity," and "ignores vulnerability, dependence and interdependence."[218] In light of this, violence is the antithesis of hospitality and the particular provision of protective hospitality.

On another level, when the relationship between protective hospitality and violence is discussed, it is appropriate to take into account the actions of nation-states and the use of hospitality as an antidote to violence and as preventative protection from aggression. While unknown to some, in the context of the nation-state, the contribution of protective hospitality as a means of prevention is not new, but was advocated by Immanuel Kant in his 1795 essay "Perpetual Peace."[219] Leonardo Boff goes as far as to say that for Kant: "hospitality is the central virtue of globalization."[220]

215. Ibid.

216. Ibid., 26.

217. Boersma, *Violence, Hospitality, and the Cross*, 16.

218. Brock and Parker, *Proverbs of Ashes*, 9–10.

219. Kant, *Perpetual Peace*, 15–18.

220. Boff, *Virtues*, 58. Boff does not identify the source, and Kant did not use the term "globalization," but Kant's assertion is found in *Perpetual Peace*, 15–18.

Kant approached the use of protective hospitality as a means for preventing violence and establishing peace between states. Hospitality on a national scale, according to Kant, meant "the right of an alien not to be treated as an enemy upon his arrival in another's country . . . as long as he behaves peaceably."[221] Kant argued the stranger " may request the *right* to be a *permanent visitor* (which would require a special, charitable agreement to make [the stranger] a fellow inhabitant for a certain period),"[222] therefore underscoring the necessity and role of diplomacy. Moreover, "the *right to visit*, to associate," according to Kant, "belongs to all [people] by virtue of their common ownership of the earth's surface; for since the earth is a globe, they cannot scatter themselves infinitely, but , finally, tolerate living in close proximity."[223] Kant also likened the conquests of poorer nations by more developed ones as "inhospitable" and unjust,[224] and long before the words of Martin Luther King, Jr., Kant proclaimed "a transgression of rights in *one* place in the world is felt *everywhere*" as inhabitants of the Earth are part of one community.[225]

Yet, centuries later, King would differentiate between just and unjust laws, remarking, ". . . it was 'illegal' to aid and comfort a Jew in Hitler's Germany. But I am sure that if I had lived in Germany during that time I would have aided and comforted my Jewish brothers even though it was illegal."[226] Such a statement is useful in viewing the paradigm of protective hospitality toward the threatened other in a hostile context in light of Kant's observations. However, Kant's essay is less clear on his views related to what would now be called "humanitarian intervention."[227]

221. Kant, *Perpetual Peace*, 15.

222. Ibid., 15–16.

223. Ibid. The connection Kant makes between hospitality and human rights makes the establishment of protective hospitality a natural and understandable development in thought and action. Kant's ideas are, most obviously, applicable to issues related to immigration, but taken further and in the spirit of Kant's ideas, would apply in the same way to issues related to asylum and refugee contexts as well.

224. Ibid., 16.

225. Ibid., 18. King echoed a similar statement in his "Letter from Birmingham City Jail," 290.

226. King, "Letter from Birmingham City Jail," 295.

227. Within the last decade or two, there has begun a movement toward implementation of an international policy, called "The Responsibility to Protect" (shortened to R2P), in response to oppression and violence endured by a threatened population, particularly in contradiction to the long-standing precedent of the 1648 Treaty of Westhpalia which guaranteed national sovereignty and discouraged intervention. The policy of R2P has been debated on numerous levels over the years, by groups as diverse as the United Nations, religious bodies, national governments, and policy institutes. On an idealistic level, it seeks to respond to critiques which arose from contexts in

In short, protective hospitality should be an affirmation of life in all of its fullness, and while violence may be an inevitable part of the greater picture of human life, it is not inevitable within the practice of hospitality. Instead, the power of protective hospitality resides in its capacity to resist and counteract violence and injustice, tell the truth to power by considering the interests of and giving sanctuary to a threatened other, and provide a healing balm for that which violence has sought to destroy.[228]

The Babylonian Talmud notes that when one "saves one life, it is equivalent to saving an entire world,"[229] highlighting that "all people bear an obligation to save the lives of others."[230] Rabbi Irving Greenberg interprets this text by arguing that since each person is created in the image of an infinite God, each person has infinite value; and since "one individual life has infinite value, then one has saved infinity . . . [and] saving infinity is the equivalent of saving six billion times infinity as well."[231] He continues his argument by stating "if one truly, emotionally encounters the infinite value of the other, this stimulates a powerful inner urge to save that life, for that life is infinitely precious" and, in turn, the uniqueness and equality of the other "elicits the desire to protect them."[232]

The choice of sections in this chapter has been shaped by conversations on hospitality with religious leadership and laity. In light of what was discovered, this chapter has addressed the issues that arose when specific

genocide that decried the callousness of the international community for not intervening on behalf of those being killed. On a cynical level, it has been relegated as another excuse used by wealthier nations to meddle in the affairs of less fortunate areas to their own advantage (US President Bush used R2P rhetoric to justify the wars in both Afghanistan and Iraq). Pacifist groups are wary toward the policy's implementation, recognizing these two sides and speculating whether or not it is simply a military rather than preventative solution as it appears to be a revision of just war theories. For more information on R2P, see Hostetter et al., "Prevention of Genocide and Mass Atrocities and the Responsibility to Protect"; Rimmer, "Refugees, Internally Displaced Persons, and the 'Responsibility to Protect'"; and Evans et al., *Report of the International Commission on Intervention and State Sovereignty*. See also International Coalition for the Responsibility to Protect (ICRtoP) at http://www.responsibilitytoprotect.org for more information.

228. These aspects of protective hospitality stem from the characteristics of life-affirming theology found in Brock and Parker, *Proverbs of Ashes*, 8–9. Similarly, Newlands refers to Elie Wiesel's Nobel Prize acceptance speech where Wiesel declares one is required to take sides to protect human life, and that "[n]eutrality helps the oppressor, not the victim" (*Hospitable God*, 56). Often, "taking sides" in response to evil is equated to the use of violence, but it does not always have to be so.

229. *m. Sanh.* 4:5; *b Sanh.* 37a.

230. Heft, "Resources for Social Transformation," 7.

231. Greenberg, "Religion as a Force for Reconciliation and Peace," 95.

232. Ibid., 96.

practice of protective hospitality was discussed. Despite the exploratory rather than empirical approach, the overall emphasis of each section has been that allowing oneself to be exposed to the other and, ultimately, being willing to put oneself at risk for the safety of the other is an effective means whereby dignity can be affirmed, transformation can take place, and relationships of solidarity may be formed.

5

Protective Hospitality as a Religious Practice

Any human being is a sanctuary. Every human being is a dwelling of God—man or woman or child . . . Any person, by virtue of being a son or daughter of humanity, is a living sanctuary whom nobody has the right to invade.

—Elie Wiesel[1]

INTRODUCTION

The sacred texts of the Abrahamic traditions offer valuable insight into protective hospitality and its ethical complexity. This chapter draws on material from the Tanakh / Hebrew Bible and from the Qur'an and Islamic traditions to consider what Christian theology might learn about protective hospitality through a more systematic engagement with the other Abrahamic traditions. It takes up the earlier argument from Chapter Three that the clearer obligations and stronger expectations around hospitality in Jewish and Islamic traditions influence practical behavior, and that these are linked to distinctive notions of social justice and to a more explicit honor code than is found in expressions of contemporary Western Christianity.

1. Wiesel, "The Refugee," 387.

As a result, this chapter will explore in greater detail the Abrahamic examples of protective hospitality as found in the sacred texts, looking specifically at the Tanakh / Hebrew Bible, the Qur'an and extra-textual sources in Islam. The purpose of limiting to the Tanakh / Hebrew Bible and not focusing upon the New Testament examples is for two reasons. First, this limitation is invoked in order to highlight the shared textual tradition between Judaism and Christianity that shapes the practice of protective hospitality. Second, the limitation is a practical one related to the need for brevity. While there are significant passages in the New Testament that could be included, this work is not an exhaustive analysis of all texts but an analysis of sample texts that problematize, shape, and speak specifically to the provision of protection.[2]

To do this it, the first section looks at four texts from the Tanakh / Hebrew Bible: Joshua 2:1–22; Genesis 19:1–14; Judges 19:14–27; and the deuteronomic witness related to the Cities of Refuge. Through these texts, I will argue hosts can be required to go to extraordinary lengths to protect those who are guests, that one needs to be willing to give oneself over for the value of the life of another, and that the cities of refuge texts, despite the textual issues present in their witness, still capture the imagination for a better, more just world.

The second section examines material in the Qur'an and extra-textual sources in Islam, which highlight the importance of a vision of a just society and the mandate to protect others. More specifically, the issue of protection mandated by God will be identified as well as a thematic analysis of the Lot/Lut narrative as it is presented in the Qur'an and extra-textual sources. Lastly, there will be a focused consideration of the Constitution of Medina and its impact upon concepts of the *ummah* ("community") and the *dhimmi* ("protected people") in the Islamic tradition, which provides a valuable contribution to the Abrahamic practice of protective hospitality.

PROTECTIVE HOSPITALITY IN THE TANAKH / HEBREW BIBLE[3]

Throughout the Tanakh / Hebrew Bible, there are texts where the practice of protective hospitality is observed. The primary texts that apply to the

2. Protective hospitality in both the Jewish and Christian traditions can be encompassed in the identified texts found in the Tanakh / Hebrew Bible, understanding, however, these texts do not exhaust the topic but are merely selections.

3. Both terms are used as this is an exercise in both the Jewish and Christian scriptures, and the usage of both terms is an intentional reminder of this.

paradigm of protective hospitality in both Judaism and Christianity are found in the narratives of Rahab and the spies in Jericho (Joshua 2 & 6), Lot's visitor's in Sodom (Genesis 19), and the Levite and the concubine in Gibeah (Judges 19), and in the provisions concerning the cities of refuge found in various places in the deuteronomic literature.[4]

Joshua 2:1–22

Chapter Three already mentioned the story of Rahab and the spies in Jericho in reference to the role of women as rewards of reciprocity in hospitality. Rahab's actions in the Joshua text also highlighted the particular delight found in the Tanakh / Hebrew Bible for the subversive. Nevertheless, attention should be paid to the general narrative of Rahab as an example of protective hospitality as well.

Rahab is designated as a prostitute in most versions of the narrative; and while it may seem a minor detail, this is a significant aspect of the story.[5] As referenced previously, the example of Rahab illustrates perfectly the realities involved with risks to one's moral and ethical purity in providing protective hospitality to the threatened other. Purity was risked on the part of Israel in that the spies were in danger and were given refuge by someone who was not only a Gentile woman, but a prostitute. Furthermore, Rahab risked her life and standing in the community, albeit the standing of someone who lived on the walls of the city and not in its center, by lying to the king of Jericho, telling his messengers she did not know where the men had gone when he commands her to give them up into his custody (2:2–4). She also took further risk by placing her trust in the spies' ability to uphold their part of the agreement—to provide protection for herself and her family in return should they return and attack the city (2:12–14).[6]

4. The paradigm of protective hospitality can be seen in other narratives as well Moses' rescue as an infant in Egypt (Exod 7:21–22), Judith's actions and role as a guest in Holofernes' tent in order to save her community (Jth 2).

5. While there are arguments against Rahab being a prostitute, on the whole, the subversive nature and character of the narrative makes much more sense if Rahab was, indeed, a prostitute. However, Josephus, *The Antiquities of the Jews* 5.1.2, labels Rahab as an innkeeper and other translations also use this similar translation. The word *zanah* used to designate Rahab, can be used for both prostitute or innkeeper/hostess. A possible solution may be that she was a madam, running a brothel rather than subsisting as a singular, solitary prostitute, or that in at least some cases the role of innkeeper and prostitute overlapped to some extent.

6. Narratively, there is a great deal going on in this story beyond the scope of this research. However, when considering this text, one should note there are questions about the spies and whether or not they're to be taken seriously or laughed at in this story.

Rahab is the hero in this narrative, not the spies. The principle of reciprocity is present in this text, but what is unique about this text is that whereas women are often mentioned in hospitality narratives as chattel to be traded, Rahab negotiates the provision of refuge, accommodation and protection to Joshua's spies in Jericho in return for her own and her family's protection when the city of Jericho will be overtaken.[7]

Furthermore, this text highlights the complexity of identifying the other. Rahab is an insider; she lives within the walls of Jericho, and the king and his messengers are aware of who she is. Yet, she is also the other, an outsider, as she is a sex worker and lives on the outer limits of the city walls, marginalized by not only her fellow city-dwellers but also by the many generations who have read this text over the centuries. Likewise, the spies are also the other, in forbidden territory and at risk of being killed, and yet, they are insiders in their own community who are able to repay Rahab's protection with protection of their own when it becomes necessary.

In the context of ancient Israel, it was customary that if one is providing hospitality, one is also required to ensure safety and protection to one's guests, at all costs.[8] Rahab had made the decision her home would be a safe place. While her motive for protecting these strangers may have been to find their favor and save herself and her family from imminent danger,[9] the text does not suggest this. In fact, the text notes Rahab had already made the decision to protect the strangers before she knew their identity

There are also questions about why the Israelites were interested in battling Jericho to begin with and the ethics of how the siege will be carried out, namely in the instructions given to destroy everyone except Rahab and her family. Furthermore, there are questions about when and for what purpose this story was written, particularly given archaeological research conducted by Kathleen Kenyon in 1952–1958 that argues Jericho was never destroyed in the manner depicted in the Book of Joshua. See Kenyon, *Digging Up Jericho*, 51–102.

7. Arterbury, *Entertaining Angels*, 77.

8. We see how this plays out (or does not play out, as the case may be) in Gen 19 and Judg 19 as well. See also Briggs, *Psalms*, 1:210; Pitt-Rivers, *Fate of Shechem*, 110; and Stone, *Sex, Honor, and Power*, 79–80.

9. Andrew Arterbury writes that not only was the provision of protection as an act of hospitality for the benefit of the stranger and his/her own safety, but also the townspeople into whose community strangers arrived had to assume, for their own protection, that these strangers had "either military resources or 'magical' powers" and that the "custom of hospitality in antiquity grew out of a desire to neutralize [these] potential threats" by either protecting one's "household or community from the wrath of the stranger" or to curry the stranger's favor. See Arterbury, "Entertaining Angels: Hospitality in Luke . . . ," 21. Arterbury refers the reader to the story of Rahab as an example. A more substantial work on Arterbury's research on hospitality can be found in his book *Entertaining Angels*. Alternatively, the townspeople can choose to attack strangers, as seen in the following cases of Gen 19 and Judg 19.

(2:1, 4). Therefore, it would be appropriate to interpret this text as a story of a woman who sells her body for a night of pleasure to two strange men, who are revealed the following day as enemies of the state and threats to the security of the homeland. Yet, Rahab knew to turn them over would be to most likely consign them to death. She risked herself further by hiding them in her own home, and later enabling them to escape from of the city and into safety (2:15–16). As a result, the narrative of Rahab is celebrated elsewhere in later texts[10] as providing exemplary hospitality.[11]

Genesis 19:1–14

For many readers, the following two texts to be explored—Genesis 19 and Judges 19—are very problematic as they give horrifying, violent, and blatantly sexist examples of protective hospitality wherein the host provides protection for his guests at the expense of women in his household.[12]

10. Heb 11:31; Jas 2:25; *I Clement* 12:1–3. See also Arterbury, *Entertaining Angels*, 77.

11. The genocide and violence committed by the Israelites in Joshua 6 cannot be ignored in this story. There are some serious issues related to the use of the *herem* (ban), which, in the eyes of the Israelites, required complete annihilation of peoples in areas they conquered. Nevertheless, the later actions of the Israelites are not similarly lauded as Rahab's actions are. In this story, hospitality trumps conquest. Docker's work *The Origins of Violence* (2008) is extremely critical of the book of Joshua and the genocide depicted in the Hebrew Bible, noting such a narrative has given inspiration to many other acts of genocide, particularly in the name of God, throughout history. Earl's *The Joshua Delusion: Rethinking Genocide in the Bible* (2011) approaches Joshua much more sympathetically as deliberate myth to affirm theological belief, preserving (or rescuing?) God from accusations of genocide, cruelty and immorality. A more objectively critical analysis can be found in Bergmann, Murray, and Rea's *Divine Evil?: The Moral Character of the God of Abraham*, which hosts conversations from critics and defenders of the problematic texts (including Joshua), and in Brueggemann's *Divine Presence Amid Violence: Contextualizing the Book of Joshua*, which takes a more literary and sociological approach.

12. As a feminist reader and interpreter, these stories disturb me greatly. In no way do I want to condone the "blatant acceptance of male-female gang rape as a responsible social act" as seen in the following texts as Berquist notes in *Controlling Corporeality*, 90. However, as is necessary in the practice of biblical hermeneutics, one must be aware of the inference present in one's own cultural and ethical understandings of a text, being careful to not let it affect the text's original intent. To condemn Lot's actions is natural and appropriate—to a point. But the reality of the status of women at this time as property of one's father or husband, with little if any sexual independence or say in who she is married off to and into whose household she is absorbed, indicates we are working with an entirely different ethical paradigm as it relates to women' roles in this text. What I seek to illuminate here are the parameters and practice of protective hospitality, even if those parameters are enforced through what are interpreted as negative, and even abhorrent, choices in our current context.

Moreover, the sexual aspects of these narratives as they have been interpreted traditionally, namely in the homosexual aspect of the men of the town wanting to have sex with, and/or rape, the host's male guests, further complicates the reading and interpretation of these texts for many.[13] Scholar Jon Berquist notes, "the fear of homosexual rape in the midst of concerns with proper hospitality" defines these passages.[14] However, biblical scholar Scott Morschauser takes a unique legal approach to the text, seeing the narrative as a detailing of procedures related to hostage-exchange in the context of threatening strangers (i.e. potentially spies or saboteurs) in the midst of a city-state.[15] These two approaches to the text—the classically held sexual subjugation argument and Morschauser's legal, hostage-exchange argument—will be analyzed side by side.

Regardless of these two arguments, however, these narratives apply to protective hospitality and are invaluable for the light they are able to shed on the practice, realities, risks, underlying values, and moral obligation for the host to protect one's guest. Additionally, according to Morschauser, the Genesis 19 text has "a clear relationship" with the deuteronomistic history corpus, sharing "a common vocabulary" with the deuteronomistic material of the Rahab narrative in Joshua 2 and 6 as explored previously, as well as Judges 19 which will be analyzed later, an indication that each of these texts is linked in a common deuteronomic witness and should be considered as a unit.[16]

The moral obligation to protect one's guests is a "core feature of ancient hospitality" according to Arterbury. Within the practice of hospitality, the host makes an "implicit vow to provide the stranger with protection" once the guest comes under the host's realm of influence.[17] Yet, in the context

13. Over the centuries, these texts have been used in anti-homosexual rhetoric, equating homosexuality with crime and depravity. Only recently has the interpretation of these texts, especially Gen. 19 in reference to the destruction of Sodom, been used to highlight the real issue here is the use of force and lack of protective hospitality practiced by the people of Sodom and not their sexual preferences. See Woggon, "A Biblical and Historical Study of Homosexuality," 158–159 and McNeill, *The Church and the Homosexual*, 42–50 for examples.

14. Berquist, *Controlling Corporeality*, 90.

15. Morschauser, "'Hospitality,' Hostiles and Hostages," 461–485.

16. Ibid., 485, ftn 78.

17. Arterbury, "Entertaining Angels: Hospitality in Luke . . . ," 20–21. "Under the host's realm of influence" implies either under the host's roof, property boundaries, or even in the town where the host lives as evidenced by the obligation for the host to escort the guest to the town gate upon his/her departure. See Genesis 18:16 for an example.

of a shared space such as a town or village, taking in guests is a public act[18] as well as a private one, as seen in these two passages. These texts give the impression the entire town is aware of the strangers' presence, and with the strangers' presence comes threat—either political or magical—as well as an opportunity to exploit or gain power over that threat.[19]

As, according to the more traditional interpretation, protection of one's guest is paramount,[20] the lengths to which one goes to ensure protection appears extreme in the following texts, particularly to the contemporary reader. The Genesis 19 text details the visit of the divine messengers to Lot's home and his family in the city of Sodom. This visit comes after the messengers have visited Abraham, announcing the imminent arrival of a son and heir (Gen. 18:1–15). As they proceed to Sodom to assess its righteousness,[21] Abraham's nephew Lot is sitting at the gate of the city (v.1), and reaches out to the visitors insisting they stay with him in his home, even after they say they wish to "spend the night in the square" (v. 2).

Morschauser notes Lot's presence at the city's gate "is not gratuitous or incidental" to this text. Instead, this description of Lot situated at the gate would indicate to an Israelite audience that Lot "was an individual of influence and standing within the social order of Sodom . . . empowered to adjudicate for the populace" and to guard the city walls from hostile entry.[22]

18. And, therefore, also political.

19. Arterbury, "Entertaining Angels: Hospitality in Luke . . . ," 20–21.

20. Arterbury cites Ps 23:5–6 as an example of the imperative that "the endangered foreigner can rest assured because 'the host is obliged to protect his guest from all enemies, at all costs.'" Briggs, *Psalms*, 1:210, quoted in Arterbury, *Entertaining Angels*, 86.

21. See Gen 18:16–33 (the pericope situated between the messengers' visit to Abraham and this text) wherein Abraham argues and bargains with God to save Sodom from destruction according to the number of righteous people who inhabit the city. See Brueggemann, *Genesis* and Fretheim, *Abraham: Trials of Family and Faith*. For a more systemic analysis of the Sodom narrative in early Jewish, Christian and Islamic writings, see Noort and Tigchelaar, *Sodom's Sin*.

22. Morschauser, "'Hospitality,' Hostiles and Hostages," 464–466. Morschauser continues by noting that "[t]ypically, a Syro-Palestinian city-state of the Bronze and Iron Ages would have been surrounded by walls marking boundaries. These structures would have been constructed primarily for defensive purposes—walls being the major fortifications against invading armies. In circumstances of attack, the citizenry and denizens of the nearby countryside would retire behind such strongholds for protection" (465). As a result, Morschauser claims those who would be responsible for "guarding 'city-gates' would have been most attentive to such problems. The responsibility for keeping vigilant at one's post for potential hostiles must have been a keen one. Undoubtedly, in times of actual warfare, there would have been heightened awareness about who, and what, was allowed behind fortifications" (466). Whether there was, however, a state of attention in Sodom reflecting this was a time of "actual warfare" is not clear, which may negate a certain amount of urgency in Morschauser's particular interpretation.

As a result, Morschauser interprets this piece of the narrative as the reason why the townsmen later threatened Lot and the guests, since Lot granting the strangers entry while essentially on "guard duty" would have caused "suspicions and roused widespread attention" as the townspeople would have feared "potential enemies [had] gained access to the site."[23] Concurrently, since Lot might have been seen as the "last line of defense against spies and saboteurs,"[24] his offer of hospitality to these strangers might have bordered on treason in the eyes of some.

Nevertheless, Lot insisted very strongly that they spend the night in his home,[25] and the messengers conceded. However, Lot's invitation appears to be conditional: they are to spend the night in his home and then "go on their way" early in the morning the following day (v. 2). Again, Morschauser argues that a "less-idealistic understanding of [Lot's] offer [of hospitality] leads one to conclude that the visitors are to be under the supervision of their erstwhile patron—under surveillance—until they are escorted out of the gates first thing in the morning."[26] This order of events could be paralleled, according to Morschauser, with the Rahab narrative, where there is an imperative placed upon the citizens of the city to turn over their guests for the safety of the city or under threat of them being spies.[27]

However, as the messengers are entertained in Lot's home, the city's men arrive at Lot's door, demanding his guests be handed over to them (v. 4–5) so that the guests can be "known."[28] The most common and traditional

23. Ibid., 467.

24. Ibid.

25. Parallel with Judg 19:20.

26. Morschauser, "'Hospitality,' Hostiles and Hostages," 469–470. Morschauser continues: "While Lot's entreaty that they not spend the night in the street is sometimes taken as an expression of 'lavish' kindness, a more realistic view is that the individuals are being prevented free access to the town . . . By granting them sanctuary, Lot, in his official capacity as a 'gate-keeper,' has assumed responsibility for his charges' welfare, and for their activities within Sodom itself. Their movements and actions are to be monitored—they are placed under a kind of temporary 'house-arrest': an implication being, lest they pose a danger to the community."

27. Ibid., 470. He refers to Josh 2:2–3 and Gen 42:5–14 as examples of this imperative that will play out in the Lot narrative, and notes "these examples demonstrate that the realities surrounding the extension of 'hospitality' are far more complex than is sometimes assumed. Strikingly enough, a common denominator in all these cases is that the privilege is withdrawn or curtailed because of fears of enemy infiltration—a telling similarity to Genesis 19."

28. Morschauser argues the Hebrew verb, *yada*, translated as "to know" is "a crux within Genesis 19" having "a number of meanings, ranging from simple 'comprehension' to the 'gaining of experience,' with its employment as a euphemism for 'intimate physical relations' often cited in this connection." In a footnote, Morschauser further explains "the meaning of [the verb *yada* 'to know' in Biblical Hebrew] as denoting

interpretation of this text is that the townsmen's intentions were to have non-consensual sex with the guests since the text appears to be loaded with overtones of rape and subjugation. Yet, Morschauser argues with this assertion, noting the townsmen insistence to "know" Lot's guests has a "judicial implication" as it potentially connotes a legal process of discovery and inquiry or interrogation.[29]

In light of the threat of the mob of men at his door, Lot offers his two virgin daughters instead as a means of protecting his guests (v. 6–8).[30] Such an offer highlights two interpretative possibilities. If the interpretation is taken as a sexual threat, it would imply that in this social context, the dishonor of having one's virgin daughters molested is more favorable than the dishonor of having one's guests molested.[31] It would also appear that only one's daughters or unmarried women in the household have the status that makes them suitable candidates for surrender.[32] While certainly not a model

---

homosexual intercourse/rape widely accepted for this verse is derived from its usage in Judg 19.22—the latter supposedly being based on Gen 19.5! The circularity of the argument is evident" (471).

29. Morschauser asserts this text "is not a cry that the parties be turned over for 'rape'—homosexual or otherwise. The implication is that the men be produced for *interrogation*: to discover (legally), and to ascertain their true identity—whether they are friends or foes; whether they truly deserve hospitality, or are to face hostility . . . Accordingly, individuals are to be held—in safekeeping—until a condition or promise is satisfactorily carried out. Failure to execute the charge or responsibility results in the forfeiture of those in custody, to the party (or parties) holding the individuals. The point of the exchange is not to mistreat those who are held but precisely the opposite: it is to ensure the execution of a prescribed duty; the value of the hostage is regarded as surety for an oath or obligation" (472–473). Morschauser cites numerous texts related to legal precedents, treaties, linguistic explorations, and Near Eastern cultural sources to solidify his argument.

30. As there is not a proliferation of stories such as these, we cannot speculate as to whether or not this was common practice, both in the case of the townsmen demanding sexual access to guests and the giving over of women of the household in exchange for the safety of the guest(s).

31. While upon a cursory reading it seems that the honor as related to the daughters sexual status and purity was disposable and flippantly given, it should be noted that such a decision could not have been easy for Lot. Throughout the rest of the Tanakh / Hebrew Bible, violations to the purity and sexual honor of women (as it affected the honor of the men in their household) were taboo and often punishable by death. See Bader, *Sexual Violation in the Hebrew Bible* for an example of this scholarship as focused on the relationships of Jacob/Dinah and David/Tamar.

32. However, his daughters were pledged to marry men, as noted in v. 14. Lot does not offer his wife, who is mentioned later in v. 15, and so one might speculate there were culturally accepted limits to what one had the power to give to protect one's guests from sexual threat. The same can be applied to the Judg 19 story to be considered later, as the Ephraimite host was most likely married, although his wife is never mentioned. As the Levite's concubine was not a wife, such an insecure marital status would make her a

for ethical behavior in our current context, this narrative never implies that Lot's willingness to offer his daughters to the mob for gang rape in order to protect his guests is a dishonorable or unethical act.[33] Instead, it illustrates that in this context, "the father controls the daughters' sexuality and can bargain with it as a commodity, in a way that Lot could not do" with the bodies and sexuality of the guests in his house.[34]

However, if Morschauser's legal-oriented argument is correct, then Lot offers his daughters as hostages, "to be given in *equal exchange* for the two envoys: they are not valueless, but exceedingly valuable" as "Lot's actions are neither an expression of patriarchal privilege, nor justification for its abuse, but are to be considered within the practice of 'hostage-exchange.'"[35] According to Morschauser's argument, the women, who are to be considered "legal detainees/captives," were "to be held safely overnight" and were "to be released, unharmed" when Lot's guests departed the following day according to Lot's instructions. Morschauser claims that "by offering his daughters as hostages—*not sacrifices*—Lot demonstrates his good faith to his fellow officials, and the gravity by which he regards his legal obligations to his guests under his watch."[36]

Yet, the situation worsens since the demands by the townsmen now include threats to Lot if he does not give them over and, interestingly, also highlight that the townsmen see Lot as a foreigner who basically has no right to meddle in their affairs (v. 9).[37] According to Berquist, household codes at this time distinguished certain persons in the household as permeable or impermeable boundaries. Male guests were impermeable and outside of the host's control; unmarried females were permeable. As such, their violation

---

permeable household boundary (see later references to Berquist) and subject her to the same possible fate as an unmarried daughter.

33. While Berquist notes the "angels' [later] action . . . prevents any rape from happening" which points to the negativity of the scenario as a whole, there is no condemnation of Lot and his offer. See Berquist, *Controlling Corporeality*, 55, 90. See particularly chapter 5, "Foreign Bodies: Reactions against the Stranger."

34. Berquist, *Controlling Corporeality*, 55.

35. Morschauser, "'Hospitality,' Hostiles and Hostages," 474. He argues with the previous possibility by stating: "There is absolutely no evidence to suggest that Lot regards his daughters' lives as being qualitatively inferior to those of his guests; to be casually expended to uphold some ill-defined concept of 'hospitality' or 'masculine honor.'"

36. Ibid., 477–78. Morschauser also notes Lot's daughters were pledged to marry men of the town as proof that Lot would not be surrendering their virginity to the sexual needs of the townsmen but instead he offers his daughters in exchange for his guests "fully anticipating that no harm will be done to his children."

37. This assertion by the townsmen would then bring into question Morschauser's claims that Lot would be considered an elder, given authority to adjudicate.

would have precipitated "a forced building of alliances" because the unmarried women of a household were considered commodities to "be traded in order to purchase protection for others."[38]

Moreover, both the offer of the daughters and their violation would constitute building connections between the households of the city and Lot's house since household codes required the rapists to pay the violated household "a purchase price and then take the women into their own households."[39] The household codes would not have allowed Lot to subject his guests to molestation of any kind—especially male-male rape—while they were under the protection of Lot's own household. "To rape these men would violate Lot's household protection, and would also destroy the boundaries of the men's own household," according to Berquist,[40] and would undoubtedly cast irreparable dishonor on both Lot and the guests.[41]

Not surprising, this particular sexual interpretation, as opposed to Morschauser's theory of hostage exchange, finds an audience with feminist theology. Theologian Elizabeth Schüssler Fiorenza has critiqued the household codes as "the ethos of kyriarchy"[42] as the codes seek to reinforce "hierarchical relationships in households, with the father, as head of household, being the one to whom all others owe obedience and submission."[43] For Schüssler Fiorenza, the primary interest in texts concerned with household codes "consists in bolstering the authority of the *kyrios*, the *pater familias*, by demanding submission and obedience from the socially weaker group—wives, slaves, and children and the whole community."[44]

38. Berquist, *Controlling Corporeality*, 93.

39. Ibid., 91, with references to Deut 22:28–29. However, this is problematic in the case of gang-rape as seen here. To whose household would the no-longer-virgin daughters go? Who in the mob would be responsible for payment and restitution? While Berquist notes this code of law as seen in Deuteronomy which would be applicable in both the case of Gen 19 and Judg 19, there are dating issues that cause one to question whether or not this deuteronomic code would have existed in the time of Lot or the period of the Judges, and therefore, may not have been the particular code at the time.

40. Ibid., 90.

41. In contrast, the cultural context seems to suggest an unmarried woman's honor could be restored or repaired once she is made honorable through marriage. The comparisons and contrasts between this scenario and current debates centered around so-called "honor killings" is not lost and would behoove further examination in another research context. See Schneider, "Of Vigilance and Virgins"; Ortner, "The Virgin and the State"; and Jafri, *Honour Killing*.

42. *Kyrios* referring to father, head of household, lord, slave master, emperor. See Schüssler Fiorenza, *Power of the Word*, 151–52.

43. Schüssler Fiorenza, *Power of the Word*, 151–52.

44. Ibid.

Nevertheless, the narrative continues with Lot and his household under threat, and to further complicate matters, Lot's guests have been sent by God to investigate the sinfulness of the city of Sodom, to announce its destruction, and to evacuate Lot and his family from imminent death.[45] Furthermore, when the threat to the protective hospitality of Lot's household becomes intractable, the messengers intervene, draw Lot back into the house from his attempts to negotiate with the crowd, and strike the townsmen blind (v. 10).[46] Ironically, in the end, the guests intervene to ensure their own safety and to preserve the honor of their host, yet the text invites one to question whether such actions were the typical or normally accepted outcome, or, instead, the result of special circumstances.

The text goes on to describe the process of evacuating Lot's household from the city of Sodom since, apparently based on the previous altercation, the messengers announce they are going to destroy the city of Sodom. Nevertheless, the text as it applies to protective hospitality more or less ends here.[47] Yet, as it applies to the previous actions, according to Morschauser, the "'outcry against Sodom' for its 'grave sin' (Gen. 18:20–21)" and its imminent destruction is justified because the "the rule of 'law' is duly rejected by the governing bodies" of Sodom for an undisclosed reason, accompanied by "threats of violence to Lot."[48] For Morschauser, "the attempted attack on Lot validates the divine *casus belli* against the city, ensuring its destruction."[49]

While Morschauser's interpretation has significant weight and removes the stigma of rape (homosexual or heterosexual) from the narrative, it stands against a well-established interpretative tradition that emphasizes the hospitality of Lot in the face of serious threat. If Morschauser's interpretation is correct, hospitality becomes less emphasized in exchange for a stronger legal paradigm that legislates the practice of hospitality out of the realm of personal or communal conviction and into the realm of unsympathetic

45. Berquist, *Controlling Corporeality*, 90.

46. Lasine, "Guest and Host in Judges 19," 54 n. 14, refers to the work of Hebrew Bible scholar Gerhard von Rad, who notes, "It is . . . a bit comical when this heroic gesture [of hospitality and protection by Lot] quickly collapses and the one who intended to protect the heavenly beings is himself protected when they quickly draw him back into the house and strike his assailants with a miraculous blindness." Von Rad also notes the word for blindness in the text is unclear but "apparently does not mean complete blinding, but rather to be dazzled, to 'see falsely' (II Kings 6:18)." Rad, *Genesis*, 219.

47. The actions of the messengers could also be classified acts of protective hospitality, but as they are described as "heavenly" or "divine" beings, constructing an authoritative ethical framework would present its own set of criteria and obstacles.

48. Morschauser, "'Hospitality,' Hostiles and Hostages," 479.

49. Ibid. *Casus belli* is a Latin term indicating the case (or justification) for war. Morschauser will also apply this argument to the Judg 19 text to be explored later.

policy. Such an interpretation is possible. However, its power to motivate contemporary audiences toward hospitality, albeit with a negative example, would be lessened.

The emphasis placed upon hospitality as the antithesis to the sexual violence in this text, in comparison to the hostage exchange aspects pointed out by Morschauser, has a long-standing tradition that should not be ignored. Despite Lot's offer of his daughters as hostages or demeaned sexual substitutes, Lot's hospitality has been commended throughout the centuries.[50] The midrash *Pirke Rabbi Eleazar* 25 praises Lot for practicing hospitality at risk to his own life, and, in comparison, Sodom was destroyed because the inhabitants systematically oppressed the poor and stranger among them, as well as those who sought to show hospitality to them.[51]

Judges 19:14–27

According to Hebrew Bible scholar Stuart Lasine, the similarities in the narratives of the preceding text (Genesis 19) and the present text (Judges 19) is "an example of 'one-sided' literary dependence" whereby the Judges 19 text "presupposes the reader's awareness of Genesis 19 in its present form, and depends on that awareness in order to be properly understood."[52] The similarities are remarkable. Guests have arrived in a host's home, and over the course of their stay, men of the town arrive at the host's door to demand access to the guest, again carrying connotations, in traditional interpretations, of male-male rape and violent subjugation.[53] Again, a daughter is offered in the guest's stead, but in this story the guest's concubine is offered as well. Yet, there are also some key differences in this text, which again provides a horrific and violent example of protective hospitality while, at the same time, having great value in shedding light on its practice.[54]

50. Rabbinic literature portrays Lot's hospitality positively. However, Lot himself gets more of a mixed opinion. See the midrash examples in *Genesis Rabbah* 41–51 for more negative interpretations of Lot. Islam portrays Lot (Lut) as positive, a righteous man, in Qur'an 11:74–83; 15:51–84; 26:161–166; 29:31–35. One would think that if Morschauser was correct in his interpretation, these earlier texts would make mention of the legal ramifications of the actions of the city of Sodom, but they do not. Instead, they highlight the abusive relationship Sodom had toward strangers in need of hospitality.

51. Alexander, "Lot's Hospitality," 289–90. See also Ezek 16:49; 22:29; 2 Pet 2:7; Josephus, *Antiquities* 1:194–5; *Genesis Rabbah* 49–51; *1 Clem* 11:1.

52. Lasine, "Guest and Host in Judges 19," 38.

53. Morschauser applies his theory to this text as well, although not in detail. His legal argument will be included where appropriate.

54. Again, it is important to note that while this research is an exercise in feminist

Initially, this text portrays the guest—the Levite and his concubine[55]—differently by relating the account of events that led to their travel and need for hospitality. The character development here suggests the utilization of tools of irony and absurdity in the narrative.[56] The author of this passage shares with the reader that the Levite's concubine has left him and returned

---

and liberation theology, the rape and death of the Levite's concubine, while horrific and deserving of attention, is not the primary focus. The subject of this research is protective hospitality, namely at what cost a guest is protected. Obviously, the concubine was not protected although she was a guest and therefore this carries importance that will be explored, but there is a limit to which attention should be paid in this context. For an exploration in the scholarship related to the rape and other issues not explored here, see Bohmbach, "Conventions/Contraventions," 83–98; and Yoo, "*Han*-Laden Women," 37–46.

55. The fact the Levite is 1) identified as a Levite, a member of the priestly tribe of Israel, and therefore expected to live up to certain codes and behaviors and 2) never given a personal name plays with the reader in the narrative development of this story. Similarly, the concubine is never given a name, and is even more anonymous than the Levite, who at least can be identified by his tribe. Throughout Judges, there is a theme of excess, people not abiding by their prescribed roles and expectations of righteousness in a context described as "every man did as he saw fit" (Judg 17:6; 19:24; 21:25). Additionally, Judg 19 begins with an assertion these were in the days when Israel "had no king," signaling a deficiency in the rule of law. As such, the author of Judges is inviting the reader into a world where moral codes have gone awry. Additionally, the narrative of Judg 19 should be read in conjunction with the following chapters of 20 and 21. However, the emphasis upon protective hospitality forces one to focus upon the events of chapter 19 only as chapters 20–21 serve to expand upon other issues presented in chapter 19 such as ethnic identity, gender violence, false justification for going to war, and issues related to the establishment of an Israelite monarchy. There are also links in this narrative with Josh 9; 1 Sam 11 and Saul's act of cutting an oxen into twelve pieces to mobilize forces (11:6–11); unjust war and death, which a generation later comes back to haunt the house of Saul and becomes a bane of King David's reign in 2 Sam 21 where he address injustice done by Saul to the Gibeonites. The original incident of violence of Saul against the Gibeonites is not told in the Hebrew Bible except in its reference in the 2 Sam 21 passage. What we do know is that the people from Gibeah had been pledged safety within Israel by Caleb as seen in Joshua 9. But according to 2 Samuel 21, Saul decided to try to "wipe them out in his zeal for the people of Israel and Judah." Nevertheless, the chain reactions of these events are beyond the scope of this research, but should be pointed out for further work as related to this passage. Nevertheless, Alice Keefe, in her article "Rapes of Women / Wars of Men," notes the "story of the concubine's rape serves effectively as propaganda to fortify the legitimacy of the Davidic lineage as Saul's birthplace, Gibeah, is defamed by association with Sodom" (93).

56. Lasine, "Guest and Host in Judges 19," 38; and Frederick, "Clinging to the Threshold of Hope," 55–71. There is a comedic factor that some interpreters have highlighted in this text, as the Levite serves as a comic character "in terms of his callousness, rigidity, absentmindedness, and inattentiveness to life, in particular, to the conventions of social life." Lasine, "Guest and Host in Judges 19," 46. Cf. Bergson, *Le Rire: Essai sur la signification du comique*; and Boling, *Judges*.

to her father's house, signaling to the reader there is something amiss.[57] The Levite notices her departure and four months later decides to pursue her to her father's home and win her back (v. 2–3). After their stay in her father's home, which illustrates its own issues with hospitality codes since they are repeatedly asked to delay their travel,[58] the Levite departs with the concubine in tow, to return home. The concubine says nothing throughout the narrative.[59]

On their way home, the Levite says he wishes to stop for the night where there are fellow Israelites and decides on Gibeah (v. 11–15).[60] Once they reach Gibeah, they take up the customary place to indicate they are in need of hospitality, the town square, where no one offers them hospitality (v.15).

57. For contemporary readers, the most likely interpretation is the concubine was in an abusive relationship with the Levite. The pattern fits, but in the context of this research, one should ask: who was protecting her? She returned to her father's house and, assumedly, was in relative safety there for four months (v. 2b). Bohmbach notes there are "textual lapses" that cause one to wonder under what circumstances the concubine left the Levite. The Masoretic text, affirmed by the Syriac, denotes she committed adultery and ran away to her father's house. Yet, if that were the case, her father would have been shamed and most likely would not have welcomed her back, especially for the four months she was there prior to the Levite arriving. Furthermore, the language used for the Levite refers to him coming to woo or speak softly to her, which would not be a typical response of infidelity but instead to suggest that the Levite was at some fault. However, the Septuagint and Old Latin versions refer to her leaving as a result of having "become angry with him" (v. 2), which reads easier in the larger narrative that gives no suggestion of adultery and seems truer to the spirit of the text. Some scholars suggest it is the Septuagint and Old Latin versions, instead of the Hebrew, that carry on the original meaning in this text. See Bohmbach, "Conventions/Contraventions," 90.

58. It was not customary or hospitable to force one's guest to stay longer than they wished to, yet the concubine's father continually persuades the Levite to stay one more day, delaying their return. In turn, this delay serves to build up the narrative tension in the text and adds to the overall theme of Judges with regards to people not abiding by the parameters set out for them for their own good. See Arterbury, *Entertaining Angels*, 82–83. However, feminist interpreters see it another way. Yani refers to the work of two authors who argue with this. Jones-Warsaw's "Toward a Womanist Hermeneutic: A Reading of Judges 19–21," 175, suggests the father may have been looking for assurances of safety for his daughter before allowing her to depart with the Levite. Likewise, Fewell and Gunn, *Gender, Power and Promise*, 133, speculate if the repeated requests to delay travel was an attempt by the father to delay the Levite because "he was hesitant to send his daughter back to possible mistreatment." Cf. Yoo, "*Han*-laden women," 40 n. 3.

59. Lot's daughters were equally silent, but were not mentioned as often, nor play as pivotal a role, as the Levite's concubine in this text. In this narrative, all the men have something to say, but the women (the concubine, the presumed existence of the concubine's mother in her father's house or the Ephramite's wife) say nothing. But the concubine has been given agency in this text as it states she left the Levite and traveled "from the remote uplands of the hill country of Ephraim down to Bethlehem, a city in the southern tribal area of Judah" (Bohmbach, "Conventions/Contraventions," 89).

60. Gibeah is a town in the area allocated to the tribe of Benjamin. See Judg 20:4.

Later that evening, however, at the town square they meet the Ephramite,[61] a non-Gibeonite living in Gibeah, who had come in through town on his way home from working in the fields (v. 16). Upon seeing the Levite and his concubine, he admonishes them to come home with him, implying that for them to remain in the town square would be unsafe (v. 20). Stone notes that, narratively speaking, the emphasis upon "a resident alien rather than a native of Gibeah [who] welcomes the travelers . . . [illustrates] the failure of the citizens of Gibeah to offer hospitality . . . [and] is a means of characterizing the city of Gibeah negatively."[62]

The subsequent scenario resembles Genesis 19 as the men of Gibeah surround the Ephramite's home and demand the surrender of the Levite, again so that the strangers may be "known." The Ephramite begs the men not to commit such wickedness (v. 23),[63] declines their demand, and offers up not only his own daughter but also the Levite's concubine (v. 24).[64]

Morschauser makes the same arguments for this text that he did for the Lot narrative. In the same way as Lot, the Ephraimite agrees to provide hospitality to his guests for the night, and later finds his house surrounded by the townsmen.[65] Again, Morschauser asserts the verb "to know" in this case alludes to interrogation, but Morschauser does concede it would be "undoubtedly in a rough and tumble manner."[66] However, as in the Lot nar-

61. Likewise, the Ephramite is never named.

62. Stone, *Sex, Honor, and Power*, 74. Stone compares this with the Lot narrative as Lot rushes to welcome the messengers while the Levite and concubine "wait in the square for some time." The same could also be said for Lot, who according to Gen 19:9 is also a foreigner in Sodom and, yet, is the one who offers hospitality in what is otherwise an inhospitable town.

63. What he is referring to as "wicked" is, however, unclear in whether he is speaking of their threatening his guest or their desire to rape another man. He presumably is not referring to male-female rape as wicked as he offers two women to the crowd, although perhaps he might see the rape of the women as being the lesser of two evils.

64. The fact the Ephramite offers the Levite's concubine is irregular, however. It would be assumed the concubine fell under the Levite's realm of control, and, therefore, she would not be within the right of the Ephramite to offer. Nevertheless, the narrative arc of this text has been moving toward ill-treatment of the concubine, so the reader is not surprised that even a stranger offers her up to violation.

65. Morschauser points out the townsmen are designated as "sons of Belial" (v. 22), which, he argues, is a "chaotic element . . . .[who] are designated by the reactor as possible disrupters of order" (480–81). In footnote 65, Morschauser expands on the term as referring to "individuals or groups considered to be subverting legitimate authority, or to those who would instigate apostasy and idolatry."

66. Morschauser, "'Hospitality,' Hostiles and Hostages," 480. He notes in footnote 66 that "suspicion expressed towards the sojourner is partially dependent upon inferences to be drawn from the surrounding literary context. In Judg 18.3–6,14–30, a Levite plays a conspicuous role in the overthrow of Laish by the Danites" implying to the reader "that such events could also transpire in Gibeah."

rative, Morschauser argues the Ephraimite offers the women as a hostage exchange, although this instance is "more exaggerated in tone" since the Ephraimite does tell the crowd they can "humble [the women] and do to them what is good" in their eyes, but to spare the Levite.[67] Morschauser asserts such language is not foreign to this context pertaining to the "transfer of legal captives to authorities," noting it signifies an admission on the part of the one who is surrendering the hostages that they are no longer within his power but there is an expectation that proper behavior will be upheld. The text appears to note the Ephraimite knows he is placing the women under the control of the "undependable . . . 'sons of Belial'" who have shown "themselves willing to overstep acceptable standards of behavior as it suits them."[68] Yet, Morschauser maintains his argument, noting the "extreme imagery employed" in this text illustrates clearly "the dire allusion contained therein—'humiliation'—*is precisely what should not occur.*"[69]

The sexual subjugation/dishonor interpretation still applies to this text however. According to another biblical scholar, Ken Stone, "sexual misconduct committed against a woman is . . . an attack upon the man under whose authority she falls."[70] The men of Gibeah only want the Levite and appear to harbor no hostility toward the Ephramite as his host. Therefore, according to Stone's argument, his offer of his daughter was rejected. In the Ephramite's eyes, "the rape of two women" was offered in order "to prevent the rape of one man."[71] As the tension increases and the Levite as the Ephramite's guest begins to feel more threatened, the Levite takes it upon himself to ensure his own safety by pushing his concubine through the door and into the mob (v. 25).[72] For his purposes, the action worked. The mob left him in peace the rest of the evening and the text invites the reader to speculate he slept peacefully. His concubine, however, was raped and abused throughout the night and was found by the Levite, with her hands on the threshold of the door, the following morning as he prepared to leave (v. 27).[73]

67. Ibid., 481–82. However, the word Morschauser translates as "humble" is translated elsewhere as "ravish," connoting sexual actions.

68. Ibid.

69. Ibid.

70. Stone, *Sex, Honor, and Power*, 81.

71. Ibid., 80. Two women were offered in Gen 19, but Lot had two guests.

72. Bohmbach notes the woman "had little, if any, choice in the matter" and that "b eing outside is a result of an action taken by her husband, a panicked maneuver meant to save his own skin" ("Conventions/Contraventions," 86).

73. Biblical scholars have asked a few questions related to this text: 1) What is the purpose of this particular narrative? 2) Does the text want us to think the Levite was cold-hearted or cowardly, or are we missing an important cultural value in our

Stone notes the men were "not interested in attacking the host; rather, they want his guest" and that is why "the offer of the concubine alone is successful."[74] As such, the rape of the Levite's concubine was an attack on him by proxy, since the men could not "dishonor the Levite directly by raping him *as if he were a woman* . . . [they could] nevertheless challenge his honor in another way: *through his woman*."[75] Stone also notes "the rape of the concubine is seen as the lesser evil of two alternatives available to the Levite"—his rape or her rape—and, therefore, requires one to consider the

---

interpretation? 3) Did the Levite assume he was consigning her to death when he pushed her into the mob, and, therefore, had no intentions of trying to find her the next day before he left? 4) Was the concubine dead when she was found on the doorstep or was she in shock or comatose and the Levite killed her later (v. 27–29)? Scholars have explored the fate of the concubine in depth, particularly the part detailing her hands were on the threshold of the door. Alice Keefe notes that "with her hands on the threshold . . . she seeks refuge with her last bit of strength," and although she has no voice in the narrative, "the description is heavy with the violence she has endured" with the Levite's callousness having "the rhetorical effect of heightening the reader's empathy for the tortured woman" ("Rapes of Women / Wars of Men," 90). The irony that the woman collapses while struggling to reach the door that ensured the protective hospitality given to the Levite is not lost either, but signals "the incongruity between her struggle and [the Levite's] indifference," according to Lasine ("Guest and Host in Judges 19," 44–45). Additionally, Frederick, in his article "Clinging to the Threshold of Hope," asserts:

> After handing over his wife, one would hope that the Levite was racked by guilt, shame or remorse, but there is no hint of that in the text. He appears to get a good night's rest and in the morning he does not even rush out to find her. In fact, only after the Levite has made provisions to leave, only at the last minute does he open the door to go on his way. Only then does he find his concubine, his wife, with her hands on the threshold. It seems ironic that in a culture so focused on biblical hospitality that none would be offered to this woman. Hospitality is as closed to her as is the door to security, the door to compassionate care and solace, the door of hope, a land where there is no king, where every man interprets truth for himself, biblical hospitality is even denied to a wife. (59)

74. Stone, *Sex, Honor, and Power*, 81. Stone goes further by noting that "[a]lthough the actions of the men of the city would, by thwarting his act of hospitality, certainly rob the host of an opportunity to increase his honor, the story turns upon the fact that the men wish to humiliate the Levite, not the host who dwells among them." Another view might be that when the two women were offered to the Gibeonites, "they were part of a negotiation process and rejected because they wanted to humiliate the Levite. Later when the Levite shoved his concubine out the door to save himself, it was not an offer in a process of negotiation, but a diversion of the Levite, using his concubine as a living shield. The mob took it because it demonstrated that the Levite did not (or could not) protect her" (Eynikel, "Judges 19–21, An 'Appendix,'" 109–10).

75. Stone, *Sex, Honor, and Power*, 81.

likelihood that the ancient and male audience of Israel may have felt the Levite's actions were justified.[76]

This particular passage ends with the Levite leaving Gibeah with his either dead or unconscious concubine in tow.[77] After a time he dismembers her into twelve parts and disperses them throughout the country to show what the Gibeonites have done.[78] Yet, if one takes the sexual subjugation/dishonor interpretation of this text, one can note it was not the violence that had been done to the woman which necessitated the grisly message, but the damage to his honor.[79] It was for that violation that he requested retaliation from the various Israelite tribes, retaliation which resulted in wars which caused the deaths of at least 25,000 soldiers and the destruction of all the towns, their residents, and livestock throughout the territory of Benjamin (20:46–48) and further destruction to other tribes (21:10–25) as a result.[80]

76. Ibid., 82. Stone notes the ancient and male audience was probably "more influenced by notions of gender-based honor than, say, Anglo-American concepts of 'chivalry' or ideas about gender equity" that makes this text so difficult for the contemporary reader.

77. Eynikel points out the Septuagint "says that the woman was dead" while "the Hebrew text does not tell us this when the Levite finds her on the threshold" ("Judges 19–21, An 'Appendix,'" 108). If one goes with the Hebrew interpretation, then it is possible the Levite killed her later as he dismembered her into twelve pieces that he then sent around to the twelve tribes of Israel, signaling the approach of civil war between the tribes. The text does not say one way or another. Trible discusses this possibility in her *Texts of Terror* as well and notes, "Of all the characters in scripture, she is the least . . . Captured, betrayed, raped, tortured, murdered, dismembered, and scattered—this woman is the most sinned against" (80–81).

78. One can only hope the irony in dismembering a dead or unconscious woman and using her body parts to show the violence that had been done to her—or the Levite's honor—was known to the author of this text.

79. Stone, *Sex, Honor, and Power*, 83. If it had been to protest the violence done to her, he would not have thrust her out to them to be abused in the first place. See the Levite's speech in Judges 20:4–7 for his side of the story.

80. Yoo refers to Trible, *Texts of Terror*, 83, which "points out rightly that the rape of one woman became the mass rape of 600 and the concubine's incident is used to justify the expansion of violence against women" ("*Han*-Laden Women," 41). It causes one to wonder: would the Levite have saved the lives of 601 women if he had not thrown out his concubine to save his own skin? Furthermore, there is scholarship which asserts that the narratives in the Hebrew Bible pertaining to a woman's rape coincides with social unrest and acts as a precursor to "war between men," as seen here, in Genesis 34 (the rape of Dinah by Shechem) and 2 Samuel 13 (the rape of Tamar by Amnon). See Keefe, "Rapes of Women/Wars of Men," 88, where she notes "Tamar's violated body, like that of Dinah and the unnamed woman [in Judges 19], functions in the narrative as the field of representation upon which brokenness in the order of human relationships and sacred meanings within Israel is made manifest."

Combined Analysis of Genesis 19 and Judges 19

Unlike the Rahab narrative in Joshua 2 and 6, Genesis 19 and Judges 19 leaves the reader with feelings devoid of hope and grace, as, despite the interpretative lens one chooses, the practice of protective hospitality toward strangers appears perverted and taken to the extremes, filled with violence and abuse. Both texts, although Judges 19 is a stronger case, illustrate protective hospitality practiced by fallible people gone horribly wrong.[81] Furthermore, the issue of women's voices in these texts is disturbing; in the Genesis 19 and Judges 19 texts, none of the women say anything, despite the risks they face, whereas in the Rahab narrative, she speaks, negotiates, maintains control of her person and is the main actor, the pivot upon which the story turns.

Most accept there are strong similarities between the Genesis 19 and Judges 19 texts, with Judges 19 dependent upon awareness of the Genesis 19 text. There are questions, however, about the "significance of that similarity,"[82] which makes the purpose of these passages unclear. If one is to go down the route of the sexual subjugation interpretation of these texts, then the issues related to household codes and a host's obligation to protect the honor and welfare of his guest apply in both texts.[83] Furthermore, both texts detail that, in the end, the guest intervenes to ensure his own safety and to preserve his own honor and the honor of his host.[84] Lasine argues that awareness of the Genesis 19 text allows the reader to contrast the hospitality of Judges 19 with it, so one can compare how the Ephraimite "inverts Lot's hospitality into inhospitality, and how the action of the Levite-guest is the inverse of the action taken by Lot's divine guests."[85] Arterbury asserts the Judges text

81. The Judg 19 text is a stronger case than the Gen 19 passage where the scenario is overturned by the magical powers of Lot's guests as they blinded/confounded and dispersed the mob instead of allowing Lot to subject his daughters to possibly the same fate. Furthermore, the Gen 19 text does not allow much narrative space for the reader to question motivations and character as the Judg 19 text does.

82. Lasine, "Guest and Host in Judges 19," 38.

83. See Berquist, *Controlling Corporeality*, 91.

84. Yet, it is easy to look unfavorably upon the Levite in this text for his actions whereas in Genesis 19 there does not appear to be the same judgment upon the messengers' or Lot's actions. This could be for one of three reasons: Either 1) the purpose of these narratives are different and seek to highlight distinct historical, ethical and situational contexts, 2) the magical/divine nature of the messengers in the Gen 19 text abdicates them from ethical responsibility in the eyes of the reader or 3) a contemporary reader is simply unable to remove the lenses of bias in the reading of the Judg 19 text. I believe it is the former two options, as the text does seem to give hints throughout the narrative that allows the reader to believe the Levite is less than honorable.

85. Lasine, "Guest and Host in Judges 19," 37.

is just one example of many texts that " may be narrating the perversion of what on the surface appear to be ideal hospitality encounters."[86] Lasine corroborates this view by noting that while one may be "astonished that Lot's 'hospitality' extends so far as to offer his virgin daughters to the mob to save his two male guests . . . there is a world of difference between Lot's offer and the analogous offer of the resident-alien host in Gibeah."[87] According to Lasine, the Ephraimite perverts Lot's example hospitality into

86. Arterbury, *Entertaining Angels*, 82–83. Arterbury notes that in Judges, "Jael kills her guest (Judg 4), the father-in-law attempts to delay his guest longer than the guest wishes to stay (Judg 19), and the Levite has to protect himself from the men of Gibeah because his host is inadequate (Judg 19). These three instances may simply serve as examples in the book of Judges of how everyone is doing what is right in his or her own eyes, thereby illustrating the perversion of the Israelites and the need for a king (Judg 21:25)." Furthermore, Arterbury also compares this narrative arc with Homer's *Odyssey* where "one way of demonstrating that a group of people was barbaric or uncivilized was to show them being either inhospitable or at least to show that they did not completely carry out the duties of hospitality (e.g., Homer, *Od.* 6.119–21; 9.175–76; 13.200–202; Cf. 9.161–505)." See also Parker, "The Hebrew Bible and Homosexuality"; Penchansky, "Up for Grabs"; Matthews, "Hospitality and Hostility in Genesis 19 and Judges 19"; and Yee, "Ideological Criticism"

However, while perhaps a minor point, I disagree with Arterbury's assertion that the "Levite has to protect himself . . . because his host is inadequate." I would argue the Ephramite was not necessarily inadequate, but was placed in an impossible position. He responded to the needs of the strangers waiting in the town square, understanding their safety was at risk. His inability to provide safety for *all* of his guests illustrates the intractability of the scenario and the cultural values at the time that placed the honor and value of the men in the household over that of the women. He can only be considered inadequate by our current standards, by not placing himself in harm's way instead, but while there are no guarantees that such an action would have been *successful* in this context, it probably would have been more *honorable*. Additionally, I am unaware of any biblical interpretation that explores the negative effects upon the Ephramite's honor as a result of the violence that occurred to the concubine. Such an exploration would be useful and interesting to this debate.

87. Lasine, "Guest and Host in Judges 19," 39. Lasine argues further:

> It is one thing to offer one's daughters to a mob in order to fulfill one's duties as host, and another to offer one's virgin daughter and the concubine of one's guest! The words and actions of the old host are almost identical to those of Lot at this point, but their effect is to invert Lot's overblown hospitality into inhospitality. The old host seems oblivious to the fact that his offer of the concubine is "inhospitable." He follows Lot's example so precisely that it is almost as though he were following a "script." The "script" calls for two women to be offered to the mob. The host has only one virgin daughter, so he must include the guest's concubine in order to act out his role! Although this characterization of the host's action exaggerates the mechanical way in which his behavior "follows" Lot's, it does highlight the ludicrous and self-defeating nature of his action, when it is compared to Lot.

a "ludicrous and absurd"[88] inhospitality by offering the Levite's concubine, and by explicitly detailing to the mob that they can "ravish," "humiliate," or "rape" the women[89] (v. 24), which Lot never did.[90] Lasine also contends that the Ephraimite is "less 'courageous than Lot" since he is never "in as much personal danger as Lot . . . [as] Lot had risked his life to go out to the crowd and shut the door behind him."[91] It was only during that negotiation and when Lot makes his offer that he was threatened. Instead, the men of Gibeah barely speak to the host and certainly never threaten him in the manner of Lot.[92] Nevertheless, while Lasine may be correct or too harsh on the Ephraimite, this text highlights the risks involved in providing hospitality and also encourages the reader to imagine what *might* have happened if the situation were different.

In light of these texts, it is necessary to note that one must carefully construct the application of protective hospitality in the current context. Obviously, the examples of Genesis 19 and Judges 19 are not to be interpreted in this context as proof that one should be willing to expend non-consenting family members to ensure the protection of one's guest. Present in these two texts are justice issues related not only to the townspeople/guest and townspeople/host relationships, but also in the relationship between family members. These texts highlight the intrinsic sexual subjugation of women in the context of ancient Israel,[93] as well as the injustice that takes place against women at the hands of those who had the responsibility to honor and protect them and their guests.

Yet, these texts also highlight the lengths to which hosts were obliged to go in order to ensure the protection of their guests. If one remains with the sexual subjugation interpretation, it is clear that the honor attached to one's hospitality was more important than the chastity of one's own virgin daughters! Concurrently, like Morschauser, Derrida highlights the role of *hostage* in this context, wherein one is offered "as a pledge . . . in a kind of captivity,"[94] which in its own way is still caught up in concepts of honor

88. Ibid., 40.

89. See Gen 34:2; 2 Sam 13:12, 14; Sarna, *Genesis*, 367 n. 6; Wyatt, 'The Story of Dinah and Shechem,' 433–58; and Seow, "A Heterotextual Perspective," 26 n. 2.

90. Lasine, "Guest and Host in Judges 19," 39. To this end, Lasine argues "[t]he 'frankness' of the old host only serves to underscore his callousness as a father and host."

91. Ibid.

92. Ibid.

93. Although I am sure it was not limited to ancient Israel but was common among most, if not all, cultures in the geographic region.

94. Derrida, *Acts of Religion*, 376.

since one commits to keep a pledge. While Derrida does not refer to these texts specifically, he does illuminate the idea that through the practice of hospitality "we substitute ourselves for the others in order to give ourselves as a pledge"[95] to the value of the life of those who have sought our sanctuary, a witness that resonates in these texts. Furthermore, while they do not provide literal examples of what one should be willing to risk in order to provide protective hospitality to the threatened other, these texts do challenge one to take seriously the notion that risk of harm to oneself, family members, or individual and communal purity is inherent in the practice. Such provision requires serious commitment and a willingness to face risk for everyone involved.

Cities of Refuge

Texts in the Tanakh / Hebrew Bible also point to the obligation to provide protective hospitality not only for the innocent, but also for the guilty. This imperative occurs primarily in the texts related to the cities of refuge. Unfortunately, scholarship surrounding the texts related to the cities of refuge is extremely limited. Found in a total of five passages in the Tanakh / Hebrew Bible, the details regarding the establishment and implementation of the cities of refuge sit in the Deuteronomic history and literary tradition and are not referred to elsewhere in the biblical text as are other deuteronomic principles, such as the year of Jubilee.[96] The silence regarding it elsewhere is curious; it indicates either that the cities of refuge were actually never implemented or that their presence was such an assumed part of life that the authors found it unnecessary to identify them further.[97]

Nevertheless, contemporary religious scholars, philosophers, activists and politically-aware individuals continue to refer to concept of the cities of refuge as an example to be replicated or from which to draw inspiration

95. Ibid.

96. The year of Jubilee is originally found in Exod 21:2; 23:10–11; Lev 25, 27; Num 36:4; Deut 15; and referenced elsewhere in Neh 10:31; Jer 34:14. It is also thought that Jesus referred to the year of Jubilee in his declaration that he has come to "proclaim the year of the Lord's favor" in Luke 4:19. Mary Douglas discusses the issues with the implementation of the year of Jubilee in her book, *In The Wilderness*, 238–47.

97. The absence of biblical scholarship related to the cities of refuge is equally curious. The reasons for its unpopularity in scholarship are mostly likely because there are only four passages where it is detailed, all of which are literally interdependent and, therefore, only coming from one biblical witness. Additionally, the lack of evidence in narrative literature, archaeology and extra-biblical attestation that it was ever actualized makes interpretation extremely difficult.

and learn. Additionally, the Jewish community refers to these texts in the religious calendar year during the Days of Awe, often drawing parallels between finding physical safety within the cities of refuge and finding spiritual safety within the Torah, likening one's contemporary realities with the biblical scenario of committing a crime or sin unintentionally and, as a result, needing redemption and sanctuary from retribution.

Before interpretation of these texts can go further, they will be explored in turn. It is generally thought the passages in Deuteronomy were written first, and therefore, they should be considered first.[98] Deut 4:41–43 explains which cities were to be designated as cities of refuge and to which tribe each city would be allocated: Bezer in the desert plateau for the Reubenites; Ramoth in Gilead for the Gadites; and Golan in Bashan for the Manassites.

Deut 19:1–10 is much more detailed regarding the three cities, yet never uses the term 'refuge' to describe them, but merely implies refuge can be taken with the phrase "*so that anyone who kills a man may flee there*." These early verses also declare the three cities should be centrally located in the land with roads built to enable greater ease of travel for those who need to travel there. The Talmud interprets this need for easier travel through the imperative in Deut 4:42 which states "*and that fleeing unto one of these cities he might live*," arguing that it was the duty of the Israelites to provide the traveler "with whatever he needs so that he may [truly] live."[99] Of note in this particular text, however, is the presence of Hebrew casuistic law, "*if/when this happens . . . you shall set aside . . .* ," signaling these passages are detailing a legal framework and system of asylum that was to be in place should the need arise.

The radicality of the idea of the cities of refuge in this text is characteristic of the deuteronomic witness. Unsurprisingly, there appears to be an emphasis placed not only on the refugee's welfare, but also that of the *go'el*, the kinsman redeemer who has a right to retribution, with the text implying an understanding that the *go'el* has the right to avenge, but reflecting a desire within the society to set up a system to keep the cycle of violence at a minimum. The deuteronomic witness goes even further in v. 8–9 in the condition—"*if you love the LORD your God and walk in God's ways*"—that three more cities should be set aside for refuge as territory expands, according to God's blessing. As a result, a direct relationship is drawn between providing refuge and being righteous. In the same vein, v. 10 emphasizes the sanctity of the land, which has been given as an inheritance by God to the

98. Although there is mention of the cities of refuge in Exod 21:13, which does not name the cities outright, but refers to a place that will be designated in the future where someone who kills another unintentionally can flee.

99. Extract from *b. Makkoth* 10a, in Levinas, *Beyond the Verse*, 34.

Israelites, and that it is their responsibility to keep from polluting the land with innocent blood and the scourge of violence.

The texts then cease in Deuteronomy but are repeated in Josh 20:1–9. The first three verses are doublets from Deuteronomy, perhaps for the sake of continuity, as the Joshua text details the coming into and taking over of land whereas the Deuteronomic passages were to reflect the law given by God to Moses while the Israelites were still wandering in the desert. As a result, the Deuteronomic texts state "*when you get to the land* . . ." while the Joshua texts state "*now that you are in the land* . . ." but are otherwise strikingly similar in wording and detail. Another doublet to the Joshua text is found in I Chr 6:57, 67, which only refers to particular cities designated as refuge that were under the oversight of the Levites.

However, a couple of details in the Joshua text are worth noting. First, the tone differs from Deuteronomy, like an instructive and firm reminder of the law—"*Now, I told you that when you get there, you* . . ."—as if there is an assumption that forgetting to implement the law might be an issue. Second, the text is much more concerned about procedural justice in the immediate context than the Deuteronomic passage, giving even more specific detail about how the system should be carried out.[100]

The final passage is Num 35:6–33, which is considered to be a much later text, most likely "belonging to the redactional unification of [the] Pentateuchal narrative and deuteronomistic historical work" and is "clearly dependent" upon the Joshua 20 text.[101] What makes this particular text unique, however, is that it appears to be the first use of the term *orei miklat*, the actual origin of the term "city of refuge." Yet, few additional details emerge in this text as the details of the cities is absorbed into the discussion of tribal allotments and the arrangements for the tribe of Levi in particular.

While some interpret the cities of refuge texts as a means to deal with blood feuds, the various texts never say this explicitly, despite the use of the term *go'el*, nor do they give a particular reason as to why the cities of refuge are declared a solution to a particular problem.[102] There is no exposition as to why this solution, as opposed to another, was given, and there is no narrative framework or further reference to the cities and their implementation. However, there appears to be an indication that the development of the

100. Including the detail that the Levites, the priestly tribe, are not to get a tribal allotment (see Joshua 21) because they do not need land to provide for themselves because God will provide for them.

101. Noth, *Numbers*, 253.

102. Was the issue of blood vengeance out of control? Was there such a high rate of accidental death—or murder that could have been blamed as an accident—that such a system needed to be put in place to adjudicate and protect those involved? The text never gives any of these details.

cities was perhaps a movement away from the practice of using the actual sanctuary altar as a place of safety.[103] Yet, there is no general agreement as to when this "transfer of asylum from altar to designated cities occurred,"[104] and, therefore, the interpretation as to the original need for and justification of this legal development remains, in essence, a mystery.

Despite the absence of detail and lack of evidence that it was ever implemented, the cities of refuge detailed in the texts above define and give structure to the "biblical institution of sanctuary"[105] for both the Jewish and Christian traditions. According to a progressive Jewish rabbi, Niles Elliot Goldstein, the establishment of the cities of refuge had three purposes:

1. "It was a protective measure, to give all of the parties involved a chance to let their passions cool" and to "let the wheels of justice . . . start to turn" as "witnesses would be called, trials held, and judgments made" by the priests who conducted the proceedings.[106]
2. "It served as quasi-form of punishment for the manslayer, since exile, even in a place of refuge, constituted a form of social death."[107] Emmanuel Levinas, in some reflections on the Talmud and its interpretation of these texts, notes this aspect as well, stating "[t]he 'avenger of blood' can no longer pursue the murderer who has taken refuge . . . ; but for the manslayer, who is also a murderer through negligence, the city of refuge is also an exile: a punishment . . . In the city of refuge, then, there is the protection of the innocent which is also a punishment for the objectively guilty party. Both at the same time."[108]
3. "It served to contain and isolate the sin that has been committed, a death—for killing was understood . . . as a contaminant to the community as a whole. The killing of a human being, even if it occurred without any malicious intent, was a moral wound to the entire household of Israel."[109]

103. Dozeman, "Numbers," 264. See 1 Kings 2:28.

104. Dozeman, "Numbers," 264.

105. Goldstein, "The New Schul—Kol Nidre 5767," 2.

106. Ibid.

107. Ibid.

108. Levinas, *Beyond the Verse*, 39.

109. Goldstein, "The New Schul—Kol Nidre 5767," 2–3. For example, Num 35:34 states the cities of refuge are to "protect from blood defilement 'for I the Lord dwell in the midst of the people of Israel.'" This emphasis upon purity and avoiding defilement is explored further by Douglas in her book *In The Wilderness*, 120, 147–48.

The issue of killing as a "contaminant" hearkens back to the previous discussion concerning issues related to purity. Since purity is based on concepts of holiness and ethical righteousness in these deuteronomic texts, the holiness of the land and its inhabitants is paramount. The importance of this aspect of holiness can be seen in the appointment of the Levites to be in charge of the cities of refuge and its resulting judicial processes as well as the underlying reason they were appointed: because there was fear that the administration of power justice by the tribes/landholders would be unfair.[110] The Levites were given the responsibility of adjudicating claims of refuge and revenge as they were perceived to be perpetual outsiders who were less inclined to side with particular tribes as a result of land issues.[111]

Nevertheless, some issues related to the cities of refuge texts need to be highlighted. The first is a textual issue: the witness of the cities of refuge texts are only from one witness, the deuteronomic source,[112] and the cities are not mentioned outside of that source in their capacity as places of refuge. Given their role as centers of justice, both socially and legally, one would think they would be mentioned later in the prophetic texts, but there is nothing.[113]

Second, one can see that the cities of refuge were to be set up as part of a more developed legal system. Now that the Israelites are based in a homeland and no longer wandering, they had the capacity to establish permanent courts and carry out justice as a rooted community. The attention paid in the Deuteronomy 19 passage defining what constituted an unintentional murder illustrates specific legal codes were being developed. Yet, since these texts mirror a social and religious progression of thought, one is aware these provisions would have continued in their development if cases in the cities of refuge were being heard.

110. Schweid, *The Philosophy of the Bible as Foundation of Jewish Culture*, 2:59–60.

111. See also Noth, *Numbers*; Barr, "Migraš in the Old Testament"; Ofer, "A Diagram of the Open Land of the Levite Cities in Nahmanides' Commentary on the Torah"; and Baker, *Tight Fists or Open Hands*, 92.

112. It is understood, however, that even the deuteronomic source is not monolithic, but probably exhibits a variety of voices and contexts over the period of its composition.

113. Unlike the year of Jubilee where its non-practice (and, as a result, Israel's deficiency of justice) is considered to be a reason why Israel fell apart and was exiled, and is referenced repeatedly outside of the deuteronomic witness. See 2 Chr 26:20–23, 36:20–23; Isa 61:1–4; Jer 25 and 29; Ezek 40:1, 46:17; Dan 9:24–27. Yet, the historical context and geographical placement of the cities may have played a role in their silence. Most prophetic literature in the Tanakh / Hebrew Bible is attributed predominantly to the Southern Kingdom of Israel and written after the Assyrian exile in 722 BCE. Since most of the cities of refuge would have been located in the Northern Kingdom of Judah and would have been under Assyrian rule at the time when the prophetic literature was being formed, it may explain why they were not mentioned in the later texts.

Thirdly, while there are few options given for conditional legal trespass and very little allowance given for the guilty to pass without judgment in the Tanakh / Hebrew Bible, there are notable exceptions where those who violate the law are either not condemned or sometimes even celebrated.[114] The text is aware that there are extenuating circumstances that override a person's better judgment and established laws and traditions. Furthermore, the laws depicted here do not seem to admit as much causal complexity as one considers human action to involve, so there is room for re-interpretation to make the laws work in each particular scenario. Levinas highlights this issue in the texts by noting the "ancient status of the city of refuge—the ambiguity of a crime which is not a crime, punished by a punishment which is not a punishment—is related to the ambiguity of human fraternity which is the source of hatred and pity.'"[115] Additionally, Levinas declares the city of refuge "is a city of civilization or of a humanity which protects subjective innocence and forgives objective guilt and all the denials that acts inflict on intentions."[116]

Nevertheless, in Elie Wiesel's essay "The Refugee," he argues the concept of sanctuary in the Jewish tradition

> refers to human beings . . . [it] is not a place . . . .Any human being is a sanctuary. Every human being is a dwelling of God—man or woman or child . . . .Any person, by virtue of being a son or daughter of humanity, is a living sanctuary whom nobody has the right to invade.[117]

Wiesel concludes the "sanctuary concept in Scripture is rooted in . . . [the] cities of refuge . . . .[and] the entire theme of sanctuary is always linked to war and peace."[118] Related to Wiesel's radical inclusion, Levinas echoes similar ideas. In a reflection upon Talmudic writings, he focuses a large proportion of his time on the cities of refuge texts. Oona Eisenstadt records Levinas' thoughts:

114. Examples such as stories of incest / endangered survival such as the Daughters of Lot (Gen 19:30–38) and Judah and Tamar (Gen 38); child sacrifice committed by Jephthah (Judg 11); a rash oath by Saul in the Saul/Jonathan narrative (1 Sam 14); and probably most interesting in this context is the account of the mark given to Cain (Gen 4:15), which served as protection from retribution despite the premeditated murder he committed. At the same time, these are all quite problematic texts in and of themselves.

115. Levinas, *Beyond the Verse*, 46–47

116. Ibid., 51–52

117. Wiesel, "The Refugee," 387.

118. Ibid.

> "Why, he asks, [is there] so much concern for the manslaughterer? He answers: because we are all manslaughterers. . . .We all participate in structures of oppression—this makes us guilty—but we participate for the most part unwillingly—this makes us innocent."[119]

Levinas continues elsewhere:

> Do not these murders, committed without the murderers' volition, occur in other ways than by the axe-head leaving the handle and coming to strike the passer-by? In Western society—free and civilized, but without social equality and a rigorous social justice—is it absurd to wonder whether the advantages available to the rich in relation to the poor . . . whether these advantages, one thing leading to another, are not the cause, somewhere, of someone's agony? Are there not, somewhere in the world, wars and carnage which result from these advantages? . . . .Does not the avenger or the redeemer of blood 'with heated heart' lurk around us, in the form of people's anger, of the spirit of revolt or even of delinquency in our suburbs, the result of the social imbalance in which we are placed?[120]

Contemporary application such as Levinas has modeled encourages one to consider how such inequalities that lead to "someone's agony" can be interrupted and addressed. The cities of refuge texts offer substantial evidence of a restorative culture, both for the perpetrator—the manslaughterer—and for the victim/survivor who has a right to justice and retribution, the *go'el*. Despite the references to guilt and innocence, Levinas highlights the questions inherent in this text and its application by universalizing the needs of the actors, and the respective rights of safety, protection, and calling for a fair accounting of events that necessitated a place of refuge in the first place.[121]

Despite the textual complications and lack of evidence that the legislation for the cities of refuge was ever enacted, these texts still capture the imagination.[122] As a result, they are continually referenced as inspiration

119. Eisenstadt, "The Problem of the Promise," 475.

120. Levinas, *Beyond the Verse*, 40.

121. For further discussion of contemporary application of the cities of refuge biblical principles, see Auckelman, "City of Refuge," 22–26; and Ryan, "The Historical Case for the Right of Sanctuary?," 209–32.

122. It should be noted, however, that the principle of refuge is not a Hebrew concept. One particular example in another culture can be found in ancient Hawaii. If someone committed *kapu*, a forbidden action such as "broke a taboo, betrayed a trust, harmed someone, or was a non-combatant during a time of war," they were at risk,

and looked to as an example of a more just society. Recent developments have been the establishment of International Cities of Refuge Network[123] (ICORN), a network of cities that welcome writers and scholars who are under threat in their home countries because of their work, and the City of Sanctuary movement in the UK,[124] which seeks to build a culture of hospitality for asylum seekers and migrants in need of sanctuary, designating various towns and cities as places of safety. Discussions are also taking place regarding the intersections between architecture, hospitality, and refuge,[125] and nations are considering the role of protection and intervention with current debates about developing international policies referred to as "Responsibility to Protect."[126] The issue of refuge and protective hospitality is certainly a part of contemporary public discourse.

PROTECTION THEMES IN QUR'AN AND ISLAMIC TRADITION

As the composition of the Qur'an differs markedly from the Tanakh / Hebrew Bible, namely in the structuring of narratives, the coverage of Qur'anic

---

"regardless of whether they'd committed an act of actual transgression, or were just in the wrong place at the wrong time." There was a place of safety—a pu'uhonua, "a place of refuge."

> Once inside the boundaries of the pu'uhonua, nobody could touch you—no blood could be shed within its walls. The place of refuge was sacred ground, and anyone who violated its sanctity would themselves become guilty of a great and terrible offense. While inside this safe haven, those who had committed wrongs were given a second chance, a new lease on life. They had time to offer prayers, perform rituals of contrition, to ask for forgiveness . . . When time passed, emotions cooled, and wrong doings were eventually forgiven, the person left the place of refuge (Goldstein, "The New Schul/Kol Nidre 5767," 2).

See also Johnson, "Religion Section of Native Hawaiians Study Commission Report"; and Morrison, Geraghty, and Crowl, *Science of Pacific Island Peoples*, vol. 2.

123. See their website http://www.icorn.org/ for more information.

124. See their website http://www.cityofsanctuary.org for more information.

125. The Skainos Project in Belfast, Northern Ireland is an attempt to transform a community through building of shared spaces in what is a divided community. For more information, see http://www.skainos.org/2009/07/09/the-skainos-name/ where the importance of hospitality in their work is articulated. Also, Martin Avila won an award for his 2012 PhD thesis at the Department for Design at Göteborgs University in Sweden titled: *Devices: On Hospitality and Hostility in Design,* available at http://www.martinavila.com/wp-content/uploads/2015/04/avila_devices_2012.pdf.

126. See the end of chapter 4 for more information.

themes of protection likewise differs. As a result, a selection of themes and pericopes will be dealt with in turn, exploring the variety of ways the Islamic tradition discusses protection.

Protection themes in the Qur'an can be divided into two different general groups: protection given by God and protection to be practiced by the Muslim, the latter of which is much more nuanced and will be given more specific attention. However, both groups are defined by a particular characteristic: an overarching concern for justice.[127] Protection in the Qur'an and the Islamic tradition are bound up in communal, social, and political ties, and those ties are defined by an understanding of justice closely connected to values of dignity and honor. Moreover, it is helpful to understand that the Qur'an's imperative for protection is informed by an ethical paradigm shaped by the recognition that right belief (orthodoxy) is a natural and required outcome of right action (orthopraxis).[128] This recognition implies orthopraxis involves striving for justice, out of which orthodoxy will arise tested by and reflective of that same justice.[129]

Divine and Human Protection in the Qur'an

Throughout, the Qur'an speaks of God as a "protector" and frequently entreats and intercedes for God's protection. Four of the ninety-nine names for God in Islam deal with protection: The Bestower of Security (*Al-Muhaymin*),[130] The Protecting Friend (*Al-Walī*),[131] The Preserver (*Al-Hafiz*)[132], and The Preventer of Harm (*Al-Mani'*).[133] Therefore, God's very nature is protective, providing security for, and preserves God's creation.

127. One may temper this assertion, however, by noting "justice for whom?" Justice within Islam is an ideal, but historically, it was often a factor in struggles for and maintenance of power. Nevertheless, this critique can be leveled at any cultural or religious tradition and is not solely an Islamic problem.

128. Qur'an 29:69. Esack, *Qur'an, Liberation, and Pluralism*, 13. This connection between justice and dignity and honor, as well as the relationship between right belief and right action are also present in Judaism and Christianity.

129. Esack, *Qur'an, Liberation, and Pluralism*, 13. Esack refers to orthopraxis that "supports justice" as "liberative praxis."

130. Qur'an 59:23.

131. Qur'an 13:11, 22:7.

132. Qur'an 11:57. This text further notes God cannot be harmed either; therefore, to molest what God protects is futile.

133. Qur'an 67:21. See Byrne, *The Names of God in Judaism, Christianity and Islam*, 128, where she argues the names of God in the Islamic tradition are grouped according to similarity in order to highlight meaning, and the "creation names" for God are linked to ideals related to protection and care.

Textual scholar Máire Byrne notes that while Muslims undoubtedly see God as an almighty Creator who "holds a dominant stance over all that has been created," it is completely logical to also believe the One who has created the world will also protect those in it. Byrne notes that within Muslim theological constructs the idea that God uses God's creative power "for protection is underlined by the Islamic idea that Allah bothered to create humanity in the first place . . . [and] it would be nonsense to go to so much effort for something that would not be safeguarded."[134]

As such, it is understood a covenant with God provides one with protection (3:112). In conjunction with the name for God *Al-Walí*, the Qur'an asserts God

> has attendant angels, before him and behind him, watching over [humanity] by God's command. God changes not what is in a people, until they change what is in themselves. Whensoever God desires evil for a people, there is no turning it back; apart from Him, they have no protector.[135]

Similarly, God is described as giving refuge to those who believe in God:

> Remember that you used to be few and oppressed, fearing that the people may snatch you, and He granted you a secure sanctuary, supported you with His victory, and provided you with good provisions, that you may be appreciative.[136]

However, if there is sin/wrongdoing involved, no one and nothing can protect the wrongdoer from God's wrath.[137] As they are associated with God, holy places such as the Ka'aba (2:125; 3:96) and Mecca (29:67) are also described as a sanctuary.[138]

Protection as it is described within the human realm as practiced by followers of Islam is more detailed and complex.[139] Most of the references

134. Byrne, *The Names of God in Judaism, Christianity and Islam*, 128.

135. Qur'an 13:11 (Arberry).

136. Qur'an 8:26 (Khalifa).

137. Qur'an 33:17, 71:25, 72:22, among many others

138. The term "sanctuary" appears most often to be applied to physical places such as Mecca, the Ka'aba, or the place where Mary dwelled.

139. An extreme example of the complexity can be seen in the case of "jihad etiquette," a term labeled in a New York Times article which detailed the various rules in place in the world of Islamic militants. Apparently, even in this context, one is not permitted to cause harm to another's guest without consent from the host. Like other aspects of religious extremism, it appears that essential values—including hospitality—still play a role, although they are most likely twisted into a shadow of its former self. See Moss and Mekhennet, "The Guidebook for Taking a Life."

to protective hospitality in the Qur'an serve as imperatives for Muslims to provide a model and as motivation for action. This method is different from the examples heretofore analyzed in the Tanakh / Hebrew Bible that situate the practice of protective hospitality within a narrative from which one extrapolates meaning and lessons for behavior. The simpler, more straightforward instructions present a default standard by which Muslims abide in relation to protection. For example, Surah 4:75 exhorts the Muslim to be a protector of the threatened by declaring:

> And what is wrong with you that you fight not in the Cause of Allah, and for those weak, illtreated and oppressed among men, women, and children, whose cry is: "Our Lord! Rescue us from this town whose people are oppressors; and raise for us from You one who will protect, and raise for us from You one who will help."[140]

Nevertheless, additional nuances in the text should be explored more closely. The following sections explore the issues present in the narrative of Lot/Lut, and analyze the development of the Constitution of Medina and the subsequent formation of legal obligations within the *ummah* and for the protection of the *dhimmi* in order to get a better understanding of the nature of protection within the Islamic tradition.

Thematic Analysis of Lot/Lut's Hospitality

Textual analysis of the Qur'an and later texts as they refer to Lot, or Lut as he is known in the Islamic tradition, has primarily focused throughout the centuries upon the issue of homosexuality and its prohibition rather than on the issue of hospitality. While some Islamic scholarship has sought to address homosexuality in a more inclusive way, the texts related to Lot were appropriated and interpreted by an anti-homosexual rhetoric that has made them difficult to reclaim for other purposes. Nevertheless, in recent years, a small yet profoundly significant amount of work has been done, primarily by Islamic scholar Scott Siraj al-Haqq Kugle in the area of a more inclusive, liberationist reading of the text that focuses on important aspects of the Lot narrative, namely the aspect of protective hospitality and related

140. From the 1977 Hilali-Khan interpretation of Qur'an (sometimes referred to as *The Noble Qur'an*) considered by some to be an amplified version, as parenthetical references are not in the original text. Note the reference to "fight in the Cause of Allah" uses the Arabic word *jihad*, implying the term is not a negative one, but simply means "to strive, battle, or struggle for." See Heck, "Jihad Revised"; and Marranci, *Jihad Beyond Islam*, for a discussion on the use and meaning of *jihad*.

issues, that have been heretofore ignored. This section will attend to these voices and the Lot texts.

The traditional and, ultimately, conventional view in the Islamic tradition is that the Qur'an, *hadith*, and other texts are "very explicit in . . . condemnation of homosexuality, leaving scarcely any loophole for theological accommodation of homosexuals in Islam."[141] However, the Lot text can be pried from the strict anti-homosexual interpretation and considered in a broader way. To detour the homosexuality debate in the texts, one can look into the text beyond the issue of same-sex intercourse and consider other factors that have contributed to the destruction of the cities besides homosexuality.[142]

Lot's persona in the Qur'an and extra-textual sources is that of a prophet, who, Kugle asserts, "hear[s] the speech of God because . . . [his] ears are opened by suffering oppression and struggling against it with endurance and patience."[143] In Islamic tradition, the prophets were those who did not "just believe in one God and reject the worship of false idols . . . [but] sacrifice[d] one's own well-being to protect the poor, the vulnerable, the strangers, and those who suffer, without which worship is incomplete, indeed hypocritical."[144]

To understand the texts that relate to Lot, one must consolidate them from many different places in the Qur'an, since the narrative is not told in full in one place but is diffuse,[145] and utilized in a variety of contexts to prove a point or refresh the memory of the reader pertaining to a particular issue. Therefore, textual interpretation is more difficult in that there are a variety

141. Ali, *Sexual Ethics and Islam*, 82, referring to the work of Duran, "Homosexuality in Islam," 181.

142. Ibid. This approach is not new to the interpretation that has been considered in the Jewish and Christian traditions in Gen 19 as explored previously. The development of more inclusive interpretations of the text in the Jewish and Christian traditions also had to take this approach at one time or another, as the Sodom and Gomorrah narratives have been used for centuries in anti-homosexual rhetoric. Only recent biblical scholarship (in the last two decades), with the help of disciplines such as anthropology and sociology, have seriously looked beyond the issue of same-sex intercourse and considered other issues present in the text.

143. Kugle, *Homosexuality in Islam*, 35–36.

144. Ibid.

145. Qur'an 6:86; 7:80; 11:70–82; 15;59–84; 21:71–75; 22:43; 26:160; Kugle, "Sexuality, Diversity and Ethics," 207–9. See also Jamal, "The Story of Lot and the Qur'an's Perception of the Morality of Same-Sex Sexuality" as a contrasting example of semantic analysis. According to Kugle, Jamal's purpose is to determine if "the Qur'anic terms that describe their wickedness and destruction are terms that specify same-sex relationships" (Kugle, "Sexuality, Diversity and Ethics in the Agenda of Progressive Muslims," 206).

of contexts to take into account. Nevertheless, Kugle refers to Islamic textual scholar Amreen Jamal and notes Jamal's argument that the terms used within the Qur'an to rebuke Lot's people "are not unique" in that some "imply . . . but are not limited to sexual activity."[146] Moreover, Jamal argues "the commentarial tradition and conventional wisdom have erred . . . [over the years] by placing undeserved emphasis on sexual deviancy as the particular sin of Lot's people," according to feminist Islamic scholar Kecia Ali.[147]

Yet, for Kugle, Jamal does not go far enough and fails to identify the exact reason for their condemnation. Kugle contends "it was not sexual behavior or sexuality for which they were all punished, but rather something far more basic."[148] According to Kugle, interpretation of the text over the centuries has included a condemnation of the tribe's rejection of Lot's authority as a prophet as seen in their prohibition of "the right to extend hospitality and protection to strangers, to the extent of demanding to use the male strangers in coercive same-sex acts."[149] Yet, such an interpretation was tempered by some classical jurists with an overarching assertion Lot's prophetical mission was "primarily to forbid anal sex between men."[150]

To circumvent this historical interpretation, Kugle asserts the use of thematic analysis in order to construct an overall narrative.[151] As portrayed by Kugle and the 12th century narrative re-construction in Muhammad ibn 'Abd Allah al Kisa'i's *Tales of the Prophets*,[152] the Lot narrative is remarkably similar to the Genesis 19 account, with one exception: Lot's prophet status places a much more serious emphasis upon his role as a model whose responsibility it is to "protect the weak, poor, and homeless with a Prophetic

146. Kugle, "Sexuality, Diversity and Ethics," 207, referring to Jamal, "The Story of Lot and the Qur'an's Perception," 1–88.

147. Ali, *Sexual Ethics and Islam*, 82, referring to Jamal, "The Story of Lot and the Qur'an's Perception," 1–88.

148. Kugle, "Sexuality, Diversity and Ethics," 207.

149. Kugle, *Homosexuality in Islam*, 50–51.

150. Ibid. Kugle argues, "[t]hese jurist interpreters created a legal term, *liwat*, as a shorthand for 'the act of the people of Lot,' meaning anal intercourse, and it corresponds to the English term 'sodomy' . . . cement[ing] the close association of Lot's Tribe with male anal intercourse." However, Kugle asserts "[the] term is [not] found in the Qur'an itself, leading sexually-sensitive interpreters to question how jurists have read into the scriptural text terms and concepts that are not literally there." The way in which biblical interpretation has effected English usage in this way as well is remarkable.

151. See Kugle, "Sexuality, Diversity and Ethics," 207, 209.

152. Al-Kisa'i, *Tales of the Prophets*, 155–59. Al-Kisa'i is thought to have lived in the 12th century, but may have been working with earlier narratives, redactions and interpretations.

ethic of generous hospitality."[153] The purpose of the *Tales of the Prophets*, according to Kugle, "is to present each Prophet as a character who upholds ethical values in the face of rejection and opposition by their community," while promoting a model for "ethical values that can and should inform the Muslim community that strives to follow the whole line of Prophets."[154]

Therefore, according to the narrative tradition, Lot was sent as a prophet to the prosperous Cities of the Plain.[155] In the Islamic tradition, Lot is also understood to be related to Abraham/Ibrahim, and, as a result, their prophetic callings were similar in their proclamation of monotheism and advocating a hospitable ethic of concern and care for those who are oppressed, vulnerable or under threat.[156] As in the Genesis version of the narrative, Lot's guests had visited Abraham previously, who had welcomed them enthusiastically,[157] and this enthusiasm for welcome by both Abraham and Lot illustrates the values held by both men in their prophetic mission which contrasted sharply with the actions of the people who were residents of the Cities of the Plain. The residents are portrayed as extremely inhospitable: instead of showing welcome and an offer to host strangers, the residents chase them away; instead of offering food to travelers, they rob them; and instead of protecting the vulnerable, they rape and coerce them "as an operation of power over them."[158]

For Kugle, the Lot narrative does not condemn the same-sex acts per se, but condemns the lengths to which the residents of the Cities of the Plain went to reject Lot's authority as a prophet. Their desire to rape his male guests was rooted in their oppression of Lot, an attempt to "prove him weak by violating his dignity and abusing his guests"[159] to whom Lot had offered protective hospitality in accordance with his prophetic authority, and over

153. Kugle, *Homosexuality in Islam*, 36.

154. Kugle, "Sexuality, Diversity, and Ethics," 215.

155. "Prosperous" is an important adjective here as in the narrative in al-Kisa'i, the cities are depicted to be prosperous precisely because of their inhospitality and injustice practiced at the expense of others.

156. Kugle, "Sexuality, Diversity, and Ethics," 212.

157. Kugle refers to a traditional Islamic attribute of Abraham whose custom it was to not eat "except with guests with whom to share his food, and he had not had any guests for three days in a row," implying Abraham had not eaten in three days ("Sexuality, Diversity, and Ethics," 212 n. 50). However, the source of this attribute is unknown.

158. Ibid. See al-Kisa'i's *Tales of the Prophets* for a vivid account of exactly how this turn of events comes to fruition in the Cities of the Plain.

159. Kugle, *Homosexuality in Islam*, 36.

whom the residents sought to "assert their own egoistic status and power, rather than by sexual desire and bodily pleasure."[160]

In the context of the Qur'an, Kugle argues ethical values which honor another's humanity arise from the belief in the unity of God, while abuse of that honor stems from idolatry. The unity of God, or *tawhid*, is "the basis for generosity, hospitality and an ethic of care for the needs of others," whereas idolatry is "the basis for pride, hoarding wealth, denying the rights of others and exploiting their weakness in every way possible (through wealth, property, coercion, objectifying others, and using them."[161] For Kugle and other readers who seek a more inclusive understanding of these texts, the Lot narrative is "clearly about infidelity through inhospitality and greed, rather than about sex acts in general or sexuality of any variation in particular."[162]

As it applies particularly to protective hospitality, Kugle's understanding of the social context resembles the previously explored interpretations of the Genesis narrative:

> As the head of a household, Lut had the duty to protect two kinds of people: his kin and his guests to whom he had offered food and shelter. Offers of hospitality were not just a matter of sharing a meal, but also cemented a social bond including the duty to protect guests from threats in the surrounding community. The people of Lut rejected his prophethood by violating his right to offer hospitality and protection to strangers and visitors. Their attempt to abduct his guests and rape them most graphically demonstrates this rejection. When Lut offers up his family members (who happen to be female daughters) in exchange for his guests (who happen to be male visitors), he displays in most extreme terms the sacredness of protecting guests who are elevated even above the status of offspring. The difference in gender between the female characters in the narrative and the male characters obscures the more important underlying message, that caring for those in need is a sacred duty that overrides the duty to protect one's own family. How many of us, homosexual or heterosexual, can claim to live up to that ethical principle?[163]

Nevertheless, the issue of Lot's daughters and the implications of consent are as equally problematic as they are in the Genesis text. Ali finds the inclusive interpretation of these texts based on the issue of consent versus

160. Ibid., 54.

161. Kugle, "Sexuality, Diversity and Ethics," 212.

162. Ibid., 213. Kugle also refers to this interpretation as being utilized by lesbian, gay, bisexual, and transgendered Muslims in his book, *Homosexuality in Islam*, 50–56.

163. Ibid., 214–15.

coercive rape problematic as the "argument that the Qur'an objects [to the actions of the residents] because they intended non-consensual violation rests on an assumption that consent is necessary for an ethical or lawful sexual relationship," which, according to Ali, was not always the case, particularly since Lot offered his daughters "without any indication that their consent mattered."[164]

To be fair, however, Kugle is not asserting that the consent is the main interpretative factor here; for Kugle, the key factor is the rejection of Lot's prophethood as seen in the *rejection of his practice of protective hospitality.* Kugle asserts his argument by asking, "Would anyone believe that a Prophet would offer his daughters to assailants intent on rape, as if their raping *women* would make the act 'pure'?"[165] The answer for Kugle is, of course, "no." In fact, it appears to be such a ridiculous possibility that Kugle suggests Lot resorts to sarcasm "to show his assailants how wrong it is to rape guests over whom he has extended protective hospitality":[166]

> And his people came to him, running towards him; and erstwhile they had been doing evil deeds. He said, 'O my people, these are my daughters; they are cleaner for you. So fear God, and do not degrade me in my guests. *What, is there not one man among you of a right mind?*'[167]

Kugle continues by arguing Lot and those at his door know that "it is far from pure to take his daughters, whose dignity [Lot] protects," and as a result, Lot utilizes the offer of his daughter to illustrate the extremity of their

164. Ali, *Sexual Ethics and Islam*, 83. Ali refers to a particular case where the Qur'anic text provides instruction related to female captives, illustrating "consent is not always relevant to the formation of licit sexual relationships." Additionally, in reference to the above cited in Kugle, "Sexuality, Diversity and Ethics," 215, 224, Ali argues the following: "One could argue that in the case of premodern patriarchal societies, only paternal consent mattered. In that case, could Lot have offered his sons to the men with equal impunity?" (83). I think this is a very insightful question. One also wonders how much of Kugle's interpretation is based upon the contemporary and inclusive Christian and Jewish examples of exegesis of the Lot narrative? His work makes no reference to similar biblical scholarship, but the similarities are so remarkable that one might wonder if there has been at least some cross-influence. Yet, it is entirely possible that Ali and Kugle's interpretations have arisen independent of Jewish and Christian scholarship in and around the same issue.

165. Kugle, *Homosexuality in Islam*, 56 (italics mine).

166. Ibid..

167. Qur'an 11:78 (italics mine). From the 1955 Arberry interpretation (*The Koran Interpreted*). The text was interpreted from Arabic by A. J. Arberry and is considered to be scholarly and highly regarded by Muslims.

actions, "that assaulting his guests is even worse in his sight than fornicating with his daughters."[168] Kugle further notes that

> Far from giving them license to rape his women, he is expressing with sarcasm born of despair, that vulnerable strangers are as valuable to him as his own children. On the surface, he may appear to talk about the correct gender for men's sexual orientation, but in reality he is preaching that both men and women deserve protection from rape and humiliation. Such protection, extended to both women and men, is a consequence of the ethic of care that fuels his Prophetic mission. This ethical message comes through clearly . . . [elsewhere in Surah 15:68–71] . . . The comparison by gender is only to emphasize to his audience that strangers of either gender deserve the same protection one gives to daughters."[169]

Interestingly, Kugle compares the Lot narrative with the story of the Prophet Salih, who "was sent to the people of Thamud, who built powerful cities that dominated wealthy trade routes . . . [and who] grew arrogant, hoarded their wealth, and refused to share equitably resources to protect the poor and vulnerable."[170] Salih, on God's order, set loose a "'sacred she-camel,' charging his people to allow this animal to roam their land and drink freely of their water, to be protected and cherished though she was vulnerable and had no owner," serving as a "living metaphor for the poor and vulnerable people living under the rule of Thamud."[171] But the people rejected Salih and his teaching, ridiculing him and God, and, "instead of attacking him directly, [the residents of Thamud] attacked his sacred she-camel, tied her up, and slaughtered her,"[172] again as a means of rejecting the prophethood of the one who protected her and was sent to them by God. In the end, the cities of Thamud suffered a fate similar to the Cities of the Plain and were destroyed.[173]

Kugle's interpretation of these texts resonates strongly with a social justice-oriented, feminist, and liberationist methodology. Therefore, it is no

168. Kugle, *Homosexuality in Islam*, 56.

169. Ibid. One cannot help but consider the applicability of this interpretation onto the Jewish and Christian interpretations of the text.

170. Ibid., 58. See Qur'an 7:73; 9:70; 11:61–95; 91:13; and al-Kisa'i, *Tales of the Prophets*, 117–27. Kugle further identifies the tribes of Thamud as those who "carved cities into the rocks of cliffs" (Qur'an 89:9) and also notes that Salih is not mentioned in the Torah "for he belonged to the other Semitic tribes who were the ancestors of the Arabs" and was unknown to the Israelite tribes (*Homosexuality in Islam*, 282 n. 44).

171. Ibid., 58.

172. Qur'an 7:77.

173. Kugle, *Homosexuality in Islam*, 58.

surprise that he refers to the foundational Islamic liberation theology work of Farid Esack as a textual interpretative model, wherein the Qur'an is found to be both "liberating and in need of liberation."[174] As Islam continues to evolve within a lived context, its relationship to its texts and tradition will also change. For Kugle, the anti-homosexual nature of the interpretation of the Lot narrative is an example of "compromise and retrogression" into the false security of oppressive power of later generations after Muhammad's radical and liberating vision of "an innovative new commonwealth, based on a brother-and-sisterhood of belief, shared wealth, and mutual protection."[175] Through the process of conquest and expansion, Kugle notes Muslims "returned to the old inequalities and hierarchies" and in the course of "a few generations, the Muslims' experimental commonwealth of liberation became an empire that rivaled Rome," rendering the radical message of liberation in the Qur'an as "an Islamic charter for domination."[176]

Another Muslim liberation theology scholar, Ashgar Ali Engineer, echoes Kugle's argument, remarking that Muhammad's practices of protective hospitality on behalf of the weak, poor, and oppressed had given away to oppressive rule, causing Islam to lose "all of its liberative thrust (except in dissident movements and rebellions)."[177] Yet for Kugle and others in his interpretive tradition, the Qur'an's liberative message that upholds the values of hospitality, generosity, dignity, honor, equality and liberation is not lost. Instead, in order to rediscover the liberative spirit, the Islamic text relies upon interpretation conducted by those who suffer as a result of injustice. Such interpretative voices are, according to Kugle, in "a privileged position as interpreters of scripture precisely because they are in a disempowered position . . . [as] oppressed within their society"[178] as evidenced by Kugle's own work regarding the Lot narrative.

174. See Esack, *The Qur'an, Liberation, and Pluralism*. Kugle argues that in order to "fulfill its promise of liberation, Muslims must first free the Qur'an from partial, limited, and corrupted interpretations that enshrine injustice." (*Homosexuality in Islam*, 38).

175. Kugle, *Homosexuality in Islam*, 36–37. This commonwealth will be explored further in the next section, which explores the Constitution of Medina and the concepts of the *ummah* and the *dhimmi*.

176. Ibid. Such principles argued by Kugle could certainly be applied to Christianity and Judaism in the context of the nation of Israel as well.

177. Engineer, *Islam and Liberation Theology*, 37.

178. Kugle, *Homosexuality in Islam*, 37. One critique of this approach, however, is that it places a great deal of burden upon the oppressed to reform a tradition that, in many cases, oppresses them.

The Constitution of Medina, the Ummah and the Dhimmi

In 622 CE, the Prophet Muhammad and his followers left Mecca under continued threat of oppression and harassment, and migrated to Yathrib, renamed Medina by Muhammad, in order to establish and grow the Islamic community under more hospitable conditions. This year and the event of migration is known as the *Hijra*, and is so important to the history of the Muslim community that the Islamic calendar hinges upon this event.[179] However, this migration to Medina also ushers in a significant change in community relations as well since it provides the opportunity for the Constitution of Medina to be written and placed into law.[180]

The importance of the Constitution of Medina is found in its usage of the principle of a social contract, which served to establish a formal relationship between different groups within Medina and, as a result, shaped the basis of a pluralist society. Scholars note the Constitution was remarkable in its concept and implementation,[181] that its aims were "entirely practical" as "it contains little that can be ascribed to the religious sphere,"[182] and yet, in the religious sphere it stands as a foundational document in the history of Islam.

Whether it is one cohesive document implemented immediately or a collection of different documents implemented over the course of several years,[183] its effect is the same in that it outlines the parameters for the establishment of a pluralist community, comprised of Muslims and non-Muslims, whose signatories commit to the mutual peace and security of each other as inhabitants of Medina. The document provides the details for a theocratic confederation (*ummah*), and according to Islam scholar Ali Khan, establishes "the reality of an actual agreement among real people of

179. Khan, "Commentary on the Constitution of Medina," 205. Technically, however, this event is the second *hijra*, as the first *hijra* was the migration of the Muslim community to Abyssinia in 615 CE.

180. The Constitution of Medina is accepted as authentic and authoritative by most scholars, although the original document has been lost. Instead, it has been included in Ibn Ishaq's 6th century biography of Muhammad. See Ibn Isḥāq, *Life of Muhammad*, 231–235.

181. Gil, *Jews in Islamic Countries*, 21; Khan, "Commentary on the Constitution of Medina," 206.

182. Gil, *Jews in Islamic Countries*, 21. Gil points out that one should remember "how difficult it is to differentiate between the religious and other aspects of life in the history of early Islam."

183. See Khan, "Commentary on the Constitution of Medina," 205–6; and Wheatley, *The Places Where Men Pray Together*. Wheatley argues the Constitution of Medina was made up of several different documents "spread over the first seven years or so of Muhammad's Madinan period" (26).

diverse ethnic and religious groups . . . in real time, in real space . . . through a real agreement, hundreds of years before the theory of . . . social contract gained widespread approval, mostly in the West."[184] Likewise, fellow Islam scholar Abdulaziz Sachedina asserts that of the Abrahamic traditions, which are rooted in the "ethos of shaping the public culture in accordance with the divine will," Islam is quite "conscious of its earthly agenda."[185]

There appears to be no solid evidence that Muhammad or his Muslim followers commonly used the term *ummah* prior to the Constitution of Medina, but scholars have noted its use in Christian contexts at that time. Its usage appears to refer to something akin to "religious community."[186] However, with the Constitution of Medina, its usage evolves from a theological concept to something that connotes a socio-religious ideal.[187] The Constitution recognized the possibility existed for several *ummahs* to exist within a greater *ummah*, as seen with the presence of the various Jewish communities situated as a distinct *ummah* alongside the emerging *ummah* of Muslims in Medina.[188] With the Jewish presence being assumed and en-

184. Khan, "Commentary on the Constitution of Medina," 206. Khan refers to Hobbes, Rousseau and Rawls' ideas of social contracts as examples the Constitution precedes. There is debate among scholars, however, as to whether or not it was a treaty or a unilateral declaration by Muhammad. Moshe Gil argues it was had been a treaty or covenant, "it would have contained the parties' oaths and pledges towards one another," or it might have been an "oral agreement (which was recorded later on)" (Gil, *Jews in Islamic Countries*, 21). See also Gil, "The Constitution of Medina."

185. Sachedina, *Islamic Roots*, 24. He notes further that "[i]n comparison to the performance of the religious-moral duties (*takālīf al-shar'iyya*) that are laid down in minute detail in the Sharī'a (the sacred law of the community), the official creed plays a secondary role in orienting the faithful in their social conduct."

186. Wheatley, *The Places Where Men Pray Together*, 369 n. 242; Denny, "The Meaning of *Ummah* in the Qur'an," 37. Both of these sources provide more background on the term and its evolution of use in the Islamic context.

187. Hassan, *Faithlines*, 87. See also van Nieuwenhuijze, "The *Ummah*—an Analytic Approach"; Von Grunebaum, *Modern Islam*; Denny, "The Meaning of *Ummah* in the Qur'an" ; Giannakis, "The Concept of the Ummah"; and Rahman, "The Principles of Shura and the Role of the Umma in Islam." Sachedina also argues that without the early development of the principles of a pluralist society and concept of the *ummah* and *dhimmi* (as will be explored in the following pages):

> The story of Islam's treatment of its religious minorities throughout history would not have been any different than Europe's treatment of the non-Christian other. One needs only to consider the violent forms that anti-Semitism generated by Christian redemptive theology took in Europe. The state policies of different Muslim dynasties are reflected in the legal decisions passed down by Muslim jurists that allowed for maximum individual as well as group autonomy in adhering to a particular religious tradition. (Sachedina, *Islamic Roots*, 25)

188. Hassan, *Faithlines*, 87. Hassan notes that eventually "the term acquired a legal

couraged within the larger *ummah*, the religious aspect of the term recedes in favor of a more social understanding.[189]

Islamic scholar Frederick Denny argues this overlapping of the term and its evolution in the early years of Islam makes it difficult to define, noting if one were to speak of the *ummah* as depicted in the Qur'an, one "cannot without qualification assume that the term means the Muslim community only, as we can when we use the term to describe post-Muhammadan Islam."[190] Concurrently, Jewish scholar Moshe Gil notes the Qur'an uses the term *ummah* "extensively in the sense of 'group,' 'community,' and especially to express the concept of 'successive revelation.'"[191] The Islamic understanding recognizes humanity has been comprised of *ummahs* to whom God has revealed God's self throughout history with messengers and warners,[192] whose "deeds [are] prescribed by God,"[193] of whom has been designated his or her "own time,"[194] and that there have been good *ummahs* and bad *ummahs*.[195] Over time, however, the term *ummah* took on more meaning in the Islamic context, coming to "symbolize and embody the very notion of the Islamic community."[196] According to Islamic scholar Riaz Hassan, the transformation of the meaning of *ummah* occurred as a result of the "change in the social structure of society . . . accompanied [by] the growth and development of the Islamic community," while further noting Muhammad "would not begin to differentiate between *ummahs* until the *ummah* he envisioned had established itself safely and concretely."[197] Whereas in the early days of Islam it was used primarily as a "universal monotheistic religious term,"[198] *ummah* began to evolve into a socio-religious-legal term in

connotation. The Muslim scholars of the classical period defined ummah as a spiritual, non-territorial community distinguished by the shared beliefs of its members." See also Dallal, "Ummah," in Esposito, *The Oxford Encyclopedia of the Modern Islamic World*.

189. See Watt, "Ideal Factors in the Origin of Islam"; Obermann, "Early Islam," in Denton, *The Idea of History in the Ancient Near East*; Serjeant, "Constitution of Medina"; and Denny, "*Ummah* in the Constitution of Medina," 44. Cf. Gil, *Jews in Islamic Countries*, 36.

190. Denny, "*Ummah* in the Constitution of Medina," 39.

191. Gil, *Jews in Islamic Countries*, 27.

192. Qur'an 4:45; 10:48; 16:38, 86, 91; 23:46; 28:75; 35:22; 40:5; 45:25. Cf. Gil, *Jews in Islamic Countries*, 27.

193. Qur'an 6:108. Cf. Gil, *Jews in Islamic Countries*, 27.

194. Qur'an 2:128, 135; 7:32; 10:50; 13:29; 15:5; 20:35, 66; 23:45. Cf. Gil, *Jews in Islamic Countries*, 27.

195. Qur'an 3:109; 7:159, 180; 7:164. Cf. Gil, *Jews in Islamic Countries*, 27.

196. Hassan, *Faithlines*, 86–87.

197. Ibid. (Italics mine).

198. Ibid. See also Watt, "Ideal Factors in the Origin of Islam," 160–74.

the later periods of the caliphs and after. Nevertheless, the precedent for an inclusive understanding of the *ummah* existed at the time and was utilized by the Prophet Muhammad.

The Constitution also details the expansion of the community, identifying in whose interest the confederation will act. Specifically, the Constitution mentions the Jewish tribes of Medina, and it grants "each tribe the right to be 'one community with the believers,'" identifying the understanding that this new state will not be understood as "an exclusively Muslim nation."[199] Khan also notes the Constitution's inclusion of each distinct Jewish tribe as signatories. For Khan, this signals that Muhammad and the formation of the new authority recognized the diversity of the Jewish population and their "equal footing" with Muslims, and bestowed "equal dignity and respect upon all Jewish tribes with whom the social contract was made, rejecting the concept that some Jews . . . [were] superior to others."[200]

Nevertheless, the Constitution was a pact first and foremost concerned about security.[201] It describes those who are a part of the pact are the believers (*mu'minun*) and Muslims (*muslimun*) of Quraysh and Yathrib as well as "those who follow, adhere to, and strive (*jāhadū*) with them."[202] Additionally, it provides no space for neutral groups; those who have signed the document are no longer responsible for their own individual security, but were responsible for the security for the signatories, the *ummah*, as a whole.[203] Such stipulations were radical at this time since it publicly overrode tribal and clan ties and formed a new concept of *ummah* as the defining communal

199. Khan, "Commentary on the Constitution of Medina," 207.

200. Ibid.

201. A criticism of this emphasis upon security is that, in the context of Muslim imperial power, security does not necessarily equal protective hospitality. In an idealized sense, it could, but political alliances based on the security of the powerful majority often do not provide an equality and justice-oriented hospitality for the minority. An awareness of the reality of the expansion of Islam (or Christianity, for that matter) through conquest and conversion must temper this discussion of security and protection within contexts of state power and authority.

202. Gil, *Jews in Islamic Countries*, 27; Denny, "*Ummah* in the Constitution of Medina," 40; and Ibn Isḥāq, *Life of Muhammad*, 232. In his article "*Ummah* in the Constitution of Medina," Denny notes that the term "Quraysh" designates in the Constitution "the Emigrants (see the preface and no. 2 of the document)" but later designates "the enemies of Muhammad from Mecca (nos. 20 and 43), who are not to receive 'neighborly protection'" as it appears that during this period "Muhammad no longer considered himself and the Emigrants to be Qurayshi except by descent" (43). Denny adds that such a move by Muhammad should not be surprising considering the treatment directed toward the Muslims by the leaders of the Quraysh prior to the *Hijrah*.

203. Gil, *Jews in Islamic Countries*, 27.

attribute.[204] Gil notes that now "precedence would be given to the ties of the *umma[h]* over kinship or family ties; from now on, the individual would need the protection of the *umma[h]*: no longer that of the clan."[205]

This new communal solidarity centered on the issue of protection. As Jews, Muslims, and pagans are now part of a greater *ummah*, the safety of the groups is of utmost importance, and each group as signatories to the pact "will act together in war and peace" under the acknowledgement of the authority of Muhammad.[206] Obviously, the peace provided by the Constitution depended upon two factors: submission to the authority of Muhammad and the consensus of the *ummah* through a spirit of equality and justice in internal matters.[207] Moreover, it was understood that God oversaw the protection provided to signatories within the boundaries of the Constitution, and God also ensured God's own protection under whose watch "there should be no discrimination."[208] Each group within the *ummah* were the "guarantors of the security" of each other in the face of those outside the pact, sometimes referred to as the *kafir*.[209]

Certain issues detailed specifically by the Constitution are of particular interest. One example can be seen in the regulation that a member of

204. Hassan, *Faithlines*, 87. The Constitution details later the particular responsibilities of each clan and the community as a whole related to blood money and the ransoming of captives, but that, even then, the community would assist if a particular contingent found itself in difficulty with their responsibilities. Gil notes the "significance . . . is that stricter attention would be paid to the taking of a life which calls for the payment of blood-money . . . [and] the redemption of prisoners would, as a matter of course, oblige the community, as people are taken prisoners only in battle and this could only occur on the orders of the leader, that is, the Prophet" (Gil, *Jews in Islamic Countries*, 29). See ibid., 27–29.

205. Gil, *Jews in Islamic Countries*, 30.

206. Brown, *A New Introduction to Islam*, 126. Brown cites the controversial 1977 work of Patricia Crone and Michael Crook, *Hagarism*, which asserts Jews and Muslims were partners in conquest, evidenced by the placement of the Dome of the Rock in Jerusalem which "hints at this relationship" (*A New Introduction to Islam*, 127). However, Wheatley notes "Muhammad expelled the Jews from al-Madinah" in the years following the *Hijrah*, which would signal that the Constitution was only successful for a limited amount of time. According to Wheatley, their expulsion was a result of their rejection of Muhammad's legitimacy as a prophet, leading Muhammad "to reject not only Jewish customs and observances but also the Jews themselves," as seen in the shift from praying toward Jerusalem to praying toward Mecca" as detailed in Qur'an 2:144 (Wheatley, *The Places Where Men Pray Together*, 28).

207. Gil, *Jews in Islamic Countries*, 31.

208. Ibid., 30

209. Ibid. The term *kafir* (and its derivatives such as *kafirun*) is somewhat ambiguous in the same way *ummah* is. It refers to "infidel," "unbeliever," or "enemy," depending on the context. In general, it carries a connotation of outside threat.

the community who provided aid to "a rebel evil-doer . . . and offered him shelter" risked invoking punishment from God to be "carried out on the Day of Judgment."[210] The purpose for such a regulation is speculated by Gil to have been an attempt to "prevent protection from being offered to people whom the Prophet eventually intended to fight" for being spies or enemies "who were plotting against him."[211]

Another regulation designated the city of Yathrib/Medina as *haram*, related to the Hebrew term *herem* (ban), referring to something that has been dedicated unto God, forbidden or sacred.[212] Somewhat reminiscent to the Hebrew concept of the city of refuge, a new legal system emerged with the Constitution that enforced the sacredness of Medina by banning hunting or bearing arms within its city boundaries and prohibiting destruction of its trees. Gil argues the intention of *haram* was to create "a holy place, without violence or the spilling of blood," forming "a sort of taboo . . . to make Medina a secure zone for both its inhabitants and its visitors."[213]

Additionally, since this pact was a "union of solidarity under Allah's protection," the welfare of each member of the *ummah* was important, carrying into this new *ummah* the "ancient obligation of the clan to avenge the blood of its members."[214] As a result, those within the pact were known as "protected people" or *dhimmi*, those to whom the *ummah* were legally bound by the confines of the contract to protect.[215]

210. Ibid., 31.

211. Ibid. One cannot help but consider the case of Rahab in Josh 2 and 6 in this scenario. Gil notes this particular purpose is shown in Muhammad's later praise of "the killers of 29 Jewish delegates from Khaybar, telling them God saved the *muslimun* from the hands of evil-doers . . . [and in the *hadith*,] the statement is preserved as directed against the [evil-doers] as well and not only against those who provided him with shelter" (ibid., 31).

212. The Hebrew term *herem* (sometimes known as the "ban") was used in reference to the acts of genocide as detailed in the book of Joshua where every living thing (man, woman, child, livestock, etc) was killed as an act of obedience and/or dedication to God. It appears, however, the Arabic use of the term is not used in this context in the same genocidal way, but simply refers to something being set aside for protection or dedication. See ibid., 32.

213. Ibid. Gil also notes that making a city haram (which existed in Mecca as well) had a practical and economic function as it was "essential for both commerce and overall urban development" ensuring "coexistence between merchants of Mecca and the nomadic tribes" (32–33).

214. Ibid., 31. Gil does state, however, that this obligation to avenge will get shifted in later Islamic tradition—along with the term *ummah*—to a more exclusivist "only Muslims" interpretation.

215. The Constitution of Medina was the first of many such pacts that would be made that designated certain groups as *dhimmi*.

The concept of the *dhimmi* began with the Constitution of Medina, but its example was implemented elsewhere in later agreements entered into by the spreading Islamic empires and the people they conquered. Often *dhimmi* are referenced in conjunction with another term *ahl al-kitab*, or "People of the Book," which "applied primarily to Jews and Christians, but was eventually enlarged to include Hindus and others living in territories that came under the sway of Islam."[216] Surah 9:6 of the Qur'an articulates the protection to be provided by them:

> And if anyone of the Mushrikun (polytheists, idolaters, pagans, disbelievers in the Oneness of Allah) seeks your protection then grant him protection, so that he may hear the Word of Allah (the Qur'an), and then escort him to where he can be secure, that is because they are men who know not.[217]

The term *dhimmi*, or more formally *ahl al-dhimma*, became a legal one after the example of the Constitution of Medina, connoting *dhimmi*'s official standing as protected under the might and will of Islamic rule. Islamic scholar John Kelsay notes the governance of *dhimmi* was established by treaties, with the understanding that if those being protected violated the terms of the agreement, such as initiating an insurrection against Islamic rule, they were justifiably subject to discipline. However, according to Kelsay, the "overarching purpose of fighting is to restore peace, order, and justice to the territory of Islam" and to return the *dhimmi* to "their rightful [protected] status."[218]

In the post-Muhammad years, the legal status of *dhimmi* ensured they lived within the state as "recognized minority communities, with their own structures of authority, religious observances, and laws."[219] Islamic rule had an obligation to treat the *dhimmi* justly and to protect them "from persecution and violence," but in exchange *dhimmi* forfeited rights and privilege that they enjoyed in their own domains,"[220] such as requirements to pay a poll tax (*jizya*), "observe restrictions on public demonstrations of worship, limit . . . build[ing] churches and synagogues, . . . and behave in ways that deemed respectful of the priority of Islam."[221] As such, in certain ways

216. Kelsay, *Arguing the Just War in Islam*, 39–40.

217. Hilali-Khan interpretation.

218. Kelsay, *Arguing the Just War in Islam*, 103.

219. Ibid., 39–40.

220. Denny, "Islam and Peacebuilding," 137.

221. Kelsay, *Arguing the Just War in Islam*, 39–40. Sachedina, *Islamic Roots*, 64, notes the "poor and dependents were exempt from paying this special tax, and it was progressive—it increased in proportion to one's wealth—but not progressive enough to avoid creating substantial hardship in some cases."

Shari'a law held no authority for the *dhimmi*, but certainly "the terms of their protection were set according to the Shari'a standard."[222]

Discrimination against the *dhimmi*, however, took root in the implementation of the provision of protection during the Caliphate period. In contrast to earlier years, the idea of "spiritual equity" lost importance, and "religious allegiance rather than righteous action" dictated social rank.[223] The power dynamic between the Muslim ruling authority and the *dhimmi* became problematic, as under this discrimination, the *dhimmi* were second-rate citizens and their protection was in the interest of the security of Muslim power.[224] Sachedina illustrates this point by noting that "even the most corrupt and misguided Muslim" would always rank higher than a non-Muslim *dhimmi*, in a court the word of a non-Muslim *dhimmi* was inferior to the testimony of a Muslim, and if a non-Muslim were murdered the crime was never treated as severely as that of the murder of a Muslim.[225]

Transgression against the practice of the early Islamic community and contrary to the principles of justice in the sacred text is visible in the policy of discrimination as seen by some scholars.[226] It is thought that the Pact (*'adh*) of 'Umar officially began the policy of discrimination in exchange for protection. The Pact of 'Umar was a document offered by the Christians of Syria to 'Umar upon the emergence of Muslim rule, although there is debate whether it can truly be attributed to the 634–644 CE rule of the second caliph 'Umar b. al-Khattab.[227] For example, 'Umar is credited with the following statement that was given to the residents of Jerusalem after their defeat in 638 CE:

> In the name of God, the Merciful, the Compassionate. This is a written document from 'Umar b. al-Khattab to the inhabitants of the Sacred House. You are guaranteed your life, your

222. Kelsay, *Arguing the Just War in Islam*, 39–40.

223. Sachedina, *Islamic Roots*, 64–65.

224. Such abuse of power in the Caliphate period at the expense of the *dhimmi* served to fuel inter-religious conflict for centuries to come, as the struggle for control over (rather than control with) dictated the terms of social interaction and legal rights for communities involved. In the contemporary context, Islamic scholar Hamid Dabashi argues that Islam "is only in power when it is not in power, and it loses legitimacy when it is in power." He continues: "The only way that this innate paradox at the heart of Islam can be put to work for a permanent good is for Islam no longer to be triumphalist but tolerant, aware of its own polyfocality, and in that awareness and tolerance not just to resist the abuse of power but also the temptation of power" (Dabashi, *Islamic Liberation Theology*, 22). Of course, the same could be said for Judaism and Christianity.

225. Sachedina, *Islamic Roots*, 64–65.

226. Ibid., 65. The Pact of 'Umar can be found in English in Lewis, *Islam* 2:217–222.

227. Sachedina, *Islamic Roots*, 65–67.

> goods, and your churches, which will neither be occupied nor destroyed, as long as you do not initiate anything [to endanger] the general security.[228]

If the rule of 'Umar had been truly discriminatory, the above letter would have made little sense.[229] Instead, according to Sachedina, the development of these practices appears to have taken effect among the jurists of the eighth and ninth century who justified these practices the "documentary evidence . . . [from] the early community, whose prestige in such matters was a source of authentication for . . . [the] jurists' extrapolations."[230] By contrast, Sachedina contends the Prophet Muhammad denounced injustice and the oppression of the *dhimmi*, saying: "On the Day of Judgment I myself will act as the accuser of any person who oppresses a person under the protection (*dhimma*) of Islam, and lays excessive [financial or other social] burdens on him."[231] Moreover, the hadith *Sahih al-Bukhari* includes a chapter heading "One should fight for the protection of the *ahl al-dhimma* and they should not be enslaved," and in that chapter Bukhari writes:

> Umar (after he was stabbed), instructed (his would-be-successor) saying, "I urge him (i.e. the new Caliph) to take care of those non-Muslims who are under the protection of Allah and His Apostle in that he should observe the convention agreed upon with them, and fight on their behalf (to secure their safety) and he should not over-tax them beyond their capability.[232]

Derrida notes that in Muslim contexts, one can draw a connection between the term *ger* (stranger, *hôte*) and the terms *giwar* and *dakhil*. Derrida describes *giwar* as a "noun of action" that "means both protection and

228. Ibid., 65, referring to an Arabic language source: Ya'qūbī, *Ta'rīkh al-ya'qūbī*, 2:135.

229. Ibid. Sachedina argues in 150 n. 9 that "most of the major historical sources that deal with the caliphate of the Umayyad 'Umar b. 'Abd al-'Aziz (717–720) and of the 'Abbasid al-Mutawakkil (847–861) mention carrying out such [discriminatory] measures against the people of the Book . . . [and t]he latter is also well known for his persecution of the Shi'ites." Therefore, one wonders if it is the wrong 'Umar to whom this pact has been attributed?

230. Sachedina, *Islamic Roots*, 65. Sachedina gives the following example: "Thus, for instance, the prohibition against building new churches or repairing old ones, which was instituted under some Umayyad and 'Abbasid caliphs, did not prevail in the early decades, because it is well documented that non-Muslims erected such places of worship following the conquest."

231. Ibid., 151 n. 12. Cf. al-Balādhūrī, *Futūh al-Buldān*, 162.

232. *Sahih Bukhari* 4:52:287. Cf. Sachedina, *Islamic Roots*, 66–67. As a result, Sachedina argues it could prove difficult to verify the authenticity of Pact of 'Umar in relation to "its representation of the situation of the non-Muslims in the early days of Islam.

neighborliness, protection of him who is *gar*."[233] Similarly, according to Derrida, *dakhil* refers to an "intimate, [an] hôte to whom protection is due, stranger, passing traveler."[234] In the same vein as *dhimmi*, the "right of *dakhil* would be a right of asylum witnessed everywhere in the Semitic world."[235] Derrida declares these two terms also "share a connotation of holiness when they are both invoked . . . to refer to the protection of a holy site or to what is protected by a holy site or by a deity," implying "the hôte or stranger is holy, divine, protected by divine blessing."[236]

In addition to the legal obligation of *dhimmi*, there is another important form of protection provided under the realm of later Islamic rule. It was traditionally accepted that any Muslim could grant "an individual or a small group of *harbīs* ('combatants,' citizens of Dar al-Harb) . . . a certificate of safe conduct," or *amān*.[237] A leader or commanding official could also grant *amān* "to a whole city, region, or to traders, religious pilgrims (e.g., to Jerusalem), and travelers as a class."[238] A certificate of *amān* was temporary, however, and upon its expiration, those under its protection who wished to remain within the jurisdiction of Muslim rule "could then assume the status" of *dhimmi*.[239] In later years, certificates of *amān* "were largely replaced by state treaties between Christian and Muslim authorities" because of an expansion in trade.[240]

233. Derrida, *Acts of Religion*, 401.

234. Ibid. Edward Said emphasizes *al-dakhil* in his writing based in the context of Palestine, giving two possible meanings that are not necessarily contrary to Derrida's claim, but portrays it in a different light. According to Said, *al-dakhil* refers to the interior, and, in the first instance, refers to the "regions of the interior of Israel, to territories and people still Palestinian despite the interdictions of the Israeli presence" (*The Edward Said Reader*, 269), whereas, in the second instance, "it refers to privacy" so that what is "on the inside is protected by both the wall of solidarity formed by members of the group, and the hostile enclosure created around us by the more powerful" (ibid., 270). It would seem *dakhil*, then, is closely linked with boundaries of protection of or from threat.

235. Derrida, *Acts of Religion*, 401.

236. Ibid.

237. Denny, "Islam and Peacebuilding," in *Religion and Peacebuilding*, 137. Denny attributes his material on *amān* is derived principally from Schacht's article "Aman," 429–30. He also notes "a great deal of important as well as detailed and fascinating information on the *amān* is contained in Al-Shaybani's (750–803/805 CE) *Siyar* (conduct of war and peace), translated by Majid Khadduri as 'The Islamic Law of Nations,' . . . [whose] contents are based on the teachings of the great Iraqi jurisconsults Abu Hanifa (d. 700–767 CE), and Abu Yusuf (d. 795), two founders of the most flexible and liberal of Sunni legal schools, the Hanafiya."

238. Denny, "Islam and Peacebuilding," 137.

239. Ibid.

240. Ibid.

Another legal obligation for protection in the context of Islamic rule occurs in the case of those who have been exiled under threat of persecution or have emigrated in order to spread the cause of Islam.[241] Surah 8:72 details a situation in which believers—although, in all likelihood, it applies to fellow Muslims—need protection, assistance, and mutual support:

> Surely, those who believed, and emigrated, and strove with their money and their lives in the cause of GOD, as well as those who hosted them and gave them refuge, and supported them, they are allies of one another. As for those who believe, but do not emigrate with you, you do not owe them any support, until they do emigrate. However, if they need your help, as brethren in faith, you shall help them, except against people with whom you have signed a peace treaty. GOD is Seer of everything you do.[242]

Later, Surah 8:74 notes those who give these individuals—refugees, exiles, and emigrants—shelter and protective hospitality are "indeed . . . true believers."[243] This text parallels Surah 4:100 which exhorts those who emigrate or are refugees for the cause of God to remember there will be many refuges available to them throughout the earth, along with a reward from God for his/her obedience, even unto death.

Ideally, the legal emphasis in Islam informs its ideals of protection and gives the various imperatives described above legal and moral authority. Development of a system of protection over the centuries formed what are now considered "human rights" in Islam, rights available to each person "regardless of his or her religion or nationality: the right to life (*nafs*), the right to religion (*din*), the right to freedom (*'aql*), the right to property (*mal*), and the right to dignity (*'ird*)."[244] Within those rights lies the imperative

241. There are some obvious parallels here with the cities of refuge idea—protection given to those who must flee, who are under threat of a persecutor—although the structure by which this protection is given as well as the connotations of manslaughter that are present in the Hebrew text are absent here. Instead, here the emphasis is upon alliance and mutual support in the cause of God.

242. From the Khalifa interpretation (*Quran: The Final Testament*), originally published in 1981 and revised in 1989, 1992. Again, the use of *jihad* is present in the phrase "strove with their money and their lives in the cause of GOD."

243. From the 1955 Sher Ali interpretation (*The Holy Qur'an*).

244. Čerić, "Judaism, Christianity and Islam," 53. In the context of human rights, Čerić gives the example of Turkey and the Ottoman empire preceding it, declaring that for centuries it has "served as major places of refuge for people suffering from persecution, Muslims and non-Muslims alike, from the fourteenth century to the present" (ibid., 52), referring to the work of Jewish scholar Stanford J. Shaw, *Turkey and the Holocaust*, 1. It would seem that in the current context related to conflict in Syria, it may continue to be true.

for protection of the threatened other as a part of Islamic spirituality and legal tradition.[245] Concurrently, the development of the idea of the *ummah* and role of the *dhimmi* in a pluralist Islamic society has an authoritative precedent in the tradition and its implementation; and the silence of a more inclusive interpretation in the development of later ideas signals additional consideration to be made regarding its recovery in a contemporary context. As has been explored here, the evolution of this radical idea that "the People are one community" provides a basis for an ethical paradigm and "theological pluralism that presupposes the divinely ordained equivalence and equal rights of all human beings," enabling the possibility for members of the faithful community to work together in order to "build a working consensus of values and goals."[246]

OBSERVATIONS

Clearly, Islam's more legal and justice-oriented approach to its relationship with the other has different emphases from the Tanakh / Hebrew Bible texts explored previously, yet this difference is not negative. In the Jewish and Christian traditions, the approach to strangers has primarily been less concrete.[247] Islam's contribution to this discussion is a more direct approach, a declaration of who is to be protected, how one should be hospitable, and the development of a culture that continues to enforce its practice.

Islamic scholar Farish Noor argues that for a religious tradition "to engage in any meaningful dialogue with the Other, [they] first begin by opening the way for dialogue within."[248] Noor's claim highlights the delusion

245. A critique to this is that in some contexts Muslims do not always grant these rights to each other, let alone anyone outside of Islam. The power dynamic (whether or not Islam is in control) and Islam's relationship to state authority historically and in the contemporary context serve to temper the ideal presented here. Nonetheless, the ideal exists, is considered authoritative by Islamic scholars as presented here, and should be analyzed. See Ahmed, *Discovering Islam;* and Friedmann, *Tolerance and Coercion in Islam*, for more moderate, yet realistic, analyses of these issues.

246. Sachedina, *Islamic Roots*, 28. Sachedina refers to the development of a "global ethic" in the form of Hans Küng, which he describes as "the fundamental consensus relating to binding values, ultimate standards, and basic personal attitudes between the religions that enable them to lead the way for society as a whole by their good example" (146 n. 12). Cf. Küng and Kuschel, *A Global Ethic*, 21.

247. At least in contemporary application. One could argue, however, that the injunctions to welcome the stranger in Leviticus and Deuteronomy *are* concrete, and certainly carry legal weight.

248. Noor, "What is the Victory of Islam?," 326. Noor is speaking on behalf of Islam, but the assertion is not unique to the Muslim context.

that each tradition—Judaism, Christianity and Islam—is pure and monolithic, a perception upheld by conservative voices fearful of risk, "dissent and heterodoxy."[249] This delusion stands in direct opposition to the reality that each tradition's internal heterogeneity requires its adherents to come to terms with internal and external pluralism if they desire health and wellbeing for their own followers and the neighbors God has commanded them to protect. Noor encourages this need to come to terms with pluralism by stating that "[r]ecognizing the multiplicity within ourselves opens the way for us to recognize the multiplicity of the other as well," and opening the eyes of the faithful to the reality that the threatened or poor "in the Muslim world may come to realize . . . their poverty [and danger] is shared by others beyond their faith community as well."[250]

For Noor, and as it has been argued in these chapters, "recognition of the other as similar to the self is the first step toward building effective collaborative coalitions and alliances" that can address the needs of the global community and ensure one another's safety as relationships are inevitably formed.[251] In order to do this, protective hospitality is a contributing factor to this outcome. The foundations are present with the Abrahamic traditions, and as the texts explored here illustrate, they continue to inspire protective hospitality centuries after their composition and canonization. It is time for this positive potential for cooperative theology and practice related to

249. Noor, "What is the Victory of Islam?," 326.

250. Ibid., 327.

251. Ibid. Noor cites the examples of the anti-apartheid struggle in South Africa or the civil rights movement in the United States where inter-religious cooperation served to address needs greater than the boundaries of particular religious communities. Furthermore, Noor argues from a Muslim context, stating:

> If we as Muslims are able to engage the world, we can help them see the tragedies in Bosnia, in Palestine, in Gurjarat, in Kashmir, and elsewhere are not just 'Muslim issues' but are human catastrophes and gross violations of universal human rights. Only if we can engage the Christian and the Jew and the Hindu and the agnostic who care about the well-being of all human beings will we get them to care about the well-being of all Muslims. That will only happen if Muslims reciprocate by being as concerned about the welfare of all as about that of Muslims. (ibid., 329)

Noor makes a very important point here: concern for the other requires an ability to look outside of one's tradition and self for the needs of others. Therefore, for example, Noor's statement would require Muslims to be concerned about the safety and security of Israeli Jews as well as the needs of the Palestinian Muslims. Similarly, fellow Islamic scholar Abdulaziz Sachedina argues for religious pluralism as a working paradigm "for a democratic, social pluralism in which people of diverse religious backgrounds are willing to form a community of global citizens". Sachedina, *Islamic Roots*, 35. See also Küng and Kuschel, *A Global Ethic*, 21.

protective hospitality to be given specific attention by the Abrahamic communities themselves.

Conclusion

What Can We Learn from This?

God welcomes us to
the table, laden and full,
Her apron dirty.[1]

This book has sought to answer the following question:

> *What are the resources and teachings in the Abrahamic traditions that take hospitality, and more specifically, its call to provide protective hospitality seriously enough to inform shared action and belief on behalf of the threatened other?*

To answer the above question, the argument presented in the previous chapters has been as follows:

> *Protective hospitality and its faith-based foundations, specifically in the Abrahamic traditions of Judaism, Christianity, and Islam, merit greater theological attention. More specifically, the practice of protective hospitality in Christianity can be enhanced by better understandings of Judaism and Islam's practice of hospitality, namely their codes and etiquettes related to honor. Additionally, the positive potential for protective hospitality's contribution to peacebuilding, conflict transformation, and reconciliation and the possibility for development of a "cooperative theology" among the Abrahamic traditions are particularly valuable.*

Throughout these pages, I have endeavoured to utilize a methodology, which emphasizes inter-religious life together, the realities of the

1. Haiku composed by author. Reaves, "Conference Response," 81.

marginalized and seemingly powerless, and the importance of grounding theological thought in lived experience. Furthermore, I have argued there is merit to the idea that there is a common theology and ethic of protective hospitality in the Abrahamic traditions, that Christian practice of protective hospitality can be enhanced by considering the same practice in Jewish and Muslim communities, and that there is a positive potential for protective hospitality to make a contribution to peacebuilding, conflict transformation, reconciliation, and the development of an inter-religious "cooperative theology" on behalf of the threatened other.

Much of the material herein has not been overtly theological in a traditional sense. Nonetheless, what has been presented here has been used to illustrate and complicate the argument presented in the introduction by exploring and analyzing the realities, triumphs and challenges of protective hospitality in the Abrahamic traditions, noting the positive potential and obstacles that exist for the development of a contextual, cooperative theology that is focused upon providing sanctuary for the threatened other.

However, in all of this, certain acknowledgements need to be made. First, the practice of hospitality existed long before organized, institutionalized religion took root. In many cases, the invasion of armies with their corresponding religious beliefs served to give additional meaning or a new lens through which to view an ethic of relating to others that would have existed in an earlier form.[2] Yet, for the purpose of what has been presented here, what is important is what adherents of the Abrahamic traditions do here and now, informed by their current religious practice. Second, it is clear that there is positive potential for faith-based resources that can inform behavior when people find it difficult to articulate why they do what they do. While most often the answer is "It's just what we do," analyzing those actions in light of the resources within the Abrahamic traditions for protective hospitality provides a means to open up new ways of thinking.

By way of conclusion, let us consider three main themes that have arisen out of the practice of protective hospitality discussed here and upon which significant observations and implications can be drawn.

2. For example, some attribute the code of besa in Albanian culture (as mentioned in chapter 2), which obligated someone to provide sanctuary to anyone who came to one's door and requested it, as an ethic made stronger by Islam. It is thought to have existed and was practiced by Albanians before the advent of Islam, but some argue that Islam helped to improve and codify it further, going so far as to say, "there is no Besa without the Qur'an" (*Islam Times*, "BESA . . . When Muslims Saved Jews").

ABSENCE OF RELIGIOUS DISCOURSE ABOUT PROTECTIVE HOSPITALITY

Throught this book, clear articulation has been given in relation to scriptural and extra-textual imperatives toward providing sanctuary to the threatened other, as well as discussions about the implications of such hospitable practice. However, as detailed in Chapter Four in relation to the focus groups conducted for this research, even religious leadership within Abrahamic communities had difficulty in detailing the reasons why protective hospitality should be practiced relative to their respective traditions, despite the fact that many had practiced it themselves. "It's just what we do" and "It's what anyone in my situation would have done" have been prevailing reasons in light of the impact of faith upon ethical behavior on behalf of the welfare of another.

The absence of articulation is significant, but it should not, however, be viewed negatively. Interpretations of culture are normal and are not predicated by articulation, or even awareness, by individuals and communities themselves as to the reasoning for their beliefs and practices. While people may not be able to detail the *why*, it does not mean that the *why* is absent. In this way, it is possible that an observer might be able to infer religious values in the experience and actions of individuals and communities of which the community itself may be unaware.[3] Similarly, while some may attribute this to the absence of religious motivation, within the context of the methodology of this research, I argue that perhaps I can say why: because they're Muslim, or Christian, or Jewish.[4]

There has been a significant amount of research on altruistic behavior in times of conflict and crisis, but more often than not, it has been conducted with a purely secular approach. Obviously, neglecting to account for or explore religious motivations for ethical behavior is short sighted. Simply because they were not included in the research does not mean that religious motivations for altruism and risks undertaken on behalf of the threatened other do not exist and were simply not articulated or included as such.[5]

3. Such an exercise of inference and interpretation is often utilized by anthropologists, who identify meaning, background and contextual information to explain cultural and social values of a community or group.

4. This, of course, does not imply that one has to be Muslim, Christian, or Jewish to practice protective hospitality. But within the confines of this research, perhaps this statement serves as an Occam's Razor moment—the simplest reason for providing sanctuary to the threatened other may be because you know your faith (or God) asks it of you.

5. Spahić-Šiljak, feminist Islamic scholar and coordinator of the Master of Arts in Religious Studies at the University of Sarajevo, interview with the author, Aug 2, 2010, Sarajevo, Bosnia.

Additionally, the practice of protective hospitality as highlighted in this research appears to hinge upon two simple facts: those who provided sanctuary commonly show their religious devotion through lived experience rather than by doctrinal adherence, and, by their example, they teach future generations to hold many of the same values even if religious adherence dwindles.[6]

Croatian Roman Catholic theologian Entoni Šeperić suspects that the nature of religious life is such that lay adherents to the respective traditions are "reluctant to conceptualize [protective hospitality] in religious terms: they either have no knowledge about it, or they do not know how to say it, or, perhaps, their faith is so simple that they do not think . . . what they did was something special."[7] Bosnian Muslim theologian Spahić-Šiljak considers it differently, asserting that perhaps it is not part of the civic discourse because humility, as seen in a principle found in the Abrahamic traditions, requires that generosity should be given in secret.[8]

Yet, religion's absence from the conversation about protective hospitality is, perhaps, a good thing. As it is often perceived to have colluded with nationalisms which fuel conflicts, the value of religion has been depreciated, and religious language had been largely appropriated by those who used it for their own gain rather than for the good of the community.[9] Accordingly, Nicaraguan theologian Juan Hernández Pico may be right when he argues that "those who are faithful to the God of history may be those whose motivating convictions stand outside religious categories," noting further that

> [In the revolutionary process] seeing people die for others, and not hearing any talk from them about faith in God being the motivating factor, liberates Christians from the prejudice of

6. In an interview, Northern Irish civil rights leader Bernadette Devlin McAliskey declared that she grew up in "a household of protective hospitality," where her mother, a devout Roman Catholic, regularly took in women and children who were victims of domestic abuse throughout Bernadette's childhood. McAliskey referred to her mother's actions as an expression of something that was "deep, ingrained within her, a part of who she was and what she believed," but that her mother never would have been able to articulate it in a religious or theological way. McAliskey then declared that although she herself is not religious, she has no doubts that her mother's hospitable acts placed "an enduring stamp on [her] and subsequent generations," providing a foundation for self-perpetuating values even in the face of sometimes declining religious devotion. Bernadette Devlin McAliskey, phone interview with the author.

7. Entoni Šeperić, Bosnian Croatian Roman Catholic theologian, interview with the author, July 27, 2010, Sarajevo, Bosnia.

8. Maimonides, *Mishneh Torah*, Hilchot Matanot Aniyim (Laws of Charity) 10:7–14; Matt 6:1–4; Al-Baydawi, *Anwar al-Tanazil*, 2:211.

9. Entoni Šeperić, interview with the author, July 27, 2010, Sarajevo, Bosnia.

> trying to encounter true love solely and exclusively within the boundaries of faith. It also helps to free them from the temptation of not considering a revolutionary process authentic unless it bears the label 'Christian.'[10]

Pico's argument highlights the reality that those who are engaged in resistance and life-affirming work such as protective hospitality may often have more in common with those of other faiths who are working toward the same goals than with those of their own religious tradition who are not. As a result, while this research considers an Abrahamic theology and practice of protective hospitality, it recognizes that such labels in certain contexts may not be helpful.

Furthermore, we must allow that overt religious adherence is not always a primary motivator. If a community or individual bases its identity and value upon the reality of living together with the other, then motivation to welcome and protect that other is paramount. Therefore, a challenge to one of the arguments of this research is that perhaps religious faith is not always the motivator for protective hospitality, but instead it may coincide with faith in the humanity of one's neighbors.

PROTECTIVE HOSPITALITY AS "GETTING IN THE WAY"

It would be easy to relegate protective hospitality to an ethic that must be practiced by a community within the confines of their own boundaried spaces, but to do so would limit its scope and power. There are numerous cases where individuals have put themselves in harm's way as a shield or hostage substitute in order to protect another, far beyond their own domains of comfort and welcome.

As mentioned in Chapter Five, Morschauser's interpretation of the Genesis 19 and Judges 19 texts argues the practice of taking a hostage was, in ideal scenarios, precisely "a guarantee of good will." Yet, in a contemporary context informed by memory of extremists taking hostages as an act of unveiled threat, one can imagine how a hostage scenario envisioned by Morschauser could be misinterpreted and go horribly wrong.

Nevertheless, the actions of placing one's self in the way of harm as a gesture of good will and as a means of providing protective hospitality is still practiced in contexts of conflict throughout the world today. Interventionist

10. Torres and Eagleson, *The Challenge of Basic Christian Communities*, 64, in Golden and McConnell, *Sanctuary*, 178.

tactics in active peacemaking, sometimes colloquially referred to working as "human shields" or "getting in the way," are utilized by individuals and communities who put themselves in the midst of a conflict, on the front-lines, and at risk of physical harm or death to provide safety or sanctuary for the other.

Such actions became headline news in January 2011 when, after a series of violent sectarian attacks on Coptic Christians in Egypt, thousands of Muslims protectively encircled churches in order to ensure that their Coptic sisters and brothers could celebrate mass without threat to their lives. "We either live together, or we die together," stated one person who stood guard.[11] Similarly, theologian Robert Schreiter writes of a group of Croatian women called Wall of Peace who, during the 1990s war in Croatia, "went ahead of the [Croatian] troops and moved into the homes of women in the Serbian villages."[12] Their purpose was to place themselves as shields and observers in order to protect Serbian women from being raped "in revenge for what had been done to Croatian women" by Serbian troops previously.[13] A final example can be seen in the direct action of organizations such as Christian Peacemaker Teams (CPT)[14] and The Israeli Committee Against House Demolitions (ICAHD)[15] who are famous for placing themselves between soldiers and civilians or bulldozers and homes, in order to bear witness to violence and injustice, and to provide safe spaces for the threatened other. It is in actions such as these that the clear connections between protective hospitality and nonviolent direct action, peacemaking tactics and principles of conflict transformation and reconciliation are visible.

PROTECTIVE HOSPITALITY CONTRIBUTES TO COLLECTIVE "DANGEROUS" MEMORY

Proportionally speaking, small communities throught the world have been able to make an enormous contributions to those in need and under

11. El-Rashidi, "Egypt's Muslims attend Coptic Christmas Mass, serving as 'human shields.'"

12. Schreiter, *The Ministry of Reconciliation*, 28.

13. Ibid. Schreiter is not clear in depicting if the Croatian women who made up the Wall of Peace had been raped by Serbian troops themselves or were simply aware that such actions happened and wanted to prevent Croatian troops from doing the same. The actions of these women are reminiscent of the actions of Le Chambon, who acted not only to protect the Jews but to also protect the perpetrators from their own violence.

14. See their website at http://cpt.org/ for more information.

15. See their website at http://icahd.org/ for more information.

threat. The two case studies of Le Chambon and the Sanctuary Movement discussed in Chapter One are perfect examples of small groups of people having an enduring, large-scale impact on the lives of others. A similar example could be the Jewish Community of Sarajevo, where a core group of about two hundred (of a community which numbered between 1,200–1,700 in total) stayed in Sarajevo during the war between 1992–1995 where they:

- opened three pharmacies and gave away 1,600,000 medical prescriptions
- cooked 110,000 hot meals (up to 300 per day) in an impromptu kitchen
- distributed 360 tons of food in the synagogue's social hall
- treated 2,500 patients in a makeshift medical clinic and made 650 house calls with the help of three staff doctors and three staff nurses
- started its own post office with the help of those who were able to travel freely (such as international workers) carrying 100,000 letters in and out of Sarajevo.
- set up a two-way radio telephone system linked with the Jewish Community in Zagreb, enabling people in the city to talk to loved ones elsewhere making 9,500 connections to the outside world and received 10,000 messages.[16]

Additionally, the Jewish Community rallied together its connections and resources, enabling it to send eleven convoys out of the city helping approximately 2,500 Sarajevans escape to safety, and less than half of that number were Jewish.[17] The community also subverted the Israeli asylum system in order to get more people to safety. First, they did this by arranging with the Israeli Jewish Agency for nearly 650 Bosnians to go to Israel and in so doing, stretched the "Who is a Jew" law in creative ways. Second, they went further by forging and sending back to Bosnia legitimate identification cards of Bosnian Jews who had already fled to Israel in order to enable others to evacuate.

The fact that the actions of the Jewish Community of Sarajevo were primarily in the vein of hospitality is not accidental. Their experience of history had taught them the necessity and value of food, safety, and open

16. Serotta, *Survival in Sarajevo*, 10–11; and Eli Tauber, leader in Jewish community of Sarajevo, interview with author, July 23, 2010, Sarajevo, Bosnia.

17. Eli Tauber, interview with the author, July 23, 2010, Sarajevo, Bosnia. Three convoys were by plane; eight were by bus.

welcome in an environment of sectarian violence as their own history was filled with experiences of anti-semitism and attempts at extermination, both from the hands of the Alhambra Decree during the Spanish Inquisition in the 1492 as well as during Nazi occupation where their numbers sharply declined from 12,000 prior to 1941 to 1,400 in 1945.[18] Similar to the experience of the Chambonais, the collective memory of the Jewish Community of Sarajevo included the horrors faced when one is not given assistance as well as taken on their behalf in the past, which served to inform their actions.[19] Those memories—not only the negative but also the positive—are an integral part of their communal narrative. As a result, their hospitable approach to their fellow Sarajevans "stands as a model for religious behavior" as well as a beacon of hope for those who work for inter-religious cooperation.[20]

Also similar to Le Chambon, the Jewish Community of Sarajevo sees itself as the paradigmatic other. They do not fit the mold or the commonly held narrative which shaped the 1990s conflict in Bosnia. But this aspect brings to light an important theme: those who put themselves at risk to provide protective hospitality for the threatened other rarely fit the mold that appears to shape mainstream society.[21] While the Jewish Community was affected by the conflict, they were not main actors; it was not their fight. Therefore, the actions they took to provide protective hospitality were enabled by the awareness within the community that they were non-combatants and that their power was not at stake by assisting a potentially threatening other. This role allowed them to escape and usher others to safety in ways, perhaps, a Bošnjak, Croat or Serb community could not have done.

18. Serotta, *Survival in Sarajevo*, 8. For more information on the Alhambra Decree and the expulsion of Jews as a result of the Spanish Inquisition, see Roth, *Conversos, Inquisition, and the Expulsion of the Jews from Spain;* and Sachar, *Farewell España.*

19. Ibid., 9, 11, 28–33, 77–79, 117–118; and Tauber, *When Neighbors Were Real Human Beings*, 40–43. Both authors give a detailed account of the story of the actions of the Muslim Hardaga family (Mustafa and Zeineba Hardaga, Mustafa's brother and sister-in-law, Izet and Bahrija Hardaga). They also tell the story of Zeineba Hardaga's father, Ahmed Sadiq-Saralop, who was arrested, deported to Jasenovac concentration camp, and killed for harboring Jewish friends and neighbors. Sadiq-Saralop, and the four Hardaga family members have been recognized as Righteous Among the Nations by Yad Vashem. Zeineba Hardaga was the remaining survivor when the family was recognized by Yad Vashem, and she and her daughter moved to Israel, and the daughter and her family converted to Judaism.

20. Little, "Cosmopolitan Compassion and Condemnation," 172.

21. The cases presented here and in chapter 1—Le Chambon and the Sanctuary Movement—show that these actions are often undertaken on the fringe, and not in the mainstream.

Furthermore, the nationalism that contributed to the 1990s war in Bosnia was often connected to efforts to protect and ensure communal purity or identity that defines the nation in question.[22] In comparison, the communal witness shared here clearly establishes that the Jewish Community of Sarajevo could never be described as nationalistic. Their secular orientation, desire to provide protective hospitality to everyone, rate of mixed marriage within the community and their decision to allow two hundred of their small number to remain and assist their fellow Sarajevans signals little concern for purity. According to Tauber, the Jewish Community operates on the idea that a "feeling of belonging is more important than purity."[23] For example, requirements for membership within the community are uniquely inclusive for the region and are as follows:

1. if one's grandmother or grandfather or a nearer relative was/is Jewish;
2. if one enters into a mixed marriage with a Jew which entitles one to the right to vote and be elected into the community even if oneself is not Jewish;
3. all members who left before the war can still be members in diaspora if they choose;
4. any Jew from the world living temporarily in Sarajevo can be a member and be a part of the community while they remain in the city.[24]

The priority of hospitality and welcome over religious, ethnic, or moral purity has previously been discussed in this research. Therefore, such a stance provides an invaluable model for how a community can value and support the diversity of an inter-religious community in constructive, hospitable ways.

Previous chapters have illustrated that the practice of protective hospitality is not a recent invention and is part of the discussion of what it means to live an ethical and faithful life as an adherent of one of the Abrahamic traditions. Yet, it is easy for the theoretical, ancient or historical examples to lose their power to illustrate the practice or inspire further action over time. This loss occurs when these examples are forgotten or disregarded as

22. See Munasinghe, "Nationalism in Hybrid Spaces," 663–92; and Mavroudi, "Nationalism, the Nation and Migration," 219–33.

23. Eli Tauber, interview with the author, July 23, 2010, Sarajevo, Bosnia.

24. Moris Albahari, interview with the author, January 18, 2004, Sarajevo, Bosnia; and Eli Tauber, interview with the author, July 23, 2010, Sarajevo, Bosnia.

an important characteristic in one's self-identification as a follower of the God of Abraham. However, if examples of protective hospitality are remembered, looked to as authoritative, and referred to in the formation of ethical practice as an example of behavior, like the Jewish Community has done, then loss is minimized.

How collective memory is formed and integrated into faithful life has been referred to previously, namely in relation to Johann Baptist Metz's concept of "dangerous memory." Scholars who have built upon Metz's idea illustrate its use in the remembrance of historical events that inform current and future action and belief.[25] Ethicist Sharon Welch argues that dangerous memory "leads to political action" as those memories "fund a community's sense of dignity; they inspire and empower those who challenge oppression" and they are "a people's history of resistance and struggle, of dignity and transcendence in the face of oppression."[26]

Furthermore, memories of "defiance and victory become dangerous as they serve as the spur to further action and critique, an ennobling reminder of the good that can be attained by ordinary people."[27] Subsequently, dangerous memory can be contagious since good is "attained by ordinary people" and provides an example for more ordinary people to act who refer to prior events as proof that their actions are not idealistic or in vain.

Moreover, within the development of a collective dangerous memory, there is an element of reciprocity inherent in building cross-community relationships. The reciprocity of protective hospitality is born out of memories of good done in the past and creates a cycle that feeds further acts of hospitality when the need arises. This understanding of dangerous memory as a component of protective hospitality is in direct opposition to the cycle of violence seen in nationalist rhetoric that fuels many conflicts.

25. Metz does this himself, in light of the events of the Holocaust, in Schuster, *Hope against Hope*. See also Schüssler Fiorenza, *In Memory of Her*; Brown and Bohn, *Christianity, Patriarchy, and Abuse*: Rigby, "Is There Joy Before Mourning?"; Johnson, *Friends of God and Prophets*, chapter 8; Keshkegian, *Redeeming Memories*; and Brock and Parker, *Proverbs of Ashes*. Schüssler Fiorenza also describes a hermeneutic of remembrance for historical reconstruction and rewriting, noting that a "hermeneutics of remembrance engages rhetorical analysis and historical re-construction for rewriting biblical history in terms of wo/men's struggles against empire and for well-being. It thereby reconstructs a different context for biblical texts and interpretations" (*The Power of the Word*, 163).

26. Welch, *A Feminist Ethic of Risk*, 154–55. Welch also refers to Martin Luther King's "Letter from Birmingham City Jail" as an example of the use of dangerous memory as "[t]he memories evoked by King are indeed dangerous. They endanger the continued acceptance of racial injustice as they propel people to courageous acts of resistance" (155).

27. Ibid., 155.

The cyclical nature of protective hospitality is hinted at by Svetlana Broz, an author who as collected stories of moral courage from Bosnia's 1992–1995 conflict, who asserts "[r]econcliation is the key issue in post-war societies" and that an "archive of stories of people who defied the evil imposed on them by warmongers can provide a model for future acts of kindness, resistance and civic courage."[28] Broz argues further that these stories

> restore faith in humanity, remind citizens that in each of us lie the seeds of goodness, and that even if we have been unkind or unethical at one point, the next moment we may find the strength to turn this around. Goodness allows for the redemption of the individual and the collective self. It creates a sense of dignity and allows us to act from a more mature perspective rather than from a stance of unmitigated blame.[29]

While peace as a passive state of being does not have the same cyclical life, I would propose that *active* peacemaking—particularly seen in the provision of protective hospitality by putting oneself at risk for the threatened other—does have a cyclical nature and is fueled by reciprocity and honor, rather than by retribution and revenge. In essence, actions are reciprocated and repeated, creating a cycle of protective hospitality, and with each movement to protect one another, life together becomes more and more solidified, like threads of a tapestry. The more threads of action taken on behalf of the other that are woven together, the stronger the fabric becomes.

CONCLUSION

Croatian journalist Slavenka Drakulić wrote that "[o]nce the concept of 'otherness' takes root, the unimaginable becomes possible,"[30] and history has taught us she is right. A concept of otherness taken to the extreme allows for dehumanization and objectification, and ultimately enables the ethnic cleansing and genocide like that which occurred in Bosnia, as well as what has happened in numerous other places across the world. However, the answer is not to homogenize and eradicate difference, but to understand and value that difference through hospitality, which, in turn, helps to form relationships of solidarity. Inter-religious cooperative theology and

28. Broz, "Moral Courage and Civil Society," 14.

29. Ibid., 14–15. Broz's point is reminiscent of the apostle Paul's admonition in Rom 12:17–21 to resist evil with good in order to obtain the redemption and repentance of the perpetrator.

30. Drakulić, *The Balkan Express*, 3.

practice in any context can only maintain credibility if each group "tangibly demonstrate[s] solidarity" as the other, rather than as the same.[31] Protective hospitality's power lies in welcoming or being welcomed by an other; protection given by the same is not hospitality but filial or communal obligation.

This work has shown the potential for protective hospitality for the threatened other to provide a foundation upon which a framework of inter-religious theology and cooperative action toward peacemaking, conflict transformation and reconciliation can be built. Yet, in the spirit of Hans Küng's global ethic,[32] a theology and ethic of protective hospitality is not just for the religious or the non-religious, and it seeks to build up a culture of honor and dignity that provides space for people to act morally and peacefully on behalf of others.

Investigating the theology and ethics of the practice of protective hospitality provided a means to bring together the two currents in contemporary Christian theologies used in this research. The first current was a contextual and political approach informed by liberation and feminist theology. The second current was a complementary and cooperative approach informed by inter-religious, Abrahamic, and hospitable principles that spoke to the reality that Christian theology exists in a pluralist world. Through these two currents, this research illustrated that hospitality is not polite accommodation but is an openness to engage with and learn from the other with compassion, dignity, honor, generosity, and risk.

The second chapter of this research highlighted the various contributions that have given meaning to hospitality as a cultural practice, looking specifically at the linguistic roots of hospitality, three central practices of hospitality, and the tensions that are inherent in its provision. These tensions, and hospitality's relationships to political power, tolerance, solidarity, and honor all give complex meaning to and confine its practice.

The third chapter focused specifically upon hospitality as found in the theology and ethics of the Abrahamic traditions of Judaism, Christianity, and Islam. By briefly examining the shared origins of each tradition, both in terms of Mediterranean and Near Eastern cultural heritages and in the patriarch of Abraham, certain common aspects and models were identified that provided a foundation for further exploration. Each religious tradition was then examined in turn, identifying and considering resources that inform hospitality as well as factors that impede its contemporary practice. By identifying aspects that are unique in each of the Abrahamic traditions'

31. Johnston and Eastvold, "History Unrequited," 232.

32. See Küng and Kuschel, *A Global Ethic*; and Küng, *A Global Ethic for Global Politics and Economics*; or Küng, *Global Responsibility*.

practice of hospitality, the absence of the role of honor in contemporary Western Christian scholarship related to hospitality was highlighted, allowing for further consideration of the importance of honor and its recovery in the Christian tradition to enhance and give additional meaning to the practice of hospitality.

The fourth chapter of this research introduced the second part, which sought to investigate the specific practice of protective hospitality. This chapter's structure was based on questions that arose in the informal conversations conducted during the course of this research in Northern Ireland and Bosnia with religious leadership and laity in the Jewish, Christian, and Islamic traditions. As a result, a foundation for an understanding of protective hospitality was established through an examination of the mechanics of protective hospitality, considering specifically the stages of its provision, the meanings and limitations inherent in protection, and the variety of motivations available to the Abrahamic traditions that inspire individuals and communities to act on behalf of the threatened other. Then particular aspects that often impede the practice of protective hospitality were analyzed: namely, concerns related to risk, the formation and enforcement of healthy boundaries, threats to spiritual, communal, or moral purity, and protective hospitality's relationship to violence, cruelty, and nonviolent action. Throughout this chapter, the reality that positive outcomes of the practice of protective hospitality are not guaranteed were highlighted, emphasizing the tremendous potential for the Abrahamic traditions to further evaluate and develop a cooperative theology and ethic of risk to address the needs of a threatened other in contexts of conflict. The overall emphasis articulated in this chapter was that by allowing oneself to be exposed to the other, and ultimately, being willing to put oneself at risk for the safety of the other is an effective means whereby dignity can be affirmed, transformation can take place, and relationships of solidarity for the greater good may be formed.

The fifth chapter surveyed samples from the Tanakh / Hebrew Bible and the Qur'an and extra-textual sources of Islam to consider the theology and ethics of protective hospitality in the sacred texts. Through this examination, the role of honor codes as discussed in earlier chapters came to the fore as interpretations of these texts emphasized the overall values of protection of one's guests and affirmation of life as an expression of honor, even in the face of serious threat. In addition, the Abrahamic textual sanctions related to the Cities of Refuge and Constitution of Medina assert the social and legal constructs that can enforce the provision refuge and protection for endangered others. As a result, the analysis suggested three points. First, there is direct relationship between protective hospitality and justice. Second, the selected texts continue to inspire belief and action related to protective hospitality in the present day, centuries after their composition and canonization. Because of this, the third point emphasizes the positive potential that exists for protective hospitality to inform and support a co-operative theology and ethic among the Abrahamic traditions of solidarity with individuals, groups, and communities who are in the midst of conflict and threatened by injustice and violence.

The conclusion served to bring several streams together for an easy distillation of the practice of protective hospitality. First, an analysis of protective hospitality makes real the risks and practicalities involved in its provision. Second, religion and its accompanying concepts related to honor play an important role in the articulation and practice of protective hospitality. Thirdly, the role of an inclusive communal memory can help develop healthy self-identification and relationships with the other, can be a strong motivator for the provision protective hospitality, and has the power to fuel an ethic of reciprocity whereby a cycle of protective hospitality develops, becoming a communal value. Fourthly, protective hospitality appears to be most effectively practiced by groups and individuals who value diversity and whose concerns about the safety and well-being of others supercede their concerns about risk or purity. Finally, the case studies highlighting the practice of Le Chambon, the Sanctuary Movement and the Jewish Community of Sarajevo have shown that protective hospitality provides a foundation upon which structures of peacemaking, conflict transformation, and reconciliation can be built and sustained.

May all of our communities be marked by our efforts at providing safe, protected places for the threatened other among us, for it is truly in the shelter of each other that we live.

Bibliography

Abu-Lughod, Lila. *Veiled Sentiments: Honor and Poetry in Bedouin Society*. Berkeley, CA: University of California Press, 1988.

Abu-Nimer, Mohammed. *Nonviolence and Peace Building in Islam: Theory and Practice*. Gainsville, FL: University of Florida Press, 2003.

———. *Reconciliation, Justice and Coexistence: Theory and Practice*. Lanham, MD: Lexington, 2001.

Admirand, Peter. "Healing the Distorted Face: Doctrinal Reinterpretation(s) and the Christian Response to the Other." *One in Christ* 42, no. 2 (2008) 302–17.

Ahmed, Akbar S. *Discovering Islam: Making Sense of Muslim History and Society*. Rev. ed. New York: Routledge, 2002.

al-Balādhūrī, Aḥmad ibn Yaḥya. *Futūh al-Buldān*. Edited by M. J. de Goeje. Leiden: Brill, 1866.

Albertz, Rainer. *Israel in Exile: The History and Literature of the Sixth Century BCE*. Atlanta, GA: Society of Biblical Literature, 2003.

Alexander, T. Desmond. "Lot's Hospitality: A Clue to His Righteousness." *Journal for Biblical Literature* 104, no. 2 (1985) 289–91.

Ali, Kecia. *Sexual Ethics and Islam: Feminist Reflections on Qur'an, Hadith, and Jurisprudence*. Oxford: Oneworld, 2006.

Al-Kaysi, Marwan Ibrahim. *Morals and Manners in Islam: A Guide to Islamic Adab*. Leicester, UK: The Islamic Foundation, 1986.

al-Kisa'i, Muhammad ibn 'Abd Allah. *Tales of the Prophets*. Translated by Wheeler M. Thackston Jr. Chicago: Kazi, 1997.

Almond, Gabriel A., et al. *Strong Religion: The Rise of Fundamentalisms Around the World*. Chicago: University of Chicago Press, 2003.

Althaus-Reid, Marcella. *The Queer God*. London: Routledge, 2003.

Anderson, Pamela Sue. "A Feminist Ethics of Forgiveness." In *Forgiveness and Truth: Explorations in Contemporary Theology*, edited by Alistair McFadyen and Marcel Sarot, 145–56. Edinburgh: T. & T. Clark, 2001.

Andijar, Gil. "'Once More, Once More:' Derrida, the Arab, the Jew." Introduction to *Acts of Religion* by Jacques Derrida, edited by Gil Andijarm, 1–39. New York: Routledge, 2002.

———. "A Note on 'Hostipitality.'" In *Acts of Religion* by Jacques Derrida, edited by Gil Andijar, 356–57. New York: Routledge, 2002.

Appiah, Kwame Anthony. *The Honor Code: How Moral Revolutions Happen*. New York: Norton, 2010.

———. "Sidling up to Difference: Social Change and Moral Revolutions." Part of the Civil Conversations Project. *On Being with Krista Tippet*, American Public Radio podcast, Aug. 15, 2013. Transcript: http://www.onbeing.org/program/sidling-up-to-difference/transcript/5876.

Appleby, R. Scott. *The Ambivalence of the Sacred: Religion, Violence, and Reconciliation*. Lanham, MD: Rowman & Littlefield, 2000.

ApRoberts, Ruth. *The Ancient Dialect: Thomas Carlyle and Comparative Religion*. Berkeley, CA: University of California Press, 1988.

Aquino, Maria Pilar, Daisy L. Machado, and Jeanette Rodriguez, eds. *A Reader in Latina Feminist Theology: Religion and Justice*. Austin, TX: University of Texas Press, 2002.

Arberry, Arthur J. *The Koran Interpreted: A Translation*. London: Oxford University Press, 1964.

Arendt, Hannah. *The Human Condition*. Chicago: University of Chicago Press, 1958.

Armstrong, Karen. "Balancing the Prophet." *Financial Times*. Arts and Weekend Section. Apr 27, 2007.

———. *Muhammad: A Biography of the Prophet*. New York: HarperCollins, 1992.

Arnautović, Marija. "Bosnia: The Village Where Hate Never Triumphed." Institute of War and Peace Reporting (IWPR). TRI issue 642, Apr 10, 2010. http://iwpr.net/report-news/Bosnia-village-where-hate-never-triumphed.

Arterbury, Andrew. *Entertaining Angels: Early Christian Hospitality in its Mediterranean Setting*. New Testament Monographs 8. Sheffield, UK: Sheffield Phoenix, 2005.

———. "Entertaining Angels: Hospitality in Luke and Acts 20." In *Christian Reflection: A Series in Faith and Ethics*, 20–26. Waco, TX: Center for Christian Ethics, Baylor University, 2007.

Auckelman, D. "City of Refuge." *Sojourners* 13 (Jan. 1984) 22–26.

Augustine. *Confessions*. Translated by Henry Chadwick. Oxford: Oxford University Press, 1992.

Augustine. *Reply to Faustus the Manichaean*. In *Nicene and Post-Nicene Fathers*. Edited by Philip Schaff and translated by Richard Stothert. First Series. Peabody, MA: Hendrickson, 1994.

Avrahami, Yael. "שוב in the Psalms—Shame or Disappointment?" *Journal for the Study of the Old Testament* 34, no. 3 (Mar 2010) 295–313.

Ayoub, Mahmoud M. "Abraham and His Children: Reply." In *Heirs of Abraham: The Future of Muslim, Jewish, and Christian Relations*, edited by Bradford E. Hinze and Irfan A. Omar, 120–124. Maryknoll, NY: Orbis, 2005.

Bader, Mary Anna. *Sexual Violation in the Hebrew Bible: A Multi-Methodological Study of Genesis 34 and 2 Samuel 13*. Studies in Biblical Literature 87. New York: Peter Lang, 2006.

Bailey, Clinton. *Bedouin Law from Sinai and the Negev: Justice without Government*. New Haven, CT: Yale University Press, 2009.

———. *A Culture of Desert Survival: Bedouin Proverbs from Sinai and the Negev*. New Haven, CT: Yale University Press, 2004.

Baker, D. L. *Tight Fists or Open Hands: Wealth and Poverty in the Old Testament Law*. Grand Rapids, MI: Eerdmans, 2009.

Barnes, Michael. *Theology and the Dialogue of Religions*. Cambridge Studies in Christian Doctrine. Cambridge: Cambridge University Press, 2002.

Barr, James. "Migraš in the Old Testament." *Journal of Semitic Studies* 29, no. 1 (Mar 1984) 15–31.

Barth, Karl. *Church Dogmatics*. Translated and edited by G. W. Bromily and T. F. Torrance. Edinburgh: T. & T. Clark, 1960.

Bass, Dorothy. "A Guide to Exploring Christian Practices." Practicing Our Faith Online Library. http://www.practicingourfaith.org/exploring-christian-practices-guide.

———. *Practicing Our Faith: A Way of Life for a Searching People*. San Francisco: Josey-Bass, 1997.

Battle, Michael. *Reconciliation: The Ubuntu Theology of Desmond Tutu*. Cleveland, OH: Pilgrim, 2009.

Bau, Ignatius. *This Ground is Holy: Church Sanctuary and Central American Refugees*. Mahwah, NJ: Paulist, 1985.

BBC News. "Libya interim leaders give ultimatum to Gaddafi forces." Aug 30, 2011. http://www.bbc.co.uk/news/world-africa-14715518.

Beck, Richard. *Unclean: Meditations on Purity, Hospitality, and Mortality*. Eugene, OR: Cascade, 2011.

Bell, Rob. *Love Wins: A Book about Heaven and Hell and the Fate of Every Person Who Ever Lived*. New York: HarperOne, 2011.

Benedict, Ruth. *The Chrysanthemum and the Sword: Patterns of Japanese Culture*. Boston: Mariner, 2006.

Benhabib, Seyla. "The Generalized and the Concrete Other: The Kohlberg-Gilligan Controversy and Feminist Theory." In *Feminism as Critique: On the Politics of Gender*, edited by Seyla Benhabib and Drucilla Cornell, 77–95. Minneapolis: University of Minnesota Press, 1987.

Bennett, John B. *Academic Life: Hospitality, Ethics, and Spirituality*. San Francisco: Anker, 2003.

Benveniste, Emile. "L'hospitaite.'" In *Le vocabulaire des institutions indo-europeennes*, vol. 1, 87–101. Paris: Editions de Minuit, 1969.

Bergmann, Michael, Michael J. Murray, and Michael C. Rea, eds. *Divine Evil?: The Moral Character of the God of Abraham*. Oxford: Oxford University Press, 2010.

Bergson, H. *Le Rire: Essai sur la signification du comique*. Paris: Presses Universitaires de France, 1969.

Berquist, Jon L. *Controlling Corporeality: The Body and the Household in Ancient Israel*. Piscataway, NJ: Rutgers University Press, 2002.

Berryhill, Carisse Mickey. "From Dreaded Guest to Welcoming Host: Hospitality and Paul in Acts." In *Restoring the First-Century Church in the Twenty-First Century: Essays on the Stone-Campbell Restoration Movement*, edited by Warren Lewis and Hans Rollmann, 71–86. Eugene, OR: Wipf & Stock, 2005.

Blok, Anton. *Honour and Violence*. New York: Polity, 2000.

Blumethal, David R. *Facing the Abusing God: A Theology of Protest*. Louisville, KY: Westminster John Knox, 1993.

Boardman, Elizabeth F. *Taking a Stand: A Guide to Peace Teams and Accompaniment Projects*. Gabriola Island, BC: New Society, 2005.

Bober, M. M. *Karl Marx's Interpretation of History*. 2nd revised edition. New York: Norton & Company, 1965.

Boersma, Hans. "Liturgical Hospitality: Theological Reflections on Sharing in Grace." *Journal for Christian Theological Research* 8 (2003) 67–77.

———. *Violence, Hospitality and the Cross: Reappropriating the Atonement Tradition*. Grand Rapids, MI: Baker, 2004.

Boff, Leonardo. *Virtues: For Another Possible World*. Eugene, OR: Cascade, 2011.

Bolchazy, Ladislaus. *Hospitality in Antiquity: Livy's Concept of Its Humanizing Force.* Chicago: Ares, 1977.

Bohmbach, Karla G. "Conventions/Contraventions: The Meanings of Public and Private for the Judges 19 Concubine." *Journal for the Study of the Old Testament* 83 (1999) 83–98.

Bolin, Thomas M. "'A Stranger and an Alien Among You' (Genesis 23:4) The Old Testament in Early Jewish and Christian Self-Identity." In *Common Life in the Early Church: Essays Honoring Graydon F. Snyder*, edited by Julian V. Hills, 57–76. Harrisburg, PA: Trinity, 1998.

Boling, Robert G. *Judges.* Garden City, NY: Doubleday, 1975.

Bonhoeffer, Dietrich. *Ethics.* New York: Touchstone, 1995.

———. *Letters and Papers from Prison.* Rev. ed. New York: Touchstone, 1997.

Borgen, Peder. "Philo of Alexandria." In *Jewish Writings of the Second Temple Period: Apocrypha, Pseudepigrapha, Qumran Sectarian Writings, Philo, Josephus*, edited by Michael E. Stone, 233–82. Philadelphia: Fortress, 1984.

Bormans, Maurice. *Guidelines for Dialogue Between Christians and Muslims.* Pontifical Council for Interreligious Dialogue. Mahwah, NJ: Paulist, 1990.

Bougarel, Xavier, Elissa Helms, and Ger Duizings, eds. *The New Bosnian Mosaic: Identities, Memories and Moral Claims in a Post-War Society.* Aldershot, UK: Ashgate, 2007.

Bowie, Fiona, and Oliver Davies. *Beguine Spirituality: Mystical Writings of Mechthild of Magdeburg, Beatrice of Nazareth, and Hadewijch of Brabant.* New York: Crossroad, 1990.

Brajovic, Zoran. "The Potential of Inter-Religious Dialogue." In *Peacebuilding and Civil Society in Bosnia-Herzegovina: Ten Years After Dayton*, edited by Martina Fischer, 185–214. Berlin: Lit Verlag, 2007.

Bretherton, Luke. *Hospitality as Holiness: Christian Witness Amid Moral Diversity.* Aldershot: Ashgate, 2006.

Briggs, Emilie Grace. *A Critical and Exegetical Commentary on the Book of Psalms.* 2 vols. Edinburgh: T. & T. Clark, 1906.

Bringa, Tone. *Being Muslim the Bosnian Way: Identity and Community in a Central Bosnian Village.* Princeton, NJ: Princeton University Press, 1995.

Brimlow, Robert W. *What About Hitler?: Wrestling with Jesus' Call to Nonviolence in an Evil World.* Grand Rapids, MI: Brazos, 2006.

Brock, Rita Nakashima, and Rebecca Ann Parker. *Proverbs of Ashes: Violence, Redemptive Suffering and the Search for What Saves Us.* Boston: Beacon, 2001.

Brown, Daniel W. *A New Introduction to Islam.* Chichester: Wiley-Blackwell, 2009.

Brown, David. *God and Enchantment of Place: Reclaiming Human Experience.* New York: Oxford, 2006.

Brown, Joanne Carlson, and Carole R. Bohn, eds. *Christianity, Patriarchy and Abuse: A Feminist Critique.* Cleveland, OH: Pilgrim, 1989.

Brown, Tricia Gates, ed. *Getting in the Way: Stories from Christian Peacemaker Teams.* Scottsdale, PA: Herald, 2005.

Broz, Svetlana. "Beacons of Humanity." *Spirit of Bosnia: An International, Interdisciplinary, Bilingual Online Journal* 1, no. 4 (Oct. 2006). http://www.spiritofBosnia.org/volume-1-no-4-2006-october/beacons-of-humanity/?output=pdf.

———. "Civil Courage: Good People in an Evil Time, Building and Promoting Resilience." In "Resilience," special issue, *African Health Sciences* 8 (Dec. 2008) 36–38.

———. *Good People in an Evil Time*. Translated by Ellen Elias-Bursać. Sarajevo: Grafičar promet, 2002.

———. "Moral Courage and Civil Society: Lessons from Yugoslavia." Translated by Ellen Elias-Bursać. Sarajevo: Gariwo, 2003.

———, ed. "Moving Forward: Essays on Civil Courage." *Spirit of Bosnia: An International, Interdisciplinary, Bilingual Online Journal* 2, no. 4 (Oct. 2007). http://www.spiritofBosnia.org/volume-2-no-4-2007-october/moving-forward-essays-on-civil-courage/.

Brueggemann, Walter. *The Covenanted Self: Explorations in Law and Covenant*. Edited by Patrick Miller. Minneapolis: Fortress, 1999.

———. *Deep Memory, Exuberant Hope*. Minneapolis: Fortress, 2000.

———. *Divine Presence Amid Violence: Contextualizing the Book of Joshua*. Eugene, OR: Cascade, 2009.

———. *Genesis*. Interpretation Biblical Commentary. Louisville, KY: John Knox, 1982

———. *Isaiah 40–66:* Westminster Bible Companion. Louisville, KY: Westminster John Knox, 1998.

———. *The Land: Place as Gift, Promise and Challenge in Biblical Faith*. Philadelphia: Fortress, 1977.

———. *Peace*. Understanding Biblical Themes. St. Louis: Chalice, 2001.

Buber, Martin. *I and Thou*. New York: Scribners, 1970.

Burrell, David B. *Knowing the Unknowable God: Ibn-Sina, Maimonides, Aquinas*. Notre Dame, IN: University of Notre Dame Press, 1986.

Burt, Donald X. *Friendship and Society: An Introduction to Augustine's Practical Philosophy*. Grand Rapids: Eerdmans, 1999.

Byrne, Brendan. *The Hospitality of God: A Reading of Luke's Gospel*. Collegeville, MN: Liturgical, 2000.

Byrne, Máire. *The Names of God in Judaism, Christianity and Islam: A Basis for Interfaith Dialogue*. London: Continuum, 2011.

Cairns, Douglas. *Aidos: The Psychology and Ethics of Honour and Shame in Ancient Greek Literature*. Oxford: Oxford University Press, 1993.

Waterworth, J., ed. "The Council of Trent: The Twenty-Fifth Session." In *The Canons and Decrees of the Sacred and Ecumenical Council of Trent*, edited and translated by J. Waterworth, 232–89. London: Dolman, 1848. http://history.hanover.edu/texts/trent/ct25.html.

Caputo, John D. *More Radical Hermeneutics: On Not Knowing Who We Are*. Studies in Continental Thought. Bloomington, IN: Indiana University Press, 2000.

———. *What Would Jesus Deconstruct?* Grand Rapids, MI: Baker Academic, 2007.

Carothers, Thomas. *In the Name of Democracy: U.S. Policy toward Latin America in the Reagan Years*. Berkeley, CA: University of California Press, 1993.

Carroll, Seforosa. "Reimagining Home: A Diasporic Perspective on Encounters with the Religious Other in Australia." In *Asian and Oceanic Christianities in Conversation: Exploring Theological Identities at Home and in Diaspora*, edited by Heup Young Kim, Fumitaka Matsuoka, and Anri Morimoto, 169–184. Amsterdam: Editions Rodopi, 2011.

Cavanaugh, William T. *Torture and Eucharist: Theology, Politics, and the Body of Christ.* Oxford: Blackwell, 1998.

Cavanaugh, William T., and Peter Scott, eds. *The Blackwell Companion to Political Theology.* Oxford: Blackwell, 2004.

Čerić, Mustafa. "Judaism, Christianity and Islam: Hope or Fear of our Times." In *Beyond Violence: Religious Sources of Social Transformation in Judaism, Christianity, and Islam,* edited by James L. Heft, 43–56. New York: Fordham University Press, 2004.

Chamberlain, J. Edward. *If This Is Your Land, Where Are Your Stories?: Reimagining Home and Sacred Space.* Cleveland: Pilgrim, 2003.

CBS News. "The Righteous." Nov 8, 2009. http://www.cbsnews.com/stories/2009/11/08/sunday/main5574960.shtml.

Chayes, Antonia, and Martha L. Minow, eds. *Imagine Coexistence: Restoring Humanity After Violent Ethnic Conflict.* San Francisco: Jossey-Bass, 2003.

Chesterton, G. K. *The Collected Works of G. K. Chesterton.* vol. 29. London: Ignatius, 1988.

Chia, Edmund Kee-Fook. "Is Interfaith Theology Possible?" *Studies in Interreligious Dialogue* 18, no. 1 (2008) 112–17.

Chicago Religious Task Force for Central America. *Organizing for Resistance: Historical and Theological Reflections and Organizing.* 1986. https://organizingforpower.files.wordpress.com/2009/06/organizing-for-resistance-chicago-manual.pdf.

Chittister, Joan. "Hospitality: The Unboundaried Heart." In *Wisdom Distilled from the Daily: Living the Rule of St. Benedict Today.* San Francisco: HarperSanFrancisco, 1990.

Chittister, Joan, et. al. *The Tent of Abraham: Stories of Hope and Peace for Jews, Christians and Muslims.* Boston: Beacon, 2006.

Chopp, Rebecca. *The Praxis of Suffering: An Interpretation of Liberation and Political Theologies.* Maryknoll, NY: Orbis, 1990.

Christensen, Michael J. "Practicing Hospitality in the City: Making the Stranger into a Friend." In *City Streets, City People.* Nashville: Abingdon, 1988.

Clark, Howard, ed. *People Power: Unarmed Resistance and Global Solidarity.* New York: Pluto, 2009.

Clark, Ian D., and David A. Cahir. "'The Comfort of Strangers': Hospitality on the Victorian Goldfields, 1850–1860." *Journal of Hospitality and Tourism Management* 15 (2008) 2–7.

Clooney, Francis X. *Comparative Theology: Deep Learning Across Religious Borders.* Chichester, UK: Wiley-Blackwell, 2010.

Cole, Darrell. "Good Wars." *First Things* 116 (Oct. 2001) 27–31.

Coleman, Will. "Being Christian in a World of Fear: The Challenge of Doing Theology within a Violent Society." In *Many Voices, One God: Being Faithful in a Pluralistic World,* edited by Walter Brueggemann and George W. Stroup, 35–45. Louisville, KY: Westminster John Knox, 1998.

Community Relations Council. *Towards Sustainable Security; Interface Barriers and the Legacy of Segregation in Belfast.* Belfast: Community Relations Council, 2008.

Cone, James. *For My People: Black Theology and the Black Church.* Maryknoll, NY: Orbis, 1984.

———. *God of the Oppressed.* Maryknoll, NY: Orbis, 1997.

———. *Speaking the Truth: Ecumenism, Liberation and Black Theology.* 2nd ed. Maryknoll, NY: Orbis, 1999.

Conner, Philip. *Huguenot Heartland: Montaubal and Southern French Calvinism During The Wars of Religion*. St. Andrews Studies in Reformation History. Farnham, UK: Ashgate, 2002.

Courville, Mathieu. *Edward Said's Rhetoric of the Secular*. London: Continuum, 2010.

Cornille, Catherine. *The Im-Possibility of Interreligious Dialogue*. New York: Crossroad, 2008.

Cornille, Catherine, and Christopher Conway, eds. *Interreligious Hermeneutics*. Eugene, OR: Cascade, 2010.

Counihan, Carole, and Penny Van Esterick, eds. *Food and Culture: A Reader*. New York: Routledge, 2007.

Crittenden, Ann. *Sanctuary: A Story of American Conscience and the Law in Collision*. New York: Grove, 1988.

Cunningham, David S. *These Three are One: The Practice of Trinitarian Theology*. Malden, MA: Blackwell, 1998.

Cunningham, Hilary. *God and Caesar at the Rio Grande: Sanctuary and the Politics of Religion*. Minneapolis: University of Minnesota Press, 1995.

Curta, Florin. *Southeastern Europe in the Middle Ages 500–1250*. Cambridge: Cambridge University Press, 2006.

Dabashi, Hamid. *Islamic Liberation Theology: Resisting the Empire*. London: Taylor & Francis, 2008.

Daly, Mary. *Beyond God the Father*. Boston: Beacon, 1973.

———. *The Church and the Second Sex*. Boston: Beacon, 1968.

Davidson, Miriam. *Convictions of the Heart: Jim Corbett and the Sanctuary Movement*. Tucson, AZ: University of Arizona Press, 1988.

Davis, Rachel, et al. "Prevention of Genocide and Mass Atrocities and the Responsibility to Protect: Challenges for the UN and the International Community in the 21st Century." The Responsibility to Protect. Occasional Paper Series. International Peace Institute, June 2008. https://www.ipinst.org/wp-content/uploads/publications/ipigeno.pdf.

Day, Dorothy. *House of Hospitality*. New York: Sheed & Ward, 1939.

Dawes, Gregory W. "The Sense of the Past in the New Testament and the Qur'an." In *Islamic and Christian Cultures: Conflict or Dialogue* (Bulgarian Philosophical Studies 3), edited by Plamen Makariev, 9–31. Washington, DC: Council for Research in Values and Philosophy, 2001.

De Gruchy, John W. *Reconciliation: Restoring Justice*. Minneapolis: Fortress, 2002.

Denffer, Ahmad von. *'Ulūm Al-Qur'ān: An Introduction to the Sciences of the Qur'ān*. London: Islamic Foundation, 1989.

Denny, Frederick M. "Islam and Peacebuilding." In *Religion and Peacebuilding*, edited by Harold Coward and Gordon S. Smith, 129–146. Albany, NY: State University of New York Press, 2004.

———. "The Meaning of *ummah* in the Qur'an." *History of Religions* 15 (1975) 34–69.

Denton, R. C., ed. *The Idea of History in the Ancient Near East*. New Haven, CT: Yale University Press, 1966.

Derrida, Jacques. *Acts of Religion*. Edited by Gil Anidjar. New York: Routledge, 2002.

———. *Adieu to Emmanuel Levinas*. Translated by Pascale-Anne Brault and Michael Naas. Stanford, CA: Stanford University Press, 1999.

———. "Hospitality." In *Deconstruction in a Nutshell: A Conversation with Jacques Derrida*, edited and with commentary by John D. Caputo, 109–12. Bronx, NY: Fordham University Press, 1997.

———. *On Cosmopolitanism and Forgiveness*. Thinking in Action. New York: Routledge, 2001.

———. *The Politics of Friendship*. New York: Verso, 2006.

———. "Violence and Metaphysics." In *Writing and Difference*, translated by Alan Bass, 79–153. Chicago: University of Chicago Press, 1978.

Derrida, Jacques, and Anne Dufourmantelle. *Of Hospitality (Cultural Memory in the Present)*. Translated by Rachel Bowlby. Palo Alto, CA: Stanford University Press, 2000.

DeSilva, David A. *Honor, Patronage, Kinship and Purity: Unlocking New Testament Culture*. Downers Grove, IL: InterVarsity, 2000.

Diamant, Anita. *Living a Jewish Life: Jewish Traditions, Customs and Values for Today's Families*. New York: Collins, 1996.

Dietler, Michael, and Brian Hayden. *Feasts: Archaeological and Ethnographic Perspectives on Food, Politics, and Power*. Tuscaloosa, AL: University of Alabama Press, 2010.

Docker, John. *The Origins of Violence: Religion, History and Genocide*. New York: Pluto, 2008.

Dodson, Jualynne E., and Cheryl Townsend Gilkes. "'There's Nothing Like Church Food': Food and the U.S. Afro-Christian Tradition: Re-membering Community and Feeding the Embodied S/spirit(s)." *Journal of the American Academy of Religion* 63, no. 3 (Fall 1995) 519–38.

Doorly, William J. *The Laws of Yahweh: A Handbook of Biblical Law*. Mahwah, NJ: Paulist, 2002.

Douglas, Mary. *Risk Acceptability According to the Social Sciences*. London: Routledge & Kegan Paul, 1985.

Douglas, Mary. *In The Wilderness: The Doctrine of Defilement in the Book of Numbers*. Journal for the Study of the Old Testament Supplement Series 158. Sheffield, UK: Sheffield Academic, 1993.

———. *Purity and Danger: An Analysis of Concepts of Pollution and Taboo*. Vol. 2 of *Mary Douglas Collected Works*. London: Routledge, 1996.

Dozeman, Thomas B. "Numbers." In vol. 2 of *New Interpreter's Bible*. Nashville: Abingdon, 1998.

Drakulić, Slavenka. *The Balkan Express: Fragments from the Other Side of War*. New York: HarperPerrenial, 1994.

Duran, Khalid. "Homosexuality in Islam." In *Homosexuality and World Religions*, edited by Arlene Swidler, 181–97. Valley Forge, PA: Trinity, 1993.

Earl, Douglas S. *The Joshua Delusion: Rethinking Genocide in the Bible*. Cambridge: Lutterworth, 2011.

Earl, Riggins R., Jr. "Under Their Own Vine and Fig Tree: The Ethics of Social and Spiritual Hospitality in Black Church Worship." *Journal of the Interdenominational Theological Center* 14, nos. 1 and 2 (Fall 1986–Spring 1987) 181–93.

Eck, Diane. *A New Religious America*. San Francisco: HarperSanFrancisco, 2001.

Ehrlich, M. Avrum. *Encyclopedia of the Jewish Diaspora: Origins, Experiences, and Culture*, vols. 1–3. Santa Barbara, CA: ABC-CLIO, 2008.

Eiesland, N. L. *The Disabled God: Toward a Liberatory Theology of Disability*. Nashville: Abingdon, 1994.

Eisenstadt, Oona. "The Problem of the Promise: Derrida on Levinas on the Cities of Refuge." *Crosscurrents*. (Winter 2000) 474–82.

El Fadl, Khaled M. Abou. *And God Knows the Soldiers: The Authoritative and Authoritarian in Islamic Discourses*. Lanham, MD: University Press of America, 2001.

Ellis, Marc. *Reading the Torah Out Loud*. Minneapolis: Fortress, 2007.

———. *Toward a Jewish Theology of Liberation*. Maryknoll, NY: Orbis, 1987.

El-Rashidi, Yasmine. "Egypt's Muslims attend Coptic Christmas mass, serving as 'human shields.'" Jan. 7, 2011. Ahram Online. http://english.ahram.org.eg/News/3365.aspx

Emerson, Ralph Waldo. "Worship." Chapter 6 in *The Conduct of Life: Nature, & Other Essays*, 1860 (rev. 1876). http://www.emersoncentral.com/worship.htm.

Engell, Helene. "Dialogue for Life: Feminist Approaches to Interfaith Dialogue." In *Theology and the Religions: A Dialogue*, edited by Viggo Mortenson, 249–256. Grand Rapids, MI: Eerdmans, 2003.

Engineer, Ashgar Ali. *Islam and Liberation Theology*. New Delhi: Sterling, 1990.

Esack, Farid. *Qur'an, Liberation and Pluralism*, Oxford: Oneworld, 1997.

Esposito, J., et al., eds. *The Oxford Encyclopedia of the Modern Islamic World*. Vol. 2. New York: Oxford University Press, 1995.

Eusebius. *The History of the Church: From Christ to Constantine*. Edited by Andrew Louth. Penguin Classics. New York: Penguin, 1990.

Evans, Gareth, Mohamed Sahnoun, et al. *The Responsibility to Protect: Report of the International Commission on Intervention and State Sovereignty* (ICIS). Ottowa: International Development Research Centre, 2001.

Eynikel, Erik. "Judges 19–21, An 'Appendix:' Rape, Murder, War and Abduction." *Communio Viatorum* 47, no. 2 (2005) 101–115.

Fast, Howard. *The Jews: Story of a People*. New York: Dell, 1992.

Feldman, Louis H. *Flavius Josephus: Translation and Commentary*. Vol. 3, *Judean Antiquities 1–4 / Translation and Commentary*. Edited by Steve Mason. Leiden: Brill, 2000.

Fewell, Danna Nolan, and David M. Gunn. *Gender, Power and Promise: The Subject of the Bible's First Story*. Nashville: Abingdon, 1993.

Firestone, Reuven. "Judaism as a Force for Reconciliation: An Examination of Key Sources." In *Beyond Violence: Religious Sources of Social Transformation in Judaism, Christianity, and Islam*. Edited by James L. Heft. New York: Fordham University Press, 2004. 74–87.

Fitzgerald, Michael L. "Relations among the Abrahamic Religions: A Catholic Point of View." In *Heirs of Abraham: The Future of Muslim, Jewish, and Christian Relations*, edited by Bradford E. Hinze and Irfan A. Omar, 55–78. Maryknoll, NY: Orbis, 2005.

Fleischner, Eva. "Can Few Become the Many? Some Catholics in France Who Saved Jews during the Holocaust." In *Remembering for the Future*, vol. 1, edited by A. Roy Eckardt and Alice Eckardt, 233–47. Oxford: Pergamon, 1989.

Fletcher, Jeannine Hill. *Monopoly on Salvation?: A Feminist Approach to Religious Pluralism*. New York: Continuum, 2005.

Fluehr-Lobban, Carolyn. *Islamic Societies in Practice*. 2nd ed. Gainsville, FL: University of Florida Press, 2004.

Fogelman, Eva. *Conscience and Courage: Rescuers of the Jews During the Holocaust*. New York: Anchor, 1995.

Fox, Marvin. *Interpreting Maimonides: Studies in Methodology, Metaphysics, and Moral Philosophy*. Chicago Studies in the History of Judaism. Chicago: University of Chicago Press, 1995.

Frankel, Jonathan, and Steven J. Zipperstein, eds. *Assimilation and Community: The Jews in Nineteenth-Century Europe*. Cambridge: Cambridge University Press, 2004.

Frantzen, Allen J. *Bloody Good: Chivalry, Sacrifice, and the Great War*. Chicago: University of Chicago Press, 2004.

Frederick, Kevin. "Clinging to the Threshold of Hope: A Sermon." *Family Matters* 17, no. 1 (Spring 2003) 55–71.

Freedman, David Noel, et al. *The Nine Commandments: Uncovering a Hidden Pattern of Crime and Punishment in the Hebrew Bible*. New York: Doubleday, 2000.

Fretheim, Terence E. *Abraham: Trials of Family and Faith*. Columbia, SC: University of South Carolina, 2007.

Fried, Charles. *Anatomy of Values*. Cambridge, MA: Harvard University Press, 1970.

Friedmann, Yohanan. *Tolerance and Coercion in Islam: Interfaith Relations in the Muslim Tradition*. Cambridge: Cambridge University Press, 2003.

Friedrich, Paul. "Sanity and the Myth of Honor: The Problem of Achilles." *Ethos* 5 (1977) 281–305.

"Friendship." Special issue, *Christian Reflection* 27 (2008).

Gandhi, Leela. *Affective Communities: Anticolonial Thought, Fin-de-Siecle Radicalism, and the Politics of Friendship*. Durham, NC: Duke University Press, 2006.

García, María Cristinia. *Seeking Refuge: Central American Migration to Mexico, the United States and Canada*. Berkeley, CA: University of California Press, 2006.

Gathje, Peter R., and Calvin Kimbrough *Sharing the Bread of Life: Hospitality and Resistance at the Open Door Community*. 25th Anniversary of the Open Door Community. Atlanta, GA: Open Door Community, 2006.

Gathogo, Julius Mutugi. "African Philosophy as Expressed in the Concepts of Hospitality and Ubuntu." *Journal of Theology for Southern Africa* 130 (March 2008) 39–53.

Geertz, Clifford. *Interpretation of Cultures*. New York: Basic, 1973.

———. *Islam Observed: Religious Development in Morocco and Indonesia*. Chicago: University of Chicago Press, 1971.

———. *Local Knowledge: Further Essays in Interpretative Anthropology*. New York: Basic, 1983.

Gershman, Norman. *Besa: A Code of Honor: Muslim Albanians Who Rescued Jews During the Holocaust*. Syracuse, NY: Syracuse University Press, 2008.

Giannakis, E. "The Concept of the Ummah." *Graeco-Arabica* 2 (1983) 99–111.

Gil, Moshe. "The Constitution of Medina: A Reconsideration." *Israel Oriental Studies* 4 (1974) 44–66.

———. *Jews in Islamic Countries in the Middle Ages*. Leiden: Brill, 2004.

Gilmore, David, ed. *Honour and Shame and the Unity of the Mediterranean*. Washington, DC: American Anthropological Association, 1987.

Golden, Judah, trans. *The Fathers according to Rabbi Nathan*. Yale Judaic Series 10. New Haven, CT: Yale University Press, 1955.

Golden, Renny and Michael McConnell. *Sanctuary: The New Underground Railroad*. Maryknoll, NY: Orbis, 1986.

Goldstein, Niles Elliot. "The New Shul—Kol Nidre 5767." http://www.newshul.org/pdfs/sermon06yk.pdf. Last accessed October 21, 2009.

Goodman, Martin, et. al. *Abraham, the Nations, and the Hagarites: Jewish, Christian, and Islamic Perspectives on Kinship with Abraham*. Leiden: Brill, 2010.

Gopin, Marc. *Between Eden and Armageddon: The Future of World Religions, Violence, and Peacemaking*. Oxford: Oxford University Press, 2000.

———. "Judaism and Peacebuilding." In *Religion and Peacebuilding*, edited by Harold G. Coward and Gordon S. Smith, 111–127. Albany, NY: State University of New York Press, 2004.

———. "The Heart of the Stranger." In *Explorations of Reconciliation*, edited by David Tombs and Joseph Liechty, 3–21. Aldershot, UK: Ashgate, 2006.

Gottleib, Lynn. *She Who Dwells Within: A Feminist Vision of a Renewed Judaism*. San Francisco: HarperSanFrancisco, 1995.

Graham, Elaine, Heather Walton, and Frances Ward, eds. *Theological Reflection: Methods*. Vol. 1. London: SCM, 2005.

Gray, John. "Pluralism and Toleration in Contemporary Political Philosophy." *Political Studies* 48, no. 2 (2000) 323–333.

Grayze, Susan R. *Women's Identities at War: Gender, Motherhood and Politics in Britain and France During the First World War*. Chapel Hill, NC: University of North Carolina Press, 1999.

Greenberg, Irving. "Religion as a Force for Reconciliation and Peace: A Jewish Analysis." In *Beyond Violence: Religious Sources of Social Transformation in Judaism, Christianity, and Islam*, edited by James L. Heft, 88–112. New York: Fordham University Press, 2004.

Gregorios, Paulos Mar. "Not a Question of Hospitality." *Ecumenical Review* 44 (1992) 46.

Grey, Mary. *To Rwanda and Back: Liberation, Spirituality and Reconciliation*. London: Darton, Longman & Todd, 2007.

Griffiths, Leslie. "Hospitality." *One in Christ* 42, no. 2 (2008) 229–45.

Gross, Michael L. *Ethics and Activism: The Theory and Practice of Political Morality*. Cambridge: Cambridge University Press, 1997.

Gross, Selwyn. "Religious Pluralism in Struggles for Justice." *New Blackfriars* 71, (September 1990) 377–86.

Grunebaum, Gustave E. von. *Modern Islam: The Search for Cultural Identity*. Berkeley, CA: University of California Press, 1962.

Guder, Darrell J., et al. *Missional Church: A Vision for the Sending of the Church in North America*. Grand Rapids, MI: Eerdmans, 1998.

Guillame, A. Introduction to *Life of Muhammad: A Translation of Ibn Ishaq's Sirat Rasul Allah*, translated and edited by A. Guillame. New York: Oxford University Press, 2002.

Gundry-Volf, Judith M., and Miroslav Volf. *A Spacious Heart: Essays on Identity and Belonging*. Harrisburg, PA: Trinity, 1997.

Gushee, David P. *Righteous Gentiles of the Holocaust: Genocide and Moral Obligation*. 2nd ed. New York: Paragon, 2003.

Gutierrez, Gustavo. *A Theology of Liberation: History, Politics, and Salvation*. Translated and edited by C. Inda and J. Eagleson. Maryknoll: Orbis, 1973.

Haddad, Yvonne Yazbeck, and John L. Esposito, eds. *Daughters of Abraham: Feminist Thought in Judaism, Christianity, and Islam*. Gainesville, FL: University Press of Florida, 2002.

Hallie, Philip. "From Cruelty to Goodness." *The Hastings Center Report* 11, no. 3 (June 1981) 23–28.

———. *In the Eye of the Hurricane: Tales of Good and Evil, Help and Harm*. Middletown, CT: Wesleyan University Press, 1997.

———. *Lest Innocent Blood Be Shed: The Story of Le Chambon and How Goodness Happened There*. New York: Harper, 1979.

Hamilton, Janet, Bernard Hamilton, and Yuri Stoyanov. *Christian Dualist Heresies in the Byzantine World, c.650–c.1450*. Manchester: Manchester University Press, 1998.

Hamilton, Jennifer, John Bell, and Ulf Hansson. "Sectarianism and Segregation: Impact on Everyday Life." *Shared Space* 6 (June 2008) 35–50.

Hand, Seán. "Working Out Interiority: Locations and Locutions of Ipseity." *Literature and Theology* 17, no. 4 (2003) 422–34.

Harder, Gary. "Competing Visions: Can We Keep Isaiah and Ezra in the Same Bible, and You and Me in the Same Church?" Vision 3, no. 1 (Spring 2002) 25–33.

Hassan, Riaz. *Faithliness: Muslim Conceptions of Islam and Society*. Oxford: Oxford University Press, 2003.

Hassan, Riffat. "Challenging the Stereotypes of Fundamentalism: An Islamic Feminist Perspective." *The Muslim World* 91, nos. 1–2 (2001) 55–69.

———. "Islamic Hagar and Her Family." In *Hagar, Sarah, and Their Children*, edited by Phyllis Trible and Letty M. Russell, 149–167. Louisville, KY: Westminster John Knox, 2006.

Hauerwas, Stanley. *The Peaceable Kingdom: A Primer in Christian Ethics*. Notre Dame, IN: University of Notre Dame, 1983.

Hauerwas, Stanley, and Samuel Wells. *The Blackwell Companion to Christian Ethics*. Blackwell Companions to Religion. Oxford: Blackwell, 2004.

Hauerwas, Stanley, and William H. Willimon. *Resident Aliens: Life in the Christian Colony*. Nashville: Abingdon, 1989.

Hawkins, Thomas. *Sharing the Search: A Theology of Christian Hospitality*. Nashville: The Upper Room, 1987.

Hayka, Muhammad Husayn. *The Life of Muhammad*. Translated by Isma'il Ragi al Faruqi. Indianapolis, IN: North American Trust, 1976.

Heck, P. L. "Jihad Revised." *Journal of Religious Ethics* 32, no. 1 (2004) 95–128.

Heft, James L. "Resources for Social Transformation in Judaism, Christianity and Islam." Introduction to *Beyond Violence: Religious Sources of Social Transformation in Judaism, Christianity, and Islam*, edited by James L. Heft, 1–14. New York: Fordham, 2004.

———, ed. *Beyond Violence: Religious Sources of Social Transformation in Judaism, Christianity, and Islam*. New York: Fordham, 2004.

Heidegger, Martin. "Letter on Humanism." In *Basic Writings*, edited by David Farrell Krell, 141–182. New York: Harper & Row, 1977.

Heim, S. Mark. *Saved from Sacrifice: A Theology of the Cross*. Grand Rapids, MI: Eerdmans, 2006.

Hellman, Peter. *When Courage Was Stronger Than Fear: Remarkable Stories of Christians and Muslims Who Saved Jews from the Holocaust*. New York: Marlowe & Company, 2004.

Helminski, Kabir. "Adab: The Courtesy of the Path." The Threshold Society, June 8, 2002. http://sufism.org/lineage/sufism/excerpts-from-the-knowing-heart/adab-the-courtesy-of-the-path-2.

Herbert, David. *Religion and Civil Society: Rethinking Public Religion in the Contemporary World*. Aldershot: Ashgate, 2003.

———. "Religion and European Identities." In *Exploring European Identities*, edited by Christina Chimisso, 183–226. Milton Keynes, UK: Open University Press, 2003.

Herman, Gabriel. *Ritualised Friendship and the Greek City*. Cambridge: Cambridge University Press, 1987.

Herman, Judith Lewis. *Trauma and Recovery*. London: Pandora, 1997.

Hershberger, Michelle. *A Christian View of Hospitality: Expecting Surprises*. Scottsdale, PA: Herald, 1999.

Heschel, Abraham Joshua. *God in Search of Man: A Philosophy of Judaism*. New York: Farrar, Straus & Giroux, 1976.

Herzfeld, Michael. "Honour and Shame: Problems in the Comparative Analysis of Moral Systems." *Man*, n. s., 15 (1980) 339–51.

Herzfeld, Michael. "'As in Your Own House': Hospitality, Ethnography, and the Stereotype of Mediterranean Society." In *Honor and Shame and the Unity of the Mediterranean*, edited by David Gilmore, 75–78. Washington: American Anthropological Association, 1987.

Hilālī, Taqī al-Dīn, et al. *Interpretation of the Meanings of the Noble Qur'ān in the English Language*. 23rd rev. ed. Riyadh, Saudi Arabia: Darussalam, 1998.

Hinze, Bradford E., and Irfan A. Omar, eds. *Heirs of Abraham: The Future of Muslim, Jewish and Christian Relations*. Maryknoll, NY: Orbis, 2005.

Hirsche, Emil, and M. Seligsohn. "Rahab." In *Jewish Encyclopedia*. http://www.jewishencyclopedia.com/articles/12535-rahab. Accessed on Sept. 1, 2015.

Hobbs, T. R. "Reflections on Honor, Shame, and Covenant Relations." *Journal of Biblical Literature* 116, no. 3 (Fall 1997) 501–503.

The Holy Rule of St. Benedict. Translated by Boniface Verheyen, 1949. Available at http://www.ccel.org/ccel/benedict/rule. Accessed on Sept. 1, 2015.

Homan, Daniel, and Lonni Collins Pratt. *Radical Hospitality: Benedict's Way of Love*. Orleans, MA: Paraclete, 2005.

hooks, bell. *Ain't I a Woman? Black Women and Feminism*. Brooklyn, NY: South End, 1981.

———. *Remembered Rapture: The Writer at Work*. London: Holt, 1999.

Horsley, Richard A. *Religion and Empire: People, Power and the Life of the Spirit*. Minneapolis: Fortress, 2003.

"Hospitality." Special issue, *Parabola: the Magazine of Myth and Tradition* 15, no. 4 (Nov. 1990).

"Hospitality." Special issue, *Weavings* 9, no. 1 (Jan./Feb. 1994).

Hughes, Edward J. *Wilfred Cantwell Smith: A Theology for the World*. London: SCM, 1986.

Hurley, Michael. *Reconciliation in Religion and Society*. Belfast: Institute of Irish Studies, 1994.

Hussain, Amir. "Muslims, Pluralism, and Interfaith Dialogue." In *Progressive Muslims: On Justice, Gender and Pluralism*, edited by Omid Safi, 251–269. Oxford: Oneworld, 2003.

Hütter, Reinhold. "Hospitality and Truth: The Disclosure of Practices in Worship and Doctrine." In *Practicing Theology: Beliefs and Practices in Christian Life*, edited by Miroslav Volf and Dorothy C. Bass, 206–227. Grand Rapids, MI: Eerdmans, 2002.

Ibn Isḥāq, Muḥammad. *The Life of Muhammad: A Translation of Ibn Ishaq's Sirat Rasul Allah*. Translated and edited by A. Guillame. New York: Oxford University Press, 2002.

Ignatieff, Michael. *The Needs of Strangers*. London: Chatto & Windus, Hogarth, 1984.

Inge, John. *A Christian Theology of Place*. Aldershot: Ashgate, 2003.

Inter-Religious Council of Bosnia-Hercegovina. "Statement of Shared Moral Commitment." http://www.mrv.ba/images/stories/documents/Statement.pdf.

Iogna-Prat, Dominique. *Order & Exclusion: Cluny and Christendom Face Heresy, Judaism, and Islam, 1000–1150*. Translated by Graham Robert Edwards. Ithaca, NY: Cornell University Press, 2003.

Irani, George E., and Nathan C. Funk. "Rituals of Reconciliation: Arab-Islamic Perspectives." In *Peace and Conflict Resolution in Islam*, edited by Abdul Aziz Said, Nathan C. Funk and Ayse S. Kadayifci, 169–192. Lanham, MD: University Press of America, 2001.

Jacobs, Janet Liebman. *Hidden Heritage: The Legacy of the Crypto-Jews*. Berkeley, CA: University of California Press, 2002.

Jafri, Amir H. *Honour Killing: Dilemma, Ritual, Understanding*. Oxford: Oxford University Press, 2008.

Jamal, Amreen. "The Story of Lot and the Qur'an's Perception of the Morality of Same-Sex Sexuality." *Journal of Homosexuality* 41, no. 1 (2001) 1–88.

Jarman, Neil. "Security and Segregation: Interface Barriers in Belfast." *Shared Space* 6 (June 2008) 21–34.

Jasam, Saima. *Honour, Shame and Resistance*. Lahore, Pakistan: ASR, 2001

Jeanrond, Werner G. "Toward an Interreligious Hermeneutics of Love." *Interreligious Hermeneutics*, edited by Catherine Cornille and Christopher Conway, 44–60. Eugene, OR: Cascade, 2010.

Johnson, Elizabeth A. *Friends of God and Prophets*. New York: Continuum, 1999.

Johnson, Rubellite. "Religion Section of Native Hawaiians Study Commission Report." *Native Hawaiians Study Commission*. Honolulu: Office of Hawaiian Affairs, Feb. 1983.

Johnson, William Stacy, ed. *Crisis, Call and Leadership in the Abrahamic Traditions*. New York: Palgrave Macmillan, 2009.

Johnston, Douglas. *Faith-based Diplomacy: Trumping Realpolitik*. Oxford: Oxford University Press, 2003.

———. *Religion: The Missing Dimension of Statecraft*. Oxford: Oxford University Press, 1995.

Johnston, Douglas M., and Jonathon Eastvold. "History Unrequited: Religion as a Provocateur and Peacemaker in the Bosnian Conflict." In *Religion and Peacebuilding*, edited by Harold Coward and Gordon S. Smith, 213–242. Albany, NY: State University of New York Press, 2004.

Jones, L. Gregory. *Embodying Forgiveness: A Theological Analysis*. Grand Rapids, MI: Eerdmans, 1995.

———. "Eucharistic Hospitality: Welcoming the Stranger into the Household of God." *Reformed Journal* 39 (May 1989) 13.

Jones, L. Gregory, Reinhard Hütter, and C. Rosalee Velloso Ewell, eds. *God, Truth, and Witness: Engaging Stanley Hauerwas*. Grand Rapids, MI: Brazos, 2005.

Jones, Martin. *Feast: Why Humans Share Food*. New York: Oxford University Press, 2008.

Jones-Warsaw, Koala. "Toward a Womanist Hermeneutic: A Reading of Judges 19–21." In *A Feminist Companion to Judges*, edited by A. Brenner, 172–86. Sheffield, UK: Sheffield Academic, 1993.

Josephus, Flavius. *Jewish Antiquities, Books I-IV*. Translated by H. St. J. Thackeray et al. Cambridge, MA: Harvard University Press, 1935.

Kang, Namsoon. "Re-constructing *Asian* Feminist Theology: Toward a *Glocal* Feminist Theology in an Era of Neo-Empire(s)." In *Christian Theology in Asia*, edited by Sebastian C. H. Kim, 205–226. Cambridge: Cambridge University Press, 2008.

Kant, Immanuel. *Perpetual Peace: A Philosophical Essay*. Translated by Ted Humphrey. Indianapolis: Hackett & Company, 2003.

Karabell, Zachary. *Peace Be Upon You: Fourteen Centuries of Muslim, Christian and Jewish Conflict and Cooperation*. New York: Vintage, 2007.

Katz, Claire Elise. *Levinas, Judaism, and the Feminine: The Silent Footsteps of Rebecca*. Indiana Series in the Philosophy of Religion. Bloomington, IN: Indiana University Press, 2003.

Kearney, Richard, and Mark Dooley, eds. *Questioning Ethics: Contemporary Debates in Philosophy*. London: Routledge, 1999.

Keefe, Alice. "Rapes of Women / Wars of Men." *Semeia* 61 (1993) 79–98.

Keen, Ralph. *Exile and Restoration in Jewish Thought: An Essay In Interpretation*. Continuum Studies In Jewish Thought. New York: Continuum, 2009.

Kellenberger, J., ed. *Inter-Religious Models and Criteria*. New York: St. Martin's, 1993.

Keller, Nuh Ha Mim. "Adab of Islam." 2001. http://www.masud.co.uk/ISLAM/nuh/adab_of_islam.htm.

Kelsay, John. *Arguing the Just War in Islam*. Cambridge, MA: Harvard University Press, 2007.

Kenyon, Kathleen. *Digging Up Jericho*. New York: Praeger, 1957.

Kern, Kathleen. *As Resident Aliens: Christian Peacemaker Teams in the West Bank 1995–2005*. Eugene, OR: Cascade, 2010.

———. *In Harm's Way: A History of Christian Peacemaker Teams*. Cambridge: Lutterworth, 2009.

Keshkegian, Flora A. *Redeeming Memories: A Theology of Healing and Transformation*. Nashville: Abingdon, 2000.

Khalifa, Rashad. *Quran: The Final Testament*. Rev. ed. Fremont, CA: Universal Unity, 1992.

Khan, Ali. "Commentary on the Constitution of Medina." In *Understanding Islamic Law: From Classical to Contemporary*, edited by Hisham M. Ramadan, 205–210. Oxford: AltaMira, 2006.

Khan, Mohammed Muqtedar. "Islam as an Ethical Tradition of International Relations." In *Peace and Conflict Resolution in Islam*, edited by Abdul Aziz Said, Nathan C. Funk and Ayse S. Kadayifci. Lanham, MD: University Press of America, 2001.

Kiefert, Patrick R. *Welcoming the Stranger: A Public Theology of Worship and Evangelism*. Minneapolis: Fortress, 1992.

Kimball, Charles. *When Religion Becomes Evil*. San Francisco: Harper, 2002.

———. *When Religion Becomes Lethal: The Explosive Mix of Politics and Religion in Judaism, Christianity and Islam*. San Francisco: Josey-Bass, 2011.

King, Martin Luther, Jr., "Letter from Birmingham City Jail, April 16, 1963." In *A Testament of Hope: The Essential Writings and Speeches of Martin Luther King, Jr.*, edited by James Melvin Washington, 289–302. San Francisco: HarperSanFrancisco, 1986.

King, Ursula. "Feminism: The Missing Dimension in the Dialogue of Religions." In *Pluralism and the Religions: The Theological and Political Dimensions*, edited by John D'Arcy May, 40–57. London: Cassell, 1998.

Kirk, David. "Hospitality: The Essence of Eastern Christian Lifestyle." *Diakonia* 16, no. 2 (1981) 104–17.

Klassen, William. *Love of Enemies: The Way to Peace*. Overtures to Biblical Theology. Philadelphia: Fortress, 1984.

Knitter, Paul F. Foreword to *An Asian Theology of Liberation*, by Aloysius Pieris. Maryknoll, NY: Orbis, 1988.

———. *No Other Name?* Maryknoll, NY: Orbis, 1985.

———. "Pluralism and Oppression: Dialogue between the Many Religions and the Many Poor." In *The Community of Religions: Voices and Images of the Parliament of the World's Religions*, edited by Wayne Teasdale and George F. Cairns, 198–208. New York: Continuum, 1996.

———. "Responsibilities for the Future: Toward an Interfaith Ethic." In *Pluralism and the Religions: The Theological and Political Dimensions*, edited by John D'Arcy May, 75–89. London: Cassell, 1998.

———. "Toward a Liberation Theology of Religions." In *The Myth of Christian Uniqueness*, edited by John Hick and P. F. Knitter, 178–200. Maryknoll, NY: Orbis, 1987.

———. "The Vocation of an Interreligious Theologian: My Retrospective on Forty Years in Dialogue." *Horizons* 31, no. 1 (2004) 135–49.

Knoppers, Gary N., and J. Gordon McConville, eds. *Reconsidering Israel and Judah: Recent Studies on Deuteronomistic History*. Sources for Biblical and Theological Study 8. Warsaw, IN: Eisenbrauns, 2000.

Koenig, John. *New Testament Hospitality: Partnership with Strangers as Promise and Mission*. Philadelphia: Fortress, 1985.

Koyama, Kosuke. "'Extend Hospitality to Strangers': A Missiology of *Theologia Crucis*." *Currents in Theology and Mission* 20, no. 3 (June 1993) 165–76.

Kugle, Scott Siraj al-Haqq. *Homosexuality in Islam: Critical Reflection on Gay, Lesbian and Transgender Muslims*. Oxford: Oneworld, 2010.

———. "Sexuality, Diversity and Ethics in the Agenda of Progressive Muslims." In *Progressive Muslims: On Justice, Gender and Pluralism*, edited by Omid Safi, 190–234. Oxford: Oneworld, 2003.

Kuschel, Karl-Josef. *Abraham: A Symbol of Hope for Jews, Christians and Muslims*. Translated by John Bowden. London: SCM, 1995.

Küng, Hans. *A Global Ethic: The Declaration of the Parliament of the World's Religions*. Edited by Hans Küng and Karl-Josef Kuschel. Special ed. New York: Continuum, 2006.

———. *A Global Ethic for Global Politics and Economics*. Oxford: Oxford University Press, 1998.

———. *Global Responsibility: In Search of a New World Ethic*. Eugene, OR: Wipf & Stock, 2004.

Küng, Hans, and Karl-Josef Kuschel, eds. *A Global Ethic: The Declaration of the Parliament of the World's Religions*. London: SCM, 1993.

Kyung, Chung Hyun. *Struggle to Be the Sun Again: Introducing Asian Women's Theology*. Maryknoll, NY: Orbis, 1990.

LaCocque, André. *The Feminine Unconventional: Four Subversive Figures in Israel's Tradition*. Minneapolis: Fortress, 1990.

LaFeber, Walter. *Inevitable Revolutions: The United States in Central America*. 2nd ed. New York: Norton, 1993.

Lawrence, Louise Joy. *An Ethnography of the Gospel of Matthew: A Critical Assessment of the Use of the Honour and Shame Model in New Testament Studies*. Doctoral thesis. Tübingen : Mohr Siebeck, 2003.

Lasine, Stuart. "Guest and Host in Judges 19: Lot's Hospitality in an Inverted World." *Journal for the Society of the Old Testament* 29 (1984) 37–59.

Lee, Jung Young. *Marginality: The Key to Multicultural Theology*. Minneapolis, MN: Fortress, 1995.

LeoGrande, William M. *Our Own Backyard: The United States in Central America, 1977–1992*. Chapel Hill, NC: University of North Carolina Press, 2000.

Levinas, Emmanuel. *Beyond the Verse: Talmudic Readings and Lectures*. Translated by Gary D. Mole. London: Athlone, 1994.

———. *Difficult Freedom: Essays on Judaism*. Translated by Sean Hand. Johns Hopkins Jewish Studies. Baltimore: Johns Hopkins University Press, 1997.

———. *Humanism of the Other*. Translated by Nidra Poller. Champaign, IL: University of Illinois Press, 2005.

———. *Time and the Other*. Translated by Richard A. Cohen. Pittsburg, PA: Duquesne University Press, 1987.

Lewis, Bernard. *Islam: From the Prophet Muhammad to the Capture of Constantinople*, vol. 2, *Religion and Society*. New York: Oxford University Press, 1987.

Lewis, Berrisford. "Forging an Understanding of Black Humanity through Relationship: An Ubuntu Perspective." *Black Theology* 8, no. 1 (Apr. 2010) 69–85.

Lake, Kirsopp. "The First Epistle of Clement to the Corinthians." In *The Apostolic Fathers*, 1–122. Cambridge, MA: Harvard University Press, 1912.

Liechty, Joseph, and Cecelia Clegg. *Moving Beyond Sectarianism: Religion, Conflict, and Reconciliation in Northern Ireland*. Dublin: Columba, 2001.

Lindbeck, George A. *The Nature of Doctrine: Religion and Theology in a Postliberal Age*. Philadelphia: Westminster, 1984.

Little, David. "Cosmopolitan Compassion and Condemnation." *Religion & Values in Public Life*. Cambridge, MA: Harvard Divinity School, 2000.

———, ed. "'Would You Shoot Me, You Idiot?': Friar Ivo Marković, Bosnia and Herzegovina." In *Peacemakers in Action: Profiles of Religion in Conflict Resolution*, 106–117. Tanenbaum Center for Interreligious Understanding. Cambridge: Cambridge University Press, 2007.

Lorentzen, Robin. *Women in the Sanctuary Movement*. Philadelphia, PA: Temple University Press, 1991.

Lottes, John D. "Toward a Christian Theology of Hospitality to Other Religions on Campus." *Currents in Theology and Mission* 32, no. 1 (2005) 26–39.

Love, Maryann Cusimano. "The Ethics of Risk." *America: The National Catholic Weekly*. Sept. 11, 2006. http://www.americamagazine.org/content/article.cfm?article_id=4943.

Maahs, Charles. "Hospitality, Power, and Mission: A Review of the Writings and Leadership of Roger W. Fjeld." *Currents in Theology and Mission* 30, no. 3 (June 2003) 168–72.

MacIntyre, Alasdair. *After Virtue: A Study in Moral Theory*. Notre Dame, IN: University of Notre Dame Press, 1984.

———. *Dependent Rational Animals: Why Human Beings Need the Virtues*. London: Duckworth, 1999.

Magnusson, Kjell. "Bosnia and Herzegovina." In *Islam Outside the Arab World*, edited by David Westerlund and Ingvar Svanberg, 295–313. New York: St. Martin's, 1999.

Mahmutćehajić, Rusmir. *Bosnia the Good: Tolerance and Tradition*. Budapest: Central European University Press, 2000.

———. *On Love: In the Muslim Tradition*. Bronx, NY: Fordham University Press, 2007.

Markham, Ian. *Plurality and Christian Ethics*. Cambridge: Cambridge University Press, 1995.

Marshall, Bruce D. *Trinity and Truth*. Cambridge: Cambridge University Press, 2000.

Marshall, Ellen Ott. *Christians in the Public Square: Faith that Transforms Politics*. Nashville: Abingdon, 2008.

Markowitz, Fran. *Sarajevo: A Bosnian Kaleidescope*. Champaign, IL: University of Illinois Press, 2010.

Marranci, Gabriele. *Jihad Beyond Islam*. Oxford: Berg, 2006.

Marty, Martin. *When Faiths Collide*. Blackwell Manifestos. Malden, MA: Blackwell, 2005.

Massignon, Louis. "The Three Prayers of Abraham, Father of all Believers." In *Testimonies and Reflections: Essays of Louis Massignon*, edited by Herbert Mason, 3–20. Notre Dame, IN: University of Notre Dame Press, 1989.

Matthews, V. "Hospitality and Hostility in Genesis 19 and Judges 19." *Biblical Theology Bulletin* 22, no. 1 (1992) 3–11.

Matthews, V., and D. Benjamin, eds. *Social World of Ancient Israel: 1250–587 BCE*. Peabody, MA: Hendrickson, 1993.

Mavroudi, Elizabeth. "Nationalism, the Nation and Migration: Searching for Purity and Diversity." *Space and Polity* 14, no. 3 (Dec. 2010) 219–233.

May, John D'Arcy. *After Pluralism: Towards an Interreligious Ethic*. Münster: LIT, 2000.

———, ed. *Pluralism and the Religions: The Theological and Political Dimensions*. London: Cassell, 1998.

McCarthy, Gerry. "A Climate of Suspicion." *The Social Edge*, May 2007. http://thesocialedge.com/commentary/gerrymccarthy/index1.shtml

McFadyen, Alistair, and Marcel Sarot. *Forgiveness and Truth: Explorations in Contemporary Theology*. Edinburgh: T. & T. Clark, 2001.

McNeill, John J. *The Church and the Homosexual*. Boston: Beacon, 1993.

McNulty, Tracy. *The Hostess: Hospitality, Femininity, and the Expropriation of Identity*. Minneapolis: University of Minnesota Press, 2007.

Meneley, Anne. "Living Hierarchy in Yemen." *Anthropologica* 42 (2000) 61–74

Menocal, Maria Rosa. *The Ornament of the World: How Muslims, Jews and Christians Created a Culture of Tolerance in Medieval Spain*. Boston: Little, Brown & Company, 2002.

Metz, Johann Baptist. *Faith in History and Society: Toward a Practical Fundamental Society*. New York: Seabury, 1980.

———. *A Passion for God: The Mystical-Political Dimension of Christianity*. Mahwah, NJ: Paulist, 1997.

Meyer, Danny. *Setting the Table: The Transforming Power of Hospitality in Business*. New York: HarperCollins, 2006.

Miller, William Ian. *Humiliation: And Other Essays on Honor, Social Discomfort, and Violence*. New York: Cornell University Press, 1993.

Moltmann, Jürgen. *On Human Dignity: Political Theology and Ethics*. London: SCM, 1984.

Morrison, R. J., et. al. *Science of Pacific Island Peoples: Land Use and Agriculture*. Vol. 2. Suva, Fiji: Institute of Pacific Studies, University of the South Pacific, 1994.

Morrison, Toni. *Beloved*. New York: Knopf, 1998.

Morschauser, Scott. "'Hospitality,' Hostiles and Hostages: On the Legal Background to Genesis 19.1–9." *Journal of the Society of the Old Testament* 21A (2003) 461–485.

Mortenson, Viggo, ed. *Theology and the Religions: A Dialogue*. Grand Rapids, MI: Eerdmans, 2003.

Moss, Michael, and Souad Mekhennet. "The Guidebook for Taking a Life." *New York Times*. June 10, 2007. http://www.nytimes.com/2007/06/10/weekinreview/10moss.html.

Moussalli, Ahmad S. "Islamic Democracy and Pluralism." In *Progressive Muslims: On Justice, Gender and Pluralism*, edited by Omid Safi, 286–305. Oxford: Oneworld, 2003.

Moyaert, Marianne. "Absorption or Hospitality: Two Approaches to the Tension between Identity and Alterity." In *Interreligious Hermeneutics*, edited by Catherine Cornille and Christopher Conway, 61–88. Eugene, OR: Cascade, 2010.

———. "The (Un-)translatability of Religions? Ricoeur's Linguistic Hospitality as a Model for Inter-Religious Dialogue." *Exchange* 37 (2008) 337–364.

Moyn, Samuel. *Origins of the Other: Emmanuel Levinas Between Revelation and Ethics*. Ithaca, NY: Cornell, 2005.

Mudge, Lewis S. *The Gift of Responsibility: The Promise of Dialogue Among Christians, Jews, and Muslims*. New York: Continuum, 2008.

Mudge, Lewis S., and James Poling, eds. *Formation and Reflection: The Promise of Practical Theology*. Minneapolis: Fortress, 1987.

Munasinghe, Viranjini. "Nationalism in Hybrid Spaces: The Production of Impurity out of Purity." *American Ethnologist* 29, no. 3 (Aug. 2002), 663–692.

Murk-Jansen, Saskia. *Brides in the Desert: The Spirituality of the Beguine*. Maryknoll, NY: Orbis, 1998.

Musser, Donald W., and D. Dixon Sutherland, eds. *War or Words? Interreligious Dialogue as an Instrument of Peace*. Cleveland, OH: Pilgrim, 2005.

Müller, Barbara. *The Balkan Peace Team: 1994–2001*. Translated by Paul Foster. Stuttgart: Ibidem, 2007.

Mzamane, Mbulelo. "Building a New Society Using the Building Blocks of Ubuntu/Botho/Vhuthu." In *Religion and Spirituality in South Africa*, 236–248. Scottsville, South Africa: University of KwaZulu-Natal Press, 2009.

Nasr, Seyyed Hossein, ed. *Islamic Spirituality: Foundations*. World Spirituality: An Encyclopedic History of the Religious Quest 19. New York: Crossroad, 1987.

Nepstad, Sharon Erickson. *Convictions of the Soul: Religion, Culture, and Agency in the Central America Solidarity Movement*. New York: Oxford University Press, 2004.

Neuffer, Elizabeth. *The Key to My Neighbor's House: Seeking Justice in Bosnia and Rwanda*. New York: Picador, 2001.

Neusner, Jacob. *Genesis Rabbah: The Judaic Commentary to the Book of Genesis, A New American Translation*. 2 vols. Atlanta: Scholars, 1985.

———. *The Idea of Purity in Ancient Judaism: The Haskell Lectures, 1972–1973*. Leiden: Brill, 1973.

———, ed. *The Fathers according to Rabbi Nathan: An Analytical Translation and Explanation*. Atlanta: Scholars, 1986.

Newlands, George, and Allen Smith. *Hospitable God: The Transformative Dream*. Aldershot: Ashgate, 2010.

Newman, Elizabeth. "Accepting Our Lives as Gift: Hospitality and Post-Critical Ethics." *Tradition and Discovery* 39, no. 1 (2002–2003) 60–72.

———. "Flannery O'Connor and the Practice of Hospitality." *Perspectives in Religious Studies* 32, no. 2 (Summer 2005) 135–147.

———. "Untamed Hospitality." In "Hospitality," special issue, *Christian Reflection* (2007) 17–18.

———. *Untamed Hospitality: Welcoming God and Other Strangers*. The Christian Practice of Everyday Life. Grand Rapids, MI: Brazos, 2007.

Nichols, Francis W., ed. *Christianity and the Stranger: Historical Essays*. Atlanta, GA: Scholars, 1995.

Nienhuis, Nancy E. "Taming 'Wild Ass-Colts': An Analysis of Theology as a Kyriarchal Weapon of Spiritual and Physical Violence." *Journal of Feminist Studies in Religion* 25, no. 1 (2009) 43–64.

Nieuwenhuijze, C. A. O. van. "The *Ummah*—An Analytic Approach." *Studia Islamica* 10 (1959) 5–22.

Nisbett, Richard E., and Dov Cohen. *Culture of Honor: The Psychology of Violence in the South*. Boulder, CO: Westview, 1996.

Noor, Farish A. "What Is the Victory of Islam? Towards a Different Understanding of the *Ummah* and Political Success in the Contemporary World." In *Progressive Muslims: On Justice, Gender, and Pluralism*, edited by Omid Safi, 320–32. Oxford: Oneworld, 2003.

Noort, Edward, and Eibert J. C. Tigchelaar. *Sodom's Sin: Genesis 18–19 and Its Interpretation*. Leiden: Brill, 2004.

Norris, H. T. *Islam in the Balkans: Religion and Society Between Europe and the Arab World*. Columbia, SC: University of South Carolina Press, 1993.

Noth, Martin. *Numbers*. The Old Testament Library. Philadelphia, PA: Westminster, 1968.

Nouwen, Henri. "Hospitality." *Monastic Studies* 10 (1974) 1–28.

———. *Peacework: Prayer, Resistance and Community*. Maryknoll, NY: Orbis, 2005.

———. *Reaching Out: The Three Movements of the Spiritual Life*. Garden City, NY: Doubleday, 1975.

Nussbaum, Martha. *Hiding from Humanity: Disgust, Shame, and the Law*. Princeton, NJ: Princeton University Press, 2004.

O'Connor, Flannery. *Mystery and Manners: Occasional Prose*. Edited by Sally Fitzgerald and Robert Fitzgerald. New York: Farrar, Straus & Giroux, 1969.

O'Connor, Kathleen M. *Lamentations and the Tears of the World*. Maryknoll, NY: Orbis, 2002.

O'Donnell, James G. "The Influence of Freud's Hermeneutic of Suspicion on the Writings of Juan Segundo." *Journal of Psychology and Theology* 10 (1982) 28–34.

O'Leary, Joseph Stephen. *Religious Pluralism and Christian Truth*. Edinburgh: Edinburgh University Press, 1996.

Ochs, Peter. "Abrahamic Hauerwas: Theological Conditions for Justifying Inter-Abrahamic Study." In *God, Truth and Witness: Engaging Stanley Hauerwas*, edited by L. Gregory Jones, Reinhold Hütter, and C. Rosalee Velloso Ewell, 309–327. Grand Rapids, MI: Brazos, 2005.

Oden, Amy G. *And You Welcomed Me: A Sourcebook on Hospitality in Early Christianity*. Nashville: Abingdon, 2002.

Oden, Thomas C. *The Rebirth of Orthodoxy: Signs of New Life in Christianity*. New York: HarperSanFrancisco, 2002.

Odenheimer, Micha. "Honor or Death." *Jerusalem Report* 9, no. 22 (March 1999) 25.

Ofer, Yosef. "A Diagram of the Open Land of the Levite Cities in Nahmanides' Commentary on the Torah." *Jewish Quarterly Review* 99, no. 2 (March 2009) 271–83.

Ogletree, Thomas W. *Hospitality to the Stranger: Dimension of Moral Understanding*. Philadelphia: Fortress, 1985.

Oh, Irene. *The Rights of God: Islam, Human Rights, and Comparative Ethics*. Washington, DC: Georgetown University Press, 2007.

Oliner, Samuel P., and Pearl M. Oliner. *The Altruistic Personality: Rescuers of Jews in Nazi Europe*. New York: Free Press, 1988.

Olyan, Saul M. "Honor, Shame, and Covenant Relations in Ancient Israel and Its Environment." *Journal of Biblical Literature* 115, no. 2 (Summer 1996) 201–218.

Ortner, S. "The Virgin and the State." *Feminist Studies* 4 (1978) 19–35.

Osiek, Carolyn, and David L. Balch. *Families in the New Testament World: Households and House Churches*. Louisville, KY: Westminster John Knox, 1997.

Ovid. *Metamorphoses*. Translated by A. D. Melville, with an introduction and notes by E. J. Kenney. Oxford: Oxford University Press, 1986.

Palmer, Parker. *Company of Strangers: Christians and the Renewal of America's Public Life*. New York: Crossroad, 1983.

Park, Andrew Sung. *From Hurt to Healing: A Theology of the Wounded*. Nashville: Abingdon, 2004.

Park, Joon-Sik. "Hospitality as Context for Evangelism." *Missiology* 30, no. 3 (July 2002) 385–395.

Parker, Simon B. "The Hebrew Bible and Homosexuality." *Quarterly Review* 11, no. 3 (Fall 1991) 4–19.

Paul, Samuel A. *The Ubuntu God: Deconstructing a South African Narrative of Oppression*. Princeton, NJ: Princeton University Press, 2009.

Pears, Angie. *Doing Contextual Theology*. London: Routledge, 2010.

Pellegrino, Marge. *Journey of Dreams*. London: Frances Lincoln Children's Books, 2009.

Penchansky, David. "Up for Grabs: A Tentative Proposal for Doing Ideological Criticism." *Semeia* 59 (1992) 35–41.

Peristiany, J. G., ed. *Honour and Shame: The Values of Mediterranean Society*. Chicago: University of Chicago Press, 1974.

Peristiany, J. G., and Julian Pitt-Rivers, eds. *Honor and Grace in Anthropology.* Cambridge: Cambridge University Press, 1992.

Peters, F. E. *Children of Abraham: Judaism, Islam, and Christianity.* Princeton, NJ: Princeton University Press, 1982.

Pew Forum on Religion and the Public Life. "The Religious Dimensions of Torture Debate." May 7, 2009. http://pewforum.org/docs/?DocID=156

Phan, Peter C. *Being Religious Interreligiously: Asian Perspectives on Interfaith Dialogue.* Maryknoll: Orbis, 2004.

———. "Living for the Reign of God: Liberation, Cultures, Religions: A Theology of Liberation for the Asian Churches." Paper delivered at Milltown Institute Conference, "Liberation Theology: Movement or Moment." Dublin, Ireland, Oct. 3–4, 2008.

Pieris, Aloysius. *An Asian Theology of Liberation.* Maryknoll, NY: Orbis, 1988.

Pitt-Rivers, Julian. "Fate of Shechem or the Politics of Sex: Essays in Anthropology of the Mediterranean." *Cambridge Studies in Social Anthropology* 19 (1977) 94–112.

———. *The Fate of Shechem or the Politics of Sex: Essays in the Anthropology of the Mediterranean.* Cambridge: Cambridge University Press, 1977.

Plaskow, Judith. *Standing Against Sinai: Judaism from a Feminist Perspective.* San Francisco: Harper, 1991.

Pohl, Christine D. "Building a Place for Hospitality." In "Hospitality," edited by Robert B. Kruschwitz, special issue, *Christian Reflection* (2007) 27–36.

———. "Hospitality, a Practice And a Way of Life." *Vision* (Spring 2002) 34–43.

———. *Making Room: Recovering Hospitality as a Christian Tradition.* Grand Rapids, MI: Eerdmanns, 1999.

Powell, Elinor D. U. *The Heart of Conflict: A Spirituality of Transformation.* Kelowna, BC: Northstone, 2003.

Rad, Gerhard von. *Genesis: A Commentary.* Old Testament Library. Philadelphia, PA: Westminster, 1972.

Rahman, F. "The Principles of Shura and the Role of the Umma in Islam." *American Journal of Islamic Studies* 1:1 (1984) 1–9.

Ramadan, Tariq. *In the Footsteps of the Prophet: Lessons Learned from the Life of Muhammad.* Oxford: Oxford University Press, 2007.

Reaves, Jayme. "Conference Response." *Being the Other: Theological Students' Conference 2011.* Experiential Learning Paper, no. 6. Irish Peace Centres. (Sept. 2011) 78–81.

———. "Room at the Table: The Role of Hospitality in Inter-Religious Life from an Open-Minded Baptist Perspective." In *The Place for Others in Our Faith and Life: Foundations for Inter-Religious Peace Education.* Building Bridges Towards Peace and Reconciliation in South-East Europe in partnership with the Conference of European Churches (CEC) and World Council of Churches' South-East European Ecumenical Partnership (SEEEP). Sarajevo: Abraham: Association for Inter-Religious Peace Work, 2004.

Renard, John, ed. *Windows on the House of Islam: Muslim Sources on Spirituality and Religious Life.* Berkley: University of California, 1998.

Reynolds, Jack. *Merleau-Ponty and Derrida: Intertwining Embodiment and Alterity.* Athens, OH: Ohio University Press, 2004.

Reynolds, Thomas E. "Improvising Together: Christian Solidarity and Hospitality as Jazz Performance." *Journal of Ecumenical Studies* 43, no. 1 (Dec. 2008) 45–66.

Ricoeur, Paul. *The Course of Recognition*. Cambridge, MA: Harvard University Press, 2007.

———. *Freud and Philosophy: An Essay on Interpretation*. Translated by Denis Savage. New Haven, CT: Yale University Press, 1970.

———. *Hermeneutics and The Human Sciences*. Translated and edited by John B. Thompson. Cambridge: Cambridge University Press, 1987.

———. *Oneself as Another*. Translated by Kathleen Blamey. Chicago: University of Chicago Press, 1995.

———. *On Translation*. Translated by Eileen Brennan. Thinking in Action. London: Routledge, 2006.

———. "Reflections on a New Ethos for Europe." In *Paul Ricoeur: The Hermeneutics of Action*, edited by Richard Kearney, 3–13. Philosophy and Social Criticism. London: Sage, 1996.

———, ed. *Tolerance Between the Intolerance and the Intolerable*. Diogenes Library 176. Providence, RI: Bergham, 1997.

———. "Universality and the Power of Difference." In *On Paul Ricoeur: The Owl of Minerva*, edited by Richard Kearney. Aldershot: Ashgate, 2004.

Rigby, Cynthia L. "Is There Joy Before Mourning? 'Dangerous Memory,' In the Work of Sharon Welch and Johann Baptist Metz." *Koinonia* 5 (Spring 1993) 1–30.

Rimmer, Susan Harris. "Refugees, Internally Displaced Persons, and the 'Responsbility to Protect.'" UNHCR. Research Paper 185. Mar. 2010. http://www.unhcr.org/4b97b0909.html.

Robeson, Angela. "Weapons of War." *New Internationalist* 244, June 1993. http://www.newint.org/features/1993/06/05/rape/.

Roclav, Pierre. *Louis Massignon et l'islam*. Damascus: Institut Français de Damas, 1993.

Rollins, Peter. *The Orthodox Heretic: And Other Impossible Tales*. Brewster, MA: Paraclete, 2009.

Romero, Oscar. *Voice of the Voiceless: The Four Pastoral Letters and Other Statements*. Translated by Michael J. Walsh. Maryknoll, NY: Orbis, 1985.

Roth, Norman. *Conversos, Inquisition, and the Expulsion of the Jews from Spain*. Madison, WI: University of Wisconsin, 2002.

Ruether, Rosemary Radford. *Mary, the Feminine Face of the Church*. Philadelphia: Westminster, 1977.

Russell, Letty M. "Children of Struggle." In *Hagar, Sarah, and Their Children*, edited by Phyllis Trible and Letty M. Russell, 185–197. Louisville, KY: Westminster John Knox, 2006.

———. "Hot-House Ecclesiology: A Feminist Interpretation of the Church." *Ecumenical Review* 53, no. 1 (Jan. 2001) 48–56.

———. *Household of Freedom: Authority in Feminist Theology*. Philadelphia: Westminster, 1987.

———. *Just Hospitality: God's Welcome in a World of Difference*. Louisville, KY: Westminster John Knox, 2009.

———. "Practicing Hospitality in a Time of Backlash." *Theology Today* 52, no. 4 (Jan. 1996) 476–84.

Ryan, William C. "The Historical Case for the Right of Sanctuary?" *Journal of Church and State* 29 (Spring 1987) 209–32.

Sachar, Howard Morley. *Farewell España: The World of the Sephardim Remembered*. Ann Arbor, MI: University of Michigan Press, 2008.

Sachedina, Abdulaziz. *The Islamic Roots of Democratic Pluralism*. Oxford: Oxford University Press, 2001.

Sacks, Jonathan. *To Heal a Fractured World: The Ethics of Responsibility*. London: Continuum, 2005.

Safi, Omid. "The Times They Are A-Changin'—A Muslim Quest for Justice, Gender Equality, and Pluralism." Introduction to *Progressive Muslims: On Justice, Gender and Pluralism*, edited by Omid Safi, 1–29. Oxford: Oneworld, 2003.

———, ed. *Progressive Muslims: On Justice, Gender, and Pluralism*. Oxford: Oneworld, 2003.

Said, Abdul Aziz, et al., eds. *Peace and Conflict Resolution In Islam: Precept and Practice*. Lanham, MD: University Press of America, 2001.

Said, Edward. *Edward Said: A Critical Reader*. Edited by Michael Sprinker. Oxford: Blackball, 1992.

Salmon, Marilyn J. *Preaching Without Contempt: Overcoming Unintended Anti-Judaism*. Fortress Resources for Preaching. Minneapolis: Fortress, 2006.

Sandmel, Samuel. *Philo's Place in Judaism: A Study of Conceptions of Abraham in Jewish Literature*. Aug. ed. New York: Ktav, 1971.

Sarna, N. M. *The JPS Torah Commentary: Genesis*. Philadelphia: JPS, 1989.

Satloff, Robert. *Among the Righteous: Lost Stories from the Holocaust's Long Reach Into Arab Lands*. New York: PublicAffairs, 2006.

Schacht, Joseph. "Aman." In *The Encyclopaedia of Islam*, 1:429–30. New ed. Leiden: Brill, 1960.

Schneider, J. "Of Vigilance and Virgins: Honor, Shame, and Access to Resources in Mediterranean Societies." *Ethnology* 10 (1971) 1–24.

Schreiter, Robert J. *The Ministry of Reconciliation: Spirituality and Strategies*. Maryknoll, NY: Orbis, 1999.

Schulman, Miriam, and Amal Barkouki-Winter. "The Extra Mile: The Ancient Virtue of Hospitality Imposes Duties on Host and Guest." *Issues in Ethics* 11, no. 1 (Winter 2000). http://www.scu.edu/ethics/publications/iie/v11n1/hospitality.html.

Schuster, Ekkehard. *Hope against Hope: Johann Baptist Metz and Elie Wiesel Speak Out on the Holocaust*. Mahwah, NJ: Paulist, 1999.

Schüssler Fiorenza, Elisabeth. *But She Said: Feminist Practices of Biblical Interpretation*. Boston: Beacon, 1993.

———. *In Memory of Her: A Feminist Theological Reconstruction of Christian Origins*. New York: Crossroad, 1983.

———. *The Power of the Word*. Minneapolis: Fortress, 2007.

Schüssler Fiorenza, Francis. "Theological and Religious Studies: The Contest of the Faculties." In *Shifting Boundaries: Contextual Approaches to the Structure of Theological Education*, edited by Barbara G. Wheeler and Edward Farley, 119–150. Louisville, KY: Westminster John Knox, 1991.

Schwartz, Regina M. *The Curse of Cain: The Violent Legacy of Monotheism*. Chicago: University of Chicago Press, 1997.

Schweid, Eliezar. *The Philosophy of the Bible as Foundation of Jewish Culture*. Vol. 2. Translated by Leonard Levin. Brighton, MA: Academic, 2008.

Scott, James M., ed. *Exile: Old Testament, Jewish, and Christian Conceptions*. Supplements to the Journal for the Study of Judaism 56. Leiden: Brill, 1997.

Scott, Jamie, and Paul Simpson-Housley, eds. *Sacred Places and Profane Spaces*. Wesport, CT: Greenwood, 1991.

Scoville, Warren C. *The Persecution of Huguenots and French Economic Development, 1680–1720*. Berkeley, CA: University of California Press, 1960.

Segundo, Juan Lois. *The Liberation of Theology*. Dublin: Gill & MacMillan, 1978.

Seow, C. L. "A Heterotextual Perspective." In *Homosexuality and Christian Community*, edited by C. L. Seow, 14–27. Louisville, KY: Westminster John Knox, 1996.

Serjeant, Robert B. "Constitution of Medina." *The Islamic Quarterly* 8: 1964. Reprinted in *Studies in Arabian History and Civilization*, 41–58. London: Variorum Reprints, 1981.

Serotta, Edward. *Survival in Sarajevo: How a Jewish Community Came to the Aid of Its City*. Vienna: Brandstätter, 1994.

Shah-Kazemi, Reza. "Light upon Light? The Qur'an and the Gospel of St. John." In *Interreligious Hermeneutics*, edited by Catherine Cornille and Christopher Conway, 116–148. Eugene, OR: Cascade, 2010.

Shanks, Hershel, ed. *Ancient Israel: From Abraham to the Roman Destruction of the Temple*. Washington, DC: Prentice Hall and Biblical Archeological Society, 1999

Shaw, Stanford J. *Turkey and the Holocaust*. London: Ipswich, 1993.

Sher Ali. *The Holy Qur'an: Arabic Text and English Translation*. Rabwah, West Pakistan: Oriental and Religious, 1955.

Sherwood, Yvonne, and Kevin Hart, eds. *Derrida and Religion: Other Testaments*. New York: Routledge, 2004.

Simons, Walter. *Cities of Ladies: Beguine Communities in the Medieval Low Countries, 1200–1565*. Philadelphia: University of Philadelphia Press, 2001.

Sobrino, Jon. *The Principle of Mercy: Taking the Crucified People from the Cross*. Maryknoll, NY: Orbis, 1994.

Smith, Archie, Jr. "Hospitality: A Spiritual Resource for Building Community." *Journal for the Interdenominational Theological Center* 25, no. 3 (Spring 1998) 139–151.

Smith, Christian. *Resisting Reagan: The U. S. Central America Peace Movement*. Chicago: University of Chicago Press, 1996.

Smith, Jonathan Z. "Religion, Religions, Religious." In Critical Terms for Religious Studies, edited by Mark C. Taylor. Chicago: University of Chicago Press, 1998.

Smooha, Sammy. *Israel: Pluralism and Conflict*. Berkeley, CA: University of California Press, 1978.

Smyth, Geraldine. "A Habitable Grief: Forgiveness and Reconciliation for a People Divided." *Milltown Studies* 53 (Summer 2004) 94–130.

Sölle, Dorothee. *Celebrating Resistance: The Way of the Cross in Latin America*. London: Mowbray, 1993.

———. *Political Theology*. Minneapolis: Fortress, 1971.

———. *The Silent Cry: Mysticism and Resistance*. Minneapolis: Augsburg Fortress, 2001.

———. *Suffering*. Minneapolis: Augsburg Fortress, 1984.

Spina, Frank Anthony. "Israelites as *gerîm*, 'Sojourners,' in Social and Historical Context." In *The Word of the Lord Shall Go Forth: Essays in Honor of David Noel Freedman in Celebration of his Sixtieth Birthday*, edited by Carol L. Meyers and M. O'Connor. Winona Lake, IN: Eisenbrauns, 1983.

Stanton, Elizabeth Cady. *The Woman's Bible: A Classic Feminist Perspective*. Mineola, NY: Dover, 2003.

Stassen, Glen, ed. *Just Peacemaking: The New Paradigm for the Ethics of Peace and War*. Cleveland, OH: Pilgrim, 2008.

Stiebert, Johanna. *The Construction of Shame in the Hebrew Bible: The Prophetic Contribution*. Journal for the Study of the Old Testament Supplement Series 346. Sheffield, UK: Sheffield Academic, 2002.

Stone, Ken. *Sex, Honor, and Power in the Deuteronomistic History: A Narratological and Anthropological Analysis*. Journal for the Study of the Old Testament Supplement Series 234. Sheffield, UK: Sheffield Academic, 1997.

Stover, Eric, and Harvey M. Weinstein, eds. *My Neighbor, My Enemy: Justice and Community in the Aftermath of Mass Atrocity*. Cambridge: Cambridge University Press, 2006.

Strom, Yale. *The Expulsion of the Jews: Five Hundred Years of Exodus*. New York: SPI, 1992.

Strhan, Anna. "And Who Is My Neighbour? Levinas and the Commandment to Love Re-examined." *Studies in Interreligious Dialogue* 19, no. 2 (2009) 145–66.

Sunshine, Glenn S. *Reforming French Protestantism: The Development of Huguenot Ecclesiastical Institutions, 1557–1572*. Kirksville, MO: Truman State University Press, 2003.

Sutherland, Arthur. *I Was a Stranger: A Christian Theology of Hospitality*. Nashville: Abingdon, 2006.

Swidler, Leonard. "Trialogue: Out of the Shadows into Blazing 'Desert' Sun." *Journal of Ecumenical Studies* 45, no. 3 (June 2010) 493–509.

———. *When Neighbors Were Real Human Beings*. Sarajevo: University of Sarajevo, Institute for the Research of Crimes Against Humanity and International Law, 2010.

Taylor, Charles. *Multiculturalism: Examining the Politics of Recognition*. Edited by Amy Gutmann. Princeton, NJ: Princeton University, 1994.

Taylor, Mildred. *Roll of Thunder, Hear My Cry*. New York: Bantam, 1984.

Tec, Nechama. *When Light Pierced the Darkness: Christian Rescue of Jews in Nazi-Occupied Poland*. Oxford: Oxford University Press, 1986.

Thambu, Valson. "Building Communities of Peace for All." *Ecumenical Review* (Apr 2005) 1–8.

Tombs, David. *Latin American Liberation Theology*. Leiden: Brill, 2002.

———. "'Shame' as a Neglected Value in Schooling." *The Journal of the Philosophy of Education Society of Great Britain* 29, no. 1 (1995) 23–32.

Tombs, David, and Joseph Liechty, eds. *Explorations in Reconciliation*. Aldershot, UK: Ashgate, 2006.

Torres, Sergio, and John Eagleson, eds. *The Challenge of Basic Christian Communities: Papers from the International Ecumenical Congress of Theology, February 29–March 2, 1980, Sao Paulo, Brasil*. Maryknoll, NY: Orbis, 1981.

Trible, Phyllis. *Texts of Terror: Literary-Feminist Readings of Biblical Narratives*. Overtures to Biblical Theology. Minneapolis: Fortress, 1984.

Trible, Phyllis, and Letty M. Russell, eds. *Hagar, Sarah, and Their Children: Jewish, Christian, and Muslim Perspectives*. Louisville, KY: Westminster John Knox, 2006.

Truth, Sojourner. "Ain't I a Woman?" Speech delivered at Women's Convention, Akron, OH, 1851. Transcript available at http://legacy.fordham.edu/halsall/mod/sojtruth-woman.asp.

Tutu, Desmond. *God Has a Dream: A Vision of Hope for Our Time*. New York: Image Doubleday, 2004.

———. *No Future Without Forgiveness*. New York: Image Doubleday, 1999.

Twain, Mark. *The Adventures of Tom Sawyer and Huckleberry Finn*. Penguin Classics. London: Penguin, 2003.

UNESCO. "The Art of Hospitality." Special issue, *UNESCO Courier* (Feb 1990).

Van Den Hengel, John W. "Paul Ricoeur's Oneself as Another and Practical Theology." *Theological Studies* 55, no. 3 (Sept. 1994) 458–80.

Van Houten, Christiana. *The Alien in Israelite Law*. Journal for the Study of the Old Testament Supplement Series 107. Sheffield, England: Sheffield Academic, 1991.

Van Seters, John. *Abraham in History and Tradition*. New Haven, CT: Yale University Press, 1975.

Van Wijk-Bos, Johanna W. H. *Reimagining God: The Case for Scriptural Diversity*. Louisville, KY: Westminster John Knox, 1995.

Velikonja, Mitja. *Religious Separation and Political Intolerance in Bosnia-Herzegovina*. Translated by Rang'ichi Ng'inja. Eastern European Studies Series. College Station, TX: Texas A&M University Press, 2003.

Volf, Miroslav. *After Our Likeness: The Church as the Image of the Trinity*. Grand Rapids, MI: Eerdmanns, 1998.

———. "A Cup of Coffee." *Christian Century* 114, no. 28 (Oct. 15, 1997) 917.

———. *Exclusion and Embrace: A Theological Exploration of Identity, Otherness, and Reconciliation*. Nashville: Abingdon, 1996.

———. "How Safe Can We Be?" *Christian Century* 127, no. 21 (Oct. 19, 2010) 66.

Volf, Miroslav, and Dorothy Bass, eds. *Practicing Theology: Beliefs and Practices in Christian Life*. Grand Rapids, MI: Eerdmanns, 2002.

Vosloo, Robert. "Identity, Otherness and the Triune God: Theological Groundwork for a Christian Ethic of Hospitality." *Journal of Theology for Southern Africa* 119 (July 2004) 69–89.

Vroom, Hendrik M. "Right Conduct as a Criterion for True Religion." *Inter-Religious Models and Criteria*, edited by J. Kellenberger, 106–134. New York: St. Martin's, 1993.

Wadell, Paul. *Friendship and the Moral Life*. Notre Dame, IN: University of Notre Dame Press, 1989.

Wadud, Amina. *Inside the Gender Jihad: Women's Reform in Islam*. Oxford: Oneworld, 2006.

———. *Qur'an and Woman: Rereading the Sacred Text from a Woman's Perspective*. New York: Oxford, 1999.

Walton, Heather. "Speaking in Signs: Narrative and Trauma in Practical Theology." *Scottish Journal of Healthcare Chaplaincy* 5, no. 2 (2002) 2–5.

Watson, James L., and Melissa L. Caldwell, eds. *The Cultural Politics of Food and Eating: A Reader*. Oxford: Blackwell, 2005.

Watt, W. M. "Ideal Factors in the Origin of Islam." *Islamic Quarterly* 2 (1955) 160–74.

Weaver, J. Denny. *The Nonviolent Atonement*. 2nd ed. Grand Rapids, MI: Eerdmans, 2011.

Weeks, Theodore. *From Assimilation to Antisemitism: The Jewish Question In Poland, 1850–1914*. DeKalb, IL: Northern Illinois University Press, 2005.

Welch, Sharon. *After Empire: The Art and Ethos of Enduring Peace*. Minneapolis: Fortress, 2004.

———. *A Feminist Ethic of Risk*. Minneapolis: Fortress, 2000.

Westerhoff, Caroline. *Good Fences: The Boundaries of Hospitality*. Harrisburg, PA: Morehouse, 2004.

Wettstein, Howard, ed. *Diasporas and Exiles: Varities of Jewish Identity*. Berkely, CA: University of California Press, 2002.

Wheatley, Paul. *The Places Where Men Pray Together: Cities in Islamic Lands, Seventh through the Tenth Centuries*. Chicago: University of Chicago Press, 2001.

Wiesel, Elie. "The Refugee." *Cross Currents* 34, no. 4 (Winter 1984/85) 385–90.

———. *The Stranger in the Bible*. Cincinnati: Hebrew Union College, Jewish Institute of Religion, 1981.

Wikler, Meir. *Aishel: Stories of Contemporary Jewish Hospitality*. Nanuet, NY: Feldheim, 1995.

Wilkins, Steve. *Face to Face: Meditations on Friendship and Hospitality*. Moscow, ID: Canon, 2002.

Will, James E. *The Universal God: Justice, Love and Peace in the Global Village*. Louisville, KY: Westminster John Knox, 1994.

Williams, Bernard. *Shame and Necessity*. Berkeley, CA: University of California Press, 1993.

Williams, Delores. *Sisters in the Wilderness: The Challenge of Womanist God-Talk*. Maryknoll, NY: Orbis, 1995.

Williams, Robert R. *Hegel's Ethics of Recognition*. Berkeley, CA: University of California Press, 2000.

Williams, Rowan. "The Suspicion of Suspicion: Wittgenstein and Bonhoeffer." In *The Grammar of the Heart: New Essays in Moral Philosophy and Theology*, edited by R. H. Bell, 36–53. San Francisco: Harper and Row, 1988.

Wimberly, Edward P. "Methods of Cross-Cultural Pastoral Care: Hospitality and Incarnation." *Journal of the Interdenominational Theological Center* 25, no. 3 (Spring 1998) 188–202.

Woggon, Harry A. "A Biblical and Historical Study of Homosexuality." *Journal of Religious Health* 20 (Summer 1981) 158–59.

Woodward, Richard. "A Lost World Made by Women." *New York Times*. July 13, 2008. Travel Section. http://travel.nytimes.com/2008/07/13/travel/13journeys.html

Wyatt, N. "The Story of Dinah and Shechem." *Ugarit-Forschungen* 22 (1990) 433–58.

Ya'qūb, Ahmad b. Abī Ya'qūb, *Ta'rīkh al-ya'qūbī*. Edited by Muhammad Sādiq Bahr al-'Ulūm. 3 vols. Najaf: al-Maktaba al-Haydariyya, 1974), vol. 2, 135

Yee, Gale. "Ideological Criticism: Judges 17–21 and the Dismembered Body." In *Judges and Method: New Approaches in Biblical Studies*, edited by Gale A. Yee, 146–70. Minneapolis: Fortress; 1995.

Yong, Amos. *Hospitality and the Other: Pentecost, Christian Practices, and the Neighbor*. Maryknoll, NY: Orbis, 2008.

Youngs, Samuel. "The Frontier of Comparative Theology." *Journal of Comparative Theology* 1 (Mar. 2010) 1–10.

Yoo, Yani. "*Han*-Laden Women: Korean 'Comfort Women' and Women in Judges 19–21." *Semeia* 78 (1997) 37–46.

Zeid, A. M. Abou. "Honour and Shame Among Bedouins of Egypt." In *Honor and Shame: The Values of Mediterranean Society*, edited by J. G. Peristiany, 245–59. London: Weidenfeld & Nicolson, 1965.

Zohar, Zion. *Sephardic and Mizrahi Jewry: From the Golden Age of Spain to Modern Times*. New York: NYU Press, 2005.

Subject and Author Index

E

Scriptural Index

HEBREW BIBLE / OLD TESTAMENT

Genesis

Exodus

Leviticus

Numbers

Deuteronomy

Joshua

Judges

1 Samuel

2 Samuel

1 Kings

2 Kings

1 Chronicles

Luke (continued)

John

Acts

Romans

1 Corinthians

Galatians

Colossians

1 Timothy

Philemon

Hebrews

James

1 Peter

1 John

2 John

3 John

QUR'AN

SAHIH AL-BUKHARI

SAHIH MUSLIM

Printed in Great Britain
by Amazon